EDEXCEL
A LEVEL
HISTORY

active Book included

endorsed for
edexcel

T0385790

Paper 3:

Rebellion and disorder under the Tudors, 1485-1603

Alison Gundy

Series editor: Rosemary Rees

ALWAYS LEARNING

PEARSON

Published by Pearson Education Limited, 80 Strand, London, WC2R 0RL

www.pearsonschoolsandfecolleges.co.uk

Copies of official specifications for all Edexcel qualifications may be found on the website: www.edexcel.com

Text © Pearson Education Limited 2016

Designed by Elizabeth Arnoux for Pearson

Typeset and illustrated by Phoenix Photosetting, Chatham, Kent

Produced by Out of House Publishing

Original illustrations © Pearson Education Limited 2016

Cover design by Malena Wilson-Max for Pearson

Cover photo/illustration © Getty Images/Culture Club

The rights of Alison Gundy to be identified as author of this work have been asserted by her in accordance with the Copyright, Designs and Patents Act 1988

First published 2016

2024

16

British Library Cataloguing in Publication Data
A catalogue record for this book is available from the British Library

ISBN 978 1 447 985433

Printed in the UK by Ashford Colour Press Ltd.

Websites

Pearson Education Limited is not responsible for the content of any external internet sites. It is essential for tutors to preview each website before using it in class so as to ensure that the URL is still accurate, relevant and appropriate. We suggest that tutors bookmark useful websites and consider enabling students to access them through the school/college intranet.

A note from the publisher

In order to ensure that this resource offers high-quality support for the associated Pearson qualification, it has been through a review process by the awarding body. This process confirms that this resource fully covers the teaching and learning content of the specification or part of a specification at which it is aimed. It also confirms that it demonstrates an appropriate balance between the development of subject skills, knowledge and understanding, in addition to preparation for assessment.

Endorsement does not cover any guidance on assessment activities or processes (e.g. practice questions or advice on how to answer assessment questions) included in the resource nor does it prescribe any particular approach to the teaching or delivery of a related course.

While the publishers have made every attempt to ensure that advice on the qualification and its assessment is accurate, the official specification and associated assessment guidance materials are the only authoritative source of information and should always be referred to for definitive guidance.

Pearson examiners have not contributed to any sections in this resource relevant to examination papers for which they have responsibility.

Examiners will not use endorsed resources as a source of material for any assessment set by Pearson.

Endorsement of a resource does not mean that the resource is required to achieve this Pearson qualification, nor does it mean that it is the only suitable material available to support the qualification, and any resource lists produced by the awarding body shall include this and other appropriate resources.

Contents

How to use this book

STRUCTURE

This book covers Paper 3, Option 31: Rebellion and disorder under the Tudors, 1485–1603 of the Edexcel A Level qualification.

You will also need to study a Paper 1 and a Paper 2 option and produce coursework in order to complete your qualification. All Paper 1/2 options are covered by other textbooks in this series.

EXAM SUPPORT

The examined assessment for Paper 3 requires you to answer questions from three sections. Throughout this book there are exam-style questions in all three section styles for you to practise your examination skills.

Section A contains a compulsory question that will assess your source analysis and evaluation skills.

> **A Level Exam-Style Question Section A**
>
> **Study Source 7 before answering this question.**
>
> Assess the value of Source 7 for revealing the extent of the challenge posed by Perkin Warbeck and the reasons for his challenge.
>
> Explain your answer, using the source, the information given about its origin and your own knowledge about the historical context. (20 marks)
>
> **Tip**
> *To consider the extent of the challenge, you could think about who Warbeck was appealing to in his proclamation.*

Section B contains a choice of essay questions that will look at your understanding of the studied period in depth.

> **A Level Exam-Style Question Section B**
>
> How accurate is it to say that it was the dissolution of the smaller monasteries in 1536 that caused the risings of 1536? (20 marks)
>
> **Tip**
> *You will need to compare the dissolution of the smaller monasteries with other reasons in order to evaluate its importance as a cause of rebellion.*

Section C will again give you a choice of essay questions but these will assess your understanding of the period in breadth.

> **A Level Exam-Style Question Section C**
>
> To what extent do you agree that the re-establishment of the Council of the North in 1537 was the key turning point in increasing royal power in the localities in the years 1485–1601? (20 marks)
>
> **Tip**
> *You need to define what is meant by the 'increase' of royal power. How can this be assessed?*

The Preparing for your exams section at the end of the book contains sample answers of different standards, with comments on how they could be improved.

FEATURES
Extend your knowledge

These features contain additional information that will help you gain a deeper understanding to the topic. This could be a short biography of an important person, extra background information about an event, an alternative interpretation, or even a research idea that you could follow up. Information in these boxes is not essential to your exam success, but still provides insights of value.

> **EXTEND YOUR KNOWLEDGE**
>
> Sir Richard Rich
> Richard Rich was a lawyer who rose at Court because of his legal and administrative capabilities. He helped to gather evidence in the trials of both More and Fisher, and used it to ensure their convictions for treason. Rich helped Cromwell in the organisation of the dissolution of the monasteries. He was appointed Chancellor of the Court of Augmentations, which was a new financial court set up by Cromwell to manage the revenues from the dissolved monasteries. Rich used his position to enrich himself. He was granted, or purchased, extensive former monastic lands, mostly in Essex. Rich's involvement in the deaths of More and Fisher, and his greed, made him a particular target for the rebels in 1536.

Knowledge check activities

These activities are designed to check that you have understood the material that you have just studied. They might also ask you questions about the sources and extracts in the section to check that you have studied and analysed them thoroughly.

ACTIVITY
KNOWLEDGE CHECK

1 In your own words, explain why the Pilgrimage of Grace was more successful than Bigod's rising.

2 Make two lists under the headings: 'Evidence that the Pilgrimage of Grace was a threat to Henry's government' and 'Evidence that the Pilgrimage of Grace was not a threat to Henry's government'.

3 'The Pilgrimage of Grace posed a serious threat to Henry VIII's government.' Write one side of A4 explaining how far you agree with this statement.

Summary activities

At the end of each chapter, you will find summary activities. These are tasks designed to help you think about the key topic you have just studied as a whole. They may involve selecting and organising key information or analysing how things changed over time. You might want to keep your answers to these questions safe – they are handy for revision.

ACTIVITY
SUMMARY

1 Design a poster showing the causes and main events of the Northern Rising. You may use illustrations on your poster, but you should ensure that there is plenty of factual detail (e.g. dates, examples).

2 Explain in your own words the consequences of the Northern Rising for each of the following:

   a) Elizabeth I and her Council

   b) moderate Catholics in England

   c) recusants

   d) moderate Protestants in England

   e) Puritans.

Thinking Historically activities

These activities are found throughout the book, and are designed to develop your understanding of history, especially around the key concepts of evidence, interpretations, causation and change. Each activity is designed to challenge a conceptual barrier that might be holding you back. This is linked to a map of conceptual barriers developed by experts. You can look up the map and find out which barrier each activity challenges by downloading the progression map from this website: www.pearsonschools.co.uk/historyprogressionsapproach.

progression map reference

THINKING HISTORICALLY Cause and consequence (6c)

Connections

Extract 1 and Sources 11–13 demonstrate some typical aspects of medieval ideas about rebellion, from the first popular revolt in 1381.

1 Read Extract 1. How might this be seen as similar to the actions of Kett's rebels?

Read Source 11.

2 What did Kett's rebels believe about the state of English society and the economy?

3 How is this similar to Langland's claims about 14th-century England?

Look at Sources 12 and 13.

4 What did Kett's rebels copy from the rebellion of 1381?

5 Make a list of other similarities between the rebellion of 1381 and Tudor popular revolts. How did their understanding of Wat Tyler's rebellion affect the attitudes and actions of Tudor rebels?

6 Why is it important for historians to see these links across time and be able to explain how causal factors can influence situations much later in time?

Getting the most from your online ActiveBook

This book comes with three years' access to ActiveBook* – an online, digital version of your textbook. Follow the instructions printed on the inside front cover to start using your ActiveBook.

Your ActiveBook is the perfect way to personalise your learning as you progress through your A Level History course. You can:

• access your content online, anytime, anywhere

• use the inbuilt highlighting and annotation tools to personalise the content and make it really relevant to you.

Highlight tool – use this to pick out key terms or topics so you are ready and prepared for revision.

Annotations tool – use this to add your own notes, for example links to your wider reading, such as websites or other files. Or, make a note to remind yourself about work that you need to do.

*For new purchases only. If the access code has already been revealed, it may no longer be valid. If you have bought this textbook secondhand, the code may already have been used by the first owner of the book.

Introduction
A Level History

WHY HISTORY MATTERS

History is about people and people are complex, fascinating, frustrating and a whole lot of other things besides. This is why history is probably the most comprehensive and certainly one of the most intriguing subjects there is. History can also be inspiring and alarming, heartening and disturbing, a story of progress and civilisation and of catastrophe and inhumanity.

History's importance goes beyond the subject's intrinsic interest and appeal. Our beliefs and actions, our cultures, institutions and ways of living, our languages and means of making sense of ourselves are all shaped by the past. If we want to fully understand ourselves now, and to understand our possible futures, we have no alternative but to think about history.

History is a discipline as well as a subject matter. Making sense of the past develops qualities of mind that are valuable to anyone who wants to seek the truth and think clearly and intelligently about the most interesting and challenging intellectual problem of all: other people. Learning history is learning a powerful way of knowing.

WHAT IS HISTORY?

History is a way of constructing knowledge about the world through research, interpretation, argument and debate.

Building historical knowledge involves identifying the traces of the past that exist in the present – in people's memories, in old documents, photographs and other remains, and in objects and artefacts ranging from bullets and lipsticks, to field systems and cities. Historians interrogate these traces and *ask questions* that transform traces into *sources of evidence* for knowledge claims about the past.

Historians aim to understand what happened in the past by *explaining why* things happened as they did. Explaining why involves trying to understand past people and their beliefs, intentions and actions. It also involves explaining the causes and evaluating the effects of large-scale changes in the past and exploring relationships between what people aimed to do, the contexts that shaped what was possible and the outcomes and consequences of actions.

Historians also aim to *understand change* in the past. People, states of affairs, ideas, movements and civilisations come into being in time, grow, develop, and ultimately decline and disappear. Historians aim to identify and compare change and continuity in the past, to measure the rate at which things change and to identify the types of change that take place. Change can be slow or sudden. It can also be understood as progressive or regressive – leading to the improvement or worsening of a situation or state of affairs. How things change and whether changes are changes for the better are two key issues that historians frequently debate.

Figure 1 Fragment of a black granite statue possibly portraying the Roman politician Mark Antony.

Debate is the essence of history. Historians write arguments to support their knowledge claims and historians argue with each other to test and evaluate interpretations of the past. Historical knowledge itself changes and develops. On the one hand, new sources of knowledge and new methods of research cause *historical interpretations* to change. On the other hand, the questions that historians ask change with time and new questions produce new answers. Although the past is dead and gone, the interpretation of the past has a past, present and future.

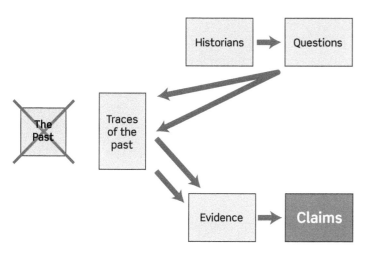

Figure 2 Constructing knowledge about the past.

THE CHALLENGES OF LEARNING HISTORY

Like all other Advanced Level subjects, A Level history is difficult – that is why it is called 'advanced'. Your advanced level studies will build on knowledge and understanding of history that you developed at GCSE and at Key Stage 3 – ideas like 'historical sources', 'historical evidence' and 'cause', for example. You will need to do a lot of reading and writing to progress in history. Most importantly, you will need to do a lot of thinking, and thinking about your thinking. This book aims to support you in developing both your knowledge and your understanding.

History is challenging in many ways. On the one hand, it is challenging to build up the range and depth of knowledge that you need to understand the past at an advanced level. Learning

about the past involves mastering new and unfamiliar concepts arising from the past itself (such as the Inquisition, Laudianism, *Volksgemeinschaft*) and building up levels of knowledge that are both detailed and well organised. This book covers the key content of the topics that you are studying for your examination and provides a number of features to help you build and organise what you know – for example, diagrams, timelines and definitions of key terms. You will need to help yourself too, of course, adding to your knowledge through further reading, building on the foundations provided by this book.

Another challenge is to develop understandings of the discipline of history. You will have to learn to think historically about evidence, cause, change and interpretations and also to write historically, in a way that develops clear and supported argument.

Historians think with evidence in ways that differ from how we often think in everyday life. In history, as Figure 2 shows, we cannot go and 'see for ourselves' because the past no longer exists. Neither can we normally rely on 'credible witnesses' to tell us 'the truth' about 'what happened'. People in the past did not write down 'the truth' for our benefit. They often had clear agendas when creating the traces that remain and, as often as not, did not themselves know 'the truth' about complex historical events.

A root of the word 'history' is the Latin word *historia*, one of whose meanings is 'enquiry' or 'finding out'. Learning history means learning to ask questions and interrogate traces, and then to reason about what the new knowledge you have gained means. This book draws on historical scholarship for its narrative and contents. It also draws on research on the nature of historical thinking and on the challenges that learning history can present for students. Throughout the book you will find 'Thinking Historically' activities designed to support the development of your thinking.

You will also find – as you would expect given the nature of history – that the book is full of questions. This book aims to help you build your understandings of the content, contexts and concepts that you will need to advance both your historical knowledge and your historical understanding, and to lay strong foundations for the future development of both.

Dr Arthur Chapman
Institute of Education
University College London

QUOTES ABOUT HISTORY

'Historians are dangerous people. They are capable of upsetting everything. They must be directed.'

Nikita Khrushchev

'To be ignorant of what occurred before you were born is to remain forever a child. For what is the worth of human life, unless it is woven into the life of our ancestors by the records of history.'

Marcus Tullius Cicero

Rebellion and disorder under the Tudors, 1485-1603

The Tudor period saw enormous political and religious change which still affects our society today. During the period 1485–1603, the Church of England was created; the importance of parliament grew and the government of England became more centralised and extensive than ever before. The Tudor period marked the beginning of our modern nation state.

SOURCE

1 Tudor attitudes to the structure of society and social order, as imagined by Diego de Valades (1533–82), Spanish Franciscan monk and writer, in his work *The Great Chain of Being*.

From the accession of the first Tudor monarch, Henry VII, in 1485 to the death of the last of the dynasty, Elizabeth I, in 1603, the monarchy faced a series of challenges from internal rebellion, the causes of which were varied. As a usurper with a weak claim to the throne, Henry VII was lucky to become king in 1485. Henry was faced with a series of challengers with a better claim to the throne than his own, and there was no certainty that he would survive as king. The initial questions for Henry, the first Tudor monarch, were how could he defeat his powerful rivals or create enough stability to build a dynasty of his own? Henry's children and grandchildren inherited a stronger claim to the throne, but they, too, faced rebellion. Discontent and popular rebellion were sometimes linked to social and economic hardship; this was the case in Kett's rebellion in 1549. Other rebellions were connected to the religious changes which began in England in the 1530s, when Henry VIII rejected the authority of the

1485 – Henry Tudor defeats Richard III at the Battle of Bosworth and becomes the first Tudor king of England

1485

1499 – The execution of Perkin Warbeck and the Earl of Warwick, rivals to Henry for the English crown

1499

1534 – Act of Supremacy made Henry VIII Head of the Church in England instead of the pope

1534

1536 – The Pilgrimage of Grace: 40,000 rebels protest against Henry VIII's religious policy

1536

1540 – The reorganisation of the Privy Council creates a more modern, professional Council to advise the monarch and run day-to-day affairs

1540

1559 – Elizabeth creates her religious settlement, a compromise designed to keep Catholics and Protestants happy

1559

1568 – Mary, Queen of Scots arrives in England posing a threat to Elizabeth's position as Queen of England

1568

1585 – The Lord Lieutenant system becomes permanent, improving England's military organisation; England enters war with Spain

1585

1594 – Outbreak of Tyrone's revolt in Ulster against English government policy in Ireland

1594

1603 – The death of Elizabeth I brings the end of the Tudor dynasty. Tyrone's revolt is ended with a peace treaty.

1603

1487	1487 – The pretender Lambert Simnel defeated at the Battle of Stoke by Henry VII
1513	1513 – The introduction of the Tudor subsidy, a more modern form of taxation
1535	1535 – First Law in Wales Act unifies Welsh and English government
1537	1537 – The reorganisation of the Council of the North creates more effective government in the region
1549	1549 – Kett's rebellion poses a serious challenge to the social and economic structures of Tudor England
1563	1563 – Statute of Artificers passed: this is a first attempt to regulate wages and employment
1569-70	1569–70 – The Revolt of the Northern Earls supports Mary, Queen of Scots and is a reaction to Elizabeth's policies in the North of England
1588	1588 – The first Spanish Armada is launched, an attempt by the Catholic Philip II of Spain to undermine Elizabeth's control of England
1598	1598 – Act for the Relief of the Poor creates an improved system of provision for the poor

pope and made himself Supreme Head of the Church in England. The Pilgrimage of Grace in 1536, the Revolt of the Northern Earls in 1569 and the Nine Years' War in Ireland from 1594 were all linked to resentment of the Crown's religious policies.

The Tudor monarchs all tried to increase and extend their authority over England and Ireland. At the start of the period, the monarchy was still reliant on powerful members of the nobility and gentry and their private armies to help them govern the localities. Central government was controlled by the king and a large council; parliament was summoned occasionally, when the monarch needed to raise money by way of taxation. The Church in England was both wealthy and powerful and was controlled by the pope in Rome. As the period progressed, central government became more streamlined and efficient, with the development of the role of Secretary and a smaller and more professional Privy Council. The Church was first brought under the direct control of the monarchy by Henry VIII in the 1534 Act of Supremacy, and later by Elizabeth I in 1559. The religious and political policies of the Crown meant that parliament was summoned more frequently, enhancing its role in Tudor government as the only institution that could grant taxation and make laws. At the same time, the Tudor monarchs tried to reduce the power of the traditional nobility and gentry by making them more reliant on access to the ruler and their patronage.

Under the Tudors, local government also underwent considerable change. From the 1530s, the monarchy started to extend its control into the more remote regions of the country, especially Wales and the North. The government also tried to improve the efficiency of local government and reduce the likelihood of rebellion by introducing changes which attempted to reduce the burden on the poorest in society. For example, a new form of tax assessment was introduced in 1513; attempts were also made to deal with the increasing problems of poverty and vagrancy through the Statute of Artificers (1563) and the Act for the Relief of the Poor (1598). However, sometimes these attempts at efficiency also contributed to the very rebellions the government was trying to avoid; as central control expanded during the period, it sometimes met with resistance and resentment. However, by the end of the Tudor period, the Crown had greater control over its subjects than it had had in 1485.

SOURCE

2 This picture shows the Irish Earl of Tyrone surrendering to the leader of the English army. Tyrone had been the leader of a rebellion against English rule in Ireland, but was defeated in 1603. The picture is labelled 'Tyrone's false submission afterwards rebelling', implying that Tyrone and the Irish were not to be trusted. This is perhaps not a surprising view, since the artist was English, but the cartoon does show contemporary attitudes towards rebellion.

3.1 Changes in governance at the centre

KEY QUESTIONS

- How effective were the key developments in Tudor government and administration?
- How did the relationship between the state and the Church change?

INTRODUCTION

The first Tudor monarch was Henry Tudor, who became Henry VII in 1485 after his victory over Richard III at the Battle of Bosworth. In the 50 years before Henry came to the throne, England had been torn apart by a civil war between two rival families, who had both claimed the right to be king. As a result of these events, by 1485 the traditional role and powers of the monarchy seemed to be under threat. Henry had many rivals with much better claims to the throne than he, who would be encouraged by his own actions in overthrowing Richard to try the same tactics themselves. But Henry VII survived and went on to found a dynasty that would last for over 100 years. Apart from a brief crisis in 1553, the throne passed from monarch to monarch by inheritance. During this period the power of the monarchy was restored and extended and, although there were challenges to it, the Tudor monarchs were always able to defeat these threats.

HOW EFFECTIVE WERE THE KEY DEVELOPMENTS IN TUDOR GOVERNMENT AND ADMINISTRATION?

The role of the monarchy, nobility and gentry in Tudor England

Tudor society was based on hierarchy; each person had their place, or rank, and was expected to be obedient to those who were their social superiors. At the top of this structure was God; under God was the monarch (see Figure 1.1). In theory, because they were chosen by God, the monarch could rule as they wished, but in practice, their power was limited because they needed the support of the nobility and gentry to rule the country. Monarchs in the Tudor period had no standing army or police force and were reliant on the nobility and gentry to carry out these roles in local government. A wise monarch would make sure that they both controlled the nobility and gentry, but also listened to them, as they were the eyes and ears of the ruler at a local level. If there was local disorder, it would be the local nobility or gentry who would be responsible for dealing with the trouble. Before Henry VII came to the throne, and during his reign, some nobles joined or led rebellions against the

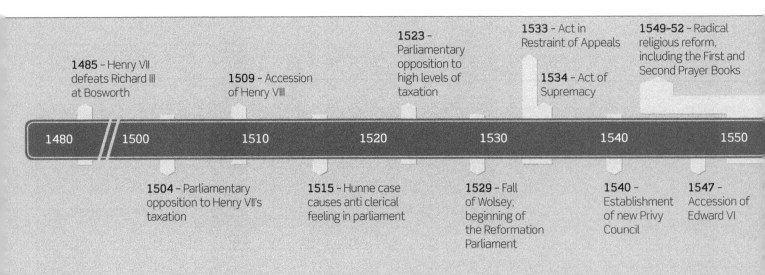

1485 – Henry VII defeats Richard III at Bosworth

1504 – Parliamentary opposition to Henry VII's taxation

1509 – Accession of Henry VIII

1515 – Hunne case causes anti clerical feeling in parliament

1523 – Parliamentary opposition to high levels of taxation

1529 – Fall of Wolsey; beginning of the Reformation Parliament

1533 – Act in Restraint of Appeals

1534 – Act of Supremacy

1540 – Establishment of new Privy Council

1547 – Accession of Edward VI

1549–52 – Radical religious reform, including the First and Second Prayer Books

1480   1500   1510   1520   1530   1540   1550

monarch. Henry Tudor himself had been a member of the nobility who was able to defeat the king. Noble challenges to the monarchy continued in the early years of his reign, but became increasingly infrequent under Henry VIII and his children. One of the political developments under the Tudors was the increasing control that the monarch was able to exert over their nobility. This was linked to the changing role of the nobility in central and local government.

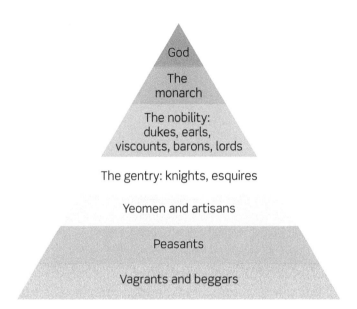

Figure 1.1 The structure of Tudor society.

Nobility and gentry

Below the monarch were the nobility and gentry. In the period from 1485 to 1603, it was these groups who helped the monarch to govern. The nobility was a group of men who held the highest titles below the king, such as duke, earl or viscount. Under the Tudors, there were between 40 and 60 men who held these titles, with the numbers fluctuating according to royal policy and natural wastage as families died out. The population of England grew from just over two million in the early 16th century to just over four million by 1600. Within this population, the nobility were a tiny, but powerful minority and it is estimated that these families held roughly ten percent of the land that was available for cultivation. The nobles saw themselves as the natural friends, advisers and military leaders of the monarch. They relied on the monarch to protect their lands and property; the monarch in turn relied on them to carry out government locally. When members of the nobility did become involved in rebellion against the monarch, it was usually because this relationship had broken down.

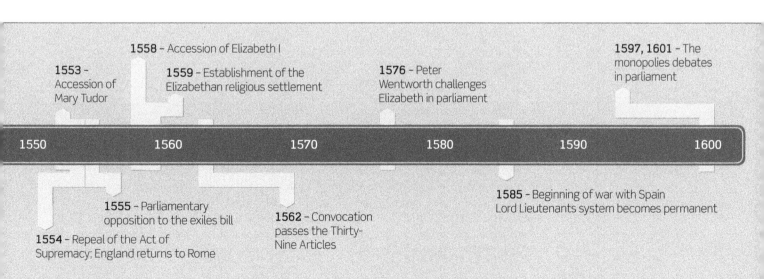

Below the nobility, there were about 5,000 gentry families, made up of knights and esquires. In 1490, there were about 375 men with the title of 'knight', which meant that they were called 'Sir'; this number had risen to 600 by 1558, and had declined slightly to 550 by 1603. Esquires were of a slightly lower rank than knights, and did not have a title. Like the nobility, the gentry originally had a military role, but by the Tudor period they too were increasingly involved in local government. The gentry were landowners as well, though their estates were generally less extensive than those of the nobility. Although Tudor society was hierarchical in nature, it was possible to rise through the ranks, through service to the king, marriage or inheritance. Conversely, it was also possible to lose rank, through political miscalculation or because of economic hardship.

Yeomen and artisans

Below the land owning elites of Tudor England were the emerging groups known as yeomen and artisans. Yeomen were prosperous farmers who tended to own their own land. Historian John Guy has estimated that there may have been about 60,000 of these men by 1600. Because they owned their lands, these farmers tended to be relatively financially secure because they were less affected by price rises or rent increases. Artisans were skilled craftsmen who often lived in towns or larger villages. Skilled craftsmen became particularly prosperous in the wool and cloth industry, which was the main English export throughout the Tudor period. In the earlier Tudor period, before 1549, it was often members of the yeomanry or skilled craftsmen who provided the leadership and shaped the demands of popular rebellion. This was because they were often better-educated and were the natural leaders of their communities. In the second half of the Tudor period, however, this group was less involved in rebellion as it became more involved in local government.

Peasants

Although Tudor towns were growing, the majority of England's population still lived and worked in rural communities, and England's economy remained based on agriculture. The peasantry worked on the land for the local landlord for wages. Usually, peasants did not own the land on which they lived and on which they were reliant for the production of food for their own survival. They were the most vulnerable to social and economic changes, such as poor harvests, epidemics and price and rent increases. It has been estimated that about two-fifths of the English population were living on the margins of subsistence; any social and economic crisis would be likely to push this group into real hardship, anger and rebellion.

Vagrants/beggars

Vagrants and beggars were people without masters who roamed the countryside. In Tudor society, they were particularly feared because every person was supposed to be under the control of their social superiors. In addition, this group was seen to be a threat to social order because their movement around England could lead to the spread of rumours and dangerous ideas. As a result, vagrants and beggars were harshly treated and punished under Tudor Acts of Parliament.

ACTIVITY
KNOWLEDGE CHECK

1 Make your own copy of the chart in Figure 1.1 and annotate it to show the roles of different social groups in Tudor society.

2 Which group do you think might pose the greatest threat to a Tudor monarch and why?

3 If you were a councillor to a Tudor monarch, what policies would you advise them to follow to improve social and political order?

The monarchy and government

Tudor monarchy was personal – as long as the monarch was able to do so, they would make key decisions about policy. Although a sensible monarch would be seen to take advice, even if they did not act on it, they still ruled England and made the important decisions on matters such as religious and foreign policy. Given the importance of the monarch in the government of England, it was essential that the ruler was adult, competent and male – it was assumed that women were incapable of ruling on their own. It was the monarch's duty to protect their country from invasion (and, if

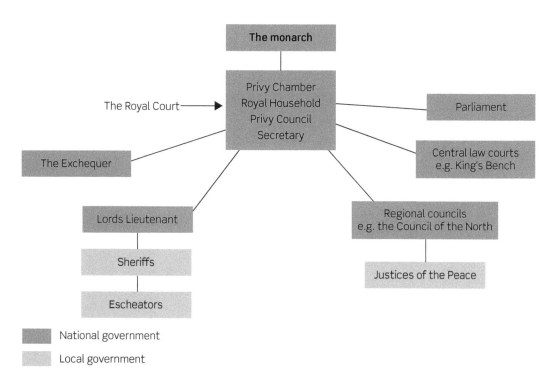

Figure 1.2 The structure of Tudor government.

ACTIVITY
KNOWLEDGE CHECK

1 Make your own copy of the diagram above. With two colours, highlight the main strengths and weaknesses of the system.

2 What changes might a Tudor monarch make in order to strengthen their control of central government?

3 As you read the next section (pages 12–19), annotate your copy of the chart to show:

   a) how each institution worked

   b) the changes made to the function of each institution

   c) continuities with earlier methods or functions (lack of change).

necessary, to lead an army into battle), and to protect the rights and privileges of their subjects; they could not rule exactly how they pleased. Their powers were curbed by Magna Carta (written in 1215) and by the development of other branches of government, such as parliament and the Royal Council. Monarchs who had tried to ignore these constraints, such as Richard II (r.1377–99) and Richard III (r.1483–85), had been labelled tyrants and overthrown.

By 1485, a complex system of government had evolved which could both help and hinder the monarch in their rule. These systems included more informal bodies, such as the Royal Court and, from Henry VII's reign, the Privy Chamber. There were also more formal institutions, such as the Council, and financial and judicial systems. These institutions were central (national) and, apart from the Court and Privy Chamber, they tended to remain in London, which was the capital city and the seat of government.

What was the Royal Court?

Not to be confused with the legal Courts of Justice, the Royal Court served the monarch; wherever the monarch was, the Court would follow. The Court was important for display and entertainment and was an informal source of power. Under the Tudors, those who wanted power or influence would tend to come to the Court in search of **patronage**. Those who succeeded in gaining patronage at Court could then build up enormous power and wealth, though they remained dependent on access

KEY TERM

Patronage
The distribution of land, offices or favours, through direct access either to the monarch or to their chief ministers.

The Eltham Ordinances
Reforms that proposed a smaller Council of 20 men who would travel with the king. It was also an attempt to reduce the number of 'hangers-on' around the king and thus reduce the size and cost of the Household. Although the Ordinances were presented as a cost-cutting measure, in reality it was another attempt by Wolsey to restrict access to the king and control the political influence of those close to him in the Chamber.

to the Court in order to secure this. The Court was also important for display. It was important for the Tudor monarchs to emphasise their power and wealth to important visitors, and the Court allowed them to do this through elaborate and expensive displays, such as tournaments and plays.

What was the role of the Royal Household?

The monarch and his family were served by a wide range of people who moved about the country with them. The Household was usually responsible for the ruler's domestic needs. Hundreds of people were employed in the kitchens, laundries and gardens, and were mostly menial servants, though they were controlled by high-level officials known as the Board of the Green Cloth. The Household could grow or shrink according to the personal needs of the monarch and his family, and was sometimes criticised when it became too large and costly. There were occasional attempts to reform how the Household worked and to reduce its expenses: for example, Thomas Wolsey issued the **Eltham Ordinances** in 1526 to try to achieve this, but they were unsuccessful because Wolsey did not have sufficient control over appointments or the desires and wishes of the king himself.

What was the role of the Privy Chamber?

Served by the Household, the monarch's living arrangements were structured in such a way that access to them was closely controlled. As the diagram of the Tudor palace of Hampton Court shows (Source 1), even the rooms of the palace were laid out to ensure that the monarch had some privacy. The Great Hall was still used for feasting and formal events, but beyond it was a series of increasingly private rooms. At Hampton Court, this included a guard room – known as the Watching Chamber – through which all visitors had to pass. There was also a Presence Chamber, which was a throne room and where the monarch would dine. It was also a place where news and gossip could flow. Beyond the Presence Chamber was the truly Privy (or private) Chamber, which was actually a series of rooms where the king and his family lived.

Changes made to the structure and function of the Household, 1485–1603

The Privy Chamber grew in political importance during the Tudor period. From 1495, when Henry VII increasingly feared betrayal from those he trusted, the Chamber was used to restrict access to the monarch. Henry created the Yeomen of the Guard, who acted as his personal bodyguards and guarded the entrance to his private rooms. Such was Henry's distrust of those around him that he also used the Chamber to collect and store royal income, which he monitored personally. This system of Chamber finance had the advantage that Henry always had access to ready money, but had the disadvantage that it was a system reliant on the monarch's ability and interest in controlling royal income. Tudor monarchs after Henry VII did not have the time or inclination to follow this system and the use of Chamber finance lapsed.

The dry stamp
An embossed stamp was made of the king's signature. This could be stamped onto documents; the signature could then be inked in. Possession of the dry stamp could give the holder considerable power over aspects of government such as grants of land, offices and titles.

Faction
An informal group of people at Court who had similar aims or ideas. Factions would seek to influence the monarch by gaining positions which allowed access to their ruler. Factions became increasingly common with the religious and political upheavals of the 1520s and 1530s. They often formed around key individuals with particular religious beliefs; in the 1530s and 1540s, historians often refer to a 'conservative' faction which sought a return to Catholicism and Rome, and a 'reformer' faction which worked for more religious change.

David Starkey's work has shown that under Henry VIII, the Privy Chamber became an important political hub. The Chamber had its own staff, who from 1518 were known as the Gentlemen of the Privy Chamber. The most important of these was the Groom of the Stool, in charge of the royal commode or toilet. Under Henry VIII, these positions were filled by Henry's most trusted friends, who were usually men from the nobility or gentry. These men were not simply servants. Because of their intimate and daily physical contact with Henry, they were also his advisers and were often also employed in more 'formal' areas of government. For example, between 1520 and 1525, Gentlemen of the Privy Chamber were sent on diplomatic missions to France and on a military expedition against the Scots.

Access to the monarch via the Privy Chamber was one route to power and influence in the Tudor period and was an opportunity to influence the direction of government. By the 1540s, this also meant control of the **dry stamp**, which was kept by Gentlemen of the Chamber. Henry VIII's aversion to paperwork had led to the introduction of the dry stamp as a method of putting the king's signature to documents quickly and easily. Control of the dry stamp could give its owner enormous power. In the 1540s, the **faction** led by Edmund Seymour, Earl of Hertford, and John Dudley, Viscount Lisle, gained control of the stamp using members of their faction within the Privy Chamber, notably Sir Anthony Denny. This enabled them to make alterations to the king's will in their favour in 1547, which brought them increased power and influence in government. Under Edward, a young boy, access to him and to the dry stamp was again controlled through the Privy Chamber, which was filled with supporters of the king's protectors, first Seymour, then Dudley.

SOURCE
1
Plan showing the layout of Hampton Court Palace as it was during the reign of King Henry VIII, from *The History of Hampton Court Palace in Tudor Times* by Ernest Law, published in 1885 (litho). The Presence Chamber and Privy Chamber can be seen on this plan.

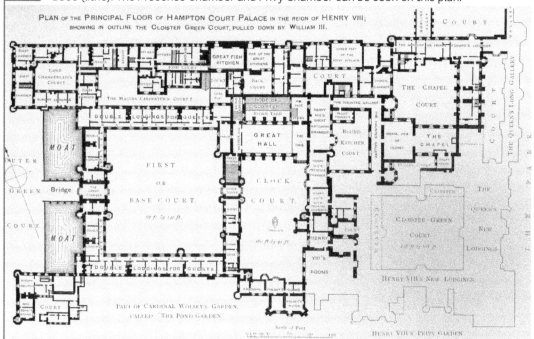

SOURCE
2
Henry VIII in his Privy Chamber, a pen and ink drawing by the artist Hans Holbein (c1497–1543). Holbein was employed by Henry as a Court artist in the 1530s and was known for his realistic portraits of Henry VIII and many of his courtiers.

ACTIVITY
KNOWLEDGE CHECK

Look at Sources 1 and 2.

1 What do these sources suggest about the role of the Privy Chamber in Tudor government?

2 Why do you think that this system might have developed?

3 What might be the advantages and disadvantages of this system?

How did the role of the Privy Chamber change under Mary and Elizabeth?

The role of the Privy Chamber began to change with the accession of female monarchs, Mary and Elizabeth. Because the role of the Chamber involved close physical contact with the ruler, under a woman these roles were filled by other women rather than men. This did not mean that the Chamber lost its political role entirely. Mary's female attendants, such as Frances Waldegrave and Frances Jerningham, were her former servants who had Catholic sympathies and were married to male members of Mary's Household, Edward Waldegrave, the Master of the Great Wardrobe, and Henry Jerningham, the Captain of the Guard. These women undoubtedly had influence with the queen. Indeed, Charles V, the Holy Roman Emperor, wrote to his ambassador Simon Renard to tell him that some of the ladies were taking advantage of their position of trust to gain patronage and favours. In one way, however, Mary kept more control over the Privy Chamber – her dry stamp was kept under lock and key and she seems never to have allowed its use by her administrators. Under Elizabeth, the Chamber continued to decline in political importance. Elizabeth did appoint the wives of her key councillors to her Privy Chamber, for example the wife of the Earl of Leicester, but reforms carried out in 1559 meant that members of her Household were also members of her Council. From then on, politics and major decisions were determined through the formal channels of her Council, rather than through the informal route of the Chamber.

What was the role of the Council?

The Royal Council was a more formal body which had existed since medieval times to advise ('counsel') the monarch. The monarch chose who should be on their Council and did not have to take their advice, though it was often in their best interests to at least listen to its views. The Council also helped the monarch with the day-to-day running of the country and could act as a judicial court when there were high-profile legal cases which could not be solved through the normal courts of law. In particular, the Council dealt with legal cases relating to the nobility. However, it could also be divided by faction, and its political importance varied depending on the style of rule adopted by different monarchs. The role of the Council did change during the period, however, becoming increasingly formal and 'professional' in its role, especially after 1540.

What was the role of the Royal Council under Henry VII?

Under Henry VII, the Royal Council was a larger, more informal body than it was to become under Henry VIII. Between 1485 and 1509, over 200 men attended Council meetings, though not all at the same time. Henry's Council consisted of a mixture of members of the nobility, churchmen, royal officials and lawyers. He was careful to include men who had served under his Yorkist predecessors, Edward IV and Richard III; Henry's Council included 22 men who had served Edward and 20 who had served Richard. As Henry was a usurper, with no experience of government, who had lived most of his life in exile, such men were crucial in helping him to establish and secure his position on the throne. Several, such as John Morton, went on to have long and distinguished careers in his service. Because Henry did not hold regular parliaments, his Councils played an important part in gathering information about popular opinion and the mood of the country, as well as advising him on the best policies to pursue. In addition, Henry also made use of 'Great Councils'. These were special gatherings of all members of the nobility and his councillors. These were used when Henry needed to be seen to consult his nobility on important issues to do with war and taxation. Henry held five Great Councils between 1487 and 1502; this was a cunning tactic as it made it seem as if he were including all the nobility in his decisions, though in fact he had already made up his mind about what to do. In 1492, for example, when he wanted to end his invasion of France, he made sure that he consulted all his nobility and made them sign a document agreeing to retreat. This tactic also made it harder for the nobility to argue with his decisions.

The Royal Council under Henry VIII

When Henry VIII came to the throne in 1509 he was nearly 18. His father, Henry VII, left a Council in place to help his young son to govern. This Council was made up of experienced administrators, such as the Archbishop of Canterbury, William Warham, and the Bishop of Winchester, Richard Fox. Both of these men were senior members of the Church hierarchy, which was common for members of the Council in this period. Both also supported Henry VII's policy of not engaging in expensive foreign wars. This was not a policy supported by the young Henry VIII, who had been trained as a warrior and wished to prove himself against England's old enemies, France and Scotland. Within two years, Fox and Warham's influence over royal policy had been undermined; they were replaced by Thomas Wolsey, who rose to power because he was able to give Henry what he wanted – war.

Wolsey remained the dominant influence in politics until 1529, when he fell from power. He was the first of the king's chief ministers and was responsible for undertaking much of the day-to-day running of government in which Henry had no interest. As a result of Wolsey's dominance, the Council retained its traditional functions. It was still a fairly large institution of perhaps 40 members, most of whom would not attend on a regular basis. However, in 1526, Wolsey was planning in the Eltham Ordinances to reduce this to 20 men who would meet daily. Although Wolsey's plans initially came to nothing, by 1540 a Council such as the one he had planned had emerged; this became known as the 'Privy Council', and by Elizabeth's reign was responsible for much of the daily running of the country, especially administration and legal matters.

The reform of the Privy Council, 1540

The role of the Privy Council changed considerably in 1540. As part of his 'Tudor revolution in government' thesis, Geoffrey Elton argued that the changes to the Council actually occurred in 1536–37, when there was a 'conscious act of administrative reform designed to modernise the existing King's Council'. Elton argued that this was part of Thomas Cromwell's attempt to modernise and reform the government of England, which brought about lasting change to how the Tudor system operated. Most historians would now reject this claim. For example, John Guy argues that although there were changes to how the Council worked in 1536, these developments were a temporary response to the crisis provoked by the Pilgrimage of Grace in that year. The smaller Council that met in 1536–37 was an emergency body filled with the king's most trusted advisers. Many of these men were political enemies of Cromwell, such as the Duke of Norfolk. If Cromwell had really instigated these changes, he would not have filled the Council with the men who resented him the most (and were responsible for his fall in 1540). It was only after Cromwell's fall and execution in 1540, that real and lasting changes to the Council took place.

The changes to the Privy Council which happened in 1540 were permanent ones which lasted for the rest of the period. After Cromwell's fall, there was a need to restructure Henry VIII's government so that it could continue to work without Cromwell, who had manipulated his position as the king's Secretary in order to wield power and influence the king. Henry's reign to 1540 had been dominated by the personalities and influence of his two chief ministers, Thomas Wolsey and Thomas Cromwell. Both of these men had come from relatively humble backgrounds, and their power was resented by the traditional members of the nobility, who saw themselves as the natural advisers of the king. After Cromwell's fall, the Privy Council turned itself into a 'chief minister'. This meant that the members of the newly formed Council were collectively responsible for much of the work which had previously been performed by Wolsey and Cromwell. For example, the Duke of Norfolk, a member of the new Council, insisted that anyone wishing to conduct business with the Council should write to them as a group, not to an individual. This change meant that no one individual was able to wield the amount of power on their own that Wolsey and Cromwell had; for the rest of Henry's reign, there was no 'chief minister'. This trend continued under Edward and Mary. Under Elizabeth, the man who could have assumed this role, William Cecil, preferred to use his position as the queen's Secretary instead, and deliberately avoided the use of the term 'chief minister', although he did act as such.

To what extent did the membership of the Council and its relationship with the monarch change from 1540?

The Council, from 1540, also changed decisively in its membership and its role. From 1540, its membership was considerably reduced and was fixed to include just the most trusted advisers of the monarch. This was in direct contrast to the Council of Henry VII, which had 227 members, many of whom attended only infrequently; before 1536, Henry VIII's Council had included up to 120 members. From 1540, the membership of the Council was reduced significantly, as Figure 1.3 shows. Although in the reigns of Edward VI and Mary it was not yet fully apparent that these changes were lasting, the trend was continued under Elizabeth, when membership of the Council narrowed still further. The reasons for these fluctuations reflected the individual styles and needs of the monarchs. The number of councillors under Edward VI grew because Edward was a child, and a larger Council was needed in order to govern the country while the king was too young to do so himself. While Edward was under the control of his uncle, Edward Seymour, Duke of Somerset, the Council's role was undermined because Somerset preferred to make decisions and rule using men from his own household such as Sir John Thynne. These men were loyal to Somerset and were given key roles in the king's household and chamber, which allowed them to influence Edward. For example, Somerset's brother-in-law, Sir Michael Stanhope, was made chief gentleman of the Privy Chamber and groom of the stool; and he also controlled the dry stamp, but Stanhope was never a member of the Council. Although these developments might seem like a reversal of the changes of 1540 and a return to government that was focused on the control of the Privy Chamber, the Council was able to reassert itself, showing that its importance in government had increased. In 1549, when rebellion broke out in the West Country and East Anglia, it was the Earl of Warwick (later the Duke of Northumberland), a member of the Council, who led the attack on Somerset which brought him down. Northumberland, who replaced Somerset as Edward's protector, was careful to be seen to govern through the Council, reasserting its new importance in Tudor government since 1540. This explains the apparent increase in Council numbers by 1552, though historian Dale Hoak has shown that actually there were about 21 active members. This did not mean that the Council was the most important institution in the country. Power still remained with the monarchy; Warwick

was careful to manipulate not only the Council, but also the king, by ensuring that key supporters such as Sir John Gates controlled access to Edward. The decision to implement the 'devise for succession' (the plan to remove Mary Tudor from the succession and replace her with Lady Jane Grey), was the work of Edward and Northumberland alone.

Under Mary, a larger number of men were appointed to the Council in an attempt by the queen to be inclusive. However, only a small core of this group were active regularly. Meetings were run by experienced administrators such as William Paget, and returned to the pattern seen in the 1540s. The average attendance at Council meetings in 1555 was 12; only eight councillors attended over 50 percent of meetings. Elizabeth's reign continued this trend; by the end of her reign, the changes begun in 1540 had become permanent. Not only had the Council become a permanent, small group of trusted advisers, but the focus of their work and their role had also changed.

Henry VII's reign	227
1509–29 (under Wolsey)	120
1536–37	19
1540	19
1548	22
1552	31
1553–58	50
1559	19
1586	19
1597	11
1603	13

Figure 1.3 The size of the council, 1485–1603.

How did the work of the Council change from 1540?

SOURCE

3

From the Council's registers, the official records of the Council's actions and business from the reign of Mary, February 1554. This section lists the business discussed and who was to be responsible for acting on decisions made by the Council. This meeting took place one month after Sir Thomas Wyatt's unsuccessful rebellion against the queen.

To call in the debts and provide for money...

... To give order for the ships and to appoint captains and others to serve in them...

To give order for victuals necessary to be sent to Calais, Berwick etc. [English garrisons]...

To consider what laws shall be established in this Parliament and to name men that shall make the books thereof...

To appoint men to continue in the examination of the prisoners [from Wyatt's rebellion].

To consider what lands shall be sold, and who shall be in the commission for that purpose...

To appoint a Council to attend and remain at London [Tower]...

To give order for the furniture and victualing of the said Tower...

Sir Thomas Wyatt's rebellion (1554)
Sir Thomas Wyatt and a group of Protestant gentry and nobility plotted a rising in protest over Mary I's marriage to Philip II of Spain. The marriage was one step in Mary's plans to return England to full Roman Catholicism, but some Protestants felt threatened by this. The plotters may even have been considering removing Mary and replacing her with her Protestant sister Elizabeth. However, the rebellion failed; Wyatt and his conspirators were imprisoned in the Tower, tried and executed for treason.

ACTIVITY
KNOWLEDGE CHECK

Read Source 3.

1 What do these tasks suggest about the relationship between the Council and the monarch?

2 With a partner, put these tasks in order of priority – which do you think would be the most important of the tasks carried out by the Council? Which would be less important?

As the list of tasks from the Council's registers (Source 3) suggests, the work of the Council from 1540 was increasingly varied. The significance of the changes made in 1540 gave new powers to the Council; it could now issue collective proclamations and orders in the monarch's name and did not have to wait for explicit instructions from the monarch before it did so. From 1540, it also had its own clerk who recorded meetings. From Mary's reign onwards, the new role of the Council in government was reflected in the fact that it had its own **seal,** though this did not override the dry stamp. Increasingly, the Council was seen as a body which served the state of England, rather than being private servants of the monarch. This did not mean that they supplanted the power of the monarch, who still took key decisions of policy relating to religion, foreign policy and the security of the realm. Moreover, the Council was very much under the control of the monarch. Elizabeth's Council would meet wherever the queen was staying; often this was at the central palaces of Whitehall or Hampton Court, but when Elizabeth went on progresses, her Council would travel with her. But as Tudor government expanded

further into the localities and the volume of administrative work increased, the amount of work done by the Council increased as well. Much of this work was day-to-day administration of the government's affairs, but the Council had to meet increasingly often to deal with this. In the period from the 1520s to the 1560s, the Council usually had meetings three or four times a week; by the 1590s, it was meeting every day, sometimes twice a day.

The development of the role of Secretary

SOURCE

 4

From Robert Beale's 'Treatise of the office of a councillor and secretary to Her Majesty' (1592). Beale was brother-in-law to Sir Francis Walsingham, the queen's Secretary. Beale worked as a clerk to the Council and would stand in for Walsingham when he was away. The 'treatise' was Beale's advice on how to behave as a Secretary and councillor.

When the Council meeteth, have a care that the time be not spent in matters of small moment, but to dispatch such things as shall be propounded unto them, for you shall find that they will not meet so often as you would desire, sometimes for sickness and sometimes for other employment... When there shall be any unpleasant matter to be imparted to her Majesty from the Council, or other matters to be done of great importance, let not the burden be laid on you alone but let the rest join with you...

A secretary must have a special cabinet whereof he is himself to keep the key, for his signets, ciphers and secret intelligences... I could wish that the secretary should make himself acquainted with some honest gentlemen in all the shires, cities and principal towns and the affection of the gentry... It is convenient for a secretary to understand the state of the whole realm...

Things to be done with her:

Have in a little paper note of such things as you are to propound to her Majesty and divide it into the titles of public and private suits [requests]... Learn before your access her Majesty's disposition by some of the privy chamber, with whom you must keep credit, for that will stand you in much stead... When her Majesty is angry or not well disposed, trouble her not with any matter which you desire to have done, unless extreme necessity urge it. When her Highness signeth it shall be good to entertain her with some relation or speech whereat she may take some pleasure.

KEY TERM

Seal
Tudor documents were made official by the use of a wax seal. Hot wax would be poured into a mould to create a design when the wax cooled. A seal also gave a measure of security for secret or controversial instructions. When the seal was broken, it would be obvious that the document had been read. There were a variety of seals which represented different institutions of government. The monarch had their own privy (private) seal; the keeper of this seal could therefore wield great power. The Lord Chancellor had control of the great seal. The fact that the Council also acquired its own seal suggests that it was becoming an important institution of government in its own right.

ACTIVITY
KNOWLEDGE CHECK

Read Source 4 then answer the following.

1 According to Beale, what were the main duties to be carried out by the Secretary? Which do you think he would consider to have been the most important?

2 Discuss with a partner: what does the type and range of tasks undertaken by the Secretary reveal about his relationship with the monarch and the Council?

3 What would be the advantages and disadvantages for Elizabeth of using a Secretary in these ways?

The role of Secretary to the Tudor monarchs first became politically important in the 1530s, when Thomas Cromwell was dominant. Originally, the role was one of personal secretary to the monarch and the Secretary was part of the Royal Household. Holding the position meant close personal access to the monarch, as well as control of the monarch's personal (or privy) seal, which made royal documents official. This meant that the Secretary could be very influential, and in the hands of Thomas Cromwell, the position grew in importance, though this importance was not sustained after Cromwell's fall.

Although Cromwell was never appointed to the highest office in Tudor government, Lord Chancellor, this did not matter because he was able to manipulate his position as Henry VIII's Secretary to make himself the most powerful man in the country next to the king. Cromwell had become Henry's Secretary by 1534. He used his position to control Council meetings and his access to the king's private correspondence meant that he had detailed knowledge of Henry's day-to-day business. However, following Cromwell's fall in 1540, the post of Secretary declined in political importance again. The post was even split between two men for the first time, Thomas Wriothesely and Ralph Sadler, neither of whom was ever as powerful as Cromwell. It is likely that the decision to split the post was partly in response to the increased amount of work which the Secretary undertook. Appointing two secretaries may also have been an attempt to ensure that no one man could exploit the position to his own advantage. The role of Secretary only became more important again when Elizabeth's most trusted adviser, William Cecil, was appointed to the role in 1558. He continued as Secretary until 1572. Later Secretaries were equally influential; Francis Walsingham, who was also Elizabeth's spymaster, held the office from 1573 until his death in 1590. He was followed by William Cecil's son, Robert. In this period, although there were always two Secretaries, one was usually much more dominant than the other.

During Elizabeth's reign, the post of Secretary became permanently important. This was because the men appointed to the post chose to use it to enhance their own power and to conduct the day-to-day running of the government on the queen's behalf. As the memorandum by Robert Beale suggests, the duties of the Secretary were many and varied. The Secretaries needed to be tactful because they had to deal with the queen; they also needed to ensure that Council meetings were well-run; besides these duties, they also had to sift through enormous amounts of information that were sent to them. Sometimes, the role of the Secretary could be a dangerous one. William Davison, who became Secretary in 1586, had the responsibility of keeping the death warrant which had been issued for the execution of Mary, Queen of Scots, Elizabeth's Catholic rival for the throne. Davison had to get Elizabeth's signature for this document, which she gave very reluctantly, telling Davison not to send the warrant, but to keep it safe. The Council decided that the warrant should be sent and Mary was executed. When she found out, Elizabeth was furious and blamed Davison. He was tried, imprisoned and forced to pay a fine of 10,000 marks, a huge amount. Although Davison was eventually released in 1589, he was never employed by the queen again.

The example of Davison shows just how exposed the Secretary's position could be, as well as the continuing importance of both the Council and the queen in government. It was always the queen who appointed the Secretary; after Walsingham's death in 1590, she refused to fill his post for six years. Nevertheless, ambitious men continued to want the role because of the great power which came with it. From 1596, when he was finally appointed, Robert Cecil used his position as Secretary to build up a network of supporters. He had access to the queen's correspondence, which included both information about offices and positions available, as well as requests for these offices. Cecil was able to ensure that patronage was distributed to his own clients, while ensuring that the followers of his rival, the Earl of Essex, were not rewarded.

The establishment of the post of Lord Lieutenant

Tudor central government also extended with increasing directness into local communities, especially through the development of the post of Lord Lieutenant. Before the mid-16th century, local government was carried out by the nobility and gentry and, increasingly, the 'middling sort' (the yeomen and artisans). The roles carried out by these groups included presiding over legal cases as Justices of the Peace (JPs) and collecting taxation. In the absence of a standing army or police force, local communities, led by members of the local gentry and nobility, were responsible for upholding law and order and raising armies to fight for the king. Because this role gave considerable power to the land owners, it was important for the monarch to be able to trust them. It was also possible for those in power locally to abuse their position; during the Wars of the Roses, noblemen had raised armies against their own king. They were also capable of manipulating the local legal system in order to protect their own families and friends. In addition, the system was reliant on local officials, who were unpaid and not necessarily well-suited to their roles. The system of Lord Lieutenants developed over the period as part of the Tudor monarchs' attempt to solve these problems, especially the recruitment for royal armies, and to increase royal control of the regions.

The first developments in the extension of royal power into the localities and the improvement of military recruitment began in the reign of Henry VIII as a response to the demands of foreign war and the threat of domestic rebellion. In 1512 and 1545, he gave commissions to members of the nobility to organise defence against the threat from France and Scotland, with whom England was at war. In 1536, he issued commissions to deal with the threat posed by the Pilgrimage of Grace rebellion. In 1549, the Duke of Northumberland, who was acting as Protector for the young Edward VI, appointed members of the nobility as Lieutenants to deal with the trouble caused by the serious rebellions of that year. Northumberland's Lieutenants were expected to have both a policing and a military role at local level. Under Mary I, there was a further attempt to formalise this system, again in response to the demands of war with France. In 1557–58, Mary's nobility and gentry found it very difficult to muster and recruit troops. Mary's response was to divide the country into ten lieutenancies, with each Lieutenant being responsible for the defence of their region and military recruitment. However, this was a temporary arrangement which did not survive once the threat of French invasion had diminished in 1558.

Under Elizabeth I, the post of Lord Lieutenant became a permanent one. Once again, the development was in response to the war with Spain, which began in 1585 and lasted until 1604. With the beginning of this war, Lord Lieutenants were appointed to each county, together with a deputy to help them in their work. Many of these appointments were for life because the war lasted so long. Initially, their work was organisation of the war effort; they were responsible for the recruitment of the national militia (army). The commission given to the Lord Lieutenants was to organise the mustering of all available men to fight in the wars; the Lieutenants also had to ensure that their armies were properly armed, trained and disciplined. All local officials were expected to help and obey the Lord Lieutenants. This system was particularly effective because it harnessed the most powerful men in the country, the nobility, in the service of the Crown. Traditionally, the nobility had always seen themselves as defenders of their country; the Lord Lieutenant system reinforced this idea. However, the Lieutenants were directly answerable to the monarch; they were raising troops for a national army, not for their own 'private' armies, as had been the case before 1585. If they disobeyed orders, they could be punished. It was also very common for members of the Council to act as Lord Lieutenants as well. This enhanced the links between the central government and the localities, especially because it was the Council who ran the war effort on Elizabeth's behalf. The Lord Lieutenants were able to gather information about local conditions, which meant that the system of recruitment and military organisation ran more smoothly, although it was possible for local communities to close ranks against the Lord Lieutenant and refuse to co-operate. This happened in both Suffolk and Wiltshire in the 1590s. Nevertheless, the introduction of the Lord Lieutenant system enhanced the ability of the monarch to control their country more directly than ever before. In some ways, however, the system was not really an innovation, because it still relied on the nobility in their traditional military role.

A Level Exam-Style Question Section C

'The key factor in upholding and extending royal authority in the years 1485–1603 was the development of the institutions of central government.'

How far do you agree with this claim? (20 marks)

Tip

You need to define what is meant by 'institutions of central government'. This could mean the Secretary, Council or Lord Lieutenants, for example.

HOW DID THE RELATIONSHIP BETWEEN THE STATE AND THE CHURCH CHANGE?

Church–state relations

Parliament was a medieval institution which had gained important powers by the start of the Tudor period. These included: the sole right to grant taxation and the sole right to pass laws (Acts of Parliament). When a monarch needed taxation to supplement their income (usually for war or another emergency), it was usual for them to summon parliament. However, monarchs also retained the right to veto any laws which they did not like, and to summon and dismiss parliament at will. In fact, there were long periods when parliament did not meet at all, and unlike parliament today, it was not involved in day-to-day government. However, most monarchs would call parliament periodically. It was an important opportunity for them to test the mood of the country and to communicate their policies to the Members of Parliament (MPs), and thus to the localities.

How was parliament organised?

Parliament had two chambers, the unelected House of Lords, where hereditary peers and bishops sat, and the House of Commons, which was filled with elected MPs. Two MPs were elected to represent each county of England, and some boroughs (towns) also had the right to send MPs to parliament. To vote in a county, it was necessary to own property which generated income worth 40 shillings (£2) per year. This meant that voting, when it happened, was restricted to those wealthy enough to own property outright. In many cases, however, MPs were elected uncontested – there was no competition for the seat. It was also common for members of the nobility to exercise patronage to ensure their clients were elected. The powerful dukes of Norfolk could usually influence the return of MPs in up to eight boroughs. Parliament tended to represent the interests of the landed gentry and nobility. To pass an Act of Parliament, a bill had to be heard in both the Commons and Lords before being given royal assent by the monarch. While parliament was usually on the same side as the monarch, this did not mean that it could always be relied on to do what the monarch wanted and, as the century progressed, the Commons became more confident and needed more careful managing. In particular, tensions arose over taxation and finance, religion and the royal succession. These developments were largely due to the changes in the balance of power between state, Church and parliament in the mid-Tudor period.

The role of parliament under Henry VII

Like most kings before him, Henry VII was forced to call parliament periodically because he needed grants of taxation to fund wars for the defence of the country from hostile foreign invasion. Because

Henry was a cautious monarch who preferred not to pursue an ambitious foreign policy, he needed to call parliament increasingly infrequently as his reign progressed. In total, Henry summoned parliament seven times in a reign lasting 24 years; parliament sat for a total of 72 weeks during that period. The last meeting of parliament in his reign was in 1504. To modern eyes, this lack of use of parliament may seem suspicious, but to Henry's contemporaries, the infrequent parliaments would have seemed entirely usual. England was at peace, Henry did not need taxation, and long gaps between parliaments were not uncommon throughout the Tudor period.

When Henry did call parliament, it was because he needed a grant of taxation. On each occasion, parliament granted the requested money without argument, except in 1504. In the parliament of 1504, Henry was forced to accept a smaller sum in taxation than he had originally asked for, as a result of opposition from the Commons, which was reluctant to grant the sum requested. These tensions had happened before in late medieval England. Since the early 14th century, the Commons had acquired the right to challenge the monarch about taxation and could even threaten to withhold taxation until their grievances had been addressed. During the period, the Commons would occasionally revert to this tactic, though it was very unusual and no Tudor monarch was ever refused taxation.

Slightly less conventionally, Henry used the first parliament that met after his victory at Bosworth to enhance his claim to be king. Parliament acknowledged his claim to the throne and passed a series of **Acts of Attainder**, convicting Henry's enemies. However, Henry was careful to use parliament only to make his claim more secure; there was never any suggestion that parliament had the power to grant him his claim to the throne. Henry's descendants would use parliament to give legal status to the Tudor succession.

EXTRACT

Sessions of Tudor parliaments, 1485–1603, taken from J. Loach, *Parliament under the Tudors*, (1991). Note that these dates show the total amount of time a particular parliament was in session before new elections were held. Parliament did not sit continuously.

Monarch	Dates of parliamentary sessions
Henry VII	1485, 1487, 1491, 1495, 1497, 1504
Henry VIII	1510, 1512-14, 1515, 1523, 1529-April 1536, June-July 1536, 1539-40, 1542-44, 1545-47
Edward VI	1547, 1548-March 1549, November 1549-50, 1552
Mary I	1553, April-May 1554, November 1554-55, 1558
Elizabeth I	1559, 1563-76, 1571, 1572-81, 1584-85, 1586-87, 1589, 1593, 1597-98, 1601

KEY TERM

Act of Attainder
A medieval innovation that allowed a king to declare someone guilty by Act of Parliament without the need to put them on trial. Under an Act of Attainder, all property of the accused was declared forfeit. This was a particularly powerful political weapon, and Henry VII used it against his Yorkist enemies and those who plotted against him. Acts of Attainder were reversible and Henry used this as a way to control those he did not trust; good behaviour could secure a complete or partial reversal of the original Act.

The early parliaments of Henry VIII, 1509–23

Parliament met only four times between 1509 and 1529: in 1510, 1512–14, 1515 and 1523. Its role in this period was mainly to grant taxation to fund Henry VIII's wars, because unlike his father, the new king wanted to prove himself on the international stage with wars against England's traditional enemies, France and Scotland. When his wars were going well, especially in 1513, it was usually not too difficult to persuade parliament to grant taxation for the defence of the realm. However, by 1517, most of the initial gains made by Henry had been lost, and as the burden of taxation increased, with little to show for it, parliament became less keen to grant increasing amounts of money. This was partly because, as landowners, the MPs feared rebellion brought about too much taxation. As members of local society, they were well aware of the amount of grumbling and resistance. In 1523, this led to Wolsey meeting stiff opposition from the Commons to exact the amount of taxation he wanted. By this date, £288,814 had been raised in taxation, not to mention 'loans' which had not been repaid, totalling £260,000. Given this burden, it is not surprising that when Wolsey tried to persuade the MPs by addressing them personally, he was met with a stubborn silence.

Apart from the tensions in 1523, however, relations between the king and parliament remained harmonious and there was little alteration in the pattern that had been established by Henry VII. This was to change dramatically from 1529, with the beginning of Henry's attempt to use parliament to get an annulment of his marriage to Catherine of Aragon.

The role of the Tudor Church before 1529

Before 1529, the Roman Catholic Church in England was enormously powerful. Since the early Middle Ages, the Church had grown in wealth and influence. The Church had its own complex structure and hierarchy. At times, this structure would work in harmony with the Tudor monarchy; at other times, there could be serious disputes over control of policy.

At the head of the Catholic Church was the pope, who it was believed was placed in this position by God. Technically, the pope had the power to appoint senior churchmen such as cardinals, archbishops and bishops. In practice, these appointments often reflected the wishes of the English monarchs, especially as England was hundreds of miles away from Rome, where the pope normally lived. Roman Catholic beliefs and practices permeated every aspect of ordinary people's lives. Children were baptised into the Church and later went through a confirmation of their Christian faith. The Church performed marriages and funerals, and was often a key source of alms (charity for the poor) and care for the sick and elderly. Church festivals celebrating important dates in the Church calendar, such as saints' days, Lent, Easter and Christmas, were key events in most people's lives, to the extent that most legal documents would be dated by referring to the closest religious festival in date rather than to a weekday or month. The Church taught that Heaven, Hell and **Purgatory** were real places; how people lived their lives on earth could affect what happened to their souls after death. The Church preached that people could help their souls by performing good works, confessing their sins to a priest, praying to the saints for help, and going on pilgrimages. Attendance at regular Church services was also crucial. The most important part of the service, known as the Mass, was a celebration of the Last Supper that Jesus had with his disciples. Bread and wine would be blessed (consecrated) by the priest and it was believed that, during this process, the bread and wine became the body and blood of Jesus. This belief was known as transubstantiation.

In addition, the Church was the main source of education and learning. The papacy guarded the Church's right to monitor and censor ideas, and would prosecute those who seemed to challenge its teaching as heretics; if found guilty of heresy, the punishment could include burning at the stake. Church services and the Bible were in Latin, not English, which meant most of the congregation would not have been able to understand what their priest was saying. However, for a clever boy, the Church was the route to power and increased status in society. Churches and monasteries offered boys the opportunity to learn to read and write, and the chance to go to one of the two English universities, Oxford or Cambridge. A career in the Church offered many opportunities to rise to the top of society, despite a lowly background – Thomas Wolsey is a good example of this route into power. He began his career as the son of an Ipswich butcher, yet through a Church education and career, he was able to rise to be Henry VIII's Chancellor and chief minister.

In the period before 1529, the Church had both supporters and critics, which has led historians to debate its continuing popularity and relevance to ordinary people's lives. On the one hand, the Church and its clergymen were undoubtedly wealthy and powerful. **Humanist** thinkers criticised this on the grounds that in the Bible, the original Church was supposed to be poor and its priests were supposed to be humble. In addition, they criticised the Church for its corruption and exploitation of people's fear of what would happen to their souls after their deaths; the practice of the sale of **indulgences** was a particular target for criticism. The Church was seen to be out of touch; services in Latin meant that ordinary worshippers could not understand what was being said, while the worship of saints was seen to be both superstitious and non-biblical. Many clergymen held multiple posts (a practice known as pluralism), which meant that they had little contact with the people they were supposed to serve. This antagonism towards the Church is often called anticlericalism.

On the other hand, it should not be assumed that the break with Rome which occurred under Henry VIII was the inevitable result of anti clerical feeling. The wealthiest in society left money in their wills to pay for priests to pray for their souls after their deaths. The Church was also endowed with vast landed estates, which meant that by the Tudor period it was the biggest landowner in England. In addition, the Church, and the traditions and festivals associated with it, were still a part of everyday life. This was particularly true in the more remote regions of England, such as Yorkshire, Lancashire, Cornwall and Devon. There is also considerable evidence that the Church retained its popularity and appeal as ordinary people continued to make contributions to their local church to buy new jewels and vestments (priests' clothing). Building or rebuilding local churches was also widespread: almost two-thirds of English parish churches were built or rebuilt during the 15th century. The English Church retained its place as an essential part of everyday life.

KEY TERMS

Purgatory
In the doctrine of the Catholic Church, it was believed that Purgatory was the intermediate place that existed between Heaven and Hell. It was believed that most people's souls would go to Purgatory on their deaths. As the name implies, Purgatory was where a soul was 'purged': the soul would undergo purification until it was pure enough to go to Heaven. Purgatory was not supposed to be a pleasant place for the soul, which was why prayers for the souls of the dead were so important in shortening the time a soul spent being purified.

Humanist
Humanist thought emerged in Europe in the later Middle Ages as part of the Renaissance (the 'rebirth' of education and thinking). Humanists such as Desiderus Erasmus did not want to break from the Catholic Church, but they were often critical of the superstition, wealth and corruption within the Church. They argued that the Church needed to be reformed from within.

Indulgences
A document that could be bought from Church officials, it offered forgiveness for sins and promised to decrease the amount of time that a soul would spend in Purgatory.

SOURCE
5

A sale of indulgences during the Tudor period in England. Indulgences were pardons for sins, sold by the Catholic Church to raise money. From a contemporary print.

ACTIVITY
KNOWLEDGE CHECK

1 Look at Source 5. On your own copy of this picture, label: a) what you can see in the picture; b) what this picture suggests about the role of the Church before 1529.

2 What are the strengths and limitations of this source for a historian trying to find out about the role of the Church in early Tudor England?

Relations between the Tudor state and Church before 1529

The relationship between the temporal power of the monarch and their government (the state) and the spiritual power of the Church was often harmonious in the period before 1529. At other times in the period, the monarchy and the Church could become rivals. Tensions tended to arise over the power and privileges of the Church, especially when they appeared to be undermining or challenging the power of the monarchy over England; particular flashpoints were the appointment of senior churchmen and the Church's rights over **sanctuary** and **benefit of clergy**. A further source of tension was the ability of the papacy, based in Rome, to intervene in English Church affairs. English monarchs tended to guard their powers and rights to control the English Church very carefully; papal, foreign intervention could be seen as an attack on the power of English kings.

As a usurper, Henry VII particularly needed the support of the Church, as this equated to support from God for his victory at the Battle of Bosworth and the death of Richard III. Henry was careful to uphold the traditional privileges of the Church, except when they seemed to threaten his own power. For example, Henry was prepared to override the sanctuary laws in order to arrest Humphrey Stafford, who had plotted to rebel against him in 1486. In 1489 and 1491, Henry passed laws tightening controls over who could claim benefit of clergy, but this seems to have been part of an attempt to ensure that those claiming this privilege were genuinely members of the clergy. It was not intended as an attack on the Church's powers. Furthermore, Henry's relationship with the papacy

KEY TERMS

Sanctuary
Under English law, anyone accused of a crime could seek sanctuary in a church. This meant that they were protected by the Church from arrest by the authorities. Someone seeking sanctuary could take advantage of this arrangement for 40 days. After this time, they had to give themselves up to the authorities for trial or confess that they were guilty and leave England. Henry VII claimed the right to override this law when the accused person had committed treason (the most serious crime).

Benefit of clergy
Any criminal who could prove that they were a member of the clergy could be tried in a Church court rather than a royal court and avoid harsher punishments.

KEY TERM

Anticlericalism
Dislike or criticism of the Church and its clergy. Anticlerical sentiment can be found as early as the 14th century; it was not new in the reign of Henry VIII. Although anticlericalism did pave the way for the growth of Protestantism, it was possible to be a member of the Roman Catholic Church, yet be critical of it.

was good. A sign of this was that he was able to ensure that the pope appointed Henry's own candidate, John Morton, to the top position in the English Church, Archbishop of Canterbury.

In the first 20 years of Henry VIII's reign, this trend continued, although there were occasional flashpoints. **Anticlericalism** did exist in Tudor England and was sometimes expressed in parliament. A good example of this was the parliaments which met in the years between 1512 and 1515. In 1512, there was another Act to limit benefit of clergy; although on its own, this Act may be seen as a continuation of the process begun by Henry VII. In the parliament that met in 1515, however, anticlerical feeling was exacerbated by the Hunne affair, in which a rich London merchant accused of heresy had been found dead while in the Bishop of London's prison. The Church claimed that he had committed suicide, but it was rumoured that Hunne had been murdered. Parliamentary criticism in this case focused on the power and corruption of the Church.

EXTEND YOUR KNOWLEDGE

The Hunne Case
Richard Hunne was a London merchant. In 1511, his infant son died, and the local parish priest asked for the usual mortuary fee (payment for burial). Hunne refused to pay and was sued in the Church courts, which found against him. Hunne was then accused of heresy and sent to the Bishop of London's prison. In December 1514, Hunne was found hanged in his cell. The Church claimed it was a case of suicide. Despite his death, Hunne was still put on trial for heresy. He was found guilty and his corpse was ceremonially burned. This case caused considerable anger and resentment in London and fuelled anticlericalism in parliament.

Despite these criticisms, state–Church relations remained relatively cordial in the early years of Henry VIII's reign. Henry regarded himself as a loyal Catholic – he even published a book, *Assertio Septem Sacramentorum* (The Defence of the Seven Sacraments), in support of the teachings of the Catholic Church and attacking the ideas of the reformer, Martin Luther. Henry's chief minister from c1511 to 1529, Thomas Wolsey, was a clergyman. Like Henry VII before him, Henry's relations with the papacy were good enough for him to be able to secure for Wolsey a whole series of top-level positions in the Church, including the bishoprics of Durham, Bath and Wells, and Tournai (France), which Wolsey held simultaneously. Wolsey was eventually promoted to the second-highest position in the English Church, the Archbishopric of York in 1514. In 1515, the pope also appointed him to the position of Cardinal; this meant that Wolsey was one of the most powerful men in the European Catholic Church, with the power to elect the next pope and even the potential to become pope himself.

As Cardinal, Wolsey was more powerful even than the Archbishop of Canterbury. Wolsey would not have achieved these positions if he had not been trusted by both Henry and the papacy, and if Henry and the papacy had not been prepared to co-operate with each other in his appointments. However, Wolsey's all-powerful position meant that it was easier for him to control both the English Church and the government of the realm, and because of his power the Church lost some of its independence from the monarchy. As a senior churchman, Wolsey's role was at times ambivalent. He was prepared to make reforms to the Church; between 1524 and 1529, he closed 30 monasteries which had decayed into corruption. But he used the money from these monasteries to found a school in Ipswich and an Oxford college in his name. Wolsey was also Henry VIII's faithful servant and chief minister. Before 1527, Wolsey was able to be loyal to both the pope and the English monarchy, but from this date, his loyalties became increasingly divided. This was because Henry wanted to get an annulment of his marriage to Catherine of Aragon from the pope; as a loyal servant of the king, Wolsey was obliged to arrange this, but as a senior member of the Church, he also owed obedience to the pope. As a result of these divided loyalties, Wolsey eventually fell from power in 1529 and died on his way to trial in 1530. In the years following his fall, English Church–state relationships changed drastically.

EXTEND YOUR KNOWLEDGE

Martin Luther and reformer ideas

Martin Luther was a German monk who challenged the teachings of the Catholic Church. His *Ninety-Five Theses* (1517) attacked practices such as the granting of indulgences. Luther went on to reject Catholic teaching on purgatory and transubstantiation. His ideas were spread widely across Europe and influenced some English courtiers, such as Thomas Cromwell, Thomas Cranmer and Anne Boleyn. Luther's reformer ideas eventually became known as 'Protestantism'.

TIMELINE: RELATIONS BETWEEN THE CHURCH AND STATE, 1485-1603

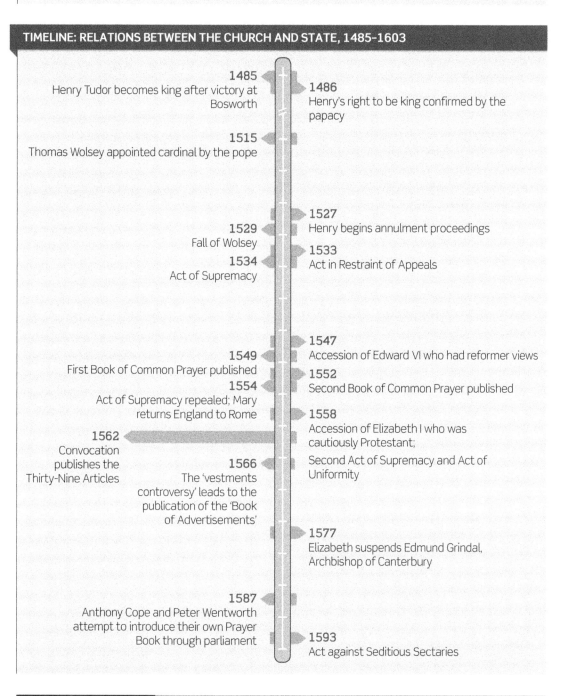

1485
Henry Tudor becomes king after victory at Bosworth

1486
Henry's right to be king confirmed by the papacy

1515
Thomas Wolsey appointed cardinal by the pope

1527
Henry begins annulment proceedings

1529
Fall of Wolsey

1533
Act in Restraint of Appeals

1534
Act of Supremacy

1547
Accession of Edward VI who had reformer views

1549
First Book of Common Prayer published

1552
Second Book of Common Prayer published

1554
Act of Supremacy repealed; Mary returns England to Rome

1558
Accession of Elizabeth I who was cautiously Protestant;

Second Act of Supremacy and Act of Uniformity

1562
Convocation publishes the Thirty-Nine Articles

1566
The 'vestments controversy' leads to the publication of the 'Book of Advertisements'

1577
Elizabeth suspends Edmund Grindal, Archbishop of Canterbury

1587
Anthony Cope and Peter Wentworth attempt to introduce their own Prayer Book through parliament

1593
Act against Seditious Sectaries

ACTIVITY
KNOWLEDGE CHECK

1 Make lists to show the strengths and weaknesses of the Church from 1485 to 1529.

2 Why do you think the relationship between the monarchy and the Church was sometimes tense? What could be done to resolve these problems?

Background to the Act of Supremacy (1534)

In 1527, Henry VIII began to challenge the legality of his marriage to Catherine of Aragon. After 18 years of marriage, Catherine had produced one living daughter, Princess Mary, but no living son. She was now past child-bearing age and Henry had fallen for the younger Anne Boleyn. During the 1520s, Henry became convinced that he was being punished by God for marrying Catherine. In Henry's eyes, God had not granted him the son and heir he so desperately wanted to secure his dynasty. As a result, Henry decided to seek an **annulment** of his marriage to Catherine from the pope. Unfortunately for Henry, he was unable to get his annulment from Catherine. The pope, Clement VII, was under the control of Catherine's nephew, Charles, the Holy Roman Emperor and ruler of Spain. Because of this, Clement was unable to give Henry an annulment. By 1529, Henry was frustrated and looking for another method to end his marriage and marry Anne. Wolsey had fallen from power as a result of his inability to help Henry; in his place, Thomas Cromwell began to rise in Henry's service. It was Cromwell who found the solution to Henry's problems by using parliament to break from papal control and to place Henry at the head of the English Church. This, in turn, allowed Henry to announce that his marriage to Catherine was void. Although neither Henry nor Cromwell was thinking of the long-term consequences of their actions, the results of the break with Rome would have a permanent impact on the relationships between the state, Church and parliament.

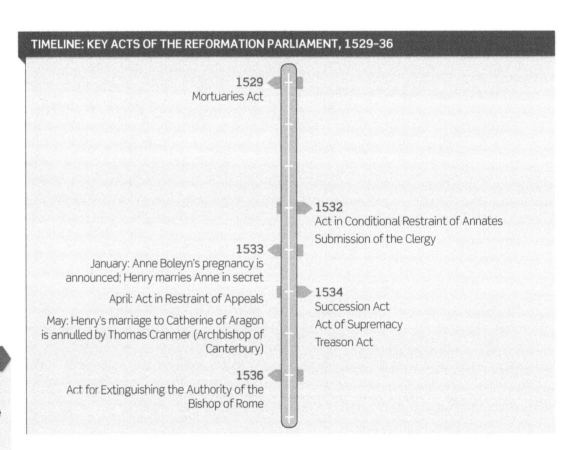

TIMELINE: KEY ACTS OF THE REFORMATION PARLIAMENT, 1529–36

1529
Mortuaries Act

1532
Act in Conditional Restraint of Annates
Submission of the Clergy

1533
January: Anne Boleyn's pregnancy is announced; Henry marries Anne in secret

April: Act in Restraint of Appeals

May: Henry's marriage to Catherine of Aragon is annulled by Thomas Cranmer (Archbishop of Canterbury)

1534
Succession Act
Act of Supremacy
Treason Act

1536
Act for Extinguishing the Authority of the Bishop of Rome

From 1532, Thomas Cromwell had risen to become Henry's chief minister and he took charge of the king's attempts to get an annulment from Catherine. Parliament had been called in 1529, in an attempt to put pressure on the papacy to grant an annulment. Before Cromwell's rise to power was complete, parliament had already been used to threaten the English Church through the passing of the Act in Conditional Restraint of **Annates**, which put a temporary stop to payments to Rome and was the first step on the path that was to lead to complete rejection of the pope's power in England. Cromwell took advantage of the anticlerical feeling in the Commons to take the pressure on the Church further. In 1532, he used anticlerical feeling to force the clergy of the English Church to submit to Henry. In the Submission of the Clergy, English churchmen agreed to accept Henry's power over them; they were not allowed to call **Convocation** without his permission, nor were they allowed to pass canons (Church laws) without his agreement. Through these early Acts, Henry and Cromwell restricted the legal and financial power of the English Church.

It was not until early 1533 that events leading to the final break with Rome speeded up. This was because Anne Boleyn was now pregnant and Henry was desperate to marry her and make sure the child she bore was legitimate. Cromwell's response was to persuade parliament to pass the Act in Restraint of Appeals, which stopped legal appeals in Church court cases being sent to Rome. This Act was particularly important because it was the first Act of Parliament to define the monarch's powers; the introduction to this Act may well have been written by Cromwell himself. Cromwell used current ideas about the power of the English monarch to argue that traditionally, the rulers of England had no superior but God, and that the papacy had usurped these powers. This idea, known as imperial kingship, was crucial. By passing the Act in Restraint of Appeals, Cromwell was using the power of parliament to create **statute law**, which would then have to be obeyed by all Henry's subjects. Because parliament represented the realm of England, Cromwell and Henry could argue that they had the approval of Henry's subjects for their actions. The way was being paved for Henry to become Supreme Head of the Church through parliamentary statute.

The Act of Supremacy (1534)

SOURCE

From the 1534 Act of Supremacy from J.R. Guy, *Tudor England*.

Be it enacted by authority of this present Parliament that the King our sovereign lord, his heirs and successors kings of this realm, shall be taken, accepted and reputed the only supreme head in earth of the Church of England called Anglicana Ecclesia, and shall have and enjoy annexed and united to the imperial crown of this realm as well the title and style thereof, as all honours, dignities, pre-eminences, jurisdictions, privileges, authorities, immunities, profits and commodities, to the said dignity of supreme head of the same Church belonging and appertaining.

The 1534 Act of Supremacy confirmed Henry VIII as the head of the English Church under English law. In some ways the Act was no more than a law which accepted Henry's assumption of the royal supremacy, a process which was well under way in 1532–33 with the Submission of the Clergy and the Act in Restraint of Appeals. By the time the Act of Supremacy was passed, Henry had already annulled his marriage to Catherine and married Anne. Queen Anne had given birth to a daughter, Princess Elizabeth, to Henry's disappointment. Nevertheless, Henry continued to reinforce his supremacy. The Act of Succession (1534) declared that his first marriage to Catherine had never been valid, that his marriage to Anne was valid and that the heirs to the throne were to be Henry and Anne's children, not the disinherited Princess Mary. By the time that the Act of Supremacy was passed, therefore, Henry had already been the head of the English Church for more than a year, and it could be argued that its significance was relatively limited.

In other ways, however, the Act of Supremacy was very significant for the power of both monarchy and parliament. Henry and Cromwell were careful to emphasise that Henry's right to the supremacy came from God, and not parliament. Nevertheless, by using an Act of Parliament to give the supremacy the authority of statute law, those who disobeyed this law could be punished under that law. If Henry had simply declared his supremacy by **proclamation**, it would have had lesser status and could be more easily disobeyed. The Act of Supremacy paved the way for a new Treason Act. Treason against the king was redefined to mean not only actively plotting against the king, but also speaking against him and the supremacy. By creating the Act of Supremacy, Henry and Cromwell reinforced royal power. It enabled them to demand that all English subjects owed obedience to Henry alone and not to the pope. However, they also inadvertently enhanced the power of parliament and created a precedent for future religious change. Any subsequent ruler who wished to alter or reverse the Acts passed in the 1530s would need to call parliament to do this. When Mary I wished to return England to Rome, she had to recall parliament in order to repeal (cancel) the Act of Supremacy. Every time parliament was called, its influence and confidence increased. As the Tudor period progressed, so the power and role of parliament in government grew.

The 1534 Act of Supremacy also marked a turning point in the relationship between the Church and the state. It reinforced royal control over the English Church and ensured that the first allegiance of the clergy should be to Henry VIII, not the papacy. All religious houses were forced to take the

KEY TERM

Statute law
Written law, rather than accepted custom or tradition. It can only be passed by the law-making body; in Tudor England, this was parliament.

KEY TERM

Proclamation
A command issued by the monarch that was then relayed across the country by messengers, often when parliament was not in session. It was accepted that proclamations would be obeyed, but they carried less weight than statute law. It was common for proclamations to be turned into statute law when parliament next met.

oath, enhancing Henry's control over them. In 1535, Henry took advantage of his new powers over the Church to appoint Cromwell as Vicegerent in Spirituals. This title meant that Cromwell was Henry's deputy in all spiritual matters and had the power to enforce Henry's wishes, despite not being a clergyman himself. Furthermore, traditional Church privileges, such as benefit of clergy and sanctuary, were abolished. As a result of these developments, the finances, administration, legal powers and doctrine were directly under the control of Henry VIII.

Church–state relations between 1534 and 1558

The Act of Supremacy and the break with Rome were not the only changes to the relationship between Church and state in the Tudor period. Change was also brought about by the dissolution of the monasteries between 1536 and 1539, and the move to Protestantism under Edward VI. Mary I attempted to reverse many of the changes made by Henry VIII and Edward, though her attempts were cut short by her death.

As Vicegerent in Spirituals, Cromwell masterminded the dissolution of the monasteries. This process began in 1535, when commissioners were sent out to investigate the moral, spiritual and financial state of English monasteries. The result of these investigations was that in 1536, an Act of Parliament was passed to dissolve smaller monasteries which had an income of less than £200 per annum. Although this led to the most serious rebellion of Henry's reign, the Pilgrimage of Grace, Cromwell continued the process of dissolution. The last monasteries were dissolved in 1540, and all former monastic land and property was transferred to the Crown. The dissolution of the monasteries caused lasting change in the relationship between Church and state. Henry VIII acquired £1.3 million from former monastic estates, although much of this money came from selling the land off to members of the nobility and gentry, such as the Cecil and Spencer families. This proved to be a lasting change, because those who bought the land were unwilling to give it up and so had a vested interest in maintaining the break with Rome. Monasteries, with their allegiance to the papacy, disappeared from England, increasing the control of the monarchy over England.

Cromwell was also keen to promote other doctrinal changes. The Act of Ten Articles (1536) was the first attempt to define the doctrine of the new English Church. The Articles were mostly in line with Catholic belief, but the Article on the Eucharist was deliberately ambiguous in its language, while the number of sacraments considered necessary for the salvation of the soul was decreased from seven to three, which was in line with reformer views. As vicegerent, Cromwell also issued two sets of Injunctions (instructions) to the English clergy in 1536 and 1538. These discouraged practices that were seen as superstitious by reformers, such as pilgrimages. After 1539, however, the pace of religious change under Henry slowed and was even reversed. Henry himself was not a reformer. In 1539, the Act of Six Articles was passed, which reinforced Catholic doctrines such as transubstantiation and celibacy for priests. Following Cromwell's execution in 1540, the king continued to move back towards a more Catholic doctrine, with the publication in 1543 of the King's Book. This book emphasised traditional practices such as masses for the dead. But despite this return to more traditional Catholic beliefs, there was never any suggestion that England should return to Rome and Henry retained his supremacy over the English Church.

After Henry's death in 1547, he was succeeded by his son Edward VI, whose religious beliefs were strongly influenced by reformer ideas. Although Edward was a minor and his government was controlled by Protectors, there was further religious change which shaped the relationship between the Church and state. In 1549, the Act of Uniformity introduced Thomas Cranmer's new English **Book of Common of Prayer** and made its use compulsory in all church services. By 1549, therefore, the liturgy and appearance of the English parish church was fundamentally different from that of 1547 and led, in part, to the serious rebellions of 1549. By 1552, Cranmer had produced a more Protestant version of the Book of Common Prayer. This second Prayer Book replaced the Catholic stone altar with a wooden table, and told the clergy to wear a plain surplice rather than their traditional, more decorated vestments. The Prayer Book also moved further away from the idea of transubstantiation and towards an even more Protestant interpretation, which denied the **real presence**. These changes altered the doctrine and nature of the English Church in a more fundamental way. The 1552 changes to doctrine in the Forty-Two Articles would pave the way for the Thirty-Nine Articles under Elizabeth.

Mary I attempted to reverse the changes made to the Church–state relationship by Henry VIII and Edward VI; her strong Catholic faith meant that she was determined to restore the English Church to Rome. Mary seems to have hoped that there would be a popular and spontaneous return to

KEY TERMS

The Books of Common Prayer, 1549 and 1552
Thomas Cranmer wrote both Books of Common Prayer. These set out the liturgy (wording) to be used in all Church services. The use of the Prayer Books was enforced by statute law.

Real presence
The Catholic belief that the actual presence of Christ existed in the bread and wine. This was made possible through transubstantiation.

Catholicism, but this did not happen. This was partly because she underestimated the determination of English Protestants, some of whom rebelled in 1554, led by Sir Thomas Wyatt. Mary also faced problems because she was not able to demand the return of former monastic land which had been legally sold to new owners. These problems meant that Mary had to be cautious in her approach. The result was a compromise agreement between the English Crown and the papacy that former church lands would not have to be returned. This compromise kept parliament and landed society happy but made it harder for Mary to restore the Catholic Church in England to its former landed power. Although Mary was able to repeal the 1534 Act of Supremacy by her own Act of Parliament in 1554, she was unable to make a lasting impression on Church–state relations. This was partly because Mary did not live long enough to enforce the changes; she died in 1558 and her heir was the Protestant Princess Elizabeth.

Background to the Act of Supremacy and the Elizabethan religious settlement, 1559

On Elizabeth's accession to the throne she faced a dilemma. On the one hand, as the daughter of Anne Boleyn, she was the embodiment of the break with Rome and she had been educated by tutors with reformer sympathies. Protestants who had been persecuted under Mary expected her to break with Rome once more. However, if Elizabeth broke with Rome and made England Protestant again, she would face the potential threat of invasion from hostile Catholic countries, coupled with Catholic rebellion in England. In the view of the Catholic Church, she was also illegitimate and could face deposition if she allowed religious reform to progress too far. In addition, during Mary's reign, the legislation that had created the original royal supremacy had been dismantled and England had returned to Rome. A further problem was that Elizabeth was a woman; in the minds of many political thinkers of the time, both Catholic and Protestant, women were not fit to rule, let alone be Supreme Head of the Church. Elizabeth's first task was to re-establish the royal supremacy and to find a *via media* (middle way) which would keep as many of her subjects happy as possible.

The Act of Supremacy (1559) and the Elizabethan religious settlement

Like her predecessors, Elizabeth had to use parliament to legalise her religious settlement. However, she faced some problems, mainly in the House of Lords, where there were influential Catholic sympathisers among the nobility – about half of whom were Catholic – and all the bishops appointed by Mary. Elizabeth and her closest adviser, William Cecil, realised that if they were to get a more Protestant religious settlement, they would need to find a way to convince the Lords to pass the necessary legislation.

Elizabeth and Cecil's resolution to this problem was to introduce two separate bills, the bills for supremacy and for uniformity. The aim was to ensure that even if the more controversial uniformity bill ran into trouble, the restoration of the supremacy would not be affected. But even in the supremacy bill, there was compromise, since Elizabeth took the title 'Supreme Governor' rather than 'Supreme Head' of the Church. This was an attempt to appeal to both Catholics, who only recognised the pope as supreme head, and some Protestants who did not like the idea of a woman as head of the Church either. This bill also ensured that Elizabeth's governorship would be accepted by including an oath of loyalty to be taken by all officials; the penalty for not doing so was to be loss of office. The bill was passed by both the Commons and the Lords without problems.

However, the bill of uniformity still faced problems from the Lords because it was more Protestant than the Catholic peers were prepared to allow. The bill was actually a compromise in terms of the doctrines it aimed to enforce. For example, although it reimposed the more radical 1552 Prayer Book with a fine of 12d for those who refused to attend weekly Church services, two sentences were added to the Communion service from the more moderate 1549 Prayer Book. These were 'The body/blood of our Lord Jesus Christ which was given for thee, preserve thy body and soul until everlasting life.' This was an attempt to appeal to both Catholics and Protestants. Catholics could interpret this to mean that the real presence existed in the bread and wine, while Protestants could see the Communion as more of a commemoration of the Last Supper. Even with this moderate approach, the bill only narrowly passed the Lords vote by 21 to 18. Arguably, Elizabeth and Cecil's careful management of the situation, and in particular the absence of two imprisoned Catholic bishops, plus the Abbot of Westminster who mysteriously missed the vote, was decisive in the eventual passing of the Act.

Following the successful passing of the two Acts, Elizabeth was able to enforce her settlement through the new Oath of Supremacy. All but one of Mary's bishops (the aged Bishop Llandaff) refused and were deprived of their posts. This allowed Elizabeth to extend her control over the Church by appointing Protestant sympathisers in their place, including Matthew Parker (Anne Boleyn's chaplain) as Archbishop of Canterbury. The initial acceptance of the settlement among the lower clergy can be seen in the fact that only about 300 out of 8,000 refused the Oath and were deprived of their offices. Although some of these bishops and other reformers put pressure on Elizabeth for more Protestant reform, the settlement created in 1559 was to last for the rest of the reign, and became the basis for what is known as the Elizabethan Church of England. Elizabeth's governorship of the Church of England remained in place throughout her reign and proved to be a much more durable development than the original royal supremacy established by Henry VIII. This is even more remarkable because there were both Catholic and **Puritan** attempts to challenge the settlement; in 1569, there was even a serious revolt in the North against Elizabeth's rule which was led by discontented Catholic nobles. Despite these challenges, the settlement remained intact.

KEY TERM

Puritan
The word was originally a term of abuse. Puritans saw the Reformation of the Church as incomplete and wanted further reform. They tended to emphasise the importance of preaching and the Bible.

The Elizabethan settlement from 1559 to 1563

Elizabeth used her governorship to establish royal authority over the Church. She was determined to accept no changes to the initial 1559 settlement, which contained no guidance on the doctrine of the new Church. Elizabeth preferred to leave such matters to Convocation, but was still prepared to intervene and assert her royal authority when she was unhappy with what they were doing. In 1563, Convocation met to discuss the Forty-Two Articles of faith introduced in Edward VI's reign; these were to become the Thirty-Nine Articles. At this meeting, a group of more radical Protestants, known as Puritans, tried to continue what they saw as further and necessary reform of the Church. Under Puritan pressure, Convocation passed Article 29, which denied the real presence in the Communion; this was unacceptable to both Catholics and moderate Protestants. Elizabeth was forced to step in. She ordered the article to be left out, so in fact only 38 were originally published. This kind of royal intervention would have been unthinkable before the break with Rome under Henry VIII, when matters of doctrine would have been left to the pope.

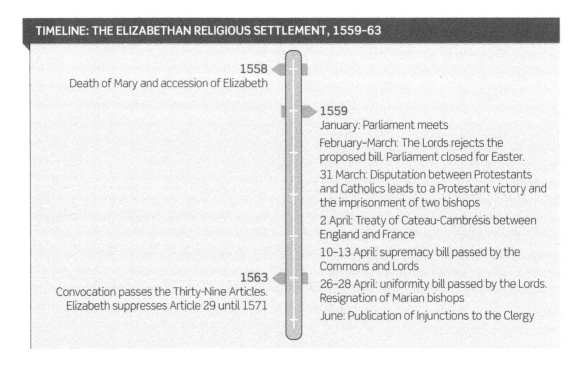

TIMELINE: THE ELIZABETHAN RELIGIOUS SETTLEMENT, 1559-63

1558
Death of Mary and accession of Elizabeth

1559
January: Parliament meets

February–March: The Lords rejects the proposed bill. Parliament closed for Easter.

31 March: Disputation between Protestants and Catholics leads to a Protestant victory and the imprisonment of two bishops

2 April: Treaty of Cateau-Cambrésis between England and France

10-13 April: supremacy bill passed by the Commons and Lords

1563
Convocation passes the Thirty-Nine Articles. Elizabeth suppresses Article 29 until 1571

26-28 April: uniformity bill passed by the Lords. Resignation of Marian bishops

June: Publication of Injunctions to the Clergy

Crown and Church, 1559-1603

Although Elizabeth I saw her 1559 settlement as definitive, and needing no further change, this did not stop the Puritan challenge to it. It did not help that some Puritans, such as Edmund Grindal, held positions of high power within the Church of England and could use their power to support further change.

The earliest forms of Puritan challenge were from within the Church itself. Some more radical clergy refused to conform to the settlement rules about vestments (clothing to be worn in Church by the clergy). Puritans preferred a simpler style, but Elizabeth saw this as a direct challenge to her authority over the Church. In 1566, she ordered Matthew Parker, the Archbishop of Canterbury, to enforce the rules. Parker issued the 'Book of Advertisements' which instructed clergy on the correct forms of dress. Thirty-seven London clergy resigned in protest, but the actions of Elizabeth and Parker put an end to the 'vestments controversy'. They were unable to end the Puritan challenge, however. Some local groups set up 'prophesyings'. These were meetings of Puritans that were aimed at encouraging better education through Bible study and Puritan clergy practising the preaching of sermons. Elizabeth thought these meetings were dangerous, because it was very difficult to control what was said and she feared the spread of radical ideas which might challenge her settlement. She ordered the new Archbishop of Canterbury, Grindal, to suppress the prophesyings. But Grindal was sympathetic to what the Puritans were trying to achieve, and refused. Elizabeth's response was to suspend him and place him under house arrest in 1577. She preferred to have no archbishop at all rather that one who appeared to encourage dangerous challenges to her authority over the Church.

Further Puritan challenges came via parliament, showing its increasing status within government. Puritans were able to get themselves elected as MPs and they used this privilege to introduce bills that would have changed the original 1559 settlement. For example, in 1571, Walter Strickland attempted to introduce a bill that would have changed the Prayer Book. The queen and her councillors intervened and the bill was suppressed. Another bill, introduced in 1587 by Anthony Cope and Peter Wentworth, attempted to remove the structure of the Church of England, which was based around a hierarchy of archbishops and bishops, with the queen as governor. Cope and Wentworth were sent to the Tower of London, and Elizabeth ordered the Speaker of the Commons to block any further discussion of the settlement.

By 1589, however, the Puritan challenge had diminished somewhat. Key supporters of the Puritans, such as Elizabeth's favourite, the Earl of Leicester, had died. Parliament itself, afraid of political instability and threats to the queen herself, passed the Act against Seditious Sectaries in 1593. This Act ordered anyone who refused to attend Church of England services to leave the country. Any exiles who returned would be executed. The fact that parliament had to pass such an Act suggests that the Tudor government was concerned about possible threats to the religious settlement. However, the decrease of Puritan activity in this period suggests that the Act was successful and that Elizabeth was ultimately able to sustain royal control over the Church and those who challenged it.

ACTIVITY
KNOWLEDGE CHECK

Comparing the impact of the 1534 and 1559 Acts of Supremacy

	What did it do?	Evidence of lasting change to the relationship between Church and Crown	Evidence of no lasting change to the relationship between Church and Crown
1534 Act of Supremacy			
1559 Act of Supremacy			

Copy and complete the table using information in this chapter.

In your opinion, which Act of Supremacy did more to change the relationship between the Crown and the Church?

Crown and parliament, 1559–1603

Elizabeth I was very careful to protect her prerogative rights and regarded with suspicion any attempts to challenge them. Apart from the Puritan attempts to change the religious settlement through parliament, her relations with her parliaments remained cordial. Like the reigns of Henry VII and the early years under Henry VIII, parliament met infrequently before 1585. However, the relationship between the monarchy and parliament did come under strain from 1585. This was because England went to war with Spain; the conflict was to last until 1604. As a result, Elizabeth

Royal prerogative
The customary rights and privileges which the Tudor monarchy claimed were due to them. These rights included the right to choose who to marry and to summon and dismiss parliament. More controversially, monarchs also claimed the right to additional financial exactions, which were not controlled by parliament. Henry VII used his royal prerogative to raise money by making demands on his nobility as his tenants (as was his right). Elizabeth used her prerogative to grant monopolies to the highest bidder. The royal prerogative and how far it could be extended was a source of tension between the monarchy and parliament.

Parliamentary bill
A bill could be introduced in the House of Lords or Commons; it would be discussed in both Houses, and if it was agreed by both Houses and the monarch, it would become an Act of Parliament. Bills were often introduced by the government, but could also be introduced as 'private' bills by any Member of Parliament.

Petition
This was different from a bill in that it was a document addressed to the monarch, complaining about a particular issue. Petitions could be made within parliament as a way to bring the monarch's attention to a complaint, but it was up to the monarch to read or listen to the petition and act on it. Using a petition was therefore a less aggressive tactic than introducing a bill, which could alter the law or prerogative.

was forced to call parliament more regularly to raise taxation. This created a new impetus for the development and confidence of parliament.

The main concerns of parliament, especially in the 1590s, were the queen's and her officials' misuse of monopolies and high levels of taxation caused by the ongoing war. Local complaints about the abuse of the **royal prerogative** to grant monopolies filtered into parliament. With the increasing demands of the war with Spain, which began in 1585, Elizabeth had less money for patronage; granting monopolies was an easy way to reward her courtiers and raise ready money, as the courtiers would pay for the privilege. The monopolies that caused the complaints were those that Elizabeth granted to her courtiers for profit. Walter Raleigh, for example, had monopolies in tin, playing cards and the licensing of taverns. The system appeared corrupt, with greedy courtiers creating huge profits for themselves by raising prices. Because they had the monopoly on a particular product, there was no competition, so monopolies forced prices up. It was resentment over monopolies, and Elizabeth's handling of the complaints in parliament, which created tension in 1597 and 1601.

By the parliament of 1597, the social and economic situation had deteriorated dramatically; the war with Spain was continuing, bringing increased fears of invasion, and Tyrone's rebellion in Ireland had broken out. Parliamentary complaints by MPs over monopolies were an expression of increasing political and economic tensions. Some MPs wanted to introduce a **parliamentary bill** to tackle the issue, but they were eventually persuaded to **petition** Elizabeth instead, which meant that they were not challenging her prerogative directly. Elizabeth managed to defuse the situation by promising that all monopoly licences would be examined. The 1597 parliament represented the first direct criticism of Elizabeth's policies, although there was no direct challenge to her prerogative, and showed the extent to which parliament's confidence had grown by this time.

In the parliament of 1601, the Commons' anger was much more extreme than in 1597. Elizabeth was forced to call parliament for more taxation, but she had done nothing to keep her promises about dealing with monopolies. The 1601 parliament was unusual because it contained 253 MPs with legal training, the highest number of such men of the whole Tudor period. These men were not only well-versed in legal procedure, but they had also come across the problems caused by monopolies in the law courts, where those with grievances against the monopolies were unable to get justice. In addition, at least 157 MPs in this session of parliament had also been present in 1597, and were therefore likely to be sympathetic to complaints about monopolies. Even worse, a mob burst into parliament, begging MPs to do something about the abuses of the monopolists. These scenes were unprecedented in any Tudor parliament and showed the extent of popular anger and the danger of the situation deteriorating into riots. Faced with such anger, Elizabeth responded cleverly. She met with a delegation of about 140 MPs, where she gave her 'golden speech', in which she admitted to some 'lapses of error', but still upheld her prerogative rights. The 'golden speech' was a triumph of political manipulation; Elizabeth managed to appear gracious, while in reality conceding very little. She also received the taxation for which parliament had originally been called. Elizabeth's careful management of parliament, although it came almost too late, was enough to keep the MPs happy. It is noticeable, however, that she did have to 'manage' her later parliaments in a way that would have been unfamiliar to earlier monarchs.

EXTEND YOUR KNOWLEDGE

Peter Wentworth (1524–97)
Wentworth was a Puritan MP in the parliaments of 1571, 1572, 1586, 1589 and 1593. He had powerful connections as he was brother-in-law to the councillor Sir Francis Walsingham, but these connections did not prevent him getting into trouble for his outbursts in parliament. Wentworth also attempted to get his tract *A Pithie Exhortation of her Majestie for establishing her successor to the crowne* published. This led to his imprisonment in 1591–92. Wentworth's final attempt to raise the issue of the succession led to his final arrest in 1593 and imprisonment until his death in 1597, because he would not apologise to the queen.

Concepts of the sovereignty of statute law and parliamentary privilege

The sovereignty of statute law became well established in the Tudor period. This means that laws passed by parliament could only be changed by a future parliament. It also meant that parliament had the sole right to pass laws and that these laws had to be obeyed by everyone in England. Before the 1530s, when parliament met relatively infrequently, it was not apparent that these changes would occur. Parliament was very much the instrument of the monarch and opposition to the Tudor rulers' policies were very rare. However, the break with Rome in the 1530s brought about significant change to the importance of statute law. Although neither the king nor Cromwell wanted to give the impression that parliament had created or granted the royal supremacy to Henry, the role and power of parliament did change as a result. The use to which parliament was put set a precedent that would have unforeseen consequences. Once parliament had been used to create the royal supremacy and break with Rome, subsequent monarchs were forced to return to it whenever they wanted to alter the religious and political settlement enforced in the 1530s. The events of the 1530s also created the notion of 'king-in-parliament'. This was the idea that the most powerful institution in the country was the king acting in conjunction with parliament rather than without it. The 'king-in-parliament' also had authority over the Church, but the king alone did not. The theory was that God had granted Henry the royal supremacy, but the people had given Henry VIII the authority to assume the supremacy through parliament. The reigns of Mary and Elizabeth reinforced this idea. Mary had to repeal the supremacy through parliament and Elizabeth reasserted it again through another Act of Parliament. Each time this happened, parliament gained more power, though it was never more powerful than the monarch. By the end of the period, parliament had gained the right to legislate on religious change and on the royal succession; this encouraged MPs to believe that they were free to discuss religious policy and the succession in parliament, though this was a privilege which Elizabeth consistently tried to deny them.

As the role of parliament became increasingly significant in Tudor government, there was more debate over its rights and privileges. Particular areas of concern were MPs' rights to freedom of speech while they were in the House of Commons, and the House of Commons' role in the granting of taxation. Since the Middle Ages, it had been acknowledged that MPs had certain privileges. They could not be arrested for debt and could not be prosecuted in the lesser law courts while they were serving as MPs. Within the Commons chamber, it was accepted that MPs would be able to speak freely, but as part of this, they had to agree not to talk about parliamentary proceedings outside the House. However, these freedoms did not grant protection from parliamentary managers, put there by the monarch who would keep the ruler informed of what was being said. This led to potential tension between parliament and the monarchy over the extent of the Commons' freedoms. As early as 1523, Thomas More, who was

acting as Speaker, made a speech requesting that Henry VIII allow MPs to speak freely (Source 7). This was the first time that the Speaker had ever made such a request. Given that the Commons was particularly angry over the monarchy's financial demands at this time, More's request was vital. Henry agreed and parliament was allowed the freedom to restrict the amount of taxation that Wolsey was granted, in which they were successful.

SOURCE

7 Thomas More's speech to parliament in 1524 requesting the right for free speech for the Commons.

My other humble request, most excellent Prince, is this. Of your commoners here assembled by your high command for your Parliament, a great number have been, in accord with the customary procedure, appointed in the House of Commons to treat and advise on the common affairs among themselves, as a separate group. And, most dear liege Lord, in accord with your prudent advice communicated everywhere by your honorable commands, due diligence has been exercised in sending up to your Highness's court of Parliament the most discreet persons out of every area who were deemed worthy of this office; hence, there can be no doubt that the assembly is a very substantial one, of very wise and politic persons. And yet, most victorious Prince, among so many wise men, not all will be equally wise, and of those who are equally wise, not all will be equally well-spoken. And often it happens that just as a lot of foolishness is uttered with ornate and polished speech, so, too, many coarse and rough-spoken men see deep indeed and give very substantial counsel... And therefore, most gracious Sovereign, considering that in your high court of Parliament nothing is discussed but weighty and important matters concerning your realm and your own royal estate, many of your discreet commoners will be hindered from giving their advice and counsel, to the great hindrance of the common affairs, unless every one of your commoners is utterly discharged of all doubt and fear as to how anything that he happens to say may happen to be taken by your Highness. And although your well known and proven kindness gives every man hope, yet such is the seriousness of the matter, such is the reverent dread that the timorous hearts of your natural-born subjects conceive toward your high Majesty, our most illustrious King and Sovereign, that they cannot be satisfied on this point unless you, in your gracious bounty, remove the misgivings of their timorous minds and animate and encourage and reassure them.

It may therefore please your most abundant Grace, our most benign and godly King, to give to all your commoners here assembled your most gracious permission and allowance for every man freely, without fear of your dreaded displeasure, to speak his conscience and boldly declare his advice concerning everything that comes up among us...

ACTIVITY
KNOWLEDGE CHECK

1 What arguments does More use to justify parliamentary freedom of speech?

2 Why do you think Henry VIII was prepared to agree to parliamentary freedom of speech?

The Tudor monarchs' parliamentary management meant that actual examples of opposition were rare, however. Crown and noble patronage meant that there was always a group of MPs who owed their obedience to a powerful patron. In the 1530s, Cromwell also introduced the concept of by-elections, when vacancies that had arisen in the Commons while parliament was in session could be filled. This process allowed the ruler and their ministers to manipulate who was elected. Even where MPs in the Commons were not directly under the control of a patron, their natural deference to their social superiors, the monarch and the Lords, meant that they tended to do what they were told. Nevertheless, parliamentary confidence in challenging their monarchs' wishes did start to grow. In 1555, Mary faced a revolt by MPs who refused to accept a bill that would have confiscated the lands of those exiled from England (who were mostly reformers). The MPs were furious at what they saw to be an attack on their rights as landowners. The MP for Gloucestershire, Sir Anthony Kingston, locked the doors to the House and forced the Speaker to take a vote defeating the bill before Mary's supporters could fetch additional support.

By Elizabeth's reign, MPs felt that their views should be heard on her marriage, the succession and religion. In most cases, Elizabeth was able to suppress these debates with the help of her councillors such as William Cecil and Francis Walsingham. Nevertheless, they could not stop all challengers, such as Peter Wentworth. In 1576, Wentworth made a speech in parliament attacking Elizabeth's attempts to control discussions in the Commons. Although this should not be seen as a defence of the modern idea of freedom of speech, it is significant that Wentworth would use traditional ideas about parliamentary privilege to justify his attempts to challenge the religious settlement. Parliament was so embarrassed by Wentworth's outburst that they imprisoned him for a month. Other MPs also expressed similar concerns about royal parliamentary management in the 1590s.

Nor could Elizabeth's councillors always ensure complete obedience from the Commons over matters of taxation. In 1593, the Commons had agreed to a bill that would allow for two subsidies to be raised, but in a meeting with representatives of the Lords, the MPs were told by Cecil that this was not enough and that they should reconsider the amount they were prepared to offer. This angered some of the MPs, who felt that the Commons should have the sole right to initiate a taxation bill and that the Lords should not intervene in the process. MPs argued that because they represented the majority of people who would pay the money, it should be they who decided whether taxation should be granted and how much should be levied. Eventually, the councillors in the Lords managed to calm down the MPs and they granted the subsidy that the Lords had requested. Although this incident was relatively minor in itself, it did demonstrate the increased confidence of the Commons; it also demonstrated the need for the Commons to be managed carefully. However, the 1593 Parliament ultimately did what it was asked, though with some grumbling.

The extent of change in the relationship between Crown and parliament

The role of parliament continued to change under the Tudors. For example, the number of MPs in the House of Commons had grown from 302 in 1512 to 402 in 1559 and 462 by 1586. This growth led to the need to 'manage' parliamentary business more, a role first undertaken by Thomas Cromwell and later by Elizabeth's councillors. In some areas of policy, parliament was growing more assertive. Encouraged by the Council, in 1563 and 1566, the Commons dared to raise the issue of marriage and the succession with the queen, something that would have been unimaginable in Henry VIII's reign. In 1566, the Council was forced to allow parliament time to debate the marriage and succession. In return, parliament agreed to discuss a grant of taxation, which it had threatened to withhold. These challenges became more serious in the second half of the reign. In 1587, Elizabeth went as far as to imprison the two Puritan MPs, Wentworth and Cope, for their attempts to change her religious settlement. It is significant that the Crown had to resort to such extreme measures against MPs who were more prepared to promote their own ideas. However, this also shows the limitations of parliamentary powers and privileges, because ultimately the queen was able to impose her will on those who disagreed with her. The use of parliament to legalise the break with Rome and the increasing frequency with which it was called to legislate on religious change meant that MPs like Wentworth and Cope grew in confidence to the point where they believed that they could use parliament to mould the English Church in the way that they wanted. Nevertheless, such men were a radical minority. Parliament was still controlled by the monarch.

Although there were some areas of dispute, it should be emphasised that Tudor monarchs and their parliaments were on the same side and that disputes between them were unusual. Under Henry VII and Henry VIII, parliament co-operated, though sometimes reluctantly. Mary faced a brief rebellion in 1555, but she was still able to reverse the supremacy and break with Rome with parliament's help. Elizabeth did try to restrict parliament's claims to freedom of speech in 1566 and 1576, but this was as much to do with her high views on her royal prerogative as an attempt to reduce parliament's powers. Where parliamentary pressure was apparently brought to bear on Elizabeth, such as the discussions about the succession and her marriage in 1563 and 1566, or debates over the fate of Mary, Queen of Scots in 1572 and 1586–87, these were the result of the Council using parliament to force the indecisive Elizabeth into making a decision rather than the Commons taking matters into its own hands. Although relations between the monarchy and parliament deteriorated somewhat in the 1590s, Elizabeth remained in control and was ultimately able to persuade parliament to do what she wanted. No parliament ever refused a Tudor monarch a grant of taxation, although they did sometimes try to limit the amounts, as in 1504 and 1523, or tie it to the discussion of their concerns, as in 1566. The power of parliament certainly increased during the Tudor period, but it was by no means the most powerful institution in the country.

ACTIVITY
KNOWLEDGE CHECK

1 With a partner, make a list of the new powers gained by parliament in the period 1485-1603.

2 Which of these new powers do you consider to be the most significant for the role and power of parliament?

3 In what ways did the power and role of parliament remain unchanged?

 THINKING HISTORICALLY Interpretations (6a)

Ever-changing history

Our interpretations of the past change as we change. This may be because our social attitudes have changed over time, or perhaps a historian has constructed a new theory, or perhaps technology has allowed archaeologists to discover something new.

Work in pairs.

Make a timeline that starts with the Act of Supremacy (1534) and ends 50 years in the future. Construct reactions that illustrate the point that time changes history. In the future box, you can speculate how people might react to the event in 50 years' time. Below is an example:

1534	1536	1555	1603	2066
Event: The Act of Supremacy	English Catholic: 'This is destroying the Catholic faith.' English reformer: 'This is the beginning of much-needed change to the Church.'	The Spanish ambassador: 'England's break with Rome was just a temporary mistake.' English gentleman: 'the pope is head of the Church again, but the queen runs the country.'	English Puritan: 'The beginning of the end of Catholicism.' English Catholic: 'A serious challenge to the Catholic Church, but there is hope for the future.'	?

Answer the following questions:

1 Identify three factors that have affected how the Act of Supremacy (1534) is interpreted over time, or might affect it in the future.

2 If a historian were to write a book proposing a radically new interpretation of the Act of Supremacy, how might other historians react? What would affect their reaction?

3 How will the future change the past?

THINKING HISTORICALLY Change (7a)

Convergence and divergence
Political change in England, 1485–1603

1485	1534	1553	1559	1601
Henry Tudor defeats Richard III at the Battle of Bosworth and becomes king	Henry VIII passes the Act of Supremacy	Crisis in the royal succession – Lady Jane Grey is overthrown by Mary Tudor	Elizabeth I passes the Act of Supremacy	Debates over monopolies in parliament; Elizabeth I gives her 'golden speech'

Religious change in England, 1485–1603

1515	1533	1536, 1539	1555	1563
The Hunne case is debated in parliament; anticlerical feeling is apparent	Act in Restraint of Appeals forbids cases being heard in Rome	Acts for the Dissolution of the Smaller and Larger Monasteries	Mary Tudor returns England to Catholicism	The Thirty-Nine Articles are published

1 Draw a timeline across the middle of a landscape piece of A3 paper. Cut out ten small rectangular cards and write the above changes on them. Then place them on the timeline, with political events above the line and religious events below. Make sure there is a lot of space between the changes and the line.

2 Draw a line and write a link between each change within each strand, so that you have four links that join up the changes in the *political* part of the timeline and four that join the religious changes. You will then have two strands of change: *political and religious*.

3 Now make as many links as possible across the timeline between political change and religious change. Think about how they are affected by one another and think about how things can link across long periods of time.

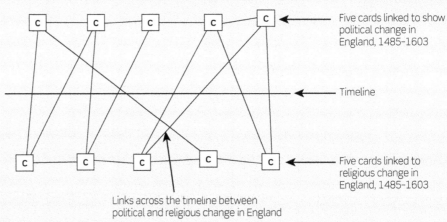

Five cards linked to show political change in England, 1485–1603

Timeline

Five cards linked to religious change in England, 1485–1603

Links across the timeline between political and religious change in England

Answer the following:

4 How far do different strands of history interact with one another? Illustrate your answer with two well-explained examples.

5 At what point do the two strands of development converge (i.e. when do the changes have the biggest impact on one another)?

6 How useful are the strands in understanding the changing relationships between the Crown, parliament and the Church in the 16th century?

A Level Exam-Style Question Section C

How far do you agree that the key turning point in the relationship between Church and state in the 16th century was the Act of Supremacy in 1559? (20 marks)

Tip

You will need to compare the 1559 Act with other developments in the period in order to decide whether it was the key turning point.

ACTIVITY
SUMMARY

1 On a sheet of A3 paper, draw a graph. The horizontal axis should show key dates from across the period 1485–1603. The vertical axis should be labelled 'Amount of power'. Draw and label three lines on your graph to represent:

   a) the changing power of the monarchy

   b) the changing power of parliament

   c) the changing power of the Church.

   Make sure that when you draw these lines, they relate to each other and show which institution was the most powerful.

   You should label the key turning points and events which caused these changes.

2 Using your graph, answer the following question:

   Which institution was the most powerful in 1485? In 1558? In 1603? You should be able to justify and explain your choice.

 WIDER READING

Guy, J. *Tudor England*, Oxford University Press (1990)

Pendrill, C. *The English Reformation, 1485–1558*, Heinemann Advanced History, Heinemann (2000)

Rex, R. *Henry VIII and the English Reformation*, Palgrave (2006)

Warren, J. *Elizabeth I: Meeting the Challenge: England 1541–1603, Access to History*, Hodder (2008)

3.2 Gaining the co-operation of the localities

KEY QUESTIONS

- How effectively were the localities governed?
- How significantly did the government of the localities change from 1485 to 1603?
- How far did the relationship between the Crown and the country change between 1485 and 1603?

INTRODUCTION

The localities were the regions of England which lay beyond London. Generally, the further away from the centre that these regions were, the harder it was for the monarch to exert direct control. The situation was made even more complex by the lack of a professional civil service to carry out the orders of the monarch. Local government was undertaken by unpaid members of the nobility and gentry. It was these men who were responsible for collecting taxation, enforcing law and order and suppressing rebellion. It was also these men who were sometimes the leaders of rebellion against Crown policies. One aim of the Tudor monarchs, therefore, was to create a successful working relationship with those in charge of local government, while also extending Crown control into the regions. From the accession of Henry VII in 1485, Tudor monarchs were usually successful in extending the power of the monarchy more directly into the localities, especially the more remote and traditionally lawless regions of England, such as Wales and the North. As part of this process, a growing number of literate yeomen and burgesses (wealthier townsmen) were drawn into government. The powers and role of the Justices of the Peace also underwent considerable change as the Tudor government sought to improve its control over tax collection, law and order and provision for the poor. At the same time, the Tudor monarchs also extended their control by encouraging the development of a complex system of patronage, through which they were able to build a successful working relationship with the nobility, who remained an integral part of Tudor government.

KEY TERM

Marcher regions
Regions on the borders of Wales and Scotland that were traditionally the first line of defence against invasion. Because of their defensive and military function, they had developed their own laws and style of government and were controlled by members of the nobility.

HOW EFFECTIVELY WERE THE LOCALITIES GOVERNED?
Relations with localities
The government of Wales under Henry VII and Henry VIII
At the accession of Henry VII, some of the most distant and hardest-to-control regions of England were the areas that had borders with Wales and Scotland. In the Middle Ages, the **marcher regions**

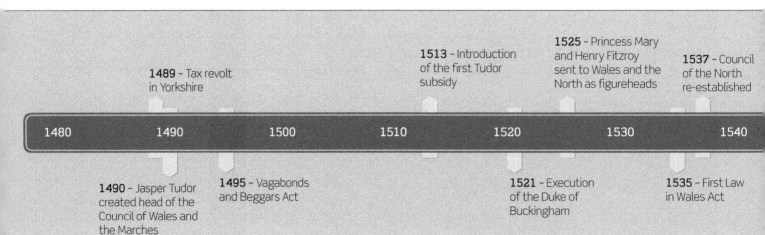

1489 – Tax revolt in Yorkshire

1513 – Introduction of the first Tudor subsidy

1525 – Princess Mary and Henry Fitzroy sent to Wales and the North as figureheads

1537 – Council of the North re-established

| 1480 | 1490 | 1500 | 1510 | 1520 | 1530 | 1540 |

1490 – Jasper Tudor created head of the Council of Wales and the Marches

1495 – Vagabonds and Beggars Act

1521 – Execution of the Duke of Buckingham

1535 – First Law in Wales Act

had developed their own laws and customs because they were the first line of defence against hostile invasion. The nobility who controlled these areas thus gained enormous legal and military power, and were almost quasi-kings in their dominance of the marcher regions. During the course of the Tudor period, these traditional powers were eroded as royal control was extended more directly into these regions.

The changes to the position of Wales had already begun before Henry VII came to the throne. By the late 15th century, Wales had been conquered by England, so there was no longer a threat of a hostile Welsh invasion. However, the government of Wales and the marcher regions of Gloucestershire, Herefordshire and Worcestershire remained out-of-step with that of England. Although the Crown controlled the **Principality of Wales**, before the 1530s Wales had its own legal system, which still depended on the local marcher lords' powers and control. This meant that in Wales and its marcher regions it was possible to commit a crime in one lordship and then escape justice by fleeing into another one. Welsh law also allowed for the continuation of blood feuds, where the family of a victim could take vengeance on the perpetrator of the crime. As a result, the area had a tendency to lawlessness. Control of Wales and the marcher regions was also vital for the Tudor monarchs because it was still possible for powerful members of the nobility to use these militarised regions to build up their own power bases, which could then be used to challenge the monarchy. This was how Henry VII himself had been able to challenge Richard III for the throne in 1485. Henry's family estates were in Pembroke, in South West Wales; when he invaded, Henry used his estate to raise an army. Henry was not the only powerful nobleman to have access to this type of military power. Edward Stafford, Duke of Buckingham, who had a claim to the throne, had landed estates in Wales. When Buckingham tried to visit his estates with 400 armed men, Henry VIII's suspicions were aroused and Buckingham was executed for treason in 1521. The threat of a powerful nobleman trying to raise an army against the Tudor monarchs was still a very real possibility, but before 1537, the Crown's attempts to deal with these problems in Wales remained very traditional in their approach.

Before the 1530s, Henry VII and Henry VIII both attempted to secure control of Wales and its marcher regions by using the Council of Wales and the Marches, which had been introduced by Edward IV in the 1470s. The Council was based at Ludlow Castle and was headed by members of the royal family and the most trusted Tudor nobility. For example, Henry VII's uncle, Jasper Tudor, Duke of Bedford, became head of the Council in 1490. Royal power in the region was reinforced in 1501, when Henry VII's 15-year-old son and heir, Prince Arthur, was sent to Wales. Arthur was the Prince of Wales, and he was supposed to enhance royal control by creating a more permanent presence in the region, although this plan was unsuccessful because Arthur died in 1502. Henry VIII was to try a similar tactic in 1525, when his nine-year-old daughter, Princess Mary, was sent to Wales as a figurehead for the Council of Wales. Like Arthur, Mary was given her own court based at Ludlow, though by 1528 she had returned to London, and the experiment of ruling Wales through the heir to the throne ended. It was not until Thomas Cromwell rose to prominence in the 1530s that a more lasting solution to extending royal authority into Wales and its Marches was found with the introduction of the Law in Wales Act.

KEY TERM

Principality of Wales
Welsh lands conquered in the 13th century that were traditionally given to the heir of the English throne, the Prince of Wales. These lands belonged to the English Crown as a result of the conquest, and included Anglesey, Caernarvon, Flint and Carmarthen. They were distinct from the marcher regions.

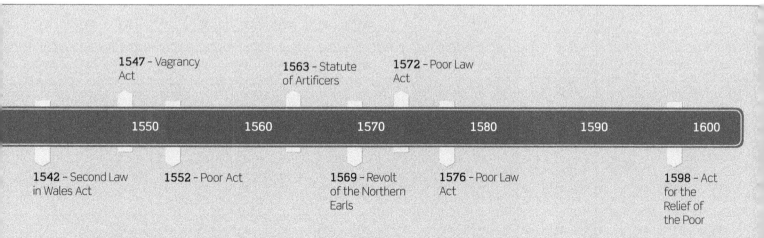

1547 – Vagrancy Act

1563 – Statute of Artificers

1572 – Poor Law Act

1550   1560   1570   1580   1590   1600

1542 – Second Law in Wales Act

1552 – Poor Act

1569 – Revolt of the Northern Earls

1576 – Poor Law Act

1598 – Act for the Relief of the Poor

The government of the North, 1485–1537

Controlling the North was an equally challenging problem for the Tudor monarchs. Geographically remote, with poor communications, it was also under threat of invasion from Scotland. The border with Scotland was so extensive that the Northern Marches were split into three: the Western, Middle and Eastern Marches. These were controlled by wardens who were responsible for their defence and keeping order. Control of this militarised zone, where cross-border raids were common, was not easy.

Henry VII faced additional problems in controlling the North because his position as a usurper made him particularly vulnerable to attempts at invasion from his rivals, who could base themselves over the border in Scotland. Regions in the North, such as Yorkshire, were also particularly unsettled because they were loyal to Richard III, who had controlled the region very successfully. The North also suffered from economic hardship; in 1489, there was a tax revolt in Yorkshire which led to the murder of Henry Percy, the Earl of Northumberland, who was in charge of money collection in the region. Because Percy's son and heir was a minor, Henry VII took the opportunity to create Thomas Howard, Earl of Surrey, as Lieutenant in the North; Surrey's role was to act as a representative of the king. He remained in this post until 1499, when power reverted to the traditional northern nobility as wardens of the Marches.

Apart from the experiment with the Earl of Surrey, the warden system continued unchanged until the 1530s. Under Henry VIII, the key noble families were the Dacres, the Cliffords, the Percy

earls of Northumberland and the Neville earls of Westmorland. These families were involved in complex feuds with each other and could not always be relied on to keep the peace; in 1525, Lord Dacre was fined £1,000 in Star Chamber (see page 73) for his tolerance of disorder in the North. However, as long as there remained the threat of invasion from Scotland, these men were needed to provide the first line of defence. An attempt to revive the Council of the North was made in 1525, when Henry Fitzroy, the six-year-old illegitimate son of the king, was made president of the Council. The young Fitzroy was brought up at Sheriff Hutton Castle in Yorkshire. However, if the king was planning to make his illegitimate son his deputy in the North, he was to be disappointed, as Fitzroy died in July 1536. It was not until the Pilgrimage of Grace (October–December 1536), the most serious rebellion of Henry's reign, that royal intervention in the government of the North became more direct and permanent.

see page 73

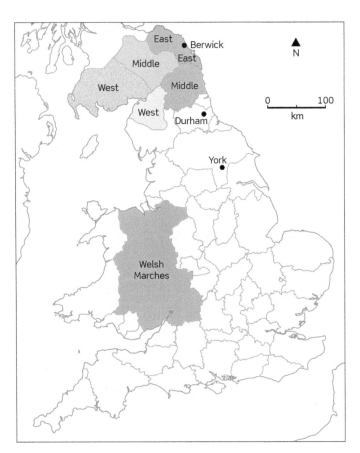

Figure 2.1 The marcher regions of Wales and the North.

ACTIVITY
KNOWLEDGE CHECK

Use the section above to add detail to this table.

	Government of Wales and the Marches	Government of the North
Role of the nobility		
Role of members of the royal family		
Use of Councils		
Successes		
Problems		

Now answer the following questions.

1 What were the main similarities and differences between the Tudor approach to the North and to Wales?

2 Why do you think there were differences in the Tudors' approaches to these regions?

3 How successfully did the Tudor monarchs manage Wales and the North before the 1530s?

The Law in Wales Act (1535)

In response to the lawlessness and the limitations of royal authority in Wales and its Marches, in 1534, Thomas Cromwell began a process that was to lead to permanent changes in the region. Cromwell began by appointing Rowland Lee to act as the Lord President of the Council of Wales. Lee was given sweeping powers to tackle crime and disorder in the region. In 1535, Cromwell introduced the first Law in Wales Act, which was passed by the English parliament in 1536. This Act is sometimes known as the Act of Union. The 1535 Act transformed the structure of Welsh government:

• The Principality of Wales and the marcher lordships were abolished, and replaced with 12 English-style counties.

- The English-style system of local government was also introduced for each new Welsh county, including **sheriffs, coroners** and Justices of the Peace.

- The Act also banned the use of Welsh in the courts – only English was to be spoken. In practice, this meant that in the more remote regions of Wales where the native language was still in common use, interpreters were widely used. However, the gentry of Wales already spoke English, so this change affected them less.

- Each new Welsh county and each Welsh county town was allocated two MPs who would sit in the English parliament. This was a change, as previously the traditional Welsh regions had not participated in English law-making.

- The main result of the Act was the end of the traditional military power of the marcher lords, a process that had already begun with the destruction of the Duke of Buckingham in 1521, but which was legalised through the 1535 Act. For the rest of the Tudor period, Wales remained directly under the control of the Crown; law and order improved and the region became less of a threat to political stability.

KEY TERMS

Sheriff
The principal agent of the Crown in the localities. One sheriff was appointed for each county and was responsible for organising royal administration and finances in their locality.

Coroner
Like their modern equivalents, Tudor coroners were responsible for investigating sudden deaths in their localities.

The Law in Wales Act (1542)

Although Cromwell fell from power and was executed in 1540, the work he had begun in extending royal control in the more remote regions of the Tudor realm continued. In 1542, a second Law in Wales Act was passed, which built on the 1535 Act. The 1542 Act introduced the system of English law into Wales, bringing an end to the traditional Welsh system, which included the use of the blood feud. In order to enforce English law, a new system of law courts was introduced called the courts of great sessions. These were sessions that were held in each new Welsh county twice a year. These courts tried criminal cases such as theft or physical attacks, and there was no right of appeal. The Act also reorganised the Council of the Marches, which was now known as the Council of Wales. The result of the 1542 Act was that the Council of Wales became a more formal body, with a president and vice president who were appointed by the monarch. Its powers were strengthened because they now rested on the authority of the king and parliament, not solely the royal prerogative. Its powers included the right to hear legal cases in a manner similar to the English Star Chamber (see page 73) and to oversee law and order in both Wales and the former marcher counties. By Elizabeth's reign, the Marcher Council had adapted further to include the Lord Lieutenants. It is a measure of the success of the Marcher Council that there was little trouble from

this region during the Tudor period. The reforms of the 1530s extended very successfully the power of the Tudor monarchs into a region which had previously been problematic.

The re-establishment of the Council of the North, 1537

Henry's inability to control the North, and the threat that this region could pose to political stability became clear in late 1536. In October 1536, rebellion broke out in Lincolnshire and spread rapidly northwards. Although the rebellion was eventually suppressed with considerable brutality, Thomas Cromwell decided to remodel the Council in 1537 in order to strengthen its powers and prevent future outbreaks of unrest. He gave it wide powers to hear and decide cases of treason, murder and **felony**. The Council became the voice of the government in London, responsible for passing on and enforcing all royal proclamations and orders made to sheriffs and JPs. It oversaw food supplies, regulated trade, organised local musters for military campaigns, and heard private cases between individuals. In addition, Cromwell extended the authority of the Council so that it governed not only Yorkshire, but also Durham, Northumberland, Cumberland and Westmorland. Finally, Henry VIII signalled the status of the new Council by giving it a permanent headquarters in York, the house of the former abbot of St Mary's priory, York, which was dissolved in 1539.

The authority of the remodelled Council was enhanced because the president was either a bishop or a member of the nobility who often came from the South or the Midlands. For example, the president from 1538 to 1540 was Robert Holgate, the bishop of Llandaff (Wales). This meant that the presidents had no vested interests in the decisions they were making and could remain relatively impartial when dealing with local disputes. The rest of the new Council was made up of local gentry, lawyers and clergy. Many of these men served for long periods of time, such as Sir Thomas Gargrave, a lawyer from Wakefield who was a councillor from 1545 to 1579. Although the president was usually not a northerner, the rest of the Council came from the region. These arrangements encouraged a consistent approach to the government of the North. Councillors were given further power and knowledge of the region under their control because they were also appointed as Justices of the Peace. As a result, the Council of the North developed as a body which could oversee the administration of the North, control border raids and manage local order through hearing court cases as a northern version of Star Chamber.

The development of the Council of the North after 1537 also signalled a longer-term decline in the power of the traditional northern lords, the Dacres, the Percies and the Nevilles.

KEY TERM

Felony
A capital crime that did not include treason. Capital crimes included offences such as murder, arson, witchcraft and heresy, and were punishable by death or forfeiture of land.

These families had dominated appointments to the wardenships of the Northern Marches since the Middle Ages. However, as the power of the monarchy increased through the power of the Council, the position of the traditional nobility was undermined. These families continued to play an important military role in the defence of the North in times of war with Scotland, when their military skills were vital, although their power declined considerably in the 1560s. Although this trend was partly the result of more peaceful relations with Scotland from 1570, increased royal control through the permanent Council meant that the traditional northern nobility were no longer able to rule the North as they pleased.

The changes to the Council seen in 1537 were not the last changes made to its role. Elizabeth I attempted to insert more southerners into the Council; this caused resentment among the traditional nobility and contributed to the outbreak of rebellion in 1569, showing that the Council was not completely in control of the North. Under Elizabeth I, the Council became responsible for combating **recusancy**. The North was the most openly Catholic region of England. There was a danger that northerners would not accept the Elizabethan settlement or would attempt to rebel against her, as they did in 1569. Although the president and the vice president, the Earl of Sussex and Thomas Gargrave respectively, had played a leading role in putting down the rebellion, the 1569 revolt led to the Council being reconstructed. In 1572, the Puritan Henry Hastings, Earl of Huntingdon, who was also Elizabeth's cousin, was made president. The result of this change was that the North became much more stable. There was no further rebellion, and the power of the traditional noble families there was much eroded, while the control of the monarchy was enhanced through the Council.

KEY TERM

Recusancy
The practice of people who refused to go to Church of England services, thus disobeying the 1559 Acts of Supremacy and Uniformity. They were mostly Catholics. Recusants could be fined, have their property confiscated, be imprisoned and even executed. Before 1569, punishments for non-attendance were relatively moderate (a fine of 12 pence per week). This was already quite a sum of money for poorer Catholics, but would not have affected wealthier members of the gentry and nobility. Before the Northern Rising, there was some tolerance to practising Catholics, with local JPs turning a blind eye to non-attendance, especially in the North.

ACTIVITY
KNOWLEDGE CHECK

1 Make a list of the key reforms made to the government of the North and Wales from the 1530s.

2 Which region saw the most change, the North or Wales? Why do you think this was?

3 'By 1603, the Tudor monarchy had complete control over both Wales and the North.' Write a paragraph explaining how far you agree with this claim.

SOURCE

From instructions given by Henry VIII to the Archbishop of York, the president of the Council of the North, and other councillors, c1544.

His Majesty, much desiring the quietness and good governance of the people there, and for speedy and indifferent administration of justice to be had between party and party, intendeth to continue his rights honourable Council called the King's Council in the North Parts. And his Highness, knowing the approved truth, wisdom and experience of the said archbishop of York, with his assured discretion and dexterity in executing of justice, hath first appointed him to be president of the said Council...

And for the more certain and brief determination if all matters that shall chance in those parts, his Majesty... ordaineth that his said Council shall by the space of one whole month in the year at least remain at York, by the space [of] one other month... at Kingston-upon-Hull, and by the space of one other month at Durham...

And... his Grace's express pleasure and commandment is, that in every sitting [of the Council]... they shall give strait charge and commandment to the people to confirm themselves in all things to the observation of such laws, ordinances and determinations as be made, passed and agreed upon by his Grace's Parliament and clergy, and specially the laws touching the abolishing of the usurped and pretended power of the bishop of Rome, whose abuses they shall so beat into their heads by continual inculcation...

ACTIVITY
KNOWLEDGE CHECK

Read the section on the remodelled Council of the North and Source 1, and answer these questions.

1 Why do you think Henry wanted the Council to spend time in different regions of the North?

2 What other functions did Henry want the Council to perform? Why might he have emphasised these?

3 What does this source reveal about the relationship between the king, the Council of the North and parliament?

Increasing borough representation in the Commons

Boroughs were towns which had the right to send two MPs to sit in parliament; this right was granted by royal charter. They were different from the shires (counties), which also sent two MPs each. During the Tudor period, the number of these boroughs increased considerably. By the end of Elizabeth's reign, there were 191 boroughs with the right to send two MPs each to parliament. This increase was part of a general trend, by which the size of the House of Commons grew from 296 members at the start of the period to 462 by the end of Elizabeth's reign. The growth of the Commons was a particularly important development because the House of Lords was decreasing in size during this period. Following the dissolution of the monasteries between 1536 and 1540, abbots were no longer summoned to the Lords; there was also a declining number of representatives of the lay nobility during the Tudor period.

Although some of the new MPs were created as a result of Henry VIII's changes to the government of Wales in the 1535 Law in Wales Act, most of the new members of the House of Commons were representatives of boroughs. For example, Edward VI created 34 new MPs representing boroughs between 1547 and 1553; Mary created 25 between 1553 and 1558; Elizabeth created 62, all in the period 1558–84. As a result of these developments, by c1600, the boroughs represented in parliament ranged in size from the largest, London, which had about 200,000 inhabitants, to middling-sized towns such as York, Bristol and Norwich, with populations of roughly 15,000, to smaller boroughs such as Exeter, Coventry and Newcastle, which had about 10,000 inhabitants each. Not all boroughs with the right to send MPs had these population levels, however. Some boroughs were so-called 'rotten' boroughs, created in the Middle Ages, but where the population had since declined, such as Dunwich (Suffolk), which was falling into the sea. In the Tudor period, some of the new borough constituencies granted a **franchise** for the first time were also rotten boroughs, such as Andover (Hampshire) and Newtown on the Isle of Wight. The reason for this lies in the growing competition for places in parliament among members of the landed gentry, and the role of Crown and noble patronage in government and the management of parliament.

Why did borough representation grow in the Tudor period?

One reason for the growth in the number of borough MPs was pressure from the towns themselves. Parliament was a place in which townsmen could ensure that the interests of their community could be promoted through the use of petitions and the creation of new laws. For example, in Edward VI's parliaments, the corporation (town council) of York was keen to ensure that laws were passed which prevented woodland areas being chopped down within 25 kilometres of the city. The MPs for York were in continuous correspondence with their corporation about such matters and seem to have paid little attention to other significant religious changes that were happening in Edward's parliaments; the two Prayer Books of 1549 and 1552 were not mentioned at all in their letters.

However, the industrial and manufacturing interests of the boroughs were not the primary reason for the growth of borough representation in the Tudor period. Most MPs who represented boroughs were not actually true 'townsmen'. Instead, they tended to be members of the landed gentry who did not even live in the towns they were supposed to represent. In the Reformation Parliament (1529–36), for example, about half of the borough MPs were townsmen; the other half were members of the gentry. This trend developed further under Elizabeth I. The historian Jennifer Loach has shown that in the 1559 parliament, only 23 percent of borough MPs were actually townsmen; by 1601, their number had decreased to just 14 percent. These developments broke the law created in the 15th century which stipulated that MPs should live in the region that they represented, but the law was ignored by the boroughs, the gentry, nobility and monarchy, because it suited the interests of all of these groups.

For boroughs, it was often financially sensible to have a member of the gentry acting as their MP. MPs could claim expenses from their constituency to cover the costs of sitting in parliament. Borough MPs could claim a wage of two shillings a day for the time they sat in parliament; they could also claim back the costs of travelling to and from London, and for their accommodation while living there. During the Reformation Parliament, it is estimated that it would have cost each town £70 to fund just one MP; these costs were doubled as each borough had two representatives. With more frequent meetings of parliament during the Tudor period, these costs grew higher. Wealthier towns such as York, Bristol or Worcester could afford to cover these costs. However, smaller and poorer boroughs looked to wealthy members of the gentry or nobility to cover these costs in return for

KEY TERM

Franchise
The qualification to vote. It varied from borough to borough, depending on the terms of the individual boroughs' charters. As a result, some boroughs had a relatively large electorate; the franchise of the borough of Gloucester allowed for between 400 and 500 men to vote. In other boroughs, the franchise was restricted to the town mayor and corporation (council) or even to the local lord. In the borough of Gatton (Surrey), the sole voter was the lord of the manor of Gatton, a member of the Copley family.

allowing them to sit as MP or nominate their own candidate. Dunwich, for example, had an annual income of £50 per annum; in 1559, its remaining residents were happy to accept the offer made to them by Sir Edmund Rowse. In return for Rowse's election in 1559 as one of the Dunwich MPs, he was prepared to cover his own expenses. This arrangement was beneficial to both parties; Dunwich was able to avoid additional expense and Rowse was able to pursue his own interests in London as an MP. Members of the gentry were increasingly keen to become MPs because of the opportunities that were available to them in London. Because the Tudor Court became an important centre of patronage, ambitious gentlemen sought election to parliament as a way to attract royal attention and to build a career.

The use of patronage by the Crown and nobility

The growth of borough representation was not solely due to increased demand from local gentry, however. Many of the local gentry who became MPs were controlled in their turn by either a member of the nobility or the monarch themselves as part of the increasingly widespread system of patronage through which the Crown extended its control over the localities. The elections for many boroughs were controlled by members of the nobility, who in turn were controlled by the Tudor monarchs. This was a method seen in the later Middle Ages, but as parliament was used more frequently, and its powers grew, it became increasingly important for the monarch to ensure that the MPs who were elected would obey the Crown's wishes. The Tudor nobility had always been able to use their landed power to control the elections to boroughs in the localities. The most powerful nobleman under Henry VIII, the Duke of Norfolk, was able to ensure that his clients were elected to boroughs such as Castle Rising, Great Yarmouth (Norfolk) and Reigate (Sussex). Similarly, in 1584, Robert Dudley, Earl of Leicester, was able to ensure the election of his candidates in the boroughs of Poole (Dorset), Tamworth (Staffordshire) and Denbigh (North Wales). This was an arrangement that was mutually beneficial to the boroughs, nobility and Tudor monarchs alike. The boroughs were able to ensure that their interests were looked after in parliament by the most powerful men in the country; for example, in 1553, the borough of Lincoln allowed the Earl of Rutland to nominate one of his own candidates as MP, and even sent the earl a barrel of wine to thank him for his support. For the nobility, the ability to place clients in positions of influence was a measure of their own power; a nobleman who could not help his own clients would rapidly lose their loyalty and support, and his own standing at the Royal Court would be compromised. Meanwhile, the Tudor monarchs could use this system to ensure that the MPs in the Commons did what they were told. These relationships help to explain why the number of boroughs increased during the Tudor period. Ambitious gentry and their noble patrons were keen to find opportunities to extend their power and influence, and the Crown was happy to encourage this. As a result, some new boroughs, such as Newtown on the Isle of Wight, were created in 1584 because of pressure from Sir George Carey. The example of Carey is particularly interesting because not only was he the governor of the Isle of Wight, but he was also Elizabeth I's cousin, and could be trusted to ensure the election of suitable MPs.

The role of the monarchy was also important in explaining the expansion of borough representation. Many of the new boroughs created in the Tudor period were in regions controlled by the Crown itself, especially the **Duchies of Cornwall and Lancaster**. The new boroughs of Grampound and Camelford, which were created in 1547, were both in the Duchy of Cornwall, for example. New boroughs in the Duchy of Lancaster included Preston (1529), Thetford (1529), Liverpool (1545) and Higham Ferrers (1545). The advantage of creating such borough seats was that the Crown could use them to place its own candidates in parliament – these men were usually loyal and experienced servants of the monarch. For example, Sir Christopher Hatton, one of Elizabeth I's most trusted courtiers, was elected as MP for Higham Ferrers for the 1571 parliament. Another of Elizabeth's trusted courtiers, Sir Walter Mildmay, ensured that his son, Humphrey Mildmay, was elected as MP for Higham Ferrers in 1584 and 1586. Sometimes, however, the Crown would try to influence borough elections in a less subtle way, in order to ensure that their favoured candidates would be elected. This was increasingly important from the period of the Reformation Parliament onwards, as the Commons became increasingly confident. The borough of Gatton, for example, whose sole elector was the Catholic Copley family, came under pressure from Elizabeth I's Privy Council to elect MPs who were acceptable to the queen. The growth of borough representation was both the result of, and an increasing challenge to, the extension of royal power into the localities. On the one hand, the Tudor monarchs encouraged and allowed the creation of new borough seats, because this kept the nobility and gentry happy and allowed increased manipulation of elections. On the other hand, by increasing the number of MPs in parliament, at a time when parliament was growing in confidence

KEY TERM

Duchies of Cornwall and Lancaster
These had once been the estates of important members of the medieval nobility. When these families died out, the estates had returned to the Crown, which used them as a source of income and patronage.

The Duchy of Cornwall had extensive estates, especially in the South West counties of Cornwall, Devon and Somerset. The main estates belonging to the Duchy of Lancaster were in Lancashire itself, Staffordshire, Yorkshire, Cheshire and Lincolnshire.

and influence, the Tudor monarchs were making it harder to control parliamentary debates, which meant that they had to develop new methods to manage the Commons that were not needed at the start of the period.

ACTIVITY
KNOWLEDGE CHECK

1 Draw a diagram to show the reasons why there was increased borough representation during the Tudor period. Your diagram should show the roles of: the boroughs, the gentry, the nobility and the Tudor monarchs. You should aim to give precise examples for each.

2 In your opinion, what was the most important cause of the growth of parliamentary boroughs? Write a paragraph justifying your reasons.

SOURCE

2 A letter from Sir Francis Walsingham, a member of the Privy Council, to Sir William More, Sir Thomas Browne and Richard Bostock, regarding the election of MPs at Gatton, 1586.

After my very hearty commendations, whereas my lords of the council do understand that Mistress Copley hath the nomination of the two burgesses for the town of Gatton... it is not thought convenient, for that she is known to be evil affected, that she should bear any sway in the choice of the said burgesses. Her majesty's pleasure being such, as by our letters hath been signified unto you, that a special choice should be had for this present parliament of fit persons known to be well affected in religion and towards the estate. Their lordships have thought good therefore you should recommend unto the said burghers William Waad, one of the clerks of her majesty's privy council, and Nicholas Fuller, a counsel at the law, whom if they shall not be willing to make choice of for their burgesses, at the least you must see that care be had that there may discreet persons be chosen and well affected...

ACTIVITY
KNOWLEDGE CHECK

Read Source 2 and answer the following questions:

1 What does Walsingham want More, Browne and Bostock to do, and why?

2 What does this letter suggest about elections to parliament under Elizabeth I?

The impact of increasing literacy in the yeoman class

During the Tudor period, literacy rates increased, especially among yeomen. The growth of humanist ideas, which emphasised the role of education for all, led to the foundation of grammar schools for boys; girls from wealthier backgrounds would have been educated at home, where they would have been taught to read and write. Public grammar schools did not charge fees and were open to rich and poor boys; these taught reading and writing, plus English and Latin grammar. Where a grammar school did not exist, some areas were served either by an 'English' school, which taught reading, writing and English grammar. The rise of these schools allowed greater access to education for those below gentry rank; the yeoman class, in particular, benefited from this development. At the same time, university education was also expanding. Although there were still only two universities in England, Oxford and Cambridge, the number of students increased. At Oxford, student numbers increased from 1,150 in 1550 to about 2,000 by the end of the period. It is estimated that just under half the students at university were the sons of the gentry or nobility; the rest came from those below gentry status, that is, those of yeomen status or from prosperous urban artisans.

Because children were taught to write only after they could read, it is possible to measure literacy rates by the number of people who could sign their own names in Church court records. The work of the historian David Cressy has shown that illiteracy rates for men and women were at about 80 percent and 98 percent respectively in 1550; by 1600, they were at 72 percent and 92 percent. However, literacy rates varied according to region and social status. In 1530, illiteracy rates among yeomen were higher in the North of England than in the Midlands, East and South. As a result of increasing education opportunities between 1550 and the end of the period, more yeomen became literate, but there were still high rates of illiteracy among labourers and the poorest in society. Sons of yeomen also benefited from increased access to schools and university. Cressy's work on the records of Church courts has shown that in the dioceses of Essex and Hertfordshire, just 33 percent of those of yeoman status were using a mark to sign documents rather than a signature in the period 1580 to 1640. In the diocese of Norwich, it is estimated that illiteracy had fallen from 60 percent to 30 percent by the 1580s However, in Durham, 73 percent of yeomen signed with a mark in the period 1561 to 1631.

The impact of this steady growth in literacy among yeomen can be seen in the changing role of this social group in government and society. Rebellions such as the Cornish Rising of 1497 and the 1549 troubles had been mostly led by yeomen who held high status in their localities. These literate yeomen were often the people who formulated the rebel demands and acted as spokesmen in negotiations with the Crown. As literacy rates increased, the role of the yeomen in local government began to change, however. Instead of being left out of local government, yeomen were now included within it. The extension of government into the localities through parliament and statute law opened up more opportunities for those of yeoman rank to take part in local government. Prosperous and literate yeomen were increasingly taking on roles such as the administration of the Poor Law and voting in elections. As they became part of the political system, so they became more likely to defend it rather than attack it through rebellion. They were also more likely to use the legal system to resolve disputes rather than resorting to violence, which was often the case earlier in the Tudor period. The result of the growth of literacy in the Tudor period was that men of yeoman rank were less likely to become involved in rebellion, especially in Elizabeth's reign. After the Revolt of the Northern Earls in 1569 (see Chapter 6), there were no more serious rebellions on the English mainland. This was mainly because England was enjoying a period of relative social and economic stability. However, when there was further economic crisis in the 1590s, there was no mass popular rising. Although there were riots and one attempted rising in Oxfordshire in 1596, these were led by the poorest in society, not by those of yeoman rank, who would once have been the leaders of popular protest but who were now part of the system of Elizabethan government.

HOW SIGNIFICANTLY DID THE GOVERNMENT OF THE LOCALITIES CHANGE FROM 1485 TO 1603?

The changing role of the Justices of the Peace, 1485–1603

How did justice work in the localities?

In the Tudor period, justice was done in the monarch's name and it was an integral part of their role to uphold law and order. The common law of England operated using precedent, tradition and parliamentary law. By 1485, the judicial system was well-established, using a combination of central courts of law, travelling courts and local courts. The main central court was the Court of King's Bench, which prosecuted cases on behalf of the king and his laws. This was usually based in London and important cases were often held there. Judges from this central court also went on tours of the localities twice a year, to monitor local processes and hear cases in the assize courts. On top of this, local officials also played a role in keeping law and order. The most important of these were the Justices of the Peace, who were usually members of the local nobility and gentry.

The role of Justice of the Peace had first emerged in the 14th century, and they had been gathering increasing power and influence locally ever since. JPs were appointed annually for each county (this was known as the county bench) and their powers were already wide-ranging by the start of the Tudor period. They could hear and decide on cases of felony and **trespass**; they could arrest potential suspects; they supervised the fixing of prices and wages; they also had to attend sessions four times a year (quarter sessions) to perform their role. Increasingly, JPs were not just active at quarter sessions, but were using their powers more widely to monitor and control local society. Being a JP was hard work, but it was also an excellent opportunity to influence local affairs. The Tudor monarchs tried to monitor carefully who became a JP; they also used the county benches to insert members of their Court into local government to enhance their control. Members of the nobility and gentry who were appointed did not have to be resident in a region to become a JP; the qualification for selection was the ownership of land worth at least £20 a year, a sizeable amount. Some JPs were appointed because they were lawyers. These men formed the 'quorum', the group of JPs who had to be present at meetings. Increasingly in the Tudor period, JPs were also

KEY TERM

Trespass
Less serious crimes that did not carry the death penalty, such as assault, damage to property or minor theft. The word carries a different meaning from today's usage.

expected to administer the Poor Law and control vagrants. Inevitably, because the men responsible for overseeing local justice were often also those with local interests to protect, there was a certain amount of bending of the system, but this did not stop the growing range of powers given to JPs during the period.

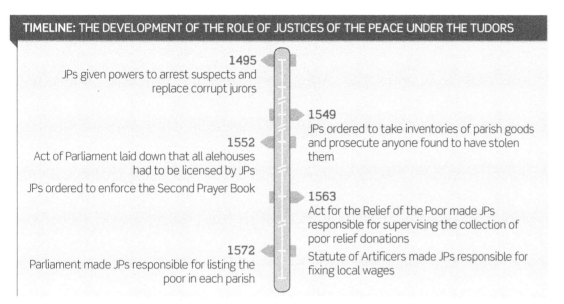

TIMELINE: THE DEVELOPMENT OF THE ROLE OF JUSTICES OF THE PEACE UNDER THE TUDORS

1495
JPs given powers to arrest suspects and replace corrupt jurors

1549
JPs ordered to take inventories of parish goods and prosecute anyone found to have stolen them

1552
Act of Parliament laid down that all alehouses had to be licensed by JPs
JPs ordered to enforce the Second Prayer Book

1563
Act for the Relief of the Poor made JPs responsible for supervising the collection of poor relief donations
Statute of Artificers made JPs responsible for fixing local wages

1572
Parliament made JPs responsible for listing the poor in each parish

What was the role of the Justices of the Peace under Henry VII and Henry VIII?

Henry VII began the extension of the powers and role of the JPs. Because his position as a usurper made him particularly vulnerable to rebellions and rival claimants, he often appointed trusted members of his Court to be JPs. For example, Sir Thomas Lovell was JP in both Yorkshire and Sussex. Lovell would not have been expected to be active at every session, but he would have acted as an important link between the centre and the localities. If politically important or sensitive cases were due to be heard before the JPs, then Lovell would have been present as a representative of the king.

Henry VII also increased the local powers of the JPs. An Act of Parliament of 1495 allowed JPs to act on information received about suspects without waiting for a **jury** to be summoned; in the same year, they were also given the power to replace jurors who they considered to be corrupt. Henry also gave the JPs power to inquire into illegal **retaining** by the nobility and to examine complaints of corruption against other local officials such as the sheriffs. The result of these developments was that by Henry's death in 1509, the judicial and administrative role of the JPs had already increased considerably.

At the beginning of Henry VIII's reign, most county benches had between 20 and 35 members. Appointment as a JP was usually for life. Occasionally, however, the government would remove a JP from the county bench. This was usually because the JP was suspected of not following government orders or of misusing his position to increase his local power. Wolsey was particularly keen to improve local justice and the quality of JPs. In 1526, for example, he summoned the JPs to hear a speech before asking them to fill in a 21-section questionnaire on law and order in their regions. Cromwell was also careful to check who was appointed as a JP, particularly since he expected them to enforce the Supremacy and the Reformation.

How did the role of the JPs develop under the later Tudors?

During the reigns of Edward, Mary and Elizabeth, the trend for placing more responsibility on the JPs continued. Social and economic crises of the late 1540s and early 1550s, including the serious rebellions of 1549, led to fears of social disorder, so in 1552, an Act of Parliament laid down that all alehouses had to be licensed by the JPs. The JPs also played an important role in enforcing Edward's religious changes. In 1549, JPs were ordered to take an inventory of parish goods in order to expose those who had illegally taken them; they were then to prosecute those responsible for the thefts. In 1552, they were ordered to enforce the Second Prayer Book. By Elizabeth's reign, both the amount of business conducted by the JPs and the size of the county benches needed to oversee this business had increased still further. The average size of the county bench had grown from 25 under Wolsey to between 40 and 50 under Elizabeth. By 1603, the number of JPs per county ranged from 40 to 90 members. Members of the local gentry had realised that becoming a JP was the key to social and political advancement. As a result, William Cecil had to keep an increasingly close eye on the membership of the benches, but he was reliant on the reports of royal judges who only visited the counties twice a year. Because government intervention was relatively limited, there was an element of corruption, though royal control over the county benches was strengthened by the appointment of leading councillors and, from 1585, Lord Lieutenants, to county benches. However, these men had multiple responsibilities in Tudor government and could not be present permanently in every locality to oversee the activities of the JPs. This led to the appointment of deputy Lieutenants, who were often JPs as well. With the outbreak of war in 1585, the JPs who also acted as deputy Lieutenants had taken on the responsibility of organising the recruitment of men to fight. By 1603, there were 309 Acts of Parliament which placed responsibility on the JPs. These responsibilities included their traditional role from the start of the period, but also new ones brought about by religious, political and social change. By the 1580s, Elizabethan JPs had acquired powers to deal with new felonies introduced by the government, including riots, damage to property, witchcraft and recusancy. They also had to deal with a wide range of more minor offences, such as damage to crops, drunkenness and abduction of heiresses. In addition, they were responsible for the administration of the Tudor Poor Laws. Because of their local status, JPs were also often appointed to additional government commissions, such as those tasked with the assessment and collection of parliamentary subsidies. By 1603, therefore, the role of the JPs in administering Tudor law and controlling the regions had expanded enormously. Through them, the power and control of the Crown expanded as well.

SOURCE

3 From Edward VI's Licensing Act, 1552.

Forasmuch as intolerable hurts and troubles to the common wealth of this realm doth daily grow and increase through such abuses and disorders as are had and used in common ale-houses and other houses called tippling-houses; It is therefore enacted... That the Justices of Peace within every shire, city, borough, town corporate, franchise, or liberty within this realm, or two of them at least, whereof one of them to be of the Quorum, shall have full power and authority... where they be Justices of Peace to remove, discharge and put away common selling of ale and beer in the said common ale-houses and tippling-houses in such town or towns and places where they shall think meet and convenient; And that none... shall be admitted or suffered to keep any common ale-house or tippling-house but such as shall be thereunto admitted and allowed in the open Sessions of the Peace, or else by two Justices of the Peace, whereof the one to be of the Quorum...

SOURCE

4 From a letter written by Edwin Sandys, Archbishop of York, to William Cecil, 1587.

I have noted in a paper, herein enclosed, such as in my opinion may be well put out of the commission [dismissed as Justices of the Peace]... I assure you some of them be the baddest sort, unworthy to govern, being so far out of order themselves. And to speak truth, although there be many gentlemen in Yorkshire, yet it is very hard to choose fit men for that purpose.

Robert Lee. He is a notable open adulterer, one that giveth offence and will not be reformed. He useth his authority as well to work private displeasure as to serve other men's turns.

Peter Stanley. A man noted to be a great fornicator. Of small wisdom, and less skill.

Thomas Wentworth. A very senseless blockhead, ever wronging his poor neighbours. He bought grain in the beginning of last year in every market, and heaped it up in his houses to sell at the dearest.

Francis Alford. This man liveth much in London. A man of small living, less skill and no countenance.

ACTIVITY
KNOWLEDGE CHECK

Read Sources 3 and 4. Using the section on the development of the JPs, complete the following activities:

1 What do Sources 3 and 4 suggest about the changing role of the JPs in local government?

2 What does Source 4 suggest about the problems faced by the central government in managing local JPs? How serious do you think these problems were?

3 What were the advantages and disadvantages for the Tudor monarchs in using unpaid JPs in local government?

How effectively was the monarchy financed?

In theory, the monarch was supposed to be financially independent, 'to live of his own', as contemporaries put it. The Crown had two main sources of income: 'ordinary revenue', which came from the royal lands and the monarch's status as a landlord, and 'extraordinary revenue', which was usually taxation granted by parliament for the monarch's special needs, usually the costs of war. 'Ordinary' income could come from rents or the sale of lands. A constant theme of the Tudor period was the tension between the Crown's income and expenditure. Even with some considerable boosts to the Crown's income, the monarchy rarely had enough money and was often reliant on parliamentary taxation. The situation was not helped by extravagant expenditure. Henry VIII spent more than £100,000 on building at Hampton Court and Whitehall, while the Royal Household in the 1550s was costing £75,000 a year to run. Raising money through taxation could cause problems for the monarchy because it could lead to dangerous unrest; this was particularly the case when there were consistently high levels of taxation over a long period of time. Poorer regions of the country, such as the West and the North, often found it difficult to meet the Crown's demands, especially when these coincided with periods of social and economic hardship brought about by poor harvests or disease. The revolts of 1489 and 1497 under Henry VII were both sparked by resentment over high levels of taxation. The Pilgrimage of Grace (1536) also took place against a background of demands for tax and poverty in the North of England. Any revolt against the Tudor monarchy was potentially serious; this led to the development of a new form of taxation from 1513, the subsidy, which was supposed to be a fairer method of raising money.

Taxation before 1513

Before 1513, there had been no real change in the methods of raising tax since the 14th century. The medieval method of raising tax was based on 'fifteenths and tenths'. Parliament was the only institution that could grant taxation; in the early Tudor period, it was accepted that the monarch could only ask for taxation in times of emergency, when England faced war or invasion. The system of tenths and fifteenths was based on property, which was often known as 'moveables', and could include both lands and other possessions. Since 1334, the amounts paid by each local community had been fixed. Boroughs were expected to pay taxation equivalent to a tenth of the value of their moveables; in the countryside, each community was expected to pay an amount equivalent to one fifteenth of the value of its goods. Under this system, each fifteenth and tenth was expected to yield £29,500. Although this system removed the need for new assessments of a community's income and property every time tax was levied, by Henry VII's reign, the system was seriously out-of-date. Local communities were paying levels of taxation that had been set 150 years before; this took no account of population or other social and economic changes. In addition, the amount payable by each community was set at a fixed rate. Because of price inflation, the amounts now received by the Crown in taxation did not meet its expenditure needs. Although parliament could grant multiple tenths and fifteenths, this still did not generate enough income. A further problem was that the tenths and fifteenths were seen as unfair. Because each community was responsible for raising a fixed sum of money, rather than each individual paying a sum based on their personal wealth, it was possible for those with wealth and power to avoid paying their share; this meant that the burden of taxation fell more harshly on the poorest in society, while wealthier nobility and gentry were able to escape payment. Another source of potential discontent was that urban communities had to pay more tax than those based in the countryside. In the early Tudor period, many towns were suffering from depopulation, while there was increasing wealth generation in the countryside as a result of the growth of the English wool and cloth trade.

Henry VII continued to use the traditional fifteenth and tenth; parliament granted him taxation in 1487, 1489–90, 1491–92 and 1497. However, these grants did not create as much income as Henry wanted, and he started to experiment with new ways of assessing and generating income through taxation. In 1497, he asked parliament for two tenths and two fifteenths. In addition to these, parliament agreed to a new tax, which was to be assessed on each individual's wealth and ability to pay, a method known as direct assessment. This combination of traditional taxation and experiment was so successful in raising additional income for the Crown that the experiment was repeated in 1504. The new taxes raised an additional £80,000 for the monarchy and paved the way for more innovation under Thomas Wolsey.

The 1513 subsidy

One of Thomas Wolsey's more lasting achievements was to create a new subsidy system which was to be used by Tudor monarchs for the rest of the period. Wolsey needed to find new ways to raise more taxation because Henry VIII was eager to go to war with France. Foreign war was very costly for a small country such as England – between 1509 and 1520, the government spent about £1 million on the war effort, but only received about £25,000 per year from its ordinary revenues before taxation. Wolsey's solution was the introduction of the subsidy, which was agreed by parliament in 1513.

- Instead of being reliant on the traditional, fixed sums of money brought in by the tenths and fifteenths, the subsidy was flexible. Each individual was assessed on their income from different possible sources of wealth – land, wages or the value of their possessions.

- The subsidy was assessed by each individual's ability to pay, based on their wealth and property. The tax each person was to pay was calculated based on these assessments, but they only had to pay tax on one category, the one in which they were wealthiest. This meant that a poor farmworker who was reliant on wages and owned no land or property would pay less than a wealthy member of the gentry who received a permanent income from their estates.

- A separate assessment was also introduced for the nobility, which was based on their rank – the higher their rank, the more they paid.

- Local officials were appointed for each county whose job it was to assess under oath what each person's wealth was.

- The local officials were often drawn from the most respected men in local society, the JPs; they in turn were monitored by national commissioners, who could change assessments.

This system reduced the amount of resentment caused by the traditional fifteenths and tenths, and ensured that the wealthier in society contributed more to taxation than its poorer members. The 1513 subsidy was so successful in raising money that it was repeated by Wolsey in 1514 and 1515, and again in 1523. Between 1513 and 1523, Wolsey raised £322,099 through the new subsidy. In comparison, fifteenths and tenths collected between 1512 and 1517 totalled just £117,936. Subsequently, Tudor monarchs adopted the subsidy as their main method of taxation for the rest of the period.

Wolsey's innovation in tax collection allowed Thomas Cromwell to develop the collection of subsidies still further. In 1534, Cromwell asked parliament for a subsidy, not to fund the king's wars, but to fund his government in peacetime. This was unprecedented in the history of Tudor or medieval government. Cromwell justified his request on the grounds that Henry had ruled England successfully for 25 years and that his loyal subjects ought to support him in this by paying tax. Parliament granted this request, though it did cause rumours and fears of further innovations that were to feed the fears of the northern rebels in the Pilgrimage of Grace. Despite this, there were further requests for peacetime subsidies in 1540, 1543, 1553 and 1555. By the start of Elizabeth's reign, parliament was regularly granting subsidies in times of peace which yielded £140,000 each time. However, this amount was not sustained, and by the end of Elizabeth's reign it was yielding only £80,000. This suggests that although the 1513 subsidy was influential in developing new methods of taxation, its effectiveness in increasing royal income from taxation was not sustained, as the Crown faced resistance from parliament and taxpayers.

Even Wolsey had problems raising his subsidies. This was mainly because of the demands of war that were placed on the English economy between 1512 and 1529, not because the subsidy itself was inefficient. As the demands of war increased, with little to show for it, parliament became more reluctant to grant the amounts Wolsey wanted. In 1523, parliament refused to grant Wolsey the £800,000 in taxation that he had requested and forced him to negotiate for a lesser sum. Although Wolsey had agreed to payment of the subsidy by instalments, by the date of the second instalment in February 1525, most of the payments were late. These problems show that even the new form of subsidy could not keep taxpayers or parliament happy when they felt that the financial burden was too great. To cover growing government costs, in 1525, Wolsey was forced to raise a non-parliamentary tax known as the 'Amicable Grant'. This provoked mass resistance in East Anglia – 10,000 men gathered to protest at Lavenham (Suffolk) and Wolsey was forced to cancel the Grant, though not the collection of the subsidy.

EXTEND YOUR KNOWLEDGE

The Amicable Grant (1525)

The Amicable Grant was controversial because it was an attempt by Wolsey to raise taxation without the consent of parliament. Parliament had grown increasingly reluctant to meet the financial demands of Wolsey and the king. Wolsey was desperate to raise money so that the king could go to war against France. The Grant was levied on top of the collection of the 1523 subsidy and was instantly unpopular. The most famous rising was at Lavenham, but there was unrest across East Anglia and in the Midlands. The local nobility, the Dukes of Norfolk and Suffolk, were forced to negotiate with the rebels. The Grant was discontinued and Henry claimed no knowledge of it, putting the blame on Wolsey.

By Elizabeth's reign, more problems emerged with the use of the subsidy. These problems were caused by Elizabeth's own caution and desire for political stability. Under Elizabeth, the assessment of the subsidy was allowed to stagnate. Instead of using Wolsey's flexible approach, which allowed for new assessments of wealth for each new subsidy, Elizabeth permitted the rates at which tax was paid to become fixed. Those who paid tax on the value of their land had to pay four shillings for every pound their land was worth. Those taxed on the value of their goods were required to pay two shillings eight pence for every pound their goods were worth. These changes meant that the amount raised by the subsidy became fixed and did not take inflation into account. The result of this was that the government's income from subsidies fell in real terms – it received less money and it was able to buy less with the money it did receive. Another problem was that the system became increasingly corrupt. After 1563, each taxpayer's assessment of their wealth was accepted as accurate; they were no longer required to take an oath to support their claims. Inevitably, this meant that most taxpayers claimed that they had less income than they really did. They were then assessed on this lower income, and so the amount of tax they paid was reduced. The decline of the subsidy system allowed some of the most wealthy to evade taxation. William Cecil, Elizabeth's most trusted councillor, had an income of around £4,000 per year, but for the purposes of his tax assessment, he claimed that his income was just £133 6s 8d. Local record-keeping added to these problems; tax records were not updated to take account of new taxpayers or those who had died. The result of this can be seen in the yields from Suffolk. In 1523, 17,000 taxpayers were assessed, but in 1566, there were just 7,700 taxpayers in the county. Elizabeth did nothing to respond to these problems; her answer was to ask for multiple subsidies, plus the medieval fifteenths and tenths. For example, in 1601, she asked for – and was granted – four subsidies and eight fifteenths and tenths. This corruption and stagnation contributed to the political tensions of the 1590s, especially as Elizabeth was forced to exploit the royal prerogative in order to fund her wars. However, it is noticeable that she did not face the same type of popular tax rebellion which Henry VII had faced in 1489 and 1497. This suggests that Tudor England was better managed, mainly because of the increased control of the localities exercised by the Crown.

ACTIVITY
KNOWLEDGE CHECK

1 List the main changes made by Wolsey in the 1513 subsidy.

2 What was the most important reason for these changes, and why?

3 How effective were these changes: a) by 1525; b) by 1603?

SOURCE

5 A letter written by Elizabeth I's Privy Council in 1598 to the commissioners collecting the subsidy.

Subsidies, of later times, have come to far less sums than those of former ages; which cannot grow but by the remiss and neglectful dealing of such as are the Commissioners for the assessment of the same... You cannot perform the trust reposed in you, nor your duties towards her Majesty and your country, if you proceed not in this service with great care, and endeavour to advance the sums and assessments as much as may be, in assessing all men indifferently that are of ability, without regard to any favour. For it hath been noted heretofore that this burden is laid upon the meaner sort who are less able to bear the burden; and the wealthier and best able to spare the same are too favourably dealt withal, the Commissioners bearing with one another, and every of them bearing with their own private friends and followers.

The growth of poverty and the government response in the localities

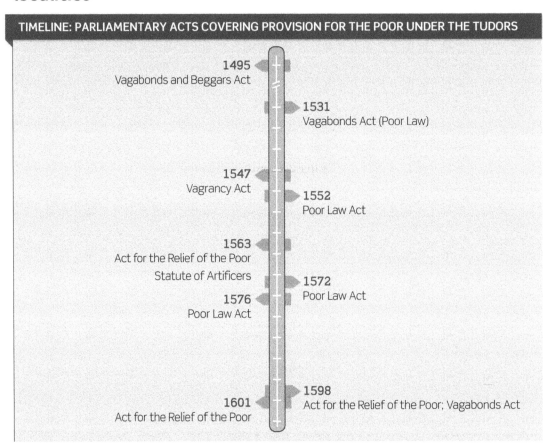

TIMELINE: PARLIAMENTARY ACTS COVERING PROVISION FOR THE POOR UNDER THE TUDORS

- 1495 Vagabonds and Beggars Act
- 1531 Vagabonds Act (Poor Law)
- 1547 Vagrancy Act
- 1552 Poor Law Act
- 1563 Act for the Relief of the Poor Statute of Artificers
- 1572 Poor Law Act
- 1576 Poor Law Act
- 1598 Act for the Relief of the Poor; Vagabonds Act
- 1601 Act for the Relief of the Poor

Poverty was an increasing problem in Tudor England, as were the associated issues of unemployment and vagabondage. The main cause of poverty in Tudor England was the increasing population in the 16th century. There was a steady growth across the period, apart from in the 1550s, where bad harvests and an influenza epidemic in Mary's reign led to a temporary decline in numbers. In 1525, the population of England was about 2.26 million; by 1551 it was 3.01 million, and by 1601 it was 4.1 million. The result of this growth was rising prices and falling wages. This was because of the basic economic principle of supply and demand. As the population grew, so more pressure was placed on resources, particularly food. The more people there were to feed, the more the demand for food grew. This meant that farmers and merchants could charge higher prices for their goods and expect them to be paid, leading to price inflation. The situation was made worse in some periods because the Tudor governments did not have the ability to ensure that its population could always be fed. In particular, harvests could be affected by bad weather, which reduced the crop yield and led to dearth. When this happened, for example in 1519–21, 1527–29, 1549–51, 1554–56 and 1586–87, as grain became scarcer, prices soared still higher. The dissolution of the monasteries in the late 1530s may also have exacerbated the spread of poverty, because the monasteries were a traditional source of support and **alms** for the poor. The result of these conditions was that unemployment rose and more people fell into poverty. This was a challenge for the national and local authorities; high levels of social and economic hardship could lead to social and political unrest. Tudor monarchs were increasingly keen to find solutions to these problems; this led to them working more closely with the local authorities and passing more social and economic legislation.

Increasing levels of poverty led to another problem for the Tudor state: vagrancy and begging. Because it was assumed that there were jobs available, but the unemployed were too lazy to work, the Tudor authorities tended to use punishment to try to control the problem. Vagrants and beggars, those who wandered from place to place, were harder to control, particularly in times of political and social unrest. This is why many Tudor laws concerning vagrancy and the poor made vagrants return to their own parishes to seek help. In their own parish, they would be known to the local authorities, and instability and the spread of seditious ideas which might undermine the Tudor state could be more easily avoided. In addition, vagrants and beggars did not have a master. In the Tudor mind, which saw society as a hierarchy, this was a threat to social order; those who were found wandering could be arrested simply because they had no master.

Social and economic legislation before 1563

Laws concerning the control and punishment of vagrants and beggars had been in place since the late 15th century. In 1495, Henry VII passed a law which ordered that beggars and the idle poor were to be put in the stocks for three days, whipped and returned to their original **parish**. In this period, poor relief in the parishes was still based on voluntary contributions by wealthier parishoners to the church alms fund. As poverty grew, so punishments became more severe. In 1531, a Poor Law was passed which ordered vagrants to be whipped. The **impotent poor** were to be licensed by the JPs and allowed to beg. In 1547, the most severe laws of the period were passed, which reflected the rising social and economic tensions of the time. Under the Vagrancy Act, a vagrant was defined as someone who was able-bodied and who had been without a master or employment for three days. The punishments for vagrants were harsh. A first offence would lead to a 'V' being branded on the person's chest. The vagrant would also be forced to work as a slave for two years for the person who had informed against them. However, the Vagrancy Act was so harsh that the local authorities found it impossible to enforce. It was repealed in 1550 and replaced in 1552 by a new Poor Law. This new law required the impotent poor to be registered for the first time. It also required parish priests and bishops to place more pressure on those who were reluctant to make voluntary contributions to alms in the parishes.

KEY TERMS

Alms
The traditional giving of food or money or other forms of charity to the poor. Voluntary alms-giving was encouraged by both the Catholic and Protestant Churches to help fund poor relief.

Parish
The area under the organisation and control of a local church. Each parish had its own priest who looked after the needs of his congregation. The parish became the centre of administration for poor relief.

Impotent poor
People who suffered physical disability or illness which made it impossible for them to work. The impotent poor also included those who were too old, infirm or too young to work.

SOURCE

6 A 16th century woodcut showing a beggar being punished by being whipped through the streets.

Meanwhile, Tudor governments also attempted to regulate wages and prices through parliamentary statute. These regulations were often the result of pressure from particular interest groups or communities who wanted their trades to be protected. For example, Acts were passed in 1547 and 1555 to regulate cloth-making in East Anglia and Worcester respectively. Social and economic legislation was not just the result of pressure from below, however. Increasingly, the central government became involved in trying to regulate such aspects of the economy as wages, employment and food prices. In 1536, for example, Cromwell introduced a radical Act which ordered local officials to find work for beggars and to organise collections for the impotent poor. This Act was so radical that it was not renewed, but it paved the way for further government attempts at regulation. In the 1540s and 1550s, food prices were starting to rise alarmingly; the government response was to try to control and encourage food production. In 1548–49, laws were passed against price and wage fixing; in 1554, an Act was introduced which forbade the export of corn (a staple product used for making bread) when prices were above a certain level.

The Statute of Artificers, 1563

Elizabeth I inherited a country that was in social and economic crisis. Poor weather had led to a series of bad harvests in the years 1554–56. The situation was exacerbated by the outbreak of an influenza epidemic between 1555 and 1559. The combination of a malnourished population and the outbreak of disease led to a decline in the population, for the only time between 1485 and 1603. In 1551, the population was about 3.01 million; by 1561, it had declined to about 2.98 million. The result of this crisis was seen in two ways. First, lack of available food led to higher prices. This affected the poorest peasants and the urban poor the most because they tended to produce just enough food from their lands to ensure survival, or else were completely reliant on being able to purchase the food they needed. The combination of poor harvests and price rises plunged these groups into poverty and vagrancy. Second, the decline in population also had the effect of pushing up wages. Those who survived and who had skills to offer were able to ask for higher wages from employers. This reduced employers' profits and forced them to raise their prices. The social and economic crises of the 1550s placed additional pressure on both the central government and local authorities. They were concerned about controlling vagrancy and the spread of social disorder; price rises also made those at the top of the Tudor hierarchy nervous because they feared that those from a lower social rank were less respectful of their place in society and their betters. An attempt at solving these problems was the Statute of Artificers (1563).

The Statute of Artificers was the first attempt by the central government to produce legislation that would address all the different problems affecting Tudor society. Rather than tackling single issues such as wages, price rises or vagrancy, it adopted a holistic approach that dealt with all of these problems together. It was also a particularly important Act because it placed even more authority and responsibility in the hands of the JPs, who were expected to enforce it. The main terms of the Act were as follows:

- All unmarried people under the age of 30 were compelled to work and to accept any job offered to them.

- At harvest time, JPs could force all those who were able to work to help bring in the crops. Anyone who refused could be punished by two days and one night in the stocks.

- Everyone between the ages of 12 and 60 was required to work on the land unless they were a member of the gentry, an heir to lands worth £10 a year or goods worth £40, already employed in a skilled craft, or worked in mining, metal-working or glass-making, or were attending a school or university.

- All wages were to be assessed and set by the local JPs annually.

- Hours of work were fixed. In summer they were to be from 5am to 7 or 8pm, with not more than 2½ hours for meal breaks. In winter they were from dawn to sunset. The penalty for absence was 1d an hour.

- Apprenticeships were set at seven years. They were to be compulsory for any skilled occupation.

How significant was the Statute of Artificers?

The Statute lasted for the rest of the Tudor period and replaced many of the earlier piecemeal attempts at social and economic legislation which had characterised earlier attempts at reform. The main impact of the Statute was to place even more importance on the role of the JPs in the regulation of social and economic affairs in their regions. The Statute was also significant because it enhanced the importance of apprenticeships and protected the status of skilled craftsmen. Under the new law, it was technically impossible to enter a skilled trade such as wheelwright, brickmaker, thatcher, goldsmith or ironmonger, without serving a seven-year training period known as an apprenticeship. Finally, the Statute was also important because of its emphasis on the need for every person to have a master and for its emphasis on the importance of food production as an essential job in which every person of a lower rank was to be involved.

However, the significance of the Statute of Artificers should not be overstated. This was partly because the Act was backward-looking in its aims. The central government had been attempting to control wage increases and social structure since the late 14th century. In addition, the government was responding to local experimentation with wage assessments and control which had begun in the 1550s. For example, the corporations of London and York had tried to stop builders' wages rising out of control in 1551–52. The social and economic crisis of the late 1550s encouraged more local authorities to try to cap wages, especially in the period 1560–62. The 1563 Statute was the central government's response to a local trend. However, it is significant that the government felt the need to respond to concerns about social order from those who represented the localities. This suggests that there was a growing partnership between the centre and the localities.

Nevertheless, the Statute of Artificers did not solve all the social and economic problems facing late Tudor England. Further Acts were needed to deal with the problem of poverty and vagabondage; these included the 1572 and 1576 Poor Laws, and the Poor Law of 1598. There were also other problems with the enforcement of the 1563 Statute. The determination of the JPs to hold down wages meant that although annual assessments of local wages were published, these did not change for years at a time, regardless of changes to social and economic conditions. The assessed wages for the county of Kent did not change once between 1563 and 1588. It was only the renewed social and economic hardship of the 1590s that forced local JPs to increase wages. In the intervening years, the control over wage increases only exacerbated poverty levels among the landless peasants at the bottom of Tudor society and meant that further Poor Laws were needed. The Statute was also unsuccessful at preventing unemployment and vagrancy. This was because it assumed that there was always work for everyone who wanted it. Some migration always happened as a result of seasonal change; for example, there was large-scale movement of people looking for work at harvest time. However, vagrancy began to increase in the late 1580s and 1590s. A group that was particularly affected was the cloth-workers, whose chances of finding employment decreased because of the disruption to European cloth exports once the war with Spain began in 1585. Poor harvests and outbreaks of disease also encouraged those who were barely surviving to move on in search of work. Although the Statute of Labourers did not create all of these problems, it did contribute to them.

ACTIVITY
KNOWLEDGE CHECK

1 Design a diagram showing the development of Tudor social and economic legislation which led to the Statute of Artificers. Make sure that you include the roles of: social and economic change; central government; local authorities.

2 In your opinion, what were the main strengths and weaknesses of the Statute of Artificers? Why do you think more legislation was still needed after 1563?

The Act for the Relief of the Poor, 1598

The 1598 Poor Law was the culmination of previous Tudor legislation to deal with the problems of vagrancy and poverty. Under Elizabeth I, attitudes towards poverty and provision for the poor had begun to change. In 1563, an Act for the Relief of the Poor moved towards making payments to poor relief in the parish almost compulsory. Special collectors of alms were to be appointed to collect contributions to the local fund. Refusal to contribute could lead to imprisonment, but the contributor could choose how large or small their payments were. Under the 1572 Poor Law, attitudes towards the able-bodied poor began to change. Punishments for unlicensed beggars remained severe: they included boring a hole through the right ear with a hot instrument. It also became harder to get a licence, as it now had to be signed by two Justices of the Peace. However, for the first time, the government recognised that there was not always enough work available for the able-bodied poor. The 1572 Act encouraged parishes with extra poor relief funds to build 'houses of correction' for vagrants and beggars. The 1570s and 1580s were a period of relative economic stability, with few poor harvests, so the government did not need to pass further laws, although the social and economic crisis of the 1590s would bring about further significant changes. There was also an increased expectation, enforced by parliamentary law, that local parishes would provide for their poor and that this provision would come from contributions from local parishioners that were almost compulsory. This move was influenced by the development of voluntary and local initiatives, especially in the larger towns. In large towns such as Norwich and York, contributions to poor relief were set up in 1549 and 1550. The town corporation of York also took over the running of a hospital for the poor which had previously been run by the Catholic Church.

However, none of these measures were effective against the severe social and economic crisis that affected England between 1594 and 1598. Cold weather caused a series of crop failures that led to famine in some regions of the North. Wages continued to fall as prices continued to rise. The price of staple foods such as wheat, barley, oats and beans rose to levels unaffordable by the poor, who relied on them the most. At the same time, there were outbreaks of plague, which added to the general misery of the period. Unsurprisingly, the result of such hardship was unrest. In 1596, there were food riots in London, the South East and the South West. The Privy Council feared that these riots would turn into camping rebellions, like those seen in 1549. In Oxfordshire, there was an attempted rising against the Lord Lieutenant. The rebels planned to attack his house, seize his weapons and march on London. Only four rebels actually turned up and they were quickly arrested, but the Council was nervous and insisted on interrogating the rebels in person. This nervousness about social unrest lay behind the decision to pass the 1598 Poor Law.

The Act for the Relief of the Poor that eventually emerged in 1598 had complex beginnings. It seems to have come from **private bills** rather than one sponsored by the Council, but the Council was prepared to allow the bill to be passed because of its fears about social unrest. In 1597, there were at least 11 draft bills dealing with poor relief, vagabondage, hospitals and houses of correction. These concerns came together to form the 1598 Poor Law. This built on and extended previous legislation and enhanced the local administration of poor relief.

- The Act introduced the post of overseer of the poor for each parish, whose job it was to assess how much poor relief was needed, and to collect and distribute the relief.

- The unpaid overseer was to be supervised by the JPs, who were given additional powers to raise compulsory contributions to local poor relief and to punish those who refused.

- The new Poor Law was combined with other laws passed at the same time, which strengthened the government's response to poverty. The 1598 Vagabonds Act ordered the most dangerous vagrants to be banished or sent to the queen's galleys; the Act for the Relief of Soldiers and Mariners provided pensions for wounded former soldiers, which was a real necessity in a country that had been at war since 1585.

- There were also Acts which provided for the building of hospitals for those who were ill, and houses of correction for the able-bodied poor.

The result of the 1598 Poor Law was that for the first time, there was now a national system of relief for the poor. However, the Poor Law in itself was not an innovation. It was the result of the panic felt by those with land and property as a result of the social and economic crises of the 1590s. It also built on 50 years of experimentation with methods of dealing with poverty and vagrancy; many of its measures had already been tried before 1598, often in private and local initiatives which were then adopted by the national government. Nevertheless, the 1598 Poor Law was the first Act to make contributions to poor relief fully compulsory; it was also the first time that all local provision for the poor had been brought into line by the national government. The 1598 Poor Law, which was confirmed and slightly revised by a second Act in 1601, was to last until 1834.

KEY TERM

Private bill
A bill introduced to parliament by an individual MP. Often, it would be an attempt by the individual or the community they represented to pass legislation on a local social or economic issue. Many private bills would fail because of a lack of wider support in the Commons, but some, such as the bills concerning the poor in 1597–98, were successful. This was because these bills received wider backing, from other MPs and, most importantly, the Council. Under Elizabeth I, two-fifths of Acts of Parliament were based on private bills.

HOW FAR DID THE RELATIONSHIP BETWEEN THE CROWN AND THE COUNTRY CHANGE BETWEEN 1485 AND 1603?

The development of a network of personal relationships by patronage and the granting of lands, titles and positions at Court

During the Tudor period, the relationship between the monarchy and the nobility changed considerably. In 1485, the nobility were traditional medieval military leaders, whose power was based on their ownership of landed estates. Ownership of land equated to power because the nobility used their estates to raise armies for the king. During the Wars of the Roses, however, this relationship had become corrupted as the nobility rose against their monarchs. The Tudor monarchs sought to alter the balance of power between the monarchy and the landed elites who ruled the localities. By Elizabeth's reign, a new type of nobleman had emerged. The power of the new nobility was based on their ability to gain access to the monarch and the supply of grants of lands, offices and titles which underpinned the Tudor system of patronage. The new nobility were courtiers, although many still retained their traditional role as military leaders as well. By the end of the Tudor period, however, it had become much harder, though not impossible, for the nobility to raise an army against their monarch. Increasingly, they were reliant on the monarchy for favour and access to patronage, which meant that they needed to be continually present at Court. This does not mean that the Tudor monarchs were trying to get rid of the nobility altogether; they still had a vital role to play in the government of the localities, especially as a link between the centre and the regions. Similarly, the role of the gentry in local government was enhanced. They were the men who ran local government through their roles as JPs. The gentry looked to the nobility for advancement in their careers because the nobility had greater access to royal patronage. Generally, the monarchy, nobility and gentry were on the same side; they all wanted security, good order and political stability. The development of a network of personal relationships through patronage mostly enhanced these relationships and strengthened the relationship between the monarchy and the men who ruled the localities on its behalf.

The relationship between Henry VII and the nobility

Henry VII's general attitude to most of the nobility was one of distrust. He was reluctant to give out many rewards and preferred to use a small group of trusted nobility, gentry and lawyers to help him control the localities. For example, Henry trusted his uncle, Jasper Tudor, to control Wales and the Marches on his behalf. Jasper Tudor was promoted from Earl of Pembroke to Duke of Bedford by Henry. However, when Jasper Tudor died childless in 1495, Henry did not promote anyone else to the title. Instead, he preferred to let the title lapse, and Bedford's considerable lands and possessions in Wales returned to the Crown, enhancing Henry's ability to control this region personally and adding to

the Crown's wealth. Administrators such as Sir Reginald Bray were also rewarded by Henry, and used their positions within the central government to build up land, power and influence. Bray was a royal councillor and the Chancellor of the Duchy of Lancaster. Through these positions he was able to acquire lands in 18 counties which brought him an income of at least £1,000 per annum. However, he was only able to do this because Henry trusted him. Bray was able to use his local lands to extend royal influence more directly into the localities.

Members of the nobility outside Henry's inner circle had to work hard to earn his trust. Thomas Howard, Earl of Surrey, had fought against Henry at Bosworth and was imprisoned in the Tower; his lands and title were forfeited to Henry. Howard refused to take the opportunity to escape and join the 1487 rebellion against Henry and was rewarded to some extent because he was released and given back some of his estates in East Anglia. Howard was also restored to his title as earl, but was not given his father's title of Duke of Norfolk. Henry's distrustful attitude towards the control of the localities and the role of the nobility is demonstrated in the position Surrey occupied for much of the reign. Henry was not prepared to restore Surrey's full lands and titles to him; nor, until 1499, was he prepared to allow Surrey to control the region where his estates were most extensive, East Anglia. Instead, Surrey was sent to run the North on Henry's behalf. This was a region where Surrey had no connections with the local gentry or landed power. The earl was entirely reliant on Henry's goodwill for his continued political rehabilitation. Once Surrey had proved his trustworthiness in the North, Henry did allow him to return to his traditional estates; in 1501, Surrey was made a councillor and served Henry for the rest of the reign. However, such was Henry's distrust, that Surrey was never able to regain the title of duke; he only achieved this in 1513, as a reward for leading Henry VIII's army against the Scots in the important English victory of Flodden. In fact, Henry was so reluctant to promote and extend the power of the nobility that the number of representatives of noble families dropped from 55 to 42 during his reign. In some ways, it can be argued that Henry was successful in his policy; after 1497, there was no open rebellion against him, although resentment at his style of rule did lead to some plotting and resentment that was voiced openly after his death.

The development of patronage under Henry VIII

Henry VIII's relationship with his nobility was very different from his father's. Henry VIII saw his nobility as companions in the pastimes he enjoyed – hunting, jousting and military campaigning. Where Henry VII was notoriously careful with money, Henry VIII was generous with his grants, rewarding his friends and companions. As a result, the style of Tudor government and the relationship between the king and his nobility started to change. From the early years of Henry VIII's reign, the Chamber became increasingly politicised. This meant that the men serving the new king in seemingly humble positions, such as the Groom of the Stool, were also his friends, with an unrivalled opportunity to influence the king informally. This influence included suggestions about where the king's patronage should be deployed. For example, Sir William Compton, who was a Gentleman of the Chamber and Groom of the Stool, was able to raise his income from his estates from £10 per year to nearly £1,700 a year by acquiring grants of royal lands and offices. Compton's success made his family's fortune; his grandson was promoted into the peerage by Elizabeth I. Similarly, one of Henry's closest friends was Charles Brandon. Brandon's father had been killed at Bosworth fighting for Henry VII. The young Charles was brought up with the future Henry VIII at Court. Henry rewarded his friend generously, making him the Duke of Suffolk and granting him extensive estates in East Anglia. Brandon was in such favour with Henry that he was even able to get away with marrying the king's sister, Mary, without permission. Henry used his good relationship with Suffolk to extend his control in the localities. Although Brandon had originally been granted estates in East Anglia, after 1536, he was ordered by the king to give up these lands. Suffolk was granted estates in Lincolnshire instead. The reason for this move was that the political unrest that turned into the Pilgrimage of Grace had begun in Lincolnshire, which was without an active and resident member of the nobility. Suffolk's move into the region was designed to reassert royal power there through the presence of a trusted member of the king's Court.

However, the role of the nobility under Henry VIII was starting to change. Power and influence were dictated by the ability to gain access to Henry, or to one of his chief ministers, Thomas Wolsey or Thomas Cromwell. This led to the development of a group of men who owed their positions to their influence at Court rather than because of their landed estates. Cromwell himself got his start in royal service through Wolsey's patronage. Professional administrators, especially those with legal training, also became increasingly influential because of their access to royal patronage. For example, two of Henry's councillors, William Paget and Thomas Wriothesley, rose to the top because of their legal expertise; both were ennobled – Paget became Baron Paget and Wriothesley became the Earl of Southampton, but neither came from a traditional military background. Paget and Wriothesley were civil servants, diplomats and courtiers. Both used their position to acquire landed estates, but the basis of their power was their personal relationship with Henry. The power of the traditional nobility was further undermined by royal attacks on those whom Henry distrusted, especially the nobles with lands in the militarised regions of the Welsh and Northern Marches. The Duke of Buckingham was executed for treason in 1521, and his lands in Wales and the Marches were forfeited to the king. Similarly, the childless Henry Percy, Earl of Northumberland, who suffered from repeated bouts of ill health and was in debt, was persuaded to bequeath his estates to the king. Although the earldom and the Percy estates eventually passed to Northumberland's nephew, this did not happen until 1557. In the meantime, the Crown had control of the Percy estates and was able to use these lands to grant rewards to its loyal followers, enhancing royal control in the North.

The growth of the royal estates under Henry VIII also added to his ability to manipulate patronage in order to control the localities. The Crown traditionally held the Duchies of Lancaster and Cornwall, but after the political turmoil of the period 1535–46, which saw increasing numbers of executions for treason, forfeitures of land and the dissolution of the monasteries, there was a substantial shift in the Crown's available income from its estates. The nobility's share of income from land only rose from 8 to 9 percent; the Crown's rose from 9 to 27 percent. However, this was a temporary change, as most of the monastic estates were later sold by Henry VIII and his successors. But even the sale of the monastic lands helped to strengthen the royal position. The former monastic estates were used to create a group of gentry and nobility who had a vested interest in supporting the royal supremacy and break with Rome because they had benefited from it. A good example of this is the rise of the Russell family. Sir John Russell had spent his life in the service of Henry VIII, as a Gentleman of the Bedchamber, a diplomat and a soldier. In the 1530s, Henry used his control of the Duchy of Cornwall to grant Russell a series of offices in the South West, a region that was distant from the centre and was difficult for the Tudors to control. When Henry Courtenay, the key noble in the South West, was executed for treason in 1538, Russell replaced him in the region. Russell was made Baron Russell and was granted the former estates of the abbey at Tavistock (Devon). Russell's rise continued under Edward VI, when he was made Earl of Bedford. With Russell, the Tudors had a trusted member of the nobility who owed his advancement to royal patronage. Russell rewarded them with loyal service, though even he was unable to prevent the rebellion that broke out in the South West in 1549.

What problems were created by Henry's use of royal patronage?

The Tudor system of patronage did have its disadvantages, however. It relied on the presence of a strong, active and decisive monarch who promoted men who were both reliable and loyal. A ruler who was too old, too young, too ill or too easily manipulated could find that ambitious courtiers around them would seek to advance their careers solely for their own ends and not to the advantage of the monarchy. Patronage, when badly handled, could cause jealousy and lead to political instability. This was increasingly the case in the last years of Henry VIII's reign, when the ageing and infirm king began to lose his grip on affairs, and under his son, Edward VI, who was just nine years old when he came to the throne. Under Henry VIII, there was increased rivalry between factions formed of members of the nobility, who each wanted to influence Henry's policy, especially his religious policy. The group led by Edward Seymour, Earl of Hertford, tended to support a reformer line. The conservative faction, which favoured a return to Rome, was led by the third Duke of Norfolk. Each side tried to use its influence with the king to gain patronage for its own followers and to undermine its rivals. The result was Court intrigue and plots, which Seymour's faction ultimately won. Seymour's faction used their control of access to the dying Henry VIII to manipulate the royal will in Seymour's favour. Henry had wanted a regency council to rule while his son was a minor; Seymour and his faction were in such a position of power that they were able to override this. Seymour made himself Lord Protector and Duke of Somerset. He also used his control of patronage to reward his own supporters; John Dudley, Viscount Lisle, was made Earl of Warwick, for example. Seymour now had complete control of patronage and of access to the young king. In this case, Henry's patronage created a member of the nobility who was almost too powerful, and who was able to further his own career at the expense of the royal will, though by 1549 he had pushed his ambitions too far and was overthrown in the aftermath of the 1549 rebellions. Ultimately, Seymour's power rested too much on his influence and position at Court; when these failed, he could not sustain his position. Similarly, Seymour's replacement as Lord Protector, John Dudley, found that despite his control of Edward VI and royal patronage, he was unable to overturn the royal succession in 1553 by placing his own candidate on the throne instead of Mary Tudor. The patronage of Henry VII and Henry VIII had succeeded in creating loyalty to the Tudor monarchy and weakening the traditional military power of the nobility. Neither Seymour nor Dudley was able to raise an army in support of their ambitions, and both were executed for treason.

EXTEND YOUR KNOWLEDGE

The 'Devise for the Succession' and Lady Jane Grey
In 1553, it became clear that the 15-year-old Edward VI was dying. According to Henry VIII's Acts of Succession, the next heir should have been Edward's sister, Mary. But Mary was a Catholic, whereas Edward and his Protector were reformers. Edward and his Protector, John Dudley, Duke of Northumberland, hatched a plan to ensure that Mary did not become queen. The Protestant Lady Jane Grey, Edward's cousin (the daughter of Charles Brandon and Mary, sister of Henry VIII), was proposed as the next heir in a document written by Edward known as the 'Devise for the Succession'. When Edward died, Jane, who was married to Northumberland's son, Guildford Dudley, was proclaimed queen. Mary Tudor was not prepared to accept this, and began raising troops in East Anglia. Local gentry, Protestant and Catholic alike, flocked to support her because she was seen as the rightful heir to the throne. Support for Jane and Northumberland quickly drained away. Northumberland was executed for treason; Jane and her husband were executed the following year. Mary's successful challenge for the throne is sometimes called the only successful Tudor rebellion.

The development of networks under Elizabeth I

Elizabeth I used a complex system of patronage and a network of informal and formal connections to tie the centre and the localities more closely together. Her nobility were both courtiers and politicians, active locally and in central government. Led by William Cecil (who himself became Baron Burghley in 1571), a key group of noblemen served Elizabeth as councillors, MPs, Lord Lieutenants and JPs. Often, these men would hold multiple positions simultaneously, but they drew their power and influence from their close working relationship with the queen. For example, William Cecil was a JP in Lincolnshire and Northamptonshire; the Earl of Bedford acted as JP in Devon and Cornwall. A new element was added to the importance of patronage by the fact that Elizabeth was not married. Her 'favourites' were men with whom she had flirtatious relationships and who were expected to admire her unconditionally. This was a good way for Elizabeth to keep control as a woman in a man's world. A good example of the role of patronage at Elizabeth's Court was Robert Dudley, earl of Leicester. Dudley is best known as a potential husband for Elizabeth, though they never married. Although he was one of her favourites, with personal access to her presence, he was also a hard-working member of her government. He was her Master of the Horse, which meant that he rode beside her when she travelled; he was also a member of her Royal Household. In 1562, he became a Privy councillor as well. Dudley was also a landowner with considerable estates in the Midlands and Wales. He benefited from Elizabeth's personal favour in that he received generous grants, such as Kenilworth Castle and Denbigh in Wales; he was also given control in the region around Chester. However, Leicester was only given these grants because he was trusted to be the queen's eyes and ears in the localities where he was dominant. Elizabeth was careful to keep the distribution of patronage in her own hands. Although she allowed William Cecil and Robert Dudley to develop their own networks of patronage, these networks were based on the ability of Cecil and Dudley to gain access to the queen and to keep her trust. By distributing patronage fairly equally between these two potential rivals, Elizabeth was also able to maintain political stability until the 1590s.

Another important aspect of Elizabeth's patronage was the continuing extension of royal power into the localities, especially hard-to-control regions such as the North. The South West and Wales were now subdued and under royal control through the Russell and Dudley families, but the power of the traditional northern nobility remained a threat. An added problem was that some of these nobles, such as Thomas Percy, Earl of Northumberland, had Catholic sympathies, and could not be trusted to be loyal to the Protestant Elizabeth. The North in general remained Catholic in its sympathies. Elizabeth's answer to these problems in the 1560s was to impose southern 'outsiders' on the North. For example, Elizabeth's cousin, Henry Carey, Lord Hunsdon, was put in charge of the key fortress of Berwick. Hunsdon had no lands in the North, and was given this position because he was completely trustworthy. Similarly, another member of the southern nobility, Francis Russell, Earl of Bedford (the son of John), was named Warden of the East March. To rub salt in the wound, the traditional northern nobility were deprived of their positions; for example, Thomas Percy lost the wardenship of the Middle March. In the short term, this policy backfired. Elizabeth's use of patronage created resentment among the northern nobility and led to a Court-based plot against William Cecil, who was blamed for the policy. Eventually, the resentment of the northern lords boiled over into what became the Revolt of the Northern Earls in 1569. Although this was serious at the time, in the longer term, the revolt played into Elizabeth's hands, as she now had the perfect excuse to destroy the power of the traditional northern nobility for good. The lands and offices forfeited by the rebels were granted to loyal members of the nobility and gentry. The Council of the North was also reformed, with the Puritan Earl of Huntingdon at its head. Huntingdon was another of Elizabeth's cousins; he was also unconnected to the North and had the queen's support. He used this support to enforce a crack down on Catholic recusancy, to promote Protestantism and to improve the government of the North, especially regarding the provision of poor relief. The result was that after 1569, the North was quiet and posed no further threat to Elizabeth.

However, in the 1590s, Elizabeth's system of patronage began to break down as the aging queen began to lose control of government. Many of her most trusted councillors had died by 1590, including Robert Dudley and Francis Walsingham. William Cecil was ageing too, and increasingly incapacitated by ill health.

In the place of Cecil and Dudley rose two new, young and ambitious members of the Court: Robert Cecil, the son of William, and Robert Devereux, Earl of Essex, who was Dudley's step son. Like the situation in the 1540s, the rivalry between the Cecils and Essex over the control of patronage caused serious political tension in the last years of Elizabeth's reign, which culminated in Essex's eventual rebellion and execution in 1601.

William Cecil used his position of influence with the queen to advance his son's career. In 1591, the queen admitted Robert Cecil to the Privy Council. However, Elizabeth was not prepared to give in to all the demands that the Cecil faction placed on her. Robert Cecil was hoping to be appointed as the queen's Secretary, a position that had been held by Walsingham until his death in 1590. Elizabeth, however, left the position vacant until 1596, when Robert Cecil finally achieved his aim. Meanwhile, the rise of the Earl of Essex created a rival to the Cecils' influence with the queen. Essex was a member of an old noble family. Although he was a member of the nobility, he was not well-off, and was reliant on the queen for enough patronage to support himself and his followers. In 1588, he was given the lucrative monopoly on sweet wines which had belonged to Leicester. Essex was appointed to the Council in 1593. He also became a Lord Lieutenant. But crucially, Essex always remained reliant on the queen for his power and influence. He did not have the resources to build up a following in the localities and his power was based at Court. The Cecils, however, were able to build up power much more effectively, mainly because William Cecil monopolised so many positions in government: until 1596, he was Lord Treasurer, Master of the Court of Wards (which controlled the estates and custody of minors and was a rich source of patronage), and acting Secretary in the absence of a permanent appointment. After 1596, when Robert Cecil became Secretary, the Cecil family were able tighten their grip on the distribution of patronage still further, causing Essex to become increasingly resentful. In February 1601, Essex and about 140 supporters planned to use an armed force to surround and capture the Court and the queen. He may even have intended to overthrow her. His plan failed when he did not gather any popular support and he was executed for treason, leaving the Cecil faction dominant at Court. Essex's failed rebellion shows that the Tudor system of patronage, when mismanaged, could lead to serious political instability. However, the fact that Essex was unable to raise any opposition to the queen shows both the loyalty which the Tudor monarchs had generated and also the changing nature of the role of the nobility, who were now completely reliant for power on access to the monarch at Court.

The use of royal progresses by the Tudor monarchs, 1485–1603

All the Tudor monarchs used progresses in order to enhance respect for and obedience to the monarchy in the localities. Progresses were journeys made by the ruler and their Court to the regions of England that lay beyond London. In an age before photographs and newspapers, when most of their subjects would only have known what their monarch looked like by their image on coins, progresses played an important part in increasing the Tudors' visibility. Progresses were also a way of showing off the

power, wealth and prestige of the Court. A population which was politically restless might be subdued by the physical presence of their ruler, which would remind them of their obedience and loyalty to their monarch. A progress was also a good way for the monarch to remind their subjects of their military and legal power. Finally, progresses were an important way for the Tudors to make and sustain more direct contact with the localities. Local communities were able to show their loyalty to the monarch by greeting them with elaborate and expensive festivities and pageants. Progresses were also an opportunity for those with local grievances to bring them to the attention of the monarch, or for those with ambitions to seek patronage. Meanwhile, the ruler had the opportunity to address local instability and misgovernment through direct intervention.

In the early years of his reign, Henry VII moved around constantly. In the first year after Bosworth, he went on an extended progress to the Midlands and the North, the regions from which he faced the greatest challenges to his rule. When he travelled, he ensured that he did so with as much magnificence as possible. On other occasions in his reign, Henry VII's progresses also had a military purpose. When faced with challenges to his throne in 1487 and 1497, he marched at the head of his army to deal with the rebellions himself. The sight of their king and his army would undoubtedly have encouraged obedience, if not loyalty among his subjects.

Before Henry VIII became too old and ill to travel, he, too, used progresses, though to a lesser extent. He and his Court went on a progress every summer, largely to escape the smells and disease of London. Often, he stayed at one of his own royal palaces, for example, the palaces of Richmond and Hampton Court; he also travelled beyond the outskirts of London into Essex and the Thames valley, where he had over 40 royal residences to choose from. When Henry travelled, his Court came too; this could include up to 1,000 people, who all had to be housed and fed by the communities they visited. Henry's visits to the rest of England were more limited, however. In 1535, he visited Gloucestershire and the Bristol Channel, Salisbury, Winchester and Southampton. This particular progress may well have prevented rebellion in the religiously conservative South West of England. In 1536, the South West, which had received a visit from Henry, did not rise up in rebellion, but the North of England, which he had neglected, rose up in the most serious rebellion of his entire reign. Significantly, one of the demands of the rebels was that a parliament be held in the North; this reflected the region's feeling of neglect by a government which was too much based in the South. Henry rectified his neglect of the North in 1541, when he went on a progress there which included a stay at York. However, it took him five years to venture to the North following the Pilgrimage of Grace, and he was only persuaded to travel there following the reports of further political unrest in 1541. Nevertheless, progresses remained an important political tool for Henry.

Royal progresses under the later Tudors

The reigns of Edward VI and Mary I saw fewer progresses, as a result of their youth and increasing ill health respectively, but the tradition of the progress was revived and brought to its height by Elizabeth I. Elizabeth and her entire Court went on progresses nearly every summer. In Elizabeth's case, her progresses were driven not just by political concerns, but also by her desire to save money, because she could stay in the houses of her leading local nobility and gentry, who would have to pay for the privilege. Like Henry VIII, the majority of Elizabeth's travels were in the South, East and Midlands, where she also had royal palaces. Her longest progresses in the North were to Staffordshire and Lincolnshire, and in the West to Bristol and Gloucestershire. She also varied her routes to some extent; for example, in 1560 and 1569 she visited Hampshire, in 1572 she went to the Midlands and in 1578 she visited East Anglia. However, she never ventured to the farthest regions of her country, such as Yorkshire or Cornwall, though she had other methods of enhancing royal control through the use of her councillors, the Lord Lieutenants and JPs. Significantly, Elizabeth used her progresses to strengthen the bonds of trust and royal authority with her leading councillors. She visited the homes of Robert Dudley and William Cecil the most; she stayed with Cecil 20 times and with Dudley 23 times. About 200 prominent members of local government who acted as JPs, MPs or Lord Lieutenants also played host to Elizabeth on her progresses. In an age of personal monarchy, these visits enhanced Elizabeth's authority and improved her relationship with the men whom she trusted to run local government on her behalf.

SOURCE

7

Edward Hall (1497–1547), an English lawyer, MP and historian, wrote *The Union of the Two Noble and Illustre Families of Lancastre and Yorke*, often known as Hall's Chronicle. Here he describes Henry VIII's summer progress in 1515.

This summer the king took his progress Westward and visited his towns, castles there and heard the complaints of his poor commonality and ever as he rode, he hunted and liberally departed with venison; and in the middle of September he came to his manor of Woking and thether came to him the Archbishop of York whom he heartily welcomed and showed him great pleasures.

SOURCE

8

Arrival of Queen Elizabeth I at Nonsuch Palace, 1598 (hand-coloured copper engraving), by the Flemish artist Joris Hoefnagel (1542–1600).

PALATIVM REGIVM IN ANGLIÆ REGNO APPELLATVM NONCIVTZ, *Hoc est nusquam simile*.

ACTIVITY
KNOWLEDGE CHECK

Look at Sources 7 and 8.

1 What do they suggest about the role of royal progresses in Tudor England?

2 How did royal progresses help the Tudor monarchs to govern England more effectively?

A Level Exam-Style Question Section C

How far do you agree that the introduction of the Statute of Artificers (1563) was the most significant improvement in the government of the localities in the years 1485–1603? (20 marks)

Tip
Consider the ways in which the Statute of Artificers could be said to have 'improved' the government of the localities. Were other changes more 'significant' or lasting than the subsidy?

Imposing realities

Queen Elizabeth I (1533–1603) in parliament, English School (16th-century engraving).

Answer the following:

1 Explain why the conversation in the picture above would not have happened.

The shape of history is imposed by people looking back. People who lived through the 'history' did not always perceive the patterns that later historians identify. For example, some people living through the Industrial Revolution may have understood that great change was taking place, but they would not have been able to understand the massive economic, social and political consequences of industrialisation.

Consider the beginning of the growth of parliamentary power in the Tudor period:

2 Who would have made the decision as to when parliament's power began to grow?

3 Could anybody have challenged this decision?

4 Explain why someone living in the 16th century would have been unable to make a judgement about the beginning of a new era.

5 Who living at the present time might regard changes in the Tudor parliament as an important event?

6 What does this picture tell us about the structure of history as we understand it?

A Level Exam-Style Question Section C

To what extent do you agree that the re-establishment of the Council of the North in 1537 was the key turning point in increasing royal power in the localities in the years 1485–1601? (20 marks)

Tip

You need to define what is meant by the 'increase' of royal power. How can this be assessed?

ACTIVITY
SUMMARY

Copy and complete the following grid.

Key development	What did it do?	How did it enhance royal control of the localities?	How did it weaken royal control of the localities?
1513 subsidy			
Re-establishment of the Council of the North			
Laws in Wales Acts			
Statute of Artificers			
Act for the Relief of the Poor (1598)			

1 Which of the key developments do you think did the most to enhance royal control of the localities? Write a side of A4 justifying your answer.

2 'The use of patronage undermined, rather than strengthened, the power of the monarchy.' What evidence can you find to support and contradict this claim? Use your evidence to explain how far you agree with this view.

 WIDER READING

Foster, R.E. 'Majesty through Magistracy: Maintaining Order in Tudor England', *History Review*, 71 (2011)

Graves, M.A.R. *Tudor Parliaments: The Crown, Lords and Commons, 1485–1603*, Longman (1985)

Gunn, S.J. *Early Tudor Government, 1485–1558*, Macmillan (1995)

Tittler, R. and Jones, N. (eds) *A Companion to Tudor Britain*, Blackwell (2008)

3.3

Challenging the succession, 1485-99

KEY QUESTIONS

- How effectively did Henry Tudor secure his hold on the throne in the years 1485–87?
- How serious was the threat posed by Lambert Simnel and Perkin Warbeck?
- What was the significance of foreign support for the pretenders?

INTRODUCTION

In 1485, Henry Tudor challenged Richard III for the throne at the Battle of Bosworth. Richard was killed and Tudor became Henry VII. However, the new king was far from secure on the throne. His claim to the throne was very weak, and there were rival claimants to the throne who had a much stronger right to be king than he did. Henry's first task, therefore, was to secure his position on the throne. He did this through a combination of rewards and punishments. But these methods were not entirely successful, because Henry faced two serious challenges to his throne, from Lambert Simnel and Perkin Warbeck, who were backed by powerful domestic and foreign support. Henry was able to overcome these challenges, but it was not until 1499 that his hold on the throne was really secure.

HOW EFFECTIVELY DID HENRY TUDOR SECURE HIS HOLD ON THE THRONE IN THE YEARS 1485-87?

Henry VII's claim to the throne was weak in 1485, and he owed his crown to the fact that he had beaten his rival Richard III on the battlefield. This put him in a particularly difficult position, because his success in challenging for the throne could encourage rival claimants to do the same. Henry's claim came through the Beaufort family, who were descendants of the third son of Edward III, John of Gaunt, the founder of the House of Lancaster. The Beauforts were illegitimate, but they had been made legitimate at the end of the 14th century, on the the condition that they, and their descendants, would not be able to claim the English throne. Henry's mother, Margaret, the last of the Beauforts, married Edmund Tudor. Edmund had no claim to the throne at all; he was the son of Catherine, the widow of Henry V, who had remarried a Welsh gentleman, Owen Tudor. Neither Catherine nor her husband had a claim to the throne. Henry Tudor's claim to the throne was based on his descent from Edward III via an illegitimate line. It did not help that Henry's claim had also been transmitted to him through a woman; in the medieval period, women were not thought to be able to rule, but they could pass on a claim to their sons, however, this claim would not be as strong as one that had come through a man.

1483 - Richard III usurps the throne; disappearance of the Princes in the Tower; Buckingham's revolt against Richard III

1486 – Challenge to Henry VII by the Staffords

1487 – Battle of Stoke

1482	1483	1484	1485	1486	1487	1488	1489	1490

1485 – Battle of Bosworth

1489 – Treaty of Medina del Campo; Yorkshire tax revolt

Henry's position in 1485 was not helped by the fact that his rivals for the throne had a stronger claim to be king than he did.

- John de la Pole, Earl of Lincoln, was the leading **Yorkist** claimant. He was the nephew of Edward IV and Richard III, and during Richard's reign had been the **heir presumptive**. De la Pole was a real threat to Henry as a potential figurehead of a Yorkist rising, and rapidly became the focus of opposition to Henry in the first two years of the reign.

- Edward Plantagenet, Earl of Warwick, was also a nephew of Edward IV and Richard III. In 1485, Warwick was just 10 years old. Warwick's youth made it easier for Henry to control him; Warwick was placed in the Tower, where he was to spend the rest of his life, though this did not stop him from becoming the focus of plots against Henry.

- The other remaining Yorkist challengers were Edward IV's own children. His two sons, Edward and Richard (known as the Princes in the Tower) had disappeared at the start of Richard III's reign in 1483, and it is probable that they were dead. This did not stop Henry's enemies from attempting to use the princes as a focus for rallying support against the king.

- Edward IV's daughters also had Yorkist blood, but it was assumed that they could not rule in their own right. But they could still pass on their claim to the throne to their children, which made them dangerous to Henry.

Despite being a **Lancastrian**, Henry had been able to rally Yorkist support behind him in 1485 by promising to marry Elizabeth of York, Edward's eldest daughter. However, Henry did have one advantage in 1485; this was that he had won the throne in the Battle of Bosworth, during which several leading supporters of Richard III had been killed or captured.

KEY TERMS

Yorkist and Lancastrian
The two families who claimed the throne during the 15th century were both descended from sons of Edward III: John of Gaunt, Duke of Lancaster, and Edmund, Duke of York. The Houses of York and Lancaster and their supporters became rivals for the throne in the 1450s; this led to the Wars of the Roses, a civil war which disrupted England until 1487. Henry VII was a representative of the House of Lancaster, and his victory at Bosworth was part of the ongoing struggle between the two sides.

Heir presumptive
Someone who is likely to be the next monarch, but who can be displaced in the line of succession by the birth of a child to the current ruler. John de la Pole was heir presumptive because Richard III had no surviving children.

ACTIVITY
KNOWLEDGE CHECK

1 Use the family tree (on the next page) to work out which of the following people had the best claim to the throne. You should be prepared to justify your decision.

   a) Henry VII

   b) John de la Pole, Earl of Lincoln

   c) Edward, Earl of Warwick

   d) Elizabeth of York

   e) Edward and Richard, sons of Edward IV

2 What does this suggest about Henry VII's position in 1485–87?

3 What do you think Henry should have done about these rival claimants?

1491 – Fall of Brittany; emergence of Perkin Warbeck

1494 – Italian wars begin

1496 – Intercursus Magnus with Burgundy; invasion by James IV

1499 – Executions of Perkin Warbeck and the Earl of Warwick

| 1491 | 1492 | 1493 | 1494 | 1495 | 1496 | 1497 | 1498 | 1499 |

1492 – Treaty of Etaples

1495 – Warbeck lands at Deal

1497 – Cornish rising; Truce of Ayton

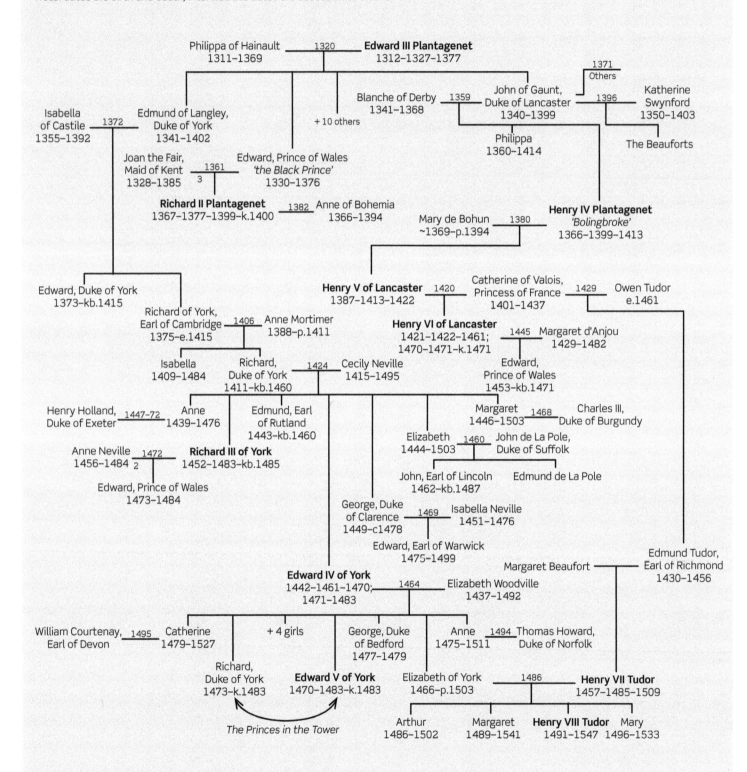

Figure 3.1 Family tree showing the claims to the throne of Henry VII and his rivals.

EXTEND YOUR KNOWLEDGE

Richard III and the Princes in the Tower
When Richard III took the throne in 1483, he did so by usurping the rightful heir, Edward V, the eldest son of Edward IV (Richard's brother). Richard claimed that Edward IV's children were illegitimate; this allowed him to claim the throne as the next rightful heir. Edward V, and his younger brother Richard, Duke of York, aged 12 and 9 respectively, were placed in the Tower. Gradually, they were seen less and less, until they disappeared completely. The likelihood is that they had been murdered. The disappearance of the young princes created considerable anger and outrage; in 1483, it sparked an attempted rebellion against Richard III. Many Yorkists transferred their support to Henry Tudor as a result of Richard III's actions in 1483.

The impact of the Battle of Bosworth, 1485

SOURCE
1

A portrait of Henry VII, painted from life in 1505 by an unknown artist from the Netherlands. Henry is holding a Tudor rose in his hand.

The Battle of Bosworth was fought on 22 August 1485. Henry Tudor had the smaller force, of about 5,000 men; Richard may have had twice this number. Richard's superior numbers ought to have been decisive, but he lost the battle because of his miscalculation and the actions of some of his leading nobility, Thomas, Lord Stanley, Stanley's brother, Sir William, and Henry Percy, Earl of Northumberland. Richard had expected these men to fight for him. However, the Stanleys' loyalties were split. Thomas Stanley had married Henry's widowed mother, Margaret Beaufort. The Stanleys chose to watch the battle from the sidelines, before Sir William eventually committed his troops in support of Henry. Northumberland brought troops to the battle, but did not fight at all.

Henry was also helped by Richard's impetuous actions; Richard saw the opportunity to finish the battle by killing Henry. He came very close to doing so, but in his charge, became separated from the majority of his troops. It was at this point that Sir William Stanley chose to intervene, directing his troops to attack Richard and possibly saving Henry's life in the process. Richard was killed in the fierce fighting that followed. Although Henry had won, Bosworth showed the difficulties of the task he faced. Powerful nobility like the Stanleys and Northumberland, whom Richard had thought he could trust, had betrayed their king and acted in their own best interests. This meant that Henry, a ruler with a very weak claim to the throne, was not able to trust his nobility completely. If they had betrayed Richard, they could easily betray Henry. In addition, Henry drew some of his support from Yorkists who had turned against Richard when he usurped the throne from his nephews. This anti-Ricardian faction included the Woodville family, who had risen to prominence when Elizabeth Woodville married Edward IV. Although the Woodvilles and other Yorkists might support Henry as a method of getting rid of Richard, there

EXTEND YOUR KNOWLEDGE

The Woodville family
In 1464, Edward IV secretly married Elizabeth Woodville. The marriage was controversial because Elizabeth was a commoner and also a widow, with two small children, Thomas and Richard Grey. Kings were supposed to use their marriages to promote international alliances; by marrying one of his subjects, Edward IV promoted the rise of faction and jealousy at Court. This was exacerbated by the Woodvilles' ambition. Elizabeth had 12 brothers and sisters; they were married off to some of the most powerful members of the English nobility, dominating the marriage market and causing resentment among other members of the English nobility. Elizabeth's father and brothers were also ennobled.

When Richard III seized the throne in 1483, the Woodvilles were targeted. Elizabeth's brother, Anthony, and her younger son from her first marriage, Richard Grey, were both executed. Her sons by Edward IV, Edward V and Richard, disappeared in the Tower of London. Another of Elizabeth's brothers, Edward Woodville, and her elder son by her first marriage, Thomas Grey, Marquess of Dorset, escaped and joined Henry Tudor in exile.

Elizabeth Woodville, with her surviving daughters, went into sanctuary at Westminster. They were eventually persuaded by Richard III to return to Court, but Elizabeth plotted with Margaret Beaufort, Henry's mother, to unite the rival Houses of York and Lancaster through the marriage of Elizabeth's eldest daughter, another Elizabeth, to Margaret's son, Henry. Richard III was rumoured to have wanted to marry the younger Elizabeth (his own niece) himself. These rumours added to his unpopularity.

was no guarantee that they would keep supporting Henry once Richard was dead.

However, Bosworth did also have a positive impact on Henry's rule. The 15th century was an age in which it was believed that God's will dictated events. Although Richard III was a king anointed by God, his defeat at Bosworth was seen as God's punishment for the methods he had used in seizing the throne. Henry was able to present his victory as one given by God; this helped to enhance his positon. Another advantage for Henry was that Richard III was killed in battle. This removed a potential political rival and focus for Yorkist support. The Wars of the Roses had been prolonged by the existence of two rival kings (Henry VI and Edward IV). With Richard dead, Henry did not have to worry about this, especially since Richard's only legitimate son and heir, Edward Prince of Wales, had died in 1484. Several other powerful supporters were also killed, for example, John Howard, the first Duke of Norfolk, and Sir Richard Ratcliffe, one of Richard's closest advisers. Other Ricardians were captured at the battle, such as John Howard's son, Thomas. Furthermore, it is estimated that less than a quarter of the nobility actually fought for Richard at Bosworth, suggesting that support for him was lukewarm at best. This did not mean that Henry could automatically rely on noble support for his rule, however. In addition, some of Richard's supporters did escape in the confusion; these included his councillor Francis, Lord Lovell, and the brothers Sir Humphrey and Thomas Stafford. Lovell and the Staffords would join the early opposition to Henry's rule in 1486–87.

The measures Henry used to secure his throne

In the months after Bosworth, Henry needed to reinforce the idea that God wanted him to be king, so his actions were focused primarily on securing and justifying his claim to the throne. After Bosworth, Henry's first move was to ensure that he was crowned in a formal ceremony. The process of crowning a monarch involved a coronation oath in which the monarch swore to protect his realm and to uphold its laws. The coronation of a monarch was the moment at which they were considered to have been chosen and anointed by God, and was thus an important step for Henry in reasserting his God-given right to be king. Henry followed up his coronation with his first parliament. It was part of the royal prerogative to summon parliament, but parliament did not have the right to appoint the monarch. The parliament of 1485 declared that Henry was king, confirming the events of the previous two months; Henry was careful to avoid any suggestion that parliament had given him the throne, however (Source 3). Henry also used his first parliament to punish his opponents at Bosworth. Parliament declared that Henry's reign had begun on 21 August 1485, the day before Bosworth. This turned Richard III into a usurper and Henry into the rightful king on the day the battle was fought; all those who had fought for Richard were traitors and could be punished as such. Finally, Henry cemented his dynastic position. First, he used parliament to cancel the *Titulus Regius* which had been passed by Richard III. The *Titulus Regius* had declared that Edward's marriage to Elizabeth Woodville was invalid and that their children were illegitimate. If Henry had

allowed the *Titulus Regius* to stand, then his future wife, Elizabeth of York (Edward and Elizabeth Woodville's daughter), would have been illegitimate under the law. Henry could not allow this to happen as he needed any children from his marriage to Elizabeth to be undeniably legitimate, so that they could inherit the throne. Once the *Titulus Regius* had been repealed, Henry was able to cement his support from the Yorkists by marrying Elizabeth of York in January 1486. This marriage united the two feuding factions, especially when Elizabeth gave birth to a healthy son and heir, Arthur, later that year. Arthur, and his younger brothers and sisters, were the representatives of the new Tudor dynasty. Even if some Yorkists were reluctant to support Henry, a representative of the House of Lancaster, they were more likely to be loyal to his children, who had both Yorkist and Lancastrian blood.

SOURCE 2

An elaborately decorated manuscript page made for Henry VIII c1516, celebrating the union of the Houses of York and Lancaster, and the combination of the white rose of York with the red rose of Lancaster to create the Tudor Rose. The illumination shows a walled castle enclosing a rose tree and surrounded by sea. It incorporates symbols used by the early Tudors, including a dragon, lion, greyhound, pomegranate bush, daisy and marigold.

SOURCE 3 Parliamentary acknowledgement of Henry VII's title of king.

To the pleasure of almighty God, the wealth, prosperity and surety of this realm of England, to the singular comfort of all the king's subjects of the same, and in avoiding of all ambiguities and questions, be it ordained, established and enacted by authority of this present Parliament that the inheritance of the crowns of the realms of England and of France, with all the pre-eminence and dignity royal to the same pertaining, and all other seignories [lordships] to the king belonging beyond the sea, with the appurtenances thereto in any wise due or pertaining, be, rest, remain and abide in the most royal person of our now sovereign lord King Harry the VIIth and in the heirs of his body lawfully coming, perpetually with the grace of God so to endure, and in none other.

ACTIVITY
KNOWLEDGE CHECK

Look at Sources 2 and 3.

1 What does Source 2 suggest about the importance of Henry VII's marriage to Elizabeth of York?

2 Why do you think Henry VIII had Source 2 made?

3 According to Source 3, what is Henry's claim to the throne?

TIMELINE: KEY EVENTS OF 1485-86

1485
22 August: Battle of Bosworth
30 October: Coronation of Henry VII
7 November: meeting of parliament

1486
18 January: Henry marries Elizabeth of York
4 March: Henry begins first progress to the Midlands and the North
April: Abortive rising by Francis Lovell and the Staffords
19 September: Birth of Prince Arthur

Henry also secured his throne by rewarding his supporters. Henry's main concern was to ensure that no member of the nobility could accumulate too much power. This meant that he tended to avoid granting too many titles or estates which would allow the nobility to build up rival sources of power to the monarchy. One of the few men to accumulate any amount of landed power was Henry's uncle, Jasper Tudor, who was created Duke of Bedford in 1485 as a reward for his lifelong support. Other beneficiaries of Henry's gratitude in 1485 were Thomas Stanley, Henry's stepfather, who was made Earl of Derby. Sir William Stanley was given the trusted position of Lord Chamberlain of the Royal Household, which meant that he controlled access to Henry. Yorkist supporters were rewarded, too; Sir Thomas Lovell, who rebelled against Richard III in 1483 and had joined Henry in exile, was made Treasurer of the Household. John Morton, who had also resisted Richard, became Chancellor

and Archbishop of Canterbury. Both Lovell and Morton spent the rest of their careers serving Henry loyally. These were particularly important appointments because both men had experience of governing England, which Henry, who had been in exile for much of his life, did not.

Henry also had to deal with the men who had actively supported Richard III. He was helped in this because his coronation, and the declaration by parliament that he was king, allowed him to justify the seizure of these men's lands. Significantly, Henry did not execute many of the survivors of Bosworth. John de la Pole, Earl of Lincoln, swore loyalty to Henry and was allowed to join the Royal Council. Similarly, Henry Percy, Earl of Northumberland, who had watched Bosworth from the sidelines, was briefly imprisoned before being allowed to return to his estates in the North. Henry's treatment of Thomas Howard, Earl of Surrey, was more cautious; Surrey was kept in the Tower until 1487, but was eventually rehabilitated (see Chapter 2).

Henry also attempted to strengthen respect and obedience for the monarchy. In 1486, he embarked on a progress to the Midlands and the North, where Ricardian support was particularly strong. He was also very aware of the threat posed to him by the private armies of the nobility; in the 1485 parliament, he made the Houses of Lords and Commons swear an oath that they would not retain (recruit) men illegally. He also attempted to make the Crown's finances more secure by passing an Act of Resumption in 1486; this allowed Henry to take back all Crown lands which had been granted away since 1455. The aim of this Act was to increase the wealth of the Crown and to give Henry more spending power compared to his nobility. When Henry did grant land to his supporters, he usually did so using lands that had been forfeited by his opponents, rather than using Crown lands, the loss of which would have impoverished him while making his nobility more powerful. Thus, Henry's early rule was characterised by attempts at cautious reconciliation. He was not prepared to over-reward his supporters, but he was prepared to trust former enemies, though he soon found that this trust was misplaced, and his later reign was increasingly dominated by paranoia and suspicion of his nobility.

Roles of the Yorkist and Lancastrian factions

Yorkist supporters of Richard III in 1485	Lancastrian supporters of Henry VII in 1485	Anti-Ricardian Yorkists who supported Henry at Bosworth
Thomas Howard, Earl of Surrey John de la Pole, Earl of Lincoln Francis, Lord Lovell Thomas and Humphrey Stafford Margaret, Duchess of Burgundy	Margaret Beaufort, Henry's mother Jasper Tudor, Duke of Bedford John de Vere, Earl of Oxford Edward Courtenay, Earl of Devon	Elizabeth Woodville John Morton, Bishop of Ely Thomas Grey, Marquess of Dorset Sir Thomas Lovell Sir Giles Daubeney
Nobility with mixed/uncertain loyalties in 1485		
Thomas, Lord Stanley, Earl of Derby; Sir William Stanley; Henry Percy, Earl of Northumberland		

In the period 1485–87, the main role of Henry's Lancastrian supporters was to enhance his control of England. Henry did not have many immediate family members, apart from his mother and uncle. He was an only child and had spent much of his youth in exile abroad. In many ways this was an advantage for Henry, because he did not have to spend money or give away royal estates to support his relatives, which had been a problem for Edward IV. The people Henry relied on the most were those who had been in exile with him, such as Jasper Tudor and John de Vere. Tudor was given extensive power in the troublesome region of Wales, where he became Chief Justice. De Vere was prominent on Henry's Council and in East Anglia, but even these men were not allowed to become more powerful than the king. The Stanley family were also trusted in these early years; Thomas Stanley was considered trustworthy because he was married to Henry's mother, Margaret Beaufort. Stanley was well-rewarded with custody of the Cheshire estates of the Earl of Stafford while the Stafford heir was a minor. Margaret, too, was given additional estates in the Midlands and the West.

A greater potential problem was the anti-Ricardian Yorkists, especially the Woodvilles, who could easily have switched their allegiance to a rival claimant once Richard III himself was dead. However, this did not happen, mainly because Henry kept his promise to marry Elizabeth of York. This marriage meant that Yorkists were able to transfer their allegiance to the new Tudor dynasty. This group soon became part of the new Tudor regime and did not support the plots against Henry. The exception to this was Thomas Grey, Marquess of Dorset. Henry's attitude to him was more ambivalent because, although Grey had joined him in exile in 1484, he later tried to return to support Richard III. Grey was saved because he was half-brother of Elizabeth, Henry's wife, but Henry never fully trusted him.

However, the hard-line supporters of Richard III began to cause problems for Henry almost immediately. Men such as Thomas and Humphrey Stafford and Francis, Lord Lovell, who had fought for Richard at Bosworth, still hoped to restore a Yorkist monarchy. In 1486, rumours began to spread of plots against Henry. One rumour suggested that the Earl of Warwick, a potential rival for the throne, had escaped from the Tower and fled to the Channel Islands; agents of the Earl of Lincoln were caught smuggling gold and silver out of the country, perhaps intending to use the money to raise an army abroad. The Stafford brothers and Francis Lovell went further, however. They had all escaped after Bosworth and had entered the protection of sanctuary at Colchester. Here, they plotted together to rebel against Henry. Leaving sanctuary in April 1486, the Staffords tried to raise a rebellion in the Midlands in the name of the Earl of Warwick. This could have been dangerous as this region was the heartland of the Warwick estates; loyalty to the young earl could have brought out Yorkist support for him. Henry was near York at the time, but when he heard the news, he began to advance on the Midlands. The Staffords fled, having failed to raise any support, and tried to take refuge in sanctuary again, but they were forcibly removed by Henry. Sir Humphrey Stafford was executed, but his younger brother, Thomas, was pardoned. Meanwhile, Lovell tried to raise a rebellion in Yorkshire, exploiting the loyalties in this region to Richard III. There was little support for Lovell, however, and the attempted revolt was suppressed by

Jasper Tudor. Lovell then fled to Burgundy, where he was able to find refuge with another key Yorkist, Margaret, Duchess of Burgundy. Although these early plots and risings came to nothing, the warning signs were there for Henry. Hard-line Yorkists were not prepared to accept his rule; more worryingly, the names of his rivals for the throne, Warwick and Lincoln, were starting to be associated with this opposition.

SOURCE

4   Polydore Vergil, *Anglica Historia*, describing Henry's actions in 1485. Vergil was commissioned by Henry VII to write a history of his reign. The first version was completed by about 1513 but was not published until 1534.

After Henry had obtained power, from the very start of his reign he then set about quelling the insurrections. Accordingly, before he left Leicester, he despatched Robert Willoughby to Yorkshire with instructions to bring back Edward, the fifteen-year-old earl of Warwick, sole survivor of George, duke of Clarence whom Richard [III] had held hitherto in the castle called Sheriff Hutton. For indeed, Henry, not unaware of the mob's natural tendency always to seek changes, was fearful lest, if the boy should escape and given any alteration in circumstances, he might stir up civil discord. Having made for the castle without delay, Robert received the boy from the commander of the place and brought him to London, where the wretch, born to misery, remained in the Tower until his death... Detained in the same fortress was Elizabeth, elder daughter of King Edward [IV]... This girl too, attended by noble ladies, was brought to her mother in London. Henry meanwhile made his way to London like a triumphing general, and in the places through which he passed was greeted with the greatest joy by all. Far and wide the people hastened to assemble by the roadside, saluting him as king and filling the length of his journey with laden table and overflowing goblets...

After this he summoned a Parliament, as was the custom, in which he might receive the crown by popular consent. His chief care was to regulate well affairs of state and, in order that the people of England should not be further torn by rival factions, he publicly proclaimed that (as he had already promised) he would take for his wife Elizabeth daughter of King Edward and that he would give complete pardon and forgiveness to all those who swore obedience to his name. Then at length having won the good-will of all men and at the instigation of both nobles and people, he was made king at Westminster on 31 October and called Henry, seventh of that name.

Henry reigned twenty-three years and seven months... His spirit was distinguished, wise and prudent... In government he was shrewd and prudent, so that no one dared to get the better of him through deceit or guile... He cherished justice above all thing; as a result he vigorously punished violence, manslaughter, and every other kind of wickedness whatsoever.

ACTIVITY
KNOWLEDGE CHECK

Read Polydore Vergil's account of Henry's early years in power (Source 4) and answer the following questions.

1 According to Polydore Vergil, what were the threats to Henry's security and how did he deal with them?

2 What impression does Polydore Vergil give of Henry's style of kingship?

3 How useful is Polydore Vergil's account for explaining why Henry was able to survive as king?

EXTEND YOUR KNOWLEDGE

Polydore Vergil and the *Anglica Historia*
Polydore Vergil was an Italian humanist, scholar and historian, who came to England c1502. Although Vergil had been commissioned by Henry VII, he did not always portray the king in a favourable light. He also used research methods which would be familiar to modern academic historians, such as talking to eyewitnesses who were present at Bosworth, like the Earl of Surrey.

However, Vergil was also writing a form of propaganda to justify Henry Tudor's seizure of the throne in 1485. Because of this, Vergil tends to emphasise the unpopularity of Richard III and the popularity of Henry VII.

Vergil went on to add to his *Anglica Historia* in the reign of Henry VIII. He portrays Thomas Wolsey in a very negative light; this was partly because Wolsey had Vergil imprisoned in the Tower of London in 1515.

support of 2,000 German mercenaries, led by the experienced Martin Schwartz. The rebels and their troops then sailed for Ireland, which was a traditional Yorkist power base. In Ireland, de la Pole and Lovell met with members of the Irish nobility, such as Gerald Fitzgerald, Earl of Kildare, who were sympathetic to their aims.

The Irish and English Yorkists crowned Simnel as king in Dublin; they then launched a combined invasion of England. The rebel army arrived in the North in early June 1487 and marched South. Worryingly for Henry, Henry Percy, Earl of Northumberland, did nothing to stop the rebel army. This was the same man who had watched Bosworth from the sidelines. Percy's ambivalence was a worry for the king; Percy, as the local lord, was supposed to be the first line of defence against rebellion, but seemed to be more interested in staying neutral and protecting his own interests.

A Level Exam-Style Question Section B

To what extent had Henry VII secured his claim to the throne by 1487? (20 marks)

Tip
You will need to ensure your answer is balanced by considering ways in which Henry was secure and ways in which he was still insecure by 1487.

HOW SERIOUS WAS THE THREAT POSED BY LAMBERT SIMNEL AND PERKIN WARBECK?

The nature of the challenge by Lambert Simnel, 1486-87

Although the attempted plots and risings against Henry came to nothing in 1486, there was still a very real threat to Henry's security on the throne. Francis Lovell was on the loose, and Henry's main rival for the throne, John de la Pole, had been implicated in plots, even though he had sworn loyalty to Henry. However, de la Pole, the most likely replacement for Henry, was not yet prepared to risk everything in open rebellion. The Yorkists' solution was to find a suitable figurehead, a young boy called Lambert Simnel, who could be manipulated and used to focus opposition against Henry.

Simnel himself had no royal blood and was an imposter. He was the ten-year-old son of a joiner from Oxford who was trained by a priest, Richard Simons, to act as if he were a royal prince. The plotters made an error in making Simnel impersonate the Earl of Warwick, because Henry was able to produce the real earl from the Tower of London and parade him through the streets. However, this did not stop the Simnel rebellion from gathering momentum. John de la Pole fled to Burgundy, where he joined Francis Lovell. Margaret of Burgundy, the sister of Richard III, used her money and power to help Lovell and de la Pole to raise troops. With Margaret's help, the rebels were able to raise the

TIMELINE: THE CHALLENGE OF LAMBERT SIMNEL

1486
November: Rumours that Lambert Simnel is claiming to be the Earl of Warwick

1487
February: Henry parades the real Earl of Warwick in the streets of London; John de la Pole attends a Council meeting to discuss measures against the plot

April: De la Pole escapes to Burgundy; Henry begins to raise troops in the localities

5 May: De la Pole and Lovell land in Ireland

24 May: Lambert Simnel crowned as king in Dublin

4 June: The rebel army arrives at Furness

16 June: Henry's army defeats the rebels at the Battle of Stoke

November-December: Henry's second parliament

Henry's response to the threat from Simnel
Meanwhile, Henry had realised that the Simnel challenge was serious. His lack of experience as king had led him to trust de la Pole, even though there were rumours that de la Pole was involved in plots. De la Pole was even present at a Council in February 1487 which met to discuss the threat from Simnel and possible measures against it. However, by April, Henry had been alerted to de la Pole's involvement and was starting to raise troops to meet the potential challenge. Although Bosworth had been his only previous battle, he showed considerable tactical awareness.

- Henry ordered the coasts to be guarded (although the rebels still managed to land).

71

- As Henry began to receive intelligence that the rebels would invade from Ireland, he gradually moved northwards and westwards, gathering men and supplies as he went.

- By 8 May, Henry had arrived at Kenilworth Castle, which he adopted as his base. Here, he waited for news of the rebel landing; when he received it, he marched North, meeting the rebels at Stoke, in East Nottinghamshire.

The Battle of Stoke is often considered to be the end of the Wars of the Roses. It seems to have been quite a one-sided fight. Although the German mercenaries used by the rebels were well-trained and equipped, the Irish forces lacked body-armour and suffered many losses in the battle as a result. Accounts of the battle by Irish supporters of Simnel suggest that the rebels were easily defeated (Source 5). Even if the rebels did put up a fight, the result went decisively in Henry's favour. John de la Pole and Martin Schwartz were killed. Francis Lovell disappeared during the battle and was never seen again. Simnel was captured, but Henry was lenient to him because Simnel was just a child. Simnel was put to work in the king's kitchens and later rose through the ranks of the Royal Household to become the king's falconer. The Simnel rebellion was over almost as quickly as it had started, and Henry never had to fight another battle in England to keep his throne, though he came close during the challenge from Perkin Warbeck in 1497. Although it may not have seemed like it to Henry, the Wars of the Roses were over.

How serious was the threat from Lambert Simnel and his supporters?

In some ways, the challenge from Simnel and the men who supported him was a very serious threat to Henry's position on the throne. The rebel alliance that emerged against Henry in 1487 was a dangerous mix of rival claimants, discontented Yorkists, and foreign support. Although Simnel himself was an imposter, he was in fact a puppet for John de la Pole, a man with a much better claim to the throne than Henry VII. If the rebels had won at Stoke, it is likely that Simnel would have been replaced by de la Pole. The Simnel challenge was made more serious because the rebels actually managed to raise an army, funded by Margaret of Burgundy. The support of the Irish was particularly crucial in the early successes of the rebels. Ireland was a potential jumping off point for anyone who wanted to invade England. Without Irish support, it would have been much harder for the rebels to sustain their challenge or to find a base from which to launch their rebellion. Henry's position as king was also put under threat because he himself was slow to realise the threat from de la Pole. Although de la Pole's name was being associated with Yorkist plots in 1486, Henry did not react. He continued to trust de la Pole and to include him in his Council meetings. Henry's inexperience as king in this situation was clear. Instead of imprisoning de la Pole, he allowed him to go free; the result was that de la Pole was able to flee to Burgundy, out of Henry's reach. Henry was then forced to fight de la Pole, which was a much more dangerous and uncertain method of dealing with an opponent than imprisoning them or putting them on trial for treason.

SOURCE 5

From the *Book of Houth*, a history of Ireland, compiled by the Anglo-Irish Houth family in the 16th century. Nicholas, Lord Houth, was one of the few Irish lords who remained loyal to Henry VII in 1487. This section describes the Battle of Stoke in 1487.

The king called his Council and these men thought it good to give a general pardon to all those who would receive the same without any condition of exemption. And after the young Earl of Warwick was brought to Paul's Church through London, where many might see him that thought he was run away and that they might perceive the fondness of the Irish to move war against the king without any just matter. The king, hearing of these men's landing, decided to encounter them straightaway in case that, in long tarrying, he might enlarge their power and increase their numbers. In truth, they were but a few in the beginning. To be short, both armies came within a little to Stoke and the morrow after joined and fought very valiant on both sides, for those Germans were very good and apt soldiers and so was their Captain, Martin Schwartz; his like was not in either army. The Irishmen did as well as any naked men could do and at length they were slain, about 4,000 and more.

How and why was Henry able to overcome the challenge from Simnel and his supporters?

The threat from Simnel should not be over-stated. Henry was able to defeat the rebels because they made mistakes and lacked support, and he acted decisively once the threat was clear. The rebels' decision to claim that Simnel was in fact the Earl of Warwick was a poor one. Nevertheless, there were still some die-hard Yorkists who were prepared to back Simnel, despite the fact that he was clearly not who he said he was. These die-hards were a minority in 1487, however. The fighting force raised by de la Pole and Lovell was made up of mercenaries, men who were paid to fight, not other Yorkist loyalists. The Irish nobility such as Kildare did not accompany the army, preferring to remain in Ireland to wait and see what happened. Although the rebels faced no resistance from the Earl of Northumberland as they marched through the North, neither did supporters flock to support the rebel army. This was significant because the North was the traditional stronghold of Richard III and the Yorkists. If this region was not prepared to rise up in support of the rebels, it was unlikely that other parts of England would be any keener to support them. Even the Yorkist Earl of Surrey, who had fought for Richard III at Bosworth and was still imprisoned in the Tower, did not take the opportunity to escape and join the rebels. Surrey's attitude was typical of many of the landed elite at this time; they preferred stability and order, which Henry VII seemed to offer. The reason for this was the natural caution and self-preservation that existed among the land owning classes. After several years of political instability, they were unwilling to risk their property and lives in a rebellion against their anointed king. The result of this was that Henry was able to gather enough loyal support to defeat the rebels in a pitched battle.

Henry's own actions were also important; he was prepared to lead an army himself. He reacted swiftly to news of the rebel army and made sure that he was well-placed in the middle of England to make a military strike at the rebels, wherever they appeared. Combined with the rebels' lack of military support, Henry's tactics meant that he was able to win at Stoke fairly easily. This helped to reinforce his position as the rightful king of England, anointed by God. His victory had the added advantage that it also removed two serious Yorkist threats, de la Pole and Lovell.

Henry was able to strengthen his hold on the throne still further in the aftermath of the 1487 rebellion. In November 1487, he called the second parliament of his reign. He used this parliament to pass 28 **Acts of Attainder** against the rebels. In addition, members of the king's Council were given additional authority by Act of Parliament to deal with local disorder and, in particular, the problem of over-powerful members of the nobility and gentry through the use of the **court of Star Chamber**. Henry did not invent the court of Star Chamber, but his Act of Parliament set up a special group of justices, drawn from the Council, who were responsible for hearing cases.

KEY TERMS

Acts of Attainder
A method of using an Act of Parliament to declare someone was guilty without having to put them on trial. All estates could be confiscated under an attainder, but it was also reversible for good behaviour.

Court of Star Chamber
A flexible legal court that had been used before the reign of Henry VII to hear cases in that it would not otherwise have been possible to get a fair trial. Star Chamber had been a royal tool since the 14th century for dealing with the nobility and gentry when they used their power to undermine local judicial systems.

ACTIVITY
KNOWLEDGE CHECK

Make a spider diagram entitled 'Why was Henry able to defeat the challenge from Simnel?' Use the following headings to make notes to answer this question.

- Rebels' mistakes and weaknesses
- Henry's strengths
- Attitude of the nobility and gentry.

The nature of the threat from Perkin Warbeck and his supporters, 1491–99

In 1491, another **pretender** emerged in Ireland to challenge Henry's position as king, a young man called Perkin Warbeck. There is considerable uncertainty about Warbeck's background, which is not helped by Warbeck's own contradictory claims. The likelihood is that he was born c1472–74 in Tournai in Flanders, and was brought up in the region that is now known as the Netherlands. He was probably well-educated. At some point, he

learnt English, and by the age of 17 he had travelled to Ireland, where he first made his claim to be the rightful king of England. Warbeck claimed to be Richard, Duke of York, the younger of the two Princes in the Tower who had disappeared in 1483. This was a plausible claim; if the Prince had been alive, he would have been about Warbeck's current age. Crucially, there was also no way for Henry to disprove Warbeck's claims. The Duke of York had completely disappeared in 1483; no one knew his fate and his body had never been found. Henry could not simply produce York as he had done with the Earl of Warwick; this suited the plotters perfectly, as they could use the uncertainty surrounding Warbeck's identity to their advantage.

KEY TERM

Pretender
In this period, someone who was a claimant to the throne. Henry VII was a pretender to the throne before he won at Bosworth in 1485; Simnel and Warbeck can also be described as pretenders.

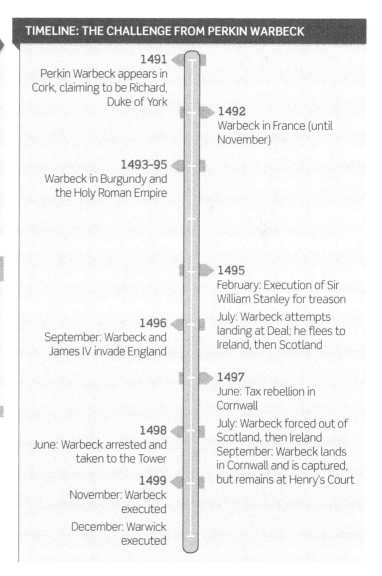

TIMELINE: THE CHALLENGE FROM PERKIN WARBECK

1491
Perkin Warbeck appears in Cork, claiming to be Richard, Duke of York

1492
Warbeck in France (until November)

1493-95
Warbeck in Burgundy and the Holy Roman Empire

1495
February: Execution of Sir William Stanley for treason
July: Warbeck attempts landing at Deal; he flees to Ireland, then Scotland

1496
September: Warbeck and James IV invade England

1497
June: Tax rebellion in Cornwall
July: Warbeck forced out of Scotland, then Ireland
September: Warbeck lands in Cornwall and is captured, but remains at Henry's Court

1498
June: Warbeck arrested and taken to the Tower

1499
November: Warbeck executed
December: Warwick executed

Like Simnel before him, Warbeck's challenge had an international dimension. From his first appearance in 1491 to his eventual capture in 1497, Warbeck received support from several foreign rulers who were prepared to use him as a way to put pressure on Henry. Warbeck's foreign supporters included, at different times, Charles VIII, king of France; the Yorkist Margaret of Burgundy, her stepson Philip of Burgundy and his father, Maximilian, Holy Roman Emperor. The Scottish king, James IV, was also prepared to offer Warbeck support, but the Irish nobles were less keen to become involved in rebellion than they had been in 1487, despite several attempts to appeal to them.

Warbeck's challenge, 1491-95

When Warbeck first appeared in Cork, Ireland in late 1491, his reception was mixed. The people of Cork were enthusiastic, but the Earl of Kildare was reluctant to get involved directly. When Irish support failed to materialise, Warbeck and the Earl of Desmond started to write to other European rulers in the hope of getting more help. Charles VIII of France invited Warbeck to France in 1492, where Warbeck was treated as if he were really a prince. However, Henry's prompt actions meant that Warbeck was soon no longer welcome there. He moved instead to Burgundy, where he received acceptance from Margaret of Burgundy and her relatives. Margaret went as far as to 'recognise' Warbeck as Richard, Duke of York, her nephew, even though she would have last seen the duke in 1480 when he was about seven years old. Margaret was determined to remove Henry VII as king and to restore the Yorkist line; Warbeck presented an opportunity for her to create a figurehead to act as a focus for opposition.

By 1494–95, Henry VII was becoming increasingly concerned by the threat from Warbeck. Although Warbeck had yet to raise an army and threaten invasion, there were signs that he was starting to gather support within England, exploiting traditional Yorkist loyalties to Edward IV and his family.

- Agents from Burgundy were able to infiltrate England, and there were cases of men trying to recruit supporters for Warbeck in 1493–94. These men were generally rounded up and put on trial.

- Sir William Stanley, Henry's step-uncle who had been responsible for helping Henry to victory at Bosworth, was implicated in a plot against Henry. Stanley's betrayal was particularly worrying for Henry because he was Chamberlain of the King's Household, and as such had daily personal access to Henry himself. In March 1493, Stanley had agreed with another man, Sir Robert Clifford, that Clifford would go abroad to speak to Warbeck. Clifford, who may have been a spy all along, then informed Henry that Stanley had been in communication with Warbeck. In January 1495, Stanley was tried and convicted of treason and executed the following month. Stanley's execution did not stop the challenge from Warbeck, however.

- In July, 1495, Warbeck attempted a landing at Deal in Kent, with a small force of 300 soldiers. When he failed to get any local support, Warbeck fled, leaving the few men who had waited for him to be captured, tried and executed.

Warbeck's challenge, 1495-97

After his failure at Deal, Warbeck moved to Scotland. James IV of Scotland was keen to cause trouble for his traditional enemy, England, and supporting Warbeck was the ideal way in which to achieve this. In Scotland, Warbeck was relatively safe from Henry, and there was a real possibility that the pretender would be able to launch an invasion from across the border. In September 1496, Warbeck tried to invade England with a small force of 1,400 men. But like Simnel before him, Warbeck was unable to raise much support in the North, and he retreated back to Scotland. The threat of Warbeck in the North created more problems for Henry, however. In 1497, the king was forced to raise taxation to fund an army to fight Warbeck. The demand for additional tax provoked rebellion in Cornwall in June 1497. The rebels, who numbered about 15,000, were protesting about the level of taxation demanded to pay for a war which was to be fought at the other end of the country. They chose to march on London, and Henry had to change his plans rapidly. He was forced to divert troops intended for the defence of the North; these troops met the rebels at Blackheath in Kent, where they won a decisive victory over the poorly equipped rebels. Accounts from the time suggest that about 1,000 rebels may have been killed.

The distraction of the revolt in Cornwall showed the potential weakness of Henry's position. Fortunately for him, James IV was tiring in his support of Warbeck, and in July 1497, Warbeck left Scotland for Ireland. When he failed to raise any support in Ireland, he decided to try his luck in Cornwall. Warbeck landed near Land's End in September 1497, aiming to take advantage of the recent unrest in the region to provoke a rebellion against the Tudor dynasty. By now, the army of 1,400 men with whom he had invaded from Scotland had shrunk to about 300. Although he attracted between 3,000 and 8,000 men from Cornwall, he was not able to attract the gentry and nobility of the South West, as Source 6 suggests. Edward Courtenay, Earl of Devon, who had been given his title as a reward for his loyalty to Henry at Bosworth, was given the job of defending Exeter against the rebels. The city came close to falling, but the rebels were driven out by the soldiers and citizens. Warbeck and his remaining men then moved on to Taunton. Here, they were trapped by advancing royal forces led by another of Henry's supporters from his days in exile, Giles Daubeney. Warbeck's remaining supporters melted away and he was quickly captured as he tried to escape.

SOURCE 6

From a letter by Raimondo de Soncino, a Venetian merchant living in London, to the Duke of Milan, 30 September 1497.

On the 6th of this month Perkin landed in Cornwall at a port called Mount St Michael with three small ships and about three hundred persons of various nationalities, who had followed him for some time before. As he had so few with him, it is thought that the Cornishmen must have invited him. In fact, eight thousand peasants soon joined him, although they were ill-disciplined and without any gentlemen, who form the governing class of England. They proclaimed Perkin as King Richard and they marched towards His Majesty, who did not hear of them until the 10th.

Significantly, Henry was at first prepared to treat Warbeck well, seeing him as the unfortunate puppet of more powerful men and women. Warbeck was accepted at Henry's Court and was not formally imprisoned. But in June 1498, Warbeck tried to escape; he was arrested and put in the Tower. In the Tower, Warbeck either tried to plot with the Earl of Warwick (who had been there since 1485) or he was tricked and framed. In 1499, both Warbeck and Warwick were tried for treason. Warbeck was convicted, and because he was considered to be a commoner, was hanged; Warwick, who had spent his whole life in prison, was allowed the 'noble' death of beheading. The deaths of Warbeck and Warwick in 1499 completed Henry's triumph over the pretenders; they also served the purpose of reassuring his main foreign ally, Spain, which was nervous about entering a marriage alliance with the son of a king who still faced challenges to his dynasty.

How Henry overcame the challenge from Warbeck and his supporters

By the time that Warbeck emerged as a threat, in late 1491, Henry VII had been on the throne for six years and he had already survived one major challenge to his position by Lambert Simnel. The longer Henry remained on the throne, the more secure he became as king. The Yorkist threat was likely to fade away as the former supporters of Richard and Edward either died or simply accepted that Henry was unlikely to be toppled. It also helped that Henry's rival, John de la Pole, was dead, and the Earl of Warwick remained safely in the Tower of London. This meant that the Yorkist faction lacked a leader who was actually prepared to challenge Henry for the throne or take advantage of Warbeck's challenge. Henry had also strengthened his own position by building his own dynasty which represented both the Yorkist and Lancastrian claims. The birth of his eldest son, Arthur, in 1486 was followed by Margaret (1489), Henry (1491) and Mary (1496). Henry used his children to create foreign alliances which helped to enhance the prestige of the Tudor dynasty in the eyes of important foreign powers. In 1489, he achieved a significant alliance with Spain in the **Treaty of Medina del Campo**. This was the first time one of the major European powers had acknowledged Henry's right to be king by signing a treaty with him.

Henry was also able to survive because he had more resources and power than Warbeck. Despite Warbeck's ability to attract a series of foreign rulers who were prepared to protect him at their courts, he was unable to sustain this support. When Warbeck did try to invade (in 1495, 1496 and 1497), he found that he was unable to attract any significant domestic support either.

Even when Warbeck did attract more support after his landing in Cornwall, Henry was too strong for him. By the early 1490s, Henry had established a network of spies who were able to keep him informed of Warbeck's movements. When Warbeck tried to land in Kent in 1495, Henry had troops and defences waiting for him. Henry also had mostly effective chains of command. When Warbeck challenged the town of Exeter, Henry was able to co-ordinate a military response which allowed him to send reinforcements to help the Earl of Devon and to drive Warbeck towards Taunton, where he would be trapped.

Finally, Henry was able to defeat Warbeck's challenge because of his successful use of a combination of punishments and rewards. Those loyal to Henry, such as Edward Courtenay, had been well-rewarded; Courtenay had helped Henry during the latter's exile, and had fought with him at Bosworth. He was one of the few men to be ennobled as a result of his support for Henry; Courtenay's lands in the South West made him an important ally in controlling a particularly remote region. Although he was unable to prevent rebellion from breaking out twice in 1497, the earl was an invaluable man on the spot for Henry; his defence of Exeter prevented Warbeck from gaining momentum in the South West. Henry was also prepared to be ruthless towards members of the nobility and gentry who were suspected of plotting against him. The king had learnt from bitter experience that even those who swore loyalty to him could not always be trusted. His spy system was active at Court, and in 1494 it caught wind of the Court plot involving Sir William Stanley. Henry did not stop with Stanley. He increasingly used the weapon of Acts of Attainder to punish those whom he thought were conspiring with Warbeck. In the wake of the Stanley betrayal, another 24 men were attainted in the parliament of 1495. Henry also used a complex system of **bonds** and **recognisances** to make his nobility obey. He targeted those whose trustworthiness was thought to be suspect. For example, Thomas Grey, Marquis of Dorset, whose loyalty to

Henry had never been complete, was forced to take out a series of recognisances to ensure his good behaviour. Grey was told to give a recognisance for £1,000, an enormous sum; he also had to find friends who were prepared to give recognisances for £10,000. Although Grey never had to pay these amounts, which would have bankrupted him and his friends, he lived under the constant fear that he would be asked to do so. Grey remained loyal in the 1490s and helped Henry to put down the 1497 risings in Cornwall; his recognisances were cancelled in 1499. In total, between 1485 and 1509, Henry placed 36 out of 62 noble families under some form of financial control. Although these methods led to an atmosphere of paranoia and distrust, they also worked because they allowed him to exert control and keep his throne in the face of Warbeck's challenge.

To what extent did Warbeck pose a threat to Henry's position on the throne?

In some ways, Warbeck did pose a considerable challenge to Henry, though he was eventually defeated. Warbeck received some support from foreign powers, and because of this he was able to evade capture from 1491 to 1497. While Warbeck was living in France, Burgundy or Scotland, under the protection of their rulers, there was very little Henry could do against him. The king was forced into a series of negotiations with these foreign powers in order to force Warbeck to move on. Henry was particularly fortunate that Warbeck was never able to raise a substantial invasion force. The most serious moments of threat were probably in 1495 and 1496–97. If Warbeck had been able to rally support at Court, then Henry may well have faced more serious armed resistance involving men such as the Marquis of Dorset and Sir William Stanley. However, Henry's stern response to the potential threat posed by these men probably deterred any other potential plotters from joining Warbeck. Similarly, in 1497, if Warbeck had arrived in Cornwall in May–June, in time to harness the anger felt at Henry's high levels of taxation, he would have been able to march at the head of a sizeable army that included at least one member of the nobility, James, Lord Audley. Henry was particularly vulnerable at this moment; for once, his spy network had let him down and he was not expecting a revolt of this size or nature. Moreover, he was distracted by a possible invasion from Scotland, at the other end of the country. Momentum was very important to any successful rebellion; in June 1497, Warbeck could have had this momentum behind him, but he did not arrive in Cornwall until September. By this time, the tax revolt had been put down and its leaders executed. Henry was much more prepared when Warbeck did finally arrive, and although there was some support for the pretender, it could not match the well-armed and organised royal army.

In comparison to the challenge from Simnel, Warbeck never managed to force Henry to fight in a pitched battle. At Stoke, in 1487, Henry had been on the throne less than two years; he had one infant son and very little experience of either fighting or ruling the country. He was also faced by John de la Pole, who had a real claim to the throne, better than Henry's own. In the 1490s, although Warbeck posed a continuous potential threat to Henry, it never became anything more serious. Henry had a growing family and mostly loyal nobility who controlled the localities; anyone

whose loyalty was suspect was dealt with harshly. Henry's reaction to Warbeck and his supporters suggests that he definitely saw the pretender as a real threat to his security on the throne, but his response, mixed with some luck, meant that Warbeck never came close to challenging for the throne.

SOURCE

Perkin Warbeck's proclamation to the English, issued in 1496, from Robert Henry's *History of Great Britain*, 1799. In this proclamation, he poses as Richard IV and portrays Henry VII as a usurper.

Richard by the Grace of God, King of England, Lord of Ireland, Prince of Wales: to all those who will see or read our present letters, greeting:

It hath pleased God… to give us means to show ourselves armed unto our lieges and people of England… For our mortal enemy, Henry Tudor, a false usurper of the crown of England, which to us be natural and lineal rights appertaineth, knowing in his own heart our undoubted right… hath not openly deprived us of our kingdom, but likewise by all foul and wicked means sought to betray us and bereave us of our life. Yet if his tyranny only extended itself to our person, although our royal blood teaches us to be sensible of injuries, it should be less to our grief. But this Tudor, who boasteth himself to have overthrown an tyrant, hath, ever since his first entrance into his usurped reign, put but little practice but tyranny and feats thereof.

For King Richard, our unnatural uncle, although desire of rule did blind him, yet in his other actions, like a true Plantagenet, was noble, and loved the honour of the realm and the contentment and comfort of his nobles and people. But this our mortal enemy, agreeable to the meanness of his birth, hath trodden underfoot the honour of this nation, selling our best confederates for money, and making merchandise of the blood, estates, and fortunes of our peers and subjects by feigned wars and dishonourable peace, only to enrich his coffers. Nor unlike hath been his hateful misgovernment and evil deportments at home. First he hath (to fortify his false quarrel) caused divers nobles of this our realm (whom he held suspect and stood in dread of) to be cruelly murdered: as our cousin, Sir William Stanley, lord chamberlain… Sir Humphrey Stafford, and many others; besides such as hath dearly bought their lives with intolerable ransoms… Also he hath long kept, and keepeth in prison, our right entirely well-beloved cousin, Edward, [Earl of Warwick] son and heir to our uncle Duke of Clarence, and others; withholding from them their rightful inheritance, to the intent that they should never be of might and power, to aid and assist us at our need, after the duty of their legiences [allegiances]…

ACTIVITY
KNOWLEDGE CHECK

Read Source 7.

1 How does Perkin Warbeck justify his challenge to Henry?

2 To whom might Warbeck be appealing in his declaration?

3 Why do you think Warbeck was not more successful in gaining support in England?

A Level Exam-Style Question Section A

Study Source 7 before answering this question.

Assess the value of Source 7 for revealing the extent of the challenge posed by Perkin Warbeck and the reasons for his challenge.

Explain your answer, using the source, the information given about its origin and your own knowledge about the historical context. (20 marks)

Tip
To consider the extent of the challenge, you could think about who Warbeck was appealing to in his proclamation.

ACTIVITY
KNOWLEDGE CHECK

1 Copy and complete this grid.

	Lambert Simnel	Perkin Warbeck
Dates active		
Supporters (domestic and foreign)		
How did they challenge Henry's position?		
Henry's response		
How serious was the threat? (10 = highest threat; 1 = no threat)		

2 Which pretender do you think posed the greatest threat to Henry? Explain your answer.

A Level Exam-Style Question Section B

How accurate is it to say that Henry survived the challenges from Lambert Simnel and Perkin Warbeck because the Yorkist faction was weak and divided in the years 1485–99? (20 marks)

Tip
You will need to weigh up the other reasons for Henry's survival against the weakness of the Yorkist faction.

WHAT WAS THE SIGNIFICANCE OF FOREIGN SUPPORT FOR THE PRETENDERS?

Support from Ireland

Irish support for Lambert Simnel

Ireland was a potential problem for any English ruler. Its separation from the mainland of England meant that it was geographically and politically remote. Successive English kings had tried to claim the right to be Lords of Ireland, but they had failed to make much impact because Ireland was too far away for it to be controlled directly from London. However, English kings found it impossible to leave Ireland alone. Its strategic position made it a very good launching pad for invasions of England. By the 15th century, English influence was only really felt in Dublin and the region around it known as the Pale. Dublin and the Pale were theoretically controlled by a representative of the English government called the **Lord Deputy**. Beyond this region, English kings had to find ways in which they could neutralise the threat from Ireland by forming working relationships with those who in reality ruled the country, the Irish nobility and gentry. Many of the Irish nobility and gentry were the descendants of English nobility who had married into Irish families. These Anglo-Irish rulers, such as the Fitzgerald earls of Kildare, were very powerful and ruled their territories almost independently from England.

KEY TERM

Lord Deputy of Ireland
An English appointee who controlled Dublin and the Pale. He was usually a member of the Anglo-Irish nobility.

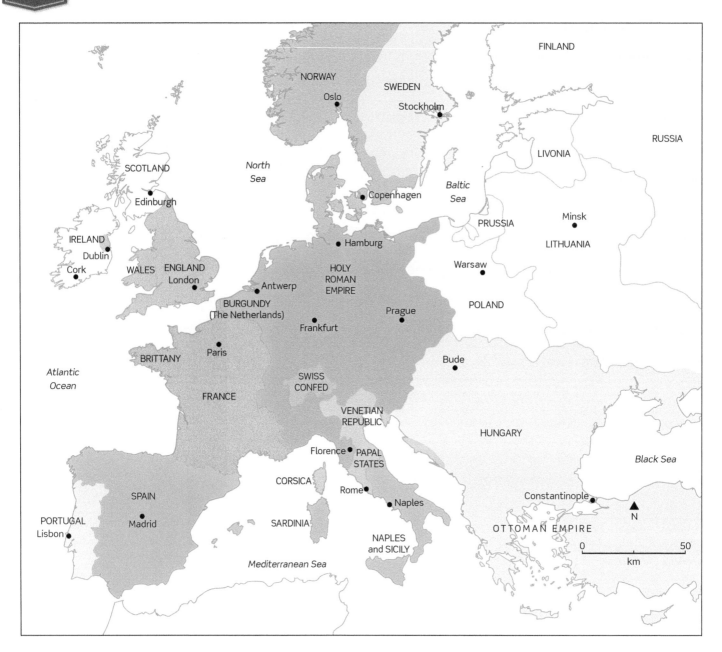

Figure 3.2 Europe in the late 15th century.

During the Wars of the Roses, the Anglo-Irish lords had taken the opportunity to increase their hold on the government of Ireland. Under Edward IV, the Fitzgeralds of Kildare were appointed Lord Deputy. This was at the expense of two rival families, the Fitzgeralds of Desmond and the Butlers of Ormond. When Henry VII seized control of England in 1485, the Fitzgeralds of Kildare were vulnerable as Yorkist supporters. Gerald Fitzgerald of Kildare, the head of the family, was now under pressure from his Anglo-Irish rivals; his response was to support Lambert Simnel, because this seemed to him to represent a better chance of political survival. If Simnel were to be successful, Kildare would be able to keep his hold over Ireland intact. This was potentially dangerous for Henry VII. Kildare was able to provide Simnel with troops and a base from which to launch an invasion. Furthermore, Kildare was out of Henry's direct reach – it would have been

logistically very difficult for Henry, a new king with a weak claim to the throne, to take an army to Ireland to fight.

Although the Irish were defeated at Stoke (1487), the significance of Ireland did not decline in the 1490s. This was because Henry did not have the military strength to interfere directly in Irish affairs. Although Kildare had helped to crown Henry's rival, he had not taken part in the invasion force to England, preferring to stay safely out of Henry's reach. In the aftermath of Stoke, Henry was forced to act cautiously regarding Ireland. He chose to pardon Kildare and other Simnel supporters. Initially, he wanted Kildare to take out bonds to ensure his future good behaviour, but Kildare refused. Henry was not in a strong enough position to argue. He was forced to accept a simple oath of loyalty from Kildare, who was allowed to remain as Deputy in Ireland.

Irish support for Perkin Warbeck

Warbeck first launched a challenge to Henry in Cork, Ireland, in 1491. He tried to return to Ireland twice more, in 1495 and 1497, each time hoping to raise military support against Henry. After his earlier escape, Kildare was reluctant to get involved directly in Warbeck's campaign; instead, he watched from the sidelines, neither helping nor stopping Warbeck. Without Kildare, Warbeck's main problem was that he was unable to raise much Irish military support and he was forced to leave Ireland rapidly on each occasion, without an invasion force.

However, Henry VII took the threat from Ireland very seriously. Realising that Kildare could not be trusted, Henry sent a small force to deal with Warbeck in 1492. Warbeck promptly fled, and Henry removed Kildare from his post as Deputy. However, Kildare was far too powerful for this to work. Henry's local replacements for Kildare could not control Ireland as Kildare had done, and Henry became worried that Warbeck would try another invasion. In 1494, Henry sent a trusted official, Sir Edward Poynings, to Ireland to enhance English royal authority there. Poynings' first job was to repel another attack by Warbeck. In 1495, Warbeck, helped by another Irish noble, the Earl of Desmond, attacked the town of Waterford. Poynings was able to rescue Waterford and Warbeck fled once more, this time to Scotland.

Poynings used the authority given to him by Henry to assert English control over Ireland. Poynings ordered the arrest of Kildare on suspicion of treason. Kildare was sent to England and imprisoned there until 1496. With Kildare, a potential figurehead for Yorkist rebellion, out of the way, Poynings introduced what became known as 'Poynings' Law' in 1495. Ireland had always had its own parliament through which Irish laws were passed. Poynings' Law stated that no Irish parliament could be summoned unless the English king had given his consent. Furthermore, the Irish parliament was not allowed to pass any laws that had not been approved by the English ruler. Poynings' control over Ireland by this point was such that he was able to persuade the Irish parliament to pass an Act that put them under the direct control of the English monarchs. After this time, Ireland did not pose a significant threat to Henry VII and he was able to recall Poynings to England at the end of 1495. Kildare was reappointed as Deputy in August 1496 and allowed to return to Ireland, though he had to leave his eldest son and heir behind at the English Court. Kildare remained loyal to Henry for the rest of the reign. When Warbeck tried one final invasion attempt at Cork in 1497, he was turned away, having gained no support at all.

ACTIVITY
KNOWLEDGE CHECK

1 Draw a graph to show the significance of the threat posed to Henry. The vertical axis should be labelled from 0–10 (10 being the most serious level of threat). On the horizontal axis, write the years from 1485 to 1499. You will add to this graph as you read through this section.

2 Draw a line on your graph to represent the level of threat to Henry from Ireland. You should write the key events on your graph.

3 Discuss with a partner when you think Ireland presented the greatest threat to Henry's security. Why was it not more of a threat?

Support from Burgundy

Burgundy in many ways posed a more consistent and serious threat to Henry's position as king than Ireland. In Ireland, he at least had a right to claim royal control over its people. But Burgundy, like France and Scotland, were independent countries with their own priorities. Burgundy and France were also richer and more powerful than England.

The Anglo-Burgundian relationship

Burgundy was a potential threat to Henry because of the presence of Margaret, Duchess of Burgundy, who was the power behind the Burgundian throne for much of the period. Margaret was the sister of Edward IV and Richard III; she had been married to Charles, Duke of Burgundy in 1468. She had no children of her own, and by 1485 she was a widow. Margaret wielded enormous influence in Burgundian politics. While the heir to Burgundy, Philip, was a minor, she virtually controlled the territories in his name. Margaret used her position to try to restore a Yorkist monarch to the throne instead of Henry VII. Henry found himself in a very difficult position; he could not easily stop Margaret protecting rival claimants, and he was reluctant to use the expensive and risky tactic of military intervention. However, Henry did have another potentially more powerful weapon, the strong trading links between England and Burgundy. The important trading port of Antwerp was under the control of the Dukes of Burgundy. Antwerp was the main destination for English wool, which was turned into some of the finest cloth in Europe. Because of their mutual reliance, England and Burgundy had always had a close relationship. However, Henry VII was always prepared to put his dynastic security ahead of trade, even if it meant upsetting the London merchants who were reliant on trade with Antwerp.

The role of Margaret of Burgundy

Because Burgundy was controlled by the Yorkist duchess Margaret, it was perhaps the most persistent threat to Henry, at least until 1496. Margaret offered protection and active support to a series of Yorkist plotters, including John de la Pole, Francis Lovell and Perkin Warbeck. In 1487, she provided mercenaries to support the Yorkist-led invasion. When Warbeck was forced out of France, she offered protection to him from 1493 to 1495. She also used her close family connection with Maximilian, the Hapsburg Holy Roman Emperor, to try to improve Warbeck's challenge. Maximilian had been married to Margaret's step daughter, Mary; Maximilian and Mary's son, Philip, was the heir to both Burgundy and the **Holy Roman Empire**. In 1493, Warbeck was invited to attend the funeral of the previous emperor, Frederick, and while there he was recognised as the rightful king of England. Warbeck even promised that if anything should happen to him, Maximilian would inherit his claim to the English throne. Although Maximilian was not interested in invading England, supporting Warbeck was a useful way to put pressure on Henry VII. Margaret of Burgundy did not stop at introducing Warbeck to other useful foreign allies. She was also prepared to back Warbeck with an armed force in 1495 for his failed landing at Deal.

Margaret's persistent support for Yorkist plots led Henry to radical action. In 1493, the young Duke Philip officially took control of government in Burgundy, but he continued to follow Margaret's policy of supporting Warbeck. Henry decided to enforce a **trade embargo**, even though this would damage English financial and trading interests. Henry took this decision because it was the best way to put pressure on Burgundy without sending an army. However, in some ways the embargo backfired; in 1494, Philip retaliated by putting his own embargo on English goods. Although the Burgundian-backed invasion of England by Warbeck in 1495 failed badly and Warbeck subsequently moved to Scotland, tensions between England and Burgundy did not start to ease until 1496. The reasons for this improvement had little to do with Henry's embargo, however. In 1494, war had broken out over control of parts of Italy. The French king, Charles VIII, had been particularly successful in his intervention in these wars; this was a direct threat to Philip and Maximilian, who feared that French successes in Italy would challenge their own ambitions there and make France too powerful. The result of this was that Philip and Maximilian became more anxious to improve their relationship with England because they did not want their war effort in Italy to be hampered by economic weakness caused by the trade embargo. In 1496, England and Burgundy signed the treaty known as *Intercursus Magnus*. In this treaty, both sides agreed to lift the trade embargo; Margaret agreed to stop supporting Warbeck and was threatened with the loss of her lands if she disobeyed. Henry also agreed not to support enemies of Burgundy and to join the anti-French alliance known as the League of Venice, though he did not have to go to war against France. This suited Henry, as he was not obliged to take an active role in fighting France and was able to stay out of the expensive Italian wars, while at the same time maintaining a friendly relationship with Burgundy. After 1496, England's relations with Burgundy reverted to a mutually beneficial trading partnership, although Margaret continued to support Warbeck, despite the ban placed on her doing so.

Support from France

France was England's traditional enemy. Traditionally, English nobles were brought up to fight for their country; a war with France would have been a good way for Henry VII to distract his nobility and unite them against a common enemy. Henry also had to consider the long-standing alliance between France and Scotland, known as the '**Auld Alliance**'. In dealing with pretenders who sought refuge in either of these countries, Henry had to consider his relationship and response to a dual threat from both France and Scotland.

KEY TERMS

Holy Roman Empire
An expansive but poor territory that covered much of modern-day Germany and Austria. It consisted of a series of small kingdoms, each governed by its own prince. The princes elected the emperor. However, all the emperors had been elected from the same family for several hundred years, the Hapsburgs.

Trade embargo
A ban on trade; England refused to export its goods to Burgundy or import Burgundian goods.

Auld Alliance
An agreement between France and Scotland. If Scotland was attacked by England, then France would come to Scotland's aid and vice versa.

However, Henry was naturally cautious and preferred to avoid war whenever possible. This was mainly because war was expensive and Henry tended to equate his own security on the throne with financial stability. Balanced against this was the threat of a French invasion of England in support of a rival claimant to the throne. The proximity of France to England meant that it would have been relatively easy for the French to mount an invasion. Although Henry had taken refuge in France in 1484 and had received French funding and troops to support his invasion in 1485, this did not mean that he could trust France as an ally. Between 1485 and 1492, relations between England and France deteriorated rapidly, and French support for Perkin Warbeck became a real possibility, which forced Henry into the only foreign campaign of his reign.

Why did Anglo-French relations deteriorate?

The reason for the deterioration in relations between England and France was the fate of the independent duchy of Brittany. Brittany had traditionally been ruled by a series of dukes, but the French kings had always claimed the right to control the region. If France succeeded in conquering Brittany, then there would be an increased threat of invasion, as the French kings would control the entire coastline opposite England. In 1487, the Duke of Brittany died, leaving a young daughter as his only heiress. France saw the opportunity to invade Brittany and Henry was forced to act. In 1489, he agreed to send 6,000 troops to help defend Brittany, though in fact he sent just 3,000. Against the might of the French army, these troops were not enough, and by 1491, France had absorbed Brittany. This was particularly serious for Henry. When he had tried to raise taxation to pay for the 1489 Brittany campaign, he had been faced with a tax revolt in Yorkshire, the heart of Richard III's former estates. The Earl of Northumberland was killed putting down the revolt. This brought home to Henry the dangers of pursuing an aggressive foreign policy; high levels of taxation for an unpopular war could lead to resistance. In 1489, Henry was lucky that there was no Yorkist rival willing to take advantage of the unrest, but the experience meant that he became even more cautious in his dealings with foreign powers. The fact that he was prepared to mount an invasion of France in 1492, therefore, shows the level of the threat that France, and its support for Warbeck, posed.

How did Henry deal with the threat from France?

Warbeck arrived in France in early 1492 and the French king, Charles VIII, welcomed him. Coupled with the French annexation of Brittany, this potential threat was too much for Henry to ignore. In October 1492, he launched an invasion of France. Henry wanted to inconvenience Charles VIII enough to make him rethink his support for Warbeck. Henry's invasion in the autumn was far too late in the year for him to have been planning a proper campaign; if he had been planning this, he would have invaded in early summer when the weather was better for fighting. When Henry and his troops landed at Calais, they marched to the town of Boulogne, which they started to besiege. Charles, however, was already beginning to consider a war in Italy; he did not want the potentially expensive distraction of a war with England. As a result, Charles immediately agreed to negotiate, which is what Henry had intended all along. The result of the negotiations was the Treaty of Etaples (1492), which was a particularly good deal for Henry. He had showed his worthiness as a military leader in taking on the traditional enemy, France, and he had restored English prestige which had been damaged by the failure to protect Brittany. Significantly for Henry, he also secured very advantageous terms in the Treaty itself.

- Charles agreed not to harbour Henry's enemies; this meant Warbeck was no longer welcome in France and had to move on.

- Henry also got an annual 'pension', which had first been paid by France to Edward IV. Under the terms of the pension, France paid Henry 50,000 crowns per annum, a useful addition to Henry's royal finances.

- The Treaty of Etaples meant that Henry had stopped the potential threat of a French-backed Yorkist challenge and he had also enhanced his financial position, which was particularly important to him.

However, Henry was also lucky in his dealings with France. From 1494, when France entered the **Italian wars**, an invasion of England was no longer likely. Henry was fortunate that his potential enemies in the 1490s were more interested in fighting for power and wealth in Italy than invading England. Furthermore, the level of potential threat from France is clear in Henry's response in 1492. Rather than negotiate, as he did with Burgundy, he was prepared to mount an invasion, which

KEY TERM

Italian Wars
The wars fought in Italy from 1494 onwards were about control of some of the wealthy Italian city states. Italy was not a unified country, and its cities such as Florence, Naples and Milan were independent powers. The rulers of France and Spain both claimed the right to govern these city states. This led to a series of wars fought in Italy which drew in most of the major European powers, especially those who wanted to undermine the increasing power of France in Europe.

was potentially costly and left England exposed to rebellion or invasion in his absence. Luckily for Henry, the final threat to his power, Scotland, was not yet in a position where it could hope to invade England, but this was to change from 1495.

Support from Scotland

Scotland was another of England's traditional enemies. Even when England and Scotland were not in an open state of warfare, the protection of the northern border presented a serious challenge to the rulers of England. The northern border with Scotland was extensive, highly fortified and a militarised zone, dominated by powerful members of the nobility whom Henry needed to trust. Richard III had been both popular and powerful in the North of England. Henry faced a double threat: Yorkist rebellion in the North coupled with an invasion by Scotland in support of a rival claimant. Luckily for Henry, Scotland was affected by its own political instabilities in the 1480s and early 1490s. It was not until 1495 that the situation in Scotland stabilised enough for its ruler, James IV, to pose a threat to Henry.

Why did relations with Scotland deteriorate?

Scotland was in a state of near-civil war from c1482. Its king was James III, but he faced a series of rebellions between 1482 and 1488, and was eventually killed fighting the rebels at the Battle of Sauchieburn in 1488. Ironically, it was James III's determination to forge an alliance with England that caused his subjects to rebel. This suited Henry VII perfectly. In 1486, Henry VII negotiated a three-year truce with James; meanwhile, any potential threat from Scotland from the anti-English rebels there was neutralised because they were busy fighting their own king. When James died in 1488, he was succeeded by his eldest son, James IV, who was just 15 years old at the time of his father's death. The young king was not yet old enough to rule for himself, and in the early years of his rule was more interested in bringing his own country under control, which he had achieved by 1493. James then became more interested in asserting his country's place in Europe. For James, this meant challenging England's power through supporting Perkin Warbeck.

Although the truce with Scotland that was negotiated in 1486 was renewed in 1493, this did not stop James IV from plotting with England's enemies, France and Burgundy. In 1495, James went a step further and welcomed Warbeck into Scotland. Warbeck was to remain in Scotland until 1497. James was so committed to supporting Warbeck that he was prepared to arrange a marriage between the pretender and one of James' own cousins, Lady Catherine Gordon. The presence of Warbeck just over the border in Scotland was a serious threat to Henry, especially because he was trying to conclude the marriage alliance with Spain, which had first been agreed in 1489. Ferdinand and Isabella, the rulers of Spain, were unlikely to allow the marriage to go ahead if they thought that Henry and his children were at risk from rival claimants. Henry became even more worried in 1496, when Warbeck invaded England at the head of an army supplied by James.

Warbeck's invasion of England in September 1496 was short-lived and unsuccessful, however. His army devastated some of the surrounding countryside before running out of supplies and being forced back by the English defenders. Nevertheless, Henry began to put measures in place to neutralise the threat from Scotland. Parliament agreed to a grant of taxation, which Henry used to fight the Scots. As military preparations for war against the Scots continued, Henry also tried to negotiate a marriage alliance between James IV and Henry's eldest daughter, Margaret. After the lack of success of the 1496 invasion, James was becoming increasingly open to the idea of a negotiated settlement and was growing disenchanted with Warbeck. However, Henry's position on the throne was shaken by the Cornish rising in May–June 1497. The rebels argued that they could not afford the amounts demanded in taxation and that they should not have to pay for the defence of a region that was so remote from their own. Although the rebellion was put down, it was a dangerous distraction for Henry when he was preparing for war at the other end of the country.

Why did the Scottish threat not continue after 1497?

The 1497 rebellion in Cornwall probably increased Henry's desire to find a peaceful solution to the threat from Scotland. By this time, James had finally grown tired of supporting Warbeck; it may be that he had believed Warbeck's claims to be Richard IV and had now found out the truth. Alternatively, James may have realised that Henry was too secure on the throne to be easily toppled and that it would be too costly to try to attempt it. On 6 July 1497, Warbeck left Scotland for good on a boat paid for by James. Warbeck's departure paved the way for a peaceful settlement with England. In September 1497, James and Henry agreed to the seven-year Truce of Ayton, and James also agreed to drop all support for Warbeck. Eventually, James was to seal the truce by marrying Princess Margaret in 1503. In 1497, however, Henry had achieved his aim of neutralising the threat from Scotland; Warbeck had now run out of foreign powers that were willing to support him, and he was captured later that year.

SOURCE 8

From a letter written to the king and queen of Spain by the Spanish **ambassador** to England in January 1500.

The English have not always remained in peaceful obedience to their king. This is because there were too many heirs to the kingdom. The claims of these heirs were so strong that there were disputes between the two sides. Now it has pleased God that all should be thoroughly and duly purged and cleansed. This is so that not a doubtful drop of royal blood remains in the kingdom except the true blood of the king and queen, and, above all, of the Lord Prince Arthur. And all of this since the execution of Perkin and the son of the Duke of Clarence.

ACTIVITY
KNOWLEDGE CHECK

Read Source 8.

1 What does it suggest about Henry's security in 1499?

2 Use the section above on Scotland to complete the graph you started earlier in this chapter.

3 Using your graph, answer the following questions:

   a) Which country posed the greatest threat to Henry, and why?

   b) In which period did Henry face the greatest number of threats from foreign powers?

   c) To what extent did the threat posed by foreign powers change over time?

A Level Exam-Style Question Section B

'The challenges from both Scotland and Burgundy in the years 1485–99 show the weakness of Henry's position on the throne.' How far do you agree with this statement? (20 marks)

Tip
Think about whether this statement is equally true for both countries for the entire date range of the question.

KEY TERM

Ambassador
A man who represented the interests of his country to other foreign monarchs. Ambassadors were usually given a considerable amount of respect at Court, but it was also important to impress them. Ambassadors often acted as unofficial spies for their own monarchs and would be in regular communication with them.

It was important for the English monarchs to ensure that foreign ambassadors received the right impression of the power and wealth of the Crown; however, most ambassadors would not have been allowed access to private meetings between the king and his councillors. Therefore, ambassadors often reported hearsay and rumour.

Cause and consequence (7a & b)

Questions and answers

Questions that historians ask vary depending on what they think is important. It is the questions that interest us that define the history that is written. These questions change with time and place. Different historians will also come up with different answers to the same questions, depending on their perspectives and methods of interpretation, as well as the evidence they use.

Below are three historians who had different areas of interest:

William Stubbs	Kenneth McFarlane	Simon Payling
A political historian who lived in the 19th century. He argued that great men shape history.	A political historian who lived in the mid-20th century. He was interested in the role of the nobility in medieval government.	A political historian active today who is interested in local history. He is interested in researching the careers of individual members of the gentry.

These are some key events from the late 15th century:

The murder of Henry VI in the Tower of London	The Battle of Bosworth	The Battle of Stoke
The Wars of the Roses between the Houses of York and Lancaster	The loss of all English territories in France except Calais	The role of parliament in impeaching (putting on trial) the king's councillors
The disappearance of the Princes in the Tower	The usurpation of the throne by Richard III	The growing role of the Justices of the Peace

Work in groups of between three and six to answer the following questions.

1 Which of these events would have been of most interest to each historian? Explain your answer.

2 Each take the role of one historian and devise a question that would interest them about each of the events.

3 Discuss each event in turn. Present the questions that have been devised for each historian and offer some ideas about how they would have answered them.

4 For each event, decide as a group which question is the most interesting and worthwhile of the three.

Answer the following questions in pairs.

5 Identify the different ways that each historian would approach writing an account of the Wars of the Roses.

6 In what ways would Stubbs and Payling differ in their explanations of the significance of the growing role of the Justices of the Peace? What would be the focus of their arguments?

Answer the following questions individually.

7 All three historians may produce very different accounts and explanations of the same piece of history. Of the three historians, whose account would you prefer to read first? Explain your answer.

8 Do the differences in these accounts mean that one is more valid than the others?

9 Explain why different historical explanations are written by different historians.

10 Explain why different explanations of the same event can be equally valid.

ACTIVITY
SUMMARY

1 How was Henry able to survive as king? Draw a Venn diagram (three overlapping circles). Label them 'Henry's actions in England', 'Henry's actions abroad' and 'Henry's luck'. Use the information from this chapter to add detail to your diagram. Use the overlapping areas of the circles to show where there were links between the different factors.

2 Copy and complete the following grid.

	France	Burgundy	Ireland	Scotland
Ruler(s)				
Why did they support Henry's rivals?				
How did they support Henry's rivals?				
What did Henry do?				
How much of a threat were they to Henry's positon as king?				

WIDER READING

Lockyer, R. *Henry VII*, Longman Seminar Studies (1983)

Penn, T. *Winter King: Henry VII and the Dawn of Tudor England*, Penguin (2011)

Wroe, A. *Perkin: A Story of Deception*, Random House (2010)

3.4 Challenging religious changes, 1533–37

KEY QUESTIONS

- How effective were Henry VIII's religious changes?
- How significant were the causes and impacts of the 1536 rebellions?
- How effective were the leaders of the rebel challenge and the government suppression?

INTRODUCTION

Between 1533 and 1537, the English Church underwent a series of changes which challenged the traditional beliefs and practices of many of Henry VIII's subjects. These changes were the results of Henry's break with Rome and included the dissolution of the monasteries. The rapid and radical nature of the changes in these years led to serious popular risings which began in Lincolnshire and spread rapidly. The leadership of the rebellions included members of the gentry and some minor members of the nobility. This, and the numbers of rebels involved, forced Henry and his advisers to negotiate, before they were in a position to suppress the rebels more brutally in 1537.

HOW EFFECTIVE WERE HENRY VIII'S RELIGIOUS CHANGES?

The impact of the break with Rome and the dissolution of the monasteries

Between 1533 and 1537, Henry VIII renounced the authority of the pope in Rome and created a Church in England of which he was the Supreme Head. The break with Rome was masterminded by Thomas Cromwell and reinforced by a series of Acts of Parliament, which legalised Henry's actions and created a means through which opponents of the supremacy could be punished (see pages 26–28).

The nature of the royal supremacy

The main result of the establishment of the royal supremacy was the change in relationship between the English monarchy and its subjects. Change happened at the centre because Henry VIII, advised by Cromwell, saw this as the best way to achieve what he wanted: the annulment of his marriage to Catherine of Aragon. Henry was not a religious reformer (or evangelical), but some of his advisers, such as Cromwell, and Thomas Cranmer, the Archbishop of Canterbury, had more radical religious views. The result of the break with Rome was that it was imposed from the top downwards. In England, reformist ideas were

1533 – Henry VIII annuls his marriage to Catherine of Aragon and marries Anne Boleyn

1535 – Compilation of the *Valor Ecclesiasticus*

Act of Uses

| 1533 | 1534 | 1535 |

1534 – Act of Supremacy; Treason Act

Collection of the 1534 subsidy

Look at Source 1 and answer the following questions:

1 What message was Henry trying to give about his position as king?

2 Who do you think the intended audience of this picture was?

3 Why do you think this image was chosen as the front page of the English Bible?

SOURCE

The title page of the Great Bible. From 1538, every parish in England was required by law to purchase a copy of an English Bible and place it in 'some convenient place' for all to see and read. To meet this demand, the Great Bible, so called because of its size, was put into production. Six editions followed, with more than 9,000 copies printed by 1541.

taking hold in London and in the South East, but in other regions, traditional Catholic practices and beliefs were still predominant. This was particularly the case in the more remote regions of England, especially the South West and the North. In these regions, the impact of the break with Rome was greater, especially for those Catholics who still believed that the pope was the head of the Church, not Henry.

Cromwell's changes to the doctrine and practices of the English Church

Following the break with Rome, Cromwell was also keen to promote not just structural changes to the English Church, but also doctrinal changes which reflected his own evangelical beliefs. In 1535, Henry appointed Cromwell to be **Vicegerent in Spirituals**. His vicegerency gave Cromwell enormous power over the Church, and he used this power to alter its **doctrine**. New bishops were appointed who shared Cromwell's religious views, such as Hugh Latimer. Cromwell used his position to launch a propaganda campaign in support of the supremacy through preaching in churches.

KEY TERMS

Vicegerent in Spirituals
This post was specially created for Cromwell and meant that he was Henry's deputy in all spiritual and religious matters, despite the fact that Cromwell was not a clergyman himself.

Doctrine
The beliefs set out by the Church.

1536 – Act of Ten Articles; Cromwell's Injunctions to the Clergy; Act for the Dissolution of the Smaller Monasteries

1537 –
16 January: Bigod's rising

1537 – Council of the North is re-established

1541 – Unrest in the North; Henry VIII visits York

1536

1537

1541

1536 –
2 October: Rebellion breaks out in Lincolnshire

11 October: Pilgrimage of Grace begins

- Preaching was controlled through government licences, and clergy were ordered to give sermons against the pope and in support of Henry's marriage to Anne Boleyn.

- In April 1535, royal letters were sent to all bishops, nobility and JPs, ordering them to imprison clergymen who continued to preach in support of the pope's authority.

- The Act of Ten Articles (1536) was the first attempt to define the doctrine of the new English Church. These were mostly in line with Catholic belief, but the Article on the **Eucharist** was deliberately ambiguous in its language, while the number of **sacraments** considered necessary for the salvation of the soul was decreased from seven to three.

- As vicegerent, Cromwell also issued a set of Injunctions (instructions) to the English clergy in 1536, which attacked traditional practices such as pilgrimages, the emphasis placed on relics and images, and the worship of saints. Holy Days, which were feast days in honour of saints when a whole community would stop work and join the celebrations, were also to be banned.

Although Henry VIII was no reformer, he was prepared to support these changes because they helped to undermine the authority of the pope and the Catholic Church, and removed an alternative focus of obedience and loyalty which might rival Henry's own supremacy. The result of these changes at the centre was that there was increasing pressure on the localities to obey Cromwell's orders. In the South, and even in the traditionally Catholic South West, most orders were followed, if reluctantly. But in the more traditional Catholic regions in the North of England, these changes were met with increasing alarm and reluctance. Many of the rebels' demands in 1536 focused on their desire to see these changes reversed, and they targeted Thomas Cromwell, together with Sir Richard Rich, as the men to blame.

EXTEND YOUR KNOWLEDGE

Sir Richard Rich
Richard Rich was a lawyer who rose at Court because of his legal and administrative capabilities. He helped to gather evidence in the trials of both More and Fisher, and used it to ensure their convictions for treason. Rich helped Cromwell in the organisation of the dissolution of the monasteries. He was appointed Chancellor of the Court of Augmentations, which was a new financial court set up by Cromwell to manage the revenues from the dissolved monasteries. Rich used his position to enrich himself. He was granted, or purchased, extensive former monastic lands, mostly in Essex. Rich's involvement in the deaths of More and Fisher, and his greed, made him a particular target for the rebels in 1536.

Opposition to the break with Rome and Henry VIII's response

Politically, the break with Rome also had an impact on England. Henry was determined to enforce obedience to his royal supremacy and the changes that were made to the royal succession, which included his daughter, Princess Mary, being declared illegitimate. The parliamentary legislation made it possible for Henry to claim that the break with Rome was legal

---

KEY TERMS

Eucharist
Sometimes known as Holy Communion or the Lord's Supper. This is a sacrament which represents the Last Supper of Jesus and his followers before his trial and crucifixion. All Christians recognise the importance of this sacrament, although they differ about how it should be interpreted.

Sacrament
A ceremony within the Christian Church which is seen as God's forgiveness of sinners ('grace'). In the Catholic Church there are seven: Eucharist, baptism, confirmation, penance, marriage, ordination and extreme unction. In the 16th-century Protestant view there were three: Eucharist, baptism and penance.

---

because it had the support of the English people. Those who dared to disobey Henry were breaking the law and could be punished accordingly. The Act of Supremacy made provision for an oath to be taken. The 1534 Treason Act made it possible to prosecute those who refused to swear the oath as traitors (see Chapter 1). The result of these political changes was that influential opponents of the supremacy were executed for treason. Both Sir Thomas More, who had once been Henry's Chancellor, and John Fisher, Bishop of Rochester, refused to accept the supremacy; both were executed in 1535.

These high-profile executions created an atmosphere of fear and suspicion. At Court, a conservative faction emerged whose aim was to see the restoration of Catholicism. Some key members of this conservative faction were Thomas Howard, Duke of Norfolk; Edward Stanley, Earl of Derby; Henry Percy, Earl of Northumberland; Thomas, Lord Darcy and John, Lord Hussey, though not all of them were to become rebels in 1536–37. Those who wanted to see a restoration of the Catholic faith saw Princess Mary, Henry's daughter, as their natural figurehead. A practising Catholic, Mary had been made illegitimate and barred from the succession in 1534; restoring her to the succession would mean the promise of a return to Rome in the future. However, there were some who may have planned to do more than simply restore Mary. In 1535–36, there was a Court-based plot which sought to remove Henry altogether and to replace him with Mary instead. These traditional feelings of loyalty at Court were echoed in the North of England, where many of these nobles, including Darcy, Hussey and Northumberland, owned extensive landed estates.

ACTIVITY
KNOWLEDGE CHECK

1 Read Source 2. Which groups in England might find it difficult to swear this oath, and why?

2 Using the section above, make a spider diagram to show the effect of the break with Rome on: Henry VIII's power; faction at Court; doctrine; opposition to Henry.

3 Using two highlighters, colour-code a copy of this page to show the advantages and disadvantages of the break with Rome for Henry's power as king.

SOURCE

The text of the Oath of Supremacy as it would have been sworn in 1534.

I (state your name) do utterly testifie and declare in my Conscience, that the Kings Highnesse is the onely Supreame Governour of this Realme, and all other his Highnesse Dominions and Countries, as well in all Spirituall or Ecclesiasticall things or causes, as Temporall: And that no forraine Prince, Person, Prelate, State or Potentate, hath or ought to have any Jurisdiction, Power, Superiorities, Preeminence or Authority Ecclesiasticall or Spirituall within this Realme. And therefore, I do utterly renounce and forsake all Jurisdictions, Powers, Superiorities, or Authorities; and do promise that from henchforth I shall beare faith and true Allegiance to the Kings Highnesse, his Heires and lawfull Successors: and to my power shall assist and defend all Jurisdictions, Priviledges, Preheminences and Authorities granted or belonging to the Kings Highnesse, his Heires and Successors or united and annexed to the Imperial Crowne of the Realme: so helpe me God: and by the Contents of this Booke.

The impact of the dissolution of the smaller monasteries, 1536

Monasteries (for men) and convents (for women) formed an important part of the spiritual life of England, but they also played a valuable social and economic role in local society, particularly in the traditional North. The role of monasteries was primarily a religious one. Monastic orders such as the **Benedictines** and the **Cistercians** followed rules of poverty, chastity and obedience. These orders usually lived in remote locations and would dedicate their lives to the service of God. Becoming a monk (or a nun) was considered to be a vocation, a calling by God. Monks and nuns prayed for the souls of the dead to shorten their time in purgatory. They also performed good works and were a particularly important part of life in socially and economically deprived parts of England, where they provided support for the poor and care for the sick and elderly. Monasteries were also important centres of education and learning. Before the introduction of the printing press in the late 15th century, monks were usually responsible for the copying and preservation of old texts and books. In addition, monasteries were local employers and landlords. Many farmers leased land from the monks, and the monasteries also provided employment on their estates for both unskilled agricultural labourers and skilled craftsmen. If the monasteries were to be dissolved, the fates of the many men and women who relied upon them for work would become uncertain.

KEY TERM

Benedictines and Cistercians
The order of the Benedictines follows the rules set out by St Benedict, which emphasise the need for stability (monks stay in one community), hard work and a simple lifestyle. Benedictine monasteries were first established in England in the 6th century. Important Benedictine monasteries included Canterbury and Fountains Abbey.

Cistercian monks arrived in England in the 12th century. They were influenced by the Benedictine style of living and worship. Important Cistercian houses included Rievaulx and Jervaux Abbeys in Yorkshire. The Cistercians were particularly known as sheep farmers.

Because of their important religious function, and the respect in which they were held, English monasteries had grown in wealth and power during the Middle Ages. By the 1530s, there were nearly 900 religious houses in England and about 12,000 people in religious orders. However, by the early 16th century, not all monasteries were beacons of learning, morality and Christianity, although they were still held in high regard, especially in the North. The North was often badly hit by social and economic hardship, and the monasteries provided a vital lifeline to local communities in times of need. Nevertheless, by the mid-1530s, the monasteries were under threat from Henry and Cromwell. Most monastic orders were controlled by foreign Catholic orders in France, Spain or Italy. Ultimately, monks and nuns owed obedience to the pope in Rome. Once the break with Rome took place, the allegiances of all monks and nuns became suspect; Henry VIII could not risk the presence in England of wealthy institutions taking orders from potentially hostile powers. Furthermore, for reformers like Cromwell, the monasteries represented the wealth and corruption of the Church. Monasteries were also felt to be promoting what the reformers felt to be a superstitious belief in purgatory. Finally, the monasteries were very wealthy; their estates and property were a tempting prize for Henry VIII. Following the break with Rome, Henry feared the threat of a Catholic invasion, involving foreign powers such as the papacy, France or Spain. Dissolving the monasteries would give him a valuable source of income, which he could use to defend England and to reward his supporters.

The process of dissolution

The process which led to the dissolution of the smaller monasteries began in 1535 with **Valor Ecclesiasticus.** *Valor* surveyed all Church property and revealed to Henry the wealth of the monasteries – between 1536 and 1547, their dissolution raised £1.3 million. *Valor* was followed by visitations of the monasteries undertaken by commissioners appointed by Cromwell, such as Thomas Legh and Richard Layton. As Source 3 suggests, the commissioners' remit was to find evidence of corruption in the monasteries to use as evidence against them. The evidence of *Valor*, coupled with that of the commissioners, was used by Cromwell to justify the 1536 Act of Parliament, which authorised the dissolution of the smaller monasteries, defined as worth less than £200 per annum. The process of dissolution involved the destruction of the monasteries' buildings – lead was stripped from the roofs and melted down, and stained glass and images were smashed. Some communities became worried that their local parish churches were under threat too. This was the case at Louth (Lincolnshire), where rebellion first broke out in 1536. The people of Louth had recently built a costly new spire for their church and feared it was about to be destroyed. Rebellion then spread rapidly to Yorkshire and other northern areas. The rebels made it very clear in their demands and actions that they wanted the monasteries that had been dissolved to be restored.

KEY TERM

Valor Ecclesiasticus
Translated from the Latin, this means 'the value of the Church'.

SOURCE
3

Letter from one of Cromwell's commissioners, Richard Layton, to Cromwell. Writing in 1535, Layton was reporting on the Priory of Maiden Bradley (Wiltshire).

By this bringer, my servant, I send you relics, first two flowers wrapped in white and black sarcenet that on Christmas Eve, at the very hour when Christ was born, will spring and burgeon and bear blossoms, which has been proved, says the Prior of Maiden Bradley. Ye shall also receive a bag of relics, wherein ye shall see strange things... as God's coat, Our Lady's smock, part of God's supper from the Lord's Supper, part of the rock on which Jesus was born in Bethlehem – belike there is in Bethlehem plenty of stones and some quarry, and make their mangers of stone. The scripture of everything shall declare you all; and all these of Maiden Bradley, where as is an holy father Prior, and hath but six children, and but one daughter married, yet of the goods of the monastery trusting shortly to marry the rest. His sons be tall men waiting upon him, and he thanks God he never meddled with married women, but all with maidens the fairest could be gotten, and always married them right well. The pope, considering his fragility, gave him licence to keep an whore...

ACTIVITY
KNOWLEDGE CHECK

1 What is Source 3 suggesting about the state of the monasteries? Why might we need to treat this source with caution?

2 Make a list of ways in which the dissolution of the monasteries might have an impact on local communities. Which of these effects do you think would have created the most anger, and why?

HOW SIGNIFICANT WERE THE CAUSES AND IMPACTS OF THE 1536 REBELLIONS?

The causes of the 1536 rebellions

Religious causes

Religious grievances undoubtedly played a significant role in explaining why so many people were prepared to rise up against Henry's government. The dissolution of the monasteries and the activities of government officials in the localities was the spark for the first rebellion, which happened on 2–3 October in Louth, Lincolnshire. Behind the anger at the dissolution of the monasteries was also wider discontent about the general direction of Henry's religious policy, which was in the hands of reformers such as Cromwell and Cranmer. Cromwell's attacks on traditional practices such as pilgrimages and worship of the saints threatened centuries of belief. Many believed that following the teachings of the Catholic Church would better prepare their souls for the afterlife, so the undermining of these traditions also threatened what they thought would happen to their souls after death. Tudor society was one in which belief in heaven, hell and purgatory as real places was usual. The reformers' attempts to alter practices which might affect what happened to a soul caused both fear and anger.

The religious aspect of both the Lincolnshire rising and the Pilgrimage of Grace can be seen in the actions and demands of the rebels. The name of the 'Pilgrimage' of Grace suggests a religious motivation: the rebels were modelling themselves on the traditional Catholic rite of peaceful pilgrimage. This impression was reinforced by the oath which the Pilgrims were required to take (see Source 4). The rebels also carried a banner which showed the five wounds that Christ received during his crucifixion (Source 5). By marching under such a banner, the rebels were making it clear that they thought they were rebelling in God's name. In addition, the trigger for many of the local risings was the closure of a smaller monastery in the region. The rebels' lists of demands also had a clear focus on religion. In one set of demands, the Pontefract Articles, 9 out of 24 of their grievances were religious.

SOURCE
4

The oath of the honourable men, 1536, taken from R.W. Hoyle, *Pilgrimage of Grace*. This oath was written by Robert Aske, the leader of the Pilgrimage of Grace in October 1536. It was taken by all Pilgrims.

Ye shall not enter into this our Pilgrimage of Grace for the commonwealth, but only for the love that ye do bear unto almighty God, his faith, and to holy church militant [and for] the maintenance thereof, to the preservation of the king's person [and] his issue, to the purifying of the nobility, and to expulse all villain blood and evil councillors against the commonwealth from his grace and his privy council of the same. And that ye shall not enter into our said Pilgrimage for no particular profit to yourself, not to do any displeasure to any private person, but by the counsel of the commonwealth, nor slay nor murder for no envy, but in your hearts put away fear and dread, and take afore you the Cross of Christ, and in your hearts his faith, the restitution of the church, the suppression of these heretics and their opinions, by the holy contents of this book.

Social and economic causes

Although grievances about the extent and speed of religious change were at the heart of both rebellions, there were also underlying social and economic factors which contributed to the discontent. The northern parts of England often suffered from social and economic hardship. These problems had been made worse by the government demands for taxation in the 1534 subsidy. Although the subsidy was supposed to be a fairer method of collecting taxation, the 1534 subsidy was particularly controversial because it had been levied during peacetime (see Chapter 2). The nature of the subsidy also led to rumours that the government was planning other new taxes. The subsidy hit the North particularly hard because it coincided with two years of bad weather and poor harvests. The methods used to collect the subsidy may also have contributed to growing resentment in the North; commissioners were used to inquire into each person's ability to pay. This meant that yet another government commission was active in the region, adding to resentment about levels of government intrusion in the localities.

SOURCE

5

The banner used by the Lincolnshire rebels and adopted by the Pilgrims in 1536 showing the five wounds that Christ received when he was crucified. It was later adopted by the northern rebels in 1569.

There were other social and economic tensions in the region as well. Some tenants were increasingly angry about the demands placed on them by their landlords. One grievance was **entry fines**. Some landlords in the regions of the West Riding of Yorkshire and the Lake District had also been enclosing their lands. **Enclosure** was the process by which a landlord could consolidate their estates. The practice of enclosure meant that some tenant farmers were forced off their lands by their landlords. However, enclosure was only an issue in some regions; it was a particular grievance in the region around York, which was a more populated area and thus felt the increased demand for land that enclosure generated.

KEY TERMS

Entry fine
This was paid to the landlord when a tenant died and was succeeded by an heir. Entry fines were a way in which landlords could raise their profits, especially in a period of rising prices. Increasing entry fines placed an increasing burden on tenant farmers who were unable or unwilling to pay.

Enclosure
Incorporating smaller holdings of land into a larger farm, with the area being 'enclosed' with fences or hedges. This larger area was then often used for profitable sheep farming.

Social and economic issues may well have contributed to the extent of the revolt and why poorer peasants and agricultural workers may have joined the rebellion, as these were the groups most affected by economic hardship. However, these issues did not affect other social groups who joined the rebellion, which included educated lawyers such as Robert Aske, and members of the gentry and nobility, so there must have been other motivating factors for them to take the risk of rebelling against their anointed king.

Political causes

Some members of the northern nobility and gentry did become involved in the revolts of 1536, such as Sir Thomas Percy, the brother of the Earl of Northumberland, and Lord Darcy. Darcy's cousin, Lord Hussey, was also implicated. The involvement in the rebellion of powerful northern nobility led the historian Geoffrey Elton to suggest that the Pilgrimage was actually the result of a Court-based plot by the conservative faction, whose aims were to restore Princess Mary to the royal succession and to remove Cromwell. The Earl of Northumberland himself did not actively support the rebels, but equally did nothing to stop them and surrendered Wressle Castle to the rebels. Northumberland had been in contact with the imperial ambassador, Eustace Chapuys, who was closely connected to the conservative faction at Court. Northumberland's brother, Sir Thomas, marched with 5,000 men to York. The support of Darcy and Hussey for the rebellion can also be explained by their links to Court. Hussey was Princess Mary's chamberlain, and he and his cousin Darcy spoke to Chapuys in 1534 about an armed rebellion; Hussey himself had Catholic beliefs. Although Hussey later claimed that he had had nothing to do with the rebellion, his connections to other men who did revolt were enough for him to be executed for treason. The Catholic sympathies of these northern nobility and gentry help to explain some of the articles which appear on the rebels' demands, such as the repeal of the 1534 Act of Supremacy and the removal of Cromwell and Richard Rich (a demand also made by the Lincolnshire rebels).

EXTEND YOUR KNOWLEDGE

Eustace Chapuys and the conservative faction at Court
Chapuys was the ambassador for Charles V, the Holy Roman Emperor, at Henry VIII's Court from 1529 to 1545. He wrote detailed letters to Charles during his time in England, but was more than just an observer of politics. Chapuys became closely attached to Catherine of Aragon, Charles' aunt, and he worked to prevent her annulment, even threatening Henry with invasion. He was linked to the conservative group at Court who supported Catherine, and after her death in 1536, her daughter Mary. This group included Thomas More, John Fisher and Lords Darcy and Hussey. Chapuys' house became a place where conservative members of Court could meet and discuss their views, which is why Northumberland, Darcy and Hussey were in contact with him.

However, most historians do not agree with Elton's claims. Although some northern gentry were sympathetic to the rebels, others who might well have supported the rebels did not rise, such as the Earl of Derby and Lord Dacre. In addition, it is possible to place too much emphasis on what was said to Chapuys, who encouraged talk of rebellions and invasions; Chapuys himself did not become involved in the rebellion. Furthermore, Elton's emphasis on the role of the nobility and the gentry was partly because he found it difficult to believe that ordinary people could organise such a wide-scale revolt. The involvement of some members of the gentry and nobility in the rebellion can be explained by their desire to try to moderate the rebellion from within because it was too large to control by the use of armed force against it. Additionally, Michael Bush has shown that most of the impetus for rebellion came from below, with the **commons** trying to recruit the gentry, not the other way round. The rebel articles that were produced in 1536 thus reflected a wide range of concerns from different social groups, but the Lincolnshire rising and the Pilgrimage were primarily popular and religious.

Another explanation for the involvement of members of the landed nobility and gentry can also be found in the Act of Uses, which had been passed in 1535. This was an attempt by Henry and Cromwell to prevent landowners avoiding the financial demands made by the king as their feudal overlord. Technically, the monarch was the feudal landlord for all of England and the landowners were his tenants. This meant that the monarch had the right to the guardianship of the tenants' lands and heir when the heir was a minor, which was a potentially very profitable source of income. Landowners had tried to get round this by creating a legal device known as an **enfeoffment to uses.** The Act of Uses restricted these enfeoffments in attempt to raise more money for the Crown and was resented by landowners, which explains the references to it in several of the rebel articles. It is unlikely, however, that this grievance would have been one which affected the majority of rebels, who did not have extensive lands or property. The inclusion of such a grievance may suggest that the rebellion was increasingly directed and controlled by the gentry and nobility, but it does not explain how or why the rebellion began.

KEY TERMS

Commons
Ordinary men and women below the ranks of nobility and gentry.

Enfeoffment to uses
A legal device in which a landowner created a group of trustees for their lands and heir. If their property was technically in the hands of someone else when the landowner died, the king could not claim custody of it or any heirs.

ACTIVITY
KNOWLEDGE CHECK

1 How far does the oath of the honourable men (Source 4) suggest that the rebellions of 1536 were motivated by religious grievances?

2 Why do you think the rebels chose to carry a banner with the five wounds of Christ (Source 5)?

3 Copy and complete this grid. You will be able to add further detail to the grid as you work through the rest of this chapter:

Causes of the 1536 rebellions	Evidence to support this as a cause for rebellion	Who was affected by this grievance?	How significant was the factor in causing the 1536 rebellion?
Religious grievances			
Social and economic grievances			
Political grievances			

The Lincolnshire Rising, October 1536

TIMELINE: THE LINCOLNSHIRE RISING, OCTOBER 1536

2–3 October
Attack on government commissioners at Louth

4 October
Lincolnshire gentry took leadership of the rebellion; murder of Dr Raynes

7 October
Lord Hussey flees Lincolnshire; rebels march to Lincoln

10 October
Royal army under the Duke of Suffolk reaches Stamford; beginning of rebellion in the East and West Ridings of Yorkshire

11 October
Lincolnshire commons persuaded to go home by the Lancaster Herald; North Riding of Yorkshire rises in revolt

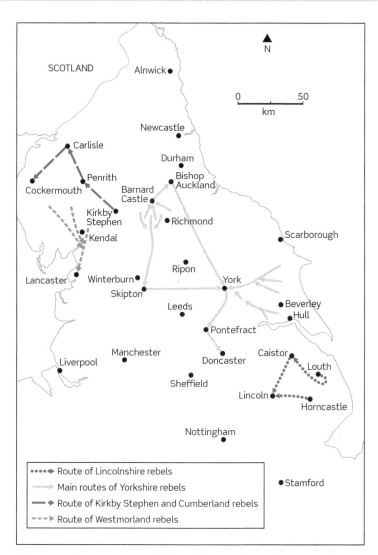

Figure 4.1 The movements of the rebels and the regions where the rebellions took place, 1536-37.

The rebellion that broke out in Lincolnshire was caused by a local reaction to the rapid and radical changes that were being imposed by Henry VIII and Cromwell in the period 1535–36. The trigger for the rising in Lincolnshire was the presence of government commissioners in the region who were overseeing the dissolution of the smaller monasteries and **visitations of the clergy**. Such a high level of government intervention focused on one region caused tension and rumours.

KEY TERM

Visitations of the clergy
An inquiry that assessed the standard of education among the clergy.

Aims and motives

The use of a set of demands to articulate the rebels' complaints was a traditional method for rebels to justify their actions, dating back to the first serious popular rebellion in 1381. The rebels used language which made it clear that they were not rebelling against Henry himself. Instead, they blamed his 'evil counsellors',

the men around Henry, whom the rebels believed had misled the king. This was a typical line for rebels to take; if they were rebelling against the king himself, then they were committing treason. If they presented themselves as loyal subjects who were concerned about the misgovernment of the realm, then there was a possibility that the king would listen to their grievances. This is why the rebels made use of the word 'commonwealth' in their demands. The commonwealth was a term used to describe what was for the good of the realm. By using this word, the rebels were claiming that they were acting for the common good, not out of self-interest. There were also other concerns, however. Another article complained about the 1534 subsidy and the inability of the Lincolnshire men to pay, mirroring the concerns of the commons who joined the rebellion. The rebels' petition reflects the fact that both gentry and landlords and the commons joined the revolt. The preoccupation with government intervention in their lives, and especially the religious changes that were occurring, was a factor that united them.

Key events

The spark for the rebellion was the arrival of the Bishop of Lincoln's officer at Louth to carry out a visitation of the clergy. Paranoia in the town was running high: an armed group of men had spent the night guarding the church treasure house at Louth, perhaps fearing that it was going to be seized by government officials. The men of Louth then showed their anger at the dissolution of the smaller monasteries by marching to the nearby Legbourne nunnery and capturing the commissioners who were there to dissolve it.

The following day, rumours spread among the commons that their weapons were going to be seized, while local priests were worried about the outcome of the visitations of the clergy and the impact on their livelihoods. The result was that 3,000 people met together at Louth and the government commissioners were forced to flee. The trouble that had started at Louth now spread to Caistor and Horncastle. On 9 October, the rebellion began to look even more serious. Dr Raynes, the chancellor of the Bishop of Lincoln, was brought to Horncastle, where he was killed by an angry mob. The rebel petition that was drawn up on 9 October makes it clear that the rebels' main grievances were over the dissolution of the smaller monasteries, the 'evil counsel' that Henry was receiving from men of 'low birth', such as Cromwell and the Chancellor, Richard Rich, and the promotion of men with reformer sympathies such as Cranmer.

Once the rebels had drawn up their petition, they marched to Lincoln itself. By this point, an estimated 10,000 men had joined the rebellion. The local members of the nobility, Lord Hussey and Lord Clinton, who should have stopped the rebels, fled. When the different rebel groups met at Lincoln, they drew up another set of articles (Source 6), which was sent to London. By this time, the king's army, led by the Duke of Suffolk, was just 40 miles away, and at this point, the members of the gentry who had assumed leadership of the rebellion started to waver. They had also received a reply from the king to their petition, which threatened the rebels with severe punishment unless they disbanded. If the rebels were to fight the king's army, it would be open treason and there would be no chance of negotiation. Rather than fight, the gentry decided to ask Suffolk for a pardon. This caused anger among the commons, but they were persuaded to go home by Suffolk's representative on 11 October. Ironically, it was just at this point that the rebellion further North in Yorkshire and Lancashire began.

SOURCE

6   The Lincoln Articles, 1536. These were the demands drawn up by the rebels who met at Lincoln on 9 October.

To the king our Sovereign lord.

1. The suppression of so many religious houses as are at this instant time suppressed, whereby the service of our God is not well [maintained] but also the [commons] of your realm be unrelieved, the which as we think is a great hurt to the common wealth...

2. The second article is that we humbly beseech your grace that the act of use[s] may be suppressed because we think by the said act that we your true subjects be clearly restrained of their liberties in the declaration of our wills concerning our lands, as well for payment of our debts, for doing of your grace service, as for helping... of our children, the which we had by the suffering of your laws by a long continuance the which as we think is a great hurt... to the common wealth.

3. The iiide [third] article is that where your grace hath a tax or a quindeyne [fifteenth] granted unto you by act of parliament payable next year, the which is and hath been ever leviable of sheep and cattle, and the sheep and cattle of your subjects within the said shire are now at this instant time in manner utterly decayed and... whereby your grace to take the said tax or quindeyn your said subjects shall be constrained to pay iiiid [four pence] for one beast and xiid [twelve pence] for xxtie [twenty] sheep, the which would be an importunate charge to them considering the poverty that they be in all ready and loss which they have sustained these ii years by past.

4. The iiiith article is that we your true subjects thinks that your grace takes of your counsel and being about you such persons as be of low birth and small reputation which hath procured the premises most especially for their own advantage, the which we suspect to be the lord Cromwell and Sir Richard Rich Chancellor of the Augmentation.

5. The vth article is that we your true subjects finds us grieved that there be diverse bishops of England of your gracious late promotion that hath falsid [made false] the faith of Christ, as we think, which are the bishop of Canterbury, the bishop of Rochester, the bishop of Worcester, the bishop of Salisbury, the bishop of Saint Davys, and the bishop of Devlyn [Dublin], and in especiall [especially] as we think the beginnings of all the trouble of this realm and the vexation that hath been taken of your subjects the bishop of Lincoln.

ACTIVITY
KNOWLEDGE CHECK

1 Read Source 6. How valuable is the source as evidence for the aims and motives of the Lincolnshire rebels?

2 What does Source 6 reveal about the social groups involved in the Lincolnshire Rising?

Supporters of the Lincolnshire Rising

The Lincolnshire Rising attracted support from a cross-section of society. The rebellion started among the ordinary men and women of Louth, and their leader was a shoemaker, Nicholas Melton. Melton was joined by the vicar of the church at Louth and at least one monk from the dissolved abbey at Louth. Monks from the Lincolnshire abbeys of Barlings, Bardney and Kirkstead also joined the rebels. Although none of these abbeys was due to be dissolved under the 1536 Act, the monks were clearly worried about the government's intentions. The abbots and some monks from all three of these abbeys were executed in the aftermath of the rebellion for their involvement. Lincolnshire parish clergy also became involved in the rebellion. Finally, some members of the local Lincolnshire gentry also joined in, though only after the rebellion had already begun. As the gentry were also JPs and responsible for keeping local order, their support meant that the rebellion was able to gather momentum. The motivation of these gentry leaders is harder to explain, mainly because they themselves gave contradictory explanations for their actions. Although the gentry were resentful about the Act of Uses, this does not explain why they would risk everything in open rebellion. Like the ordinary rebels, some gentry would have been resentful of government religious policy and intervention in the region. In a letter to the Duke of Suffolk written on 10 October, the gentry leaders in Lincolnshire claimed that they had joined the rebellion in order to control it and to prevent the rising from becoming more violent and dangerous. It is possible that these claims are true to some extent. The size of the rebellion and the speed with which it gathered momentum took the local gentry by surprise, and it took several days for outside help to arrive. Some may well have joined the rebels because they were threatened; others may genuinely have seen taking leadership of the rebellion as the best way to contain it and to ensure it remained peaceful, which would be the best way to avoid a charge of treason. However, the actions of some of the Lincolnshire gentry suggest that they took an active, not a reluctant role, in encouraging the rebellion, even to the extent of organising their own military musters. However, the chronology of the Lincolnshire rebellion suggests that whatever role the gentry took, it was a reaction to anger from the commons; the rebellion did not start with the gentry.

The threat of the Lincolnshire Rising to Henry's government

The Lincolnshire rising was potentially serious because some local Lincolnshire gentry became involved. As the rebellion gathered momentum, numbers swelled to 10,000 and the rebels were able to march to Lincoln as members of the local nobility fled. The involvement of members of the clergy and monks also added to the potential seriousness of the rebellion. The Church usually helped the Tudors to keep control because it reinforced ideas of obedience and the importance of social hierarchy. The speed with which the rebellion gathered support clearly took the local authorities by surprise, to the point where they were unable to cope. Another worrying feature of the rebellion was that the Lincolnshire rebels were in touch with men in Yorkshire who were equally discontented with government policy. This level of organisation suggests that the rebellion could have posed an even greater threat to Henry's government. It was fortunate for Henry that the Yorkshire commons were not ready to rise when the Lincolnshire Rising broke out, and that the Lincolnshire rebels ignored the letter from the Yorkshiremen telling them to delay their rebellion.

However, the Lincolnshire revolt was put down almost as swiftly as it had emerged. A royal army had quickly marched to Lincolnshire, led by the Duke of Suffolk, Henry's brother-in-law. The leadership of the gentry also turned out to be half-hearted. When they were threatened with punishment, they quickly backed down. The lack of continued support from the gentry meant that when the Suffolk herald arrived on 11 October, he was able to persuade the rebels to go home. In the meantime, the consequences of committing treason had driven a wedge between the rebels. The gentry were reluctant to risk their lives and property by risking treason; this lost them the support of the more hard-line and lower-ranking rebels, who had less to lose. The government was able to deal with the Lincolnshire Rising without risking a battle. In addition, the rebels were loyal to Henry; they did not seek to challenge his right to rule, and the local nobility did not join the rising.

However, the fact that the rebellion had spread so quickly and attracted such widespread support from all sections of society showed that it was a potential threat. The reason that the government was able to deal with it so quickly was because, at this stage, it was only the Lincolnshire commons that had risen. The relative ease with which the rising was put down may have lulled Henry into a false sense of security, because on 19 October, he disbanded a second army he had sent North to deal with the Lincolnshire rebels, leaving the Duke of Suffolk and his army to finish suppressing the trouble in Lincolnshire on his own. This proved to be a serious error of judgement.

SOURCE

A letter from Richard Cromwell to Thomas Cromwell, written on 11 October 1536, describing Henry's response to the Lincolnshire Rising. Richard Cromwell was Thomas Cromwell's nephew. He had risen in royal service because of his connection with Thomas. In 1536, he was involved in visitations of religious houses.

Last night my lord of Suffolk arrived here at Stamford. I and my train attended upon him and found Sir John Russell, Sir Francis Brian, Sir Wm. [William] Parre, and others well furnished with men. About 8 p.m. arrived also my lord Admiral who, like my lord's Grace, showed me great attention. We hear the traitors about Lincoln are so dismayed at the assembly of these noblemen that they know not what to do. The township of Boston, with others, have fled home again within these two days, to the number of ten or twelve thousand men, and I suppose the rest will flee shortly. My lord Admiral, with Russell, Brian, Parre, and me will ride towards them on Saturday. Yesterday in riding hither I met George Stanes, sometime clerk to the King's late attorney, who was one of the chief captains of those traitors, and had a letter from them to the King. I brought him before my lord's Grace who, I suppose, will send him to the King. The great traitor Sir John

Thymbleby, dwelling at Burne, seven miles from Stamford, knowing of Mr. Russell and Mr. Parre's approach, assembled all his tenants under color of doing the King service, and threatening to burn the houses of those who refused to go with him, then joined the traitors upon Monday last.

One of Sir John Thymbleby's sons has just come in, who says that five or six thousand of them have fled home, so that there remain not 10,000 at Lincoln, and his father has also come home again. Lament nothing so much as that they fly thus, as we hoped to have used them as they deserved... My lord's Grace has committed young Thymbleby to ward and, if his father come not in by 8 o'clock tomorrow, will spoil all he has and cut him in pieces.

ACTIVITY
KNOWLEDGE CHECK

1 What does Source 7 suggest about the seriousness of the threat posed by the Lincolnshire Rising?

2 Write down evidence that could be used to support each of these claims: 'The Lincolnshire Rising posed a serious threat to Henry VIII's government'; 'The Lincolnshire Rising was never a threat to Henry VIII's government'.

The Pilgrimage of Grace

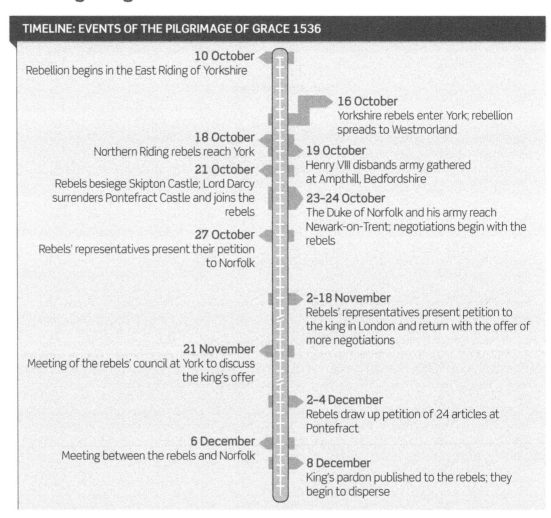

TIMELINE: EVENTS OF THE PILGRIMAGE OF GRACE 1536

10 October
Rebellion begins in the East Riding of Yorkshire

16 October
Yorkshire rebels enter York; rebellion spreads to Westmorland

18 October
Northern Riding rebels reach York

19 October
Henry VIII disbands army gathered at Ampthill, Bedfordshire

21 October
Rebels besiege Skipton Castle; Lord Darcy surrenders Pontefract Castle and joins the rebels

23-24 October
The Duke of Norfolk and his army reach Newark-on-Trent; negotiations begin with the rebels

27 October
Rebels' representatives present their petition to Norfolk

2-18 November
Rebels' representatives present petition to the king in London and return with the offer of more negotiations

21 November
Meeting of the rebels' council at York to discuss the king's offer

2-4 December
Rebels draw up petition of 24 articles at Pontefract

6 December
Meeting between the rebels and Norfolk

8 December
King's pardon published to the rebels; they begin to disperse

Aims and motives

The causes of the larger and more serious Pilgrimage of Grace were also linked to the dissolution of the smaller monasteries and religious reform. There has been debate about the extent to which there was genuine popular anger at the dissolution and the extent to which the grievances of the clergy and leaders such as Robert Aske were imposed on the commons. However, research by historians such as Michael Bush has revealed the genuine anger felt by the commons about the dissolution. The rebels also feared the social and economic consequences of the dissolution, and especially the impact on the poor, who relied on the alms provided by the monasteries, as the Pilgrims' ballads circulating in 1536 suggest. There were also wider social and economic concerns which reflected the hardship faced by the North of England. The wide-ranging Pontefract Articles complained about enclosure and unfair rises in rent imposed by landlords. They also asked for remission from the 1534 subsidy, which had hit the impoverished North particularly hard. The views of members of the clergy who joined the rebellion are also reflected in the articles in complaints about government attacks on the traditional privileges of the Church, such as benefit of clergy. The leader of the Pilgrimage of Grace, Robert Aske, an educated lawyer, was able to articulate the rebels' fears and it was he who encouraged the idea that the rebellion was a traditional 'pilgrimage'. However, the rebels' actions and the majority of the complaints made by the rebels were about the religious changes imposed by the government. The rebels wanted an end to the heresies of Luther and other thinkers, the restoration of the powers of the pope and the reversal of the dissolution of the smaller monasteries.

Key events

The Pilgrimage of Grace began on 10 October in the East Riding of Yorkshire at Beverley, and was closely connected to events in Lincolnshire. Representatives of the commons in Yorkshire were communicating with the Lincolnshire rebels as early as 2 October. By 16 October, the rebellion in the East Riding had attracted 10,000 followers and the rebels were able to take over the city of York. At York, Aske issued a proclamation stating the Pilgrims' peaceful intentions and their determination to protect the Church. The rebels in York made their intentions plain by restoring two religious houses which had been dissolved. On 19 October, the rebels captured the port of Hull and Pontefract Castle. Lord Darcy, who had been trying to defend Pontefract, wrote letters to the king asking for help, but did little else to stop the rebels, and was eventually persuaded to join them.

While the rebels in East Yorkshire were making great gains, the North Riding of Yorkshire also rose up on 11 October. Again, they had support from leading members of the local nobility and gentry, Lord Latimer and Sir Christopher Derby, plus another lawyer, Robert Bowes. The North Yorkshire rebels captured Barnard Castle before meeting up with Aske's rebels at York. Further afield, rebels were mustering in Westmorland and Cumberland. By 21 October, a rebel army was besieging Skipton Castle, where Henry Clifford, Earl of Cumberland, was trapped. On 16 October, rebellion broke out in Westmorland. By 19 October, four more rebel hosts had marched to Carlisle (Cumberland), though they failed to convince the town authorities to join them. The geographical extent of the rebellion covered most of the North and North East of England by late October. The only region where the rebels were less successful was in Lancashire, where the Earl of Derby remained loyal to Henry, despite Derby's religiously conservative beliefs. This was because Henry had given Derby huge powers in Lancashire, Cheshire and North Wales, which convinced Derby to remain loyal and put down the rebels instead. With Derby's leadership, the local gentry of Lancashire remained loyal to the government as well.

Government negotiations with the rebels

The Pilgrimage of Grace was now extremely serious for the government. Nine rebel hosts had formed across the North and all of them looked to Aske as their overall captain. The rebel army was 30,000 strong, and had in its ranks well-trained fighters who had recent military experience in the wars against Scotland. By contrast, Henry's military resources were over stretched. The Duke of Suffolk was still restoring order in Lincolnshire, and Henry's over-confidence had led him to send home a second army. The result of these government errors was that the rebels had three weeks in which to gather and prepare a strategy. The situation was made worse because so many of the northern gentry had joined the rebellion. Eventually, on 23 October, the Duke of Norfolk and the Earl of Shrewsbury marched North with an army of about 8,000 men. Because they were so outnumbered by the rebels, they had little choice but to negotiate, so Norfolk sent a letter to the rebels asking for a meeting, which took place on 27 October at Pontefract. At this meeting, the rebels presented a list of five articles and it was agreed that two representatives would take it to the king and that a truce would be called. When Henry was presented with the rebel articles, his initial response was to write an angry reply. The rebels then drew up a second set of 24 complaints to give to Norfolk (Source 8). A second meeting between Norfolk and the rebels took place at Doncaster on 6 December. The rebels asked for the king's pardon, which Norfolk was able to grant, together with a promise of a parliament to be held in the North of England and further negotiations on the fate of the monasteries. When news of the king's pardon reached the rebel camp on 8 December, many of them started going home, as Norfolk had hoped. Aske himself travelled to London, where he was received at Court and treated courteously. When Aske returned to the North, he was convinced of Henry's good intentions and that the rebels had won. However, Henry was simply biding his time until he could take his revenge.

SOURCE
8

From the Pontefract Articles, drawn up by the rebel leaders in December 1536 as given in *Letters and Papers of Henry VIII, Vol. XI*. This was the second set of demands issued by the rebels.

1. The first touching our faith to have the heresies of Luther, Wycliffe, Huss, Melancthon, Oecolampadius, Bucer, Confessio Germaniae, Apologia Melancthonis, the works of Tyndale, of Barnes, of Marshall, of Rastell, Saint German and such other heresies of Anabaptists destroyed.

2. The supremacy of the church touching the care of souls to be reserved to the See of Rome...

3. That the Lady Mary may be made legitimate...

4. The suppressed abbeys to be restored to their houses, lands, and goods

5. To have the tenths and first fruits clearly discharged of the same

6. To have the Friars Observants restored to their houses

7. To have the heretics, bishops and temporal, and their sect to have condign [fitting] punishment by fire or other such...

8. Lord Cromwell, the Lord Chancellor, and Sir Richard Riche to have condign punishment, as the subverters of the good laws of this realm and maintainers and inventors of heretics...

11. That Dr. Lighe and Dr. Layton have condign punishment for their extortions from religious houses and other abominable acts

13. The statute for inclosures and intacks to be put in execution...

14. To be discharged of the quinzine [fifteenth] and taxes now granted by Act of Parliament

15. To have a parliament at Nottingham or York...

16. The statute of the declaration of the crown by will to be repealed

18. The privileges and rights of the Church to be confirmed by Act of Parliament...

20. To have the statute 'That no man shall not will his lands' repealed

21. The statutes of treason for words and such like... to be repealed

22. That the common laws may have place as was used in the beginning of the reign...

23. That men north of Trent summoned on subpoena appear at York, or by attorney, unless it be directed upon pain of allegiance, or for like matters concerning the King.

A Level Exam-Style Question Section A

Study Source 8 before answering this question.

Assess the value of Source 8 for revealing the reasons for mass support for the Pilgrimage of Grace and the impact of the dissolution of the monasteries in 1536.

Explain your answer, using the source, the information given about its origin and your own knowledge about the historical context. (20 marks)

Tip

What is meant by 'mass support'? In what ways does the source reflect the view of different groups in society?

ACTIVITY
KNOWLEDGE CHECK

1 On your own copy of Source 8, highlight, in different colours, demands that would have been supported by: the ordinary rebels; the nobility and gentry; clergymen. Which demands would have appealed to several groups?

2 What are the similarities and differences between the Lincolnshire Articles and the Pontefract Articles? How could you explain them?

3 How valuable is Source 8 as evidence of the causes of the Pilgrimage of Grace?

Bigod's Rising, 1537

By January 1537, some of the former Pilgrims began to realise that Henry had tricked them. The Duke of Norfolk, who had returned to London, remained there for much longer than the rebels had expected. Rumours began to circulate that the king was not going to keep his promises and was planning revenge instead. In January 1537, there was a brief, unsuccessful rising led by Sir Francis

Bigod and a former Pilgrim, John Hallam, who captured Beverley (East Yorkshire). Bigod planned to capture Scarborough and Hull. Only a few hundred rebels joined Bigod and Hallam, and Bigod was captured in Cumberland in February 1537. There was also renewed unrest in the West Riding of Yorkshire, Cumberland and Westmorland, where the commons feared that the gentry who had previously led them were about to turn on them. The rebels attacked Carlisle, but were put down by a force led by Sir Christopher Dacre on 16 February.

This unrest gave Henry the excuse he needed to punish the rebels. The Duke of Norfolk was sent North and carried out a brutal suppression of the rebels. The Carlisle rebels were hanged and trials and executions were conducted throughout Cumberland. Among those conducting the trials was a former Pilgrim, Robert Bowes, who had now distanced himself from the rebellion. Some gentry leaders of the Pilgrimage were being recruited by the government to put down the risings; the gentry themselves had turned against the rebels, as they feared the impact of continuing unrest. By siding with the government, they were also able to avoid punishment themselves. However, the members of the gentry and nobility who had taken the greatest role in leading the Pilgrimage were arrested and taken to London. These men included Aske and Darcy. Since Henry had previously extended a pardon to the rebels, the government had to make up new crimes with which to charge these men. At least 144 people were executed, including Aske, Sir Thomas Percy, Bigod and Hussey. The rebellion was finally over and put down with brutal force by Henry, who was determined to take his revenge.

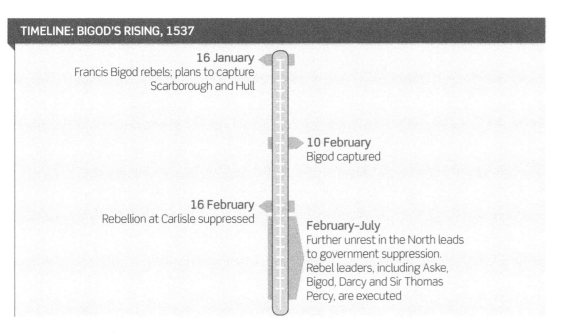

TIMELINE: BIGOD'S RISING, 1537

16 January
Francis Bigod rebels; plans to capture Scarborough and Hull

10 February
Bigod captured

16 February
Rebellion at Carlisle suppressed

February–July
Further unrest in the North leads to government suppression. Rebel leaders, including Aske, Bigod, Darcy and Sir Thomas Percy, are executed

Supporters of the Pilgrimage of Grace

The Pilgrimage of Grace was the largest mass rebellion of the Tudor period and attracted support from members of the nobility and the gentry, clergymen and monks, as well as the commons. Influential rebels from the ranks of the nobility and gentry included Lord Darcy, Lord Hussey, Sir Robert Constable, Sir Ingram Percy and Sir Thomas Percy. Darcy and Hussey were members of the conservative faction at Court (see page 91); given their conservative religious sympathies and links with other disaffected Catholics at Court, it is not surprising that they would join the rebellion. The two Percies who became involved in the rebellion were the brothers of Henry Percy, the Earl of Northumberland. The work of Michael Bush has shown that connection to the Percy family was an important factor in convincing some men to join the rebellion. The Percy power base in the North had been challenged by Henry in the 1530s, so it was perhaps unsurprising that they would choose to rebel (see Chapter 2). The high status of the Percy family in the North meant that many of their tenants and followers joined them in rebellion. Robert Aske was the earl's legal adviser, and Sir Robert Constable also acted as an adviser to the earl. Robert Aske and Robert Bowes were not knights, but had considerable status in northern society. Both Bowes and Aske were lawyers; they were well-educated and were able to articulate the grievances of the rebels effectively. They both also had links to members of the northern nobility and gentry; Aske was a cousin of Henry Clifford, Earl of Cumberland, and Bowes was the younger son of a gentry family.

However, the Pilgrimage of Grace did not start as a noble-led revolt. The first protests against the dissolution of the monasteries and Henry's government were raised by the commons of Yorkshire; they were followed by popular risings across Yorkshire, Cumberland and Westmorland. Clergymen and monks also became involved in the rebellion. The extent of Church involvement in the revolts can be seen in the number of executions of clergymen and monks in the aftermath of the revolt. In total, six abbots, 38 monks and 16 parish priests were executed for treason. The demands of the rebels in the York and Pontefract Articles show that the rebels came from very different social and economic backgrounds. Demands about the restoration of the papacy were mixed with complaints about abuses of Tudor government, high levels of taxation and greedy landlords. Nor was the Pilgrimage of Grace a rising which included all members of the conservative northern nobility and gentry. The Earl of Derby remained loyal, as did the Clifford family, who defended Skipton, Carlisle and Berwick from the rebels. Both Derby and the Cliffords had been well-rewarded by Henry in the 1530s, which may explain why they continued to support him rather than the rebels. The Earl of Northumberland himself was too ill to take a decisive part in events. He surrendered Wressle Castle to Aske without a fight and was taken into protective custody by the rebels.

The threat of the Pilgrimage of Grace to Henry's government

The Pilgrimage of Grace posed an enormous logistical challenge to Henry's government. The numbers of rebels, and the rapidity with which their armies gathered, took the government by surprise. The situation was made worse because of events in Lincolnshire, which had diverted the attention of the Duke of Suffolk and the army that he led. The Pilgrimage became even more threatening when members of the nobility and gentry decided to join it. This meant that the government could not rely on the usual mechanisms for dealing with local trouble, especially the local JPs, because so many of them were involved in the rebellion. The rebels were also well-organised. The early contact with the Lincolnshire rebels suggests that some of the commons were already making plans for a rising. The Pilgrims were able to co-ordinate their protest with considerable efficiency; all the rebel hosts acknowledged Aske as their overall leader. The speed with which the rebellion and the ideas associated with it spread suggests that the rebels were in constant contact with each other. This meant that the rebellion became harder for the government to put down. The leadership of men such as Aske ensured that the rebellion remained peaceful, which helped it to attract even more support from the landed gentry, who might have been threatened if the rebels had used violence. The size of the eventual rebel army (30,000) was larger than the army of 8,000 raised by the government. In the period between October and December 1536, the Duke of Norfolk was forced to negotiate with the rebels rather than suppress them, which would have been the usual government tactic.

However, the Pilgrimage of Grace was eventually defeated. Aske was prepared to believe the promises which Norfolk made on Henry's behalf. Norfolk was able to take advantage of the commons' sense of obedience to the monarchy and those above them in society. In 1536, the commons were still prepared to trust their social superiors, especially Norfolk and Aske. Once the rebels had dispersed, Henry was able to take advantage of further risings to exploit tensions and distrust between the landed gentry and the commons. By the time some former rebels realised that they had been tricked, it was too late because the rebel army had been dispersed. The rebels were also not interested in removing Henry from the throne. Even the plotters at Court were not prepared to go this far. Although some members of the conservative Court faction did join in the rebellion, not enough of them did for the challenge to be sustained. Henry had used his patronage to reward men such as the Earl of Derby and the Cliffords; they repaid him by remaining loyal. These splits among the northern nobility meant that Henry was able to keep enough men on his side to at least contain the situation, if not to stop the rebellion entirely.

A Level Exam-Style Question Section B

How accurate is it to say that it was the dissolution of the smaller monasteries in 1536 that caused the risings of 1536? (20 marks)

Tip
You will need to compare the dissolution of the smaller monasteries with other reasons in order to evaluate its importance as a cause of rebellion.

ACTIVITY
KNOWLEDGE CHECK

1 In your own words, explain why the Pilgrimage of Grace was more successful than Bigod's Rising.

2 Make two lists under the headings: 'Evidence that the Pilgrimage of Grace was a threat to Henry's government' and 'Evidence that the Pilgrimage of Grace was not a threat to Henry's government'.

3 'The Pilgrimage of Grace posed a serious threat to Henry VIII's government.' Write one side of A4 explaining how far you agree with this statement.

HOW EFFECTIVE WERE THE LEADERS OF THE REBEL CHALLENGE AND THE GOVERNMENT SUPPRESSION?

Robert Aske

Robert Aske quickly emerged as the most influential leader of the Pilgrimage of Grace. Aske was born c1500 into a gentry family from Selby (Yorkshire). As Aske had an elder brother, it was not expected that he would inherit the family estates. Instead, Aske entered the legal profession; he trained at Gray's Inn in London, which was one of four highly respected centres of learning for aspiring lawyers. After he had finished his training, Aske practised law in both London and Yorkshire. His knowledge of legal procedure, his intelligence and his skill as a speaker made him a natural leader of the rebels. In addition, Aske was also a committed Catholic. He was linked to the Lincolnshire rising in early October 1536, and may already have been planning a protest of his own even before the Lincolnshire rebels rose up.

The leadership of Robert Aske

Aske was an important figure in shaping the nature of the protest. He came up with the name 'The Pilgrimage of Grace for the commonwealth', which was a clever piece of propaganda because it associated the protest with the traditional Catholic ritual of a pilgrimage, which was believed to be a way to cleanse the soul. In choosing this phrase, Aske was making it clear that the protest was peaceful, Christian and in support of a restoration of the Catholic Church in England. The word 'grace' meant 'favour' from God, but Aske meant it as an appeal to Henry VIII. The Pilgrims were asking for the king's mercy for them and the commonwealth of England. Aske's leadership of the rebellion was also significant. He acted as a military captain, who began to organise musters of the commons in Yorkshire when the rebellion broke out. However, he was also very insistent that the Pilgrims should remain peaceful and orderly, and that they should be completely loyal to Henry VIII. For example, Aske forbade foot soldiers from entering York to prevent any stealing or disorder. The proclamations issued by Aske reinforced his view of the rebellion, and under his charismatic leadership the rebellion grew in size, but always remained peaceful.

Aske was also an important go-between. His legal training and position as member of a gentry family meant that he was a natural leader of the commons and that he was able to speak to and negotiate with other members of the gentry and the nobility. It was Aske who spoke to Lord Darcy at Pontefract to persuade him to join the movement. The compilation of the demands that became the Pontefract Articles was also carefully organised by Aske. He sent out messages to the different rebel armies who sent representatives to Pontefract to discuss their demands. Each of the demands was then agreed by the Pilgrim captains. What Aske had achieved was similar to a northern assembly; he also managed to ensure a balance between the demands of the gentry and those of the commons. When the rebels met with the Duke of Norfolk, it was Aske who was their spokesman and negotiator.

Aske's mistakes

However, Aske's idealism sometimes clouded his judgement. His loyalty to Henry and his absolute conviction in the moral rightness of his protest meant that he was too willing to accept the apparent concessions offered by Norfolk in December 1536. Although some of the rebels were suspicious of Norfolk and wanted to use their superior numbers to overwhelm the smaller royal army, Aske persuaded them that they could trust the Duke to represent their grievances at Court. When Aske was invited to spend Christmas at Court and was treated with great favour, he may have thought that his challenge to Henry had been forgiven and the rebels would achieve their demands. In this assumption, Aske was perhaps naive. When he returned to the North in January 1537, he told the gentry about Henry's promises for a northern parliament and a royal progress, but the lack of action by the king meant that some former rebels were becoming suspicious. This led to renewed rebellion by Sir Francis Bigod. Although Aske was not involved in any of the new risings, his prominence as the Pilgrims' leader made him particularly vulnerable to Henry's desire for revenge. Aske was arrested, charged with treason and executed in York on 12 July 1537.

Sir Francis Bigod

Francis Bigod's aims and motives in launching a new rebellion against Henry VIII were superficially very different from Aske's. Bigod was another member of the Yorkshire gentry; he had risen in the service of Thomas Wolsey. In the early 1530s, Bigod had become a committed evangelical, and he had even been involved in implementing Cromwell's reforms in the Yorkshire region. Bigod's religious convictions were in many ways the complete opposite of the Catholic Aske's. Bigod even translated religious works from the Latin so that he could use them, and paid the costs of several preachers. When the Pilgrimage of Grace broke out in October 1536, Bigod tried to escape by sea, but he was captured by the rebels. At this point, Bigod seems to have decided to support the Pilgrims, albeit reluctantly. His reformist views made him concerned about the king's supremacy over the Church, which Bigod saw as unnecessary. Bigod feared that Henry's **Erastian** view of kingship would mean more royal interference in Church affairs; as far as Bigod was concerned, only clergymen should decide on the doctrine and organisation of the Church. Ironically, in these views, Bigod was not dissimilar from the Pilgrims' opposition to the supremacy.

Why did Bigod rebel in 1537?

Bigod was one of those who feared that Henry and Norfolk could not be trusted. He was especially vulnerable because he was a gentry leader of the rebellion who also opposed the supremacy, a particularly dangerous point of view. Bigod was approached by another former rebel, John Hallam, who also distrusted the king. On 16 January 1537, Bigod and Hallam tried to start a new rebellion in the East Riding of Yorkshire. They planned to capture Hull and Scarborough, but only a few hundred men turned out to support them. The towns of Hull and Scarborough resisted the rebels' attempts to capture them and Bigod fled. He was eventually captured in Cumberland on 10 February. Bigod was taken to the Tower of London, tried and executed on 2 June 1537.

Bigod's rebellion shows the growing distrust and paranoia that was present among the former Pilgrims in late 1536–37. It also gave Henry the perfect excuse to act against the other Pilgrims, such as Aske. Bigod also failed to raise much local support; he was not a Catholic and seems to have lacked the natural ability to co-ordinate and lead a popular rising, unlike Aske. Although Bigod's rising encouraged further unrest across the North, the trouble came from the ordinary commons and lacked gentry leadership. Bigod was unable to harness this support, partly because he was a member of the gentry, who were coming under increasing suspicion from the commons, and partly because he did not share the same religious beliefs as the men he attempted to lead.

Thomas Cromwell

Thomas Cromwell's initial role in the suppression of the 1536 rising was fairly limited. His religious policies made him one of the main targets of the rebels' complaints, and this could have made him vulnerable to an attack on his position at Court and with the king. Cromwell was particularly vulnerable because the rebellion played into the hands of the conservative faction at Court, especially men like the Duke of Norfolk. However, Henry supported Cromwell in 1536, and in the following years Cromwell used his position to reinforce royal authority in the North and over religious policy. The involvement in rebellion of some members of the conservative faction (Lords Darcy and Hussey), and their subsequent executions, also strengthened Cromwell's position. Encouraged by Henry, Cromwell was able to use the rebellion to purge the remaining rival claimants to the throne with Yorkist blood, many of whom had Catholic sympathies. The main victims were members of the Pole and Courtenay families and included Henry Courtenay, Marquis of Exeter and Henry Pole, Lord Montague. Courtenay and Pole were accused of treason in 1538 and both were executed. These executions removed some of the remaining conservative elements at Court, who were a threat to Cromwell. It was also convenient for Henry to have rival claimants to the throne eliminated. However, Cromwell did still have opponents at Court, especially the Duke of Norfolk and Stephen Gardiner, Bishop of Winchester, and these men would help to bring about his downfall in 1540.

Cromwell's response to the rebellions of 1536-37

Although the unrest of 1536–37 temporarily halted the dissolution of the monasteries, Cromwell was able to use monastic involvement in the risings as a pretext to close down larger monasteries. The monasteries could now be associated with treason and disobedience to Henry and his supremacy. The closure of the larger monasteries began in 1537, but rather than using an Act of Parliament, Cromwell used a more cautious tactic of encouraging 'voluntary' closures. Abbots who willingly surrendered their monasteries to the Crown were well-rewarded with pensions. Abbots who resisted were executed. When most of the remaining monasteries had been dissolved, an Act for

KEY TERM

Erastian
Erastian ideas about kingship were based on the ideas of the 16th-century philosopher, Thomas Erastus. He argued that the secular prince of a kingdom should have control over the Church. This idea appealed to Henry VIII as he wanted to justify his supremacy. It was also an idea common among some religious evangelicals such as Cromwell. Other reformers, such as Bigod, rejected this idea, however. In particular, they were concerned that a secular leader could have control over the care of their subjects' immortal souls.

the Suppression of Religious Houses was passed in 1539. The last monastery was suppressed in 1540. The Pilgrimage of Grace had taught Cromwell and Henry that they needed a more cautious approach to the dissolution of the monasteries, but it did not change their overall policy. Cromwell also continued to impose more evangelical ideas on the Church. In 1538, he issued a second set of Injunctions to the Clergy. These ordered priests to discourage the veneration of relics or images in at least four sermons per year. Every parish church was also ordered to have a copy of the Bible in English and everyone was to be encouraged to read it. In 1539, Cromwell's reforms reached their height with the publication of the Great Bible, a revised translation of the earlier English Bible. The 1536 rebellions did not discourage Cromwell in the pursuit of his religious reforms; in fact, the risings may have encouraged him to continue with the changes as the best way to enforce the royal supremacy and Henry's power.

Henry VIII

Henry's initial response to the rebellions was one of fury. He was convinced of his own power and right to the supremacy; he was also convinced that every subject owed absolute obedience to him. However much the rebels professed their loyalty to him, to Henry, any rebellion was defiance to his rule. When the Lincolnshire rebels and the Pilgrims sent him their petitions, therefore, his reaction to both was to reject their demands and to question their loyalty. For example, when the Lincolnshire petition reached him, Henry's response was to write to the rebels threatening severe punishment unless the rebels dispersed. On this occasion, his threats were successful because they were backed up by the arrival of a royal army led by the Duke of Suffolk. This forced the rebels, especially the gentry, to think twice about how far they were prepared to take their defiance.

Henry's response to the Pilgrimage of Grace

Henry was confident enough in his own power to assume that similar tactics would work when news of the Pilgrimage of Grace reached him. Although the Pilgrimage of Grace had attracted about 30,000 supporters, and so was much larger than the Lincolnshire rising, Henry was still determined to punish the rebels and had to be persuaded to take a more cautious line by Norfolk. In his initial response to the rebels, written in his own hand, he expressed outrage that the rebels would dare to defy his rule (Source 9). He also made no mention of any concessions to the rebels' demands, other than that he would show them mercy; this mercy was not to be extended to the ringleaders of the rising, whom Henry wanted to be executed. Henry made a mistake in sending this letter. He underestimated the scale of the rising and the determination of the rebels, and thought that the threat of reprisals would deter the rebels. But Henry's letter only encouraged the rebels to continue, because without any promise of negotiation and the threat of reprisals hanging over them, they had more to gain by continuing to put pressure on the government than by giving up and going home. The rebels were also encouraged to continue because their army was so much larger than the royal army. Henry was not in a position to issue demands. Fortunately for Henry, Norfolk persuaded him to try a different tactic. Henry wrote again to the Pilgrims, this time offering further negotiation between Norfolk and 300 rebel representatives. Henry was careful not to address any of the Pilgrim articles in his reply, leaving Norfolk to find a way to negotiate and undermine the Pilgrims' position peacefully.

SOURCE

Henry VIII's handwritten letter to the Pilgrims, written on 2 November 1536 before he had taken Norfolk's advice. This was a response to the petition brought to Henry at Windsor by two of the rebel leaders.

What King hath kept you all his subjects so long in wealth and peace... so indifferently ministered justice to all, both high and low; so defended you all from outward enemies; so fortified the frontiers of this realm, to his no little, and in a manner inestimable charges? And all for your wealths and sureties.

However, Henry's actions suggest that he was always planning to take revenge on the rebels. Taking Norfolk's advice, he made a series of promises to the rebels that appeared to address many of their grievances, but nothing was ever put in writing. This was a clever tactic, as it meant that Henry was able to go back on his word more easily and the Pilgrims were unable to prove what had been promised to them. Henry's verbal promises were also of a vague nature. He was prepared to promise a northern parliament, a general pardon and a truce with the rebels. By promising a northern parliament, at a later date that was unnamed, he was able to delay discussion of particularly controversial grievances, such as the dissolution of the monasteries. The delaying tactics and Henry's promises finally convinced the rebels to go home. Henry was helped in this by Aske, who was prepared, mistakenly, to trust Henry. But as late as early December, Henry was still insisting that the ringleaders of the Pilgrimage should not be pardoned. This suggests that his true aim was always to inflict as much revenge as possible on those he considered to be disobedient. The violence of the government's suppression of the former rebels in 1537–38 reflected Henry's response to the rebellions.

ACTIVITY
KNOWLEDGE CHECK

What does Source 9 reveal about Henry's attitude to the rebellions of 1536?

The Duke of Norfolk

SOURCE
10 A portrait of Thomas Howard, Duke of Norfolk. This was painted by Hans Holbein when Norfolk was 66 years old, c1539.

Thomas Howard, third Duke of Norfolk, was the son of the Duke of Norfolk who had been rehabilitated in the reign of Henry VII (see Chapter 3). Born in 1473, the third Duke was a highly experienced statesman and military leader. His landed estates also made him the wealthiest and most powerful member of the nobility. Norfolk's religious beliefs were conservative and he tended to side with other conservatives at Court against Cromwell. These beliefs did not stop Norfolk from loyally serving Henry VIII in 1536–37. Norfolk was a political realist who realised that he had more to gain than lose by loyal service to Henry. Norfolk was well-rewarded for his loyalty; he even received grants of former monastic lands, despite his religious convictions.

Norfolk's role in 1536
Norfolk's role in 1536 was as the man-on-the-spot who advised Henry to negotiate rather than fight. In October and November 1536, Norfolk was in constant contact with Henry and Cromwell in London. When he arrived at Doncaster, his assessment of the strength of the Pilgrim host compared to that of his own army convinced the Duke that negotiation and playing for time would be the better tactic. It took Norfolk until early December to convince the furious king to agree to this approach. Norfolk even wrote to Cromwell, asking him to persuade the king to adopt these cautious tactics. It was Norfolk who suggested that Henry propose a parliament in the North, thus giving the government even more time to rearm itself. Norfolk's role as a go-between for Henry and the Pilgrims was also very important. The Duke's rank and position as a leading member of the conservative faction at Court persuaded Aske and the other noble and gentry Pilgrims that Norfolk could be trusted to put their case to Henry. Norfolk may even have taken his role as negotiator further than Henry intended in order to persuade the rebels to disperse. Although the Pilgrims were prepared to accept most of Henry's proposals, they remained concerned about the fate of the monasteries. The rebels insisted that the monasteries should not be dissolved until Parliament had discussed the matter. Norfolk had not been given permission by Henry to negotiate on this matter, but he chose to make a compromise arrangement with the Pilgrims anyway. Norfolk agreed with the rebels that the monasteries should formally surrender to the king's officials, but would then be restored again until parliament met. It was this that convinced the rebels to accept the king's pardon and promises and to return home. Norfolk had managed to defeat an army nearly four times as large as his own without needing to resort to violence.

Norfolk's role in repression, 1537
In 1537, Norfolk was sent North by Henry once again with an armed force, because the king feared that there would be further unrest. Now that the rebels had been dispersed, the smaller and less co-ordinated risings that occurred in 1537 were easily dealt with by the local gentry and nobility, who were encouraged by Norfolk's presence. Norfolk exploited the increasing divisions and distrust between the commons and the former gentry Pilgrims by recruiting some of the former leading rebels into his council. These men included formerly prominent Pilgrims: Sir Ralph Ellerker and Robert Bowes. At Henry's request, Norfolk also persuaded former rebels who were considered to be a threat, such as Aske, Darcy and Sir Robert Constable, to go to Court. These men seem to have trusted Norfolk and did not suspect that they were about to be arrested. Other rebels, such as Sir Thomas Percy, were arrested by Norfolk and then sent South. The Duke also declared **martial law**. He dealt with many of the rebels from Bigod's rising and the failed attack on Carlisle in this way. Norfolk's actions were crucial in 1536–37 in preventing the rebellion from becoming even more serious than it already was. As the king's representative, he was the noble who acted as both negotiator and enforcer in the North, and brought an end to the rebellion in a manner which reasserted royal power.

The extent of repression in 1537
Once the new risings of 1537 began, Henry VIII had the excuse to take revenge on the rebels of 1536. His anger was reflected in the severity of the punishments meted out to the ringleaders of the rebellion. At least 144 people were executed, although some sources suggest that the figure may be closer to 200. The main victims were key figures from the rebellion, including Robert Aske, Lords Darcy and Hussey, Sir Robert Constable, Sir Thomas Percy and Sir Francis Bigod. The Earl of Northumberland, who had wavered and whose brothers had rebelled, was not executed, but he was persuaded to make Henry VIII his heir, putting the Percy estates in royal hands. Several leading clerics were also executed, including Adam Sedbar, abbot of Jervaulx, and William Thirsk, abbot

> **KEY TERM**
>
> **Martial law**
> Proclaimed when a government faces a state of emergency. Ordinary legal processes are suspended, and trials and punishments are overseen by a senior military commander. This allowed Norfolk, as a senior military man, to try to punish some of the rebels himself.

of Fountains Abbey. In addition, Norfolk summarily executed 74 of the rebels who had attacked Carlisle in 1537. Cromwell himself took a personal role in the interrogation of Robert Aske, and was instrumental in finding or extracting new evidence against Aske which was then used to argue that Aske was guilty of new treason that was not covered by the 1536 pardon. The punishment meted out to Aske was particularly vicious; he was hung in chains from a gibbet until he died. Afterwards, his body was left in chains as a warning and reminder to the people of the North.

Henry's anger and suspicion led to the punishment of some other more minor figures who had the misfortune to do or say the wrong thing. The most notorious such cases were those of Thomas Miller, the Lancaster Herald, and Margaret Cheyney. Thomas Miller was a royal agent who had been completely loyal in 1536 and had helped with the negotiations with the Pilgrims. However, he was hanged for treason in 1538 because he had pointed out to the rebels that they had the military advantage. Although Miller had only been trying to point out to the rebels that they had the upper hand and were in a strong position to negotiate, his comments were taken as treasonous. Margaret Cheyney's case was even more shocking. Margaret seems to have been the mistress of Sir John Bulmer, who had been involved in the 1536 rebellion but had been pardoned. When Bulmer was summoned to Court in 1537, he panicked and tried to plot a rebellion. Margaret tried to persuade Bulmer to leave the country. These events were enough for both Bulmer and Margaret to be accused of treason. Bulmer was executed and Margaret suffered a woman's punishment for treason, which was to be burnt at the stake.

However, Henry's attitude towards the North also included some more moderate and constructive policies. Although the risings did not stop the dissolution of the monasteries, it did cause Henry and Cromwell to change their tactics. As a longer-term response, Henry and Cromwell also re-organised the Council of the North in 1537 (see Chapter 2). Some of the first members of the new Council were former Pilgrims, such as Ralph Ellerker and Robert Bowes. Resentment of his policies continued in the North, however. In 1541, there was a plot to kill the president of the Council of the North and capture Pontefract Castle, but this was quickly discovered and put down by the Council itself. Henry himself also finally went on a progress to York in 1541. These measures were enough to pacify the North, and there would not be another rebellion there until 1569.

ACTIVITY
KNOWLEDGE CHECK

1 'The risings of 1536–37 were only suppressed because the rebel leaders made crucial mistakes.' How far do you agree with this judgement?

a) To help you answer this question, copy and complete this table:

	Contribution to the leadership or suppression of the risings	Evidence	Overall significance of their contribution
Robert Aske			
Francis Bigod			
Thomas Cromwell			
Henry VIII			
Thomas Howard, Duke of Norfolk			

b) Using your completed table, write an answer to the question.

A Level Exam-Style Question Section B

How significant was the challenge posed by the risings of 1536–37 for the government of Henry VIII? (20 marks)

Tip
You will need to consider all the rebellions of 1536–37; were they all equally a threat to Henry?

THINKING HISTORICALLY — Cause and consequence (7c)

The value of historical explanations

Historical explanations derive from the historian who is investigating the past. Differences in explanations are usually about what the historians think is significant. Historians bring their own attitudes and perspectives to historical questions and see history in the light of these. It is therefore perfectly acceptable to have very different explanations of the same historical phenomenon. The way we judge historical accounts is by looking at how well argued they are and how well evidence has been deployed to support the argument.

Approach A	Approach B	Approach C
Rebellion is caused by decisions taken by politicians. It is the result of the actions of great men. Ordinary people respond to their actions and rebel against them.	Rebellion is the result of mass movements in which similar peoples with similar ideas come together to protest.	Rebellion is an inevitable part of the process of change. The great movements of history point us to this fact.

Work in groups of between three and five (you will need an even number of groups in the class).

1 In your groups, devise a brief explanation of the risings of 1536, of between 200 and 300 words, which matches one of the approaches above. Present your explanation to another group, who will decide on two things:

  a) Which of the approaches is each explanation trying to demonstrate?

  b) Considering the structure and the quality of the argument and use of evidence, which is the best of the three explanations?

2 If you choose a 'best' explanation, should you discount the other two? Explain your answer.

ACTIVITY SUMMARY

1 Create a diagram, cartoon strip or road map to show the causes and main events of the 1536–37 risings. Make sure that you include precise dates and facts.

2 Compare the risings of 1536–37 with those faced by Henry VII and answer the following questions:

  a) Which king faced the most serious threat to his throne, and why: Henry VII or Henry VIII?

  b) What are the main similarities and differences between the rebellions faced by Henry VII and Henry VIII? Think about: the causes of the rebellions; the aims of the rebels; who was involved; how easily the government managed to suppress the risings; the extent and location of the rebellions.

WIDER READING

Lipscomb, S. *1536: The Year that Changed Henry VIII*, Lion Hudson (2009)

Rex, R. *Henry VIII and the English Reformation*, 2nd edition, Palgrave Macmillan (2006)

Wood, A. *Riot, Rebellion and Popular Politics in Early Modern England*, Palgrave Macmillan (2001)

3.5

Agrarian discontent: Kett's rebellion, 1549

KEY QUESTIONS

- What was the significance of the social and economic causes of Kett's rebellion?
- To what extent did Kett's rebellion pose a challenge to the government?
- What were the roles of Kett, the Duke of Somerset and the Earl of Warwick?

INTRODUCTION

The rebellion in East Anglia, led by Robert Kett, was a different type of rising from those seen under Henry VII and Henry VIII. Whereas earlier rebellions had attracted some noble or gentry support, Kett's rebellion was against the power and influence of the landed elites. Historian John Guy has described the rebellion as 'the closest thing Tudor England saw to a class war'. Kett and his rebels were reacting to the social and economic conditions of the 1540s. Their anger was inflamed by the actions of the **Protector** of England, the Duke of Somerset. The result was a serious rebellion across the South East, which the government struggled to suppress. Eventually, it was John Dudley, Earl of Warwick, who restored order, but the rebellion led to Somerset's fall from power.

WHAT WAS THE SIGNIFICANCE OF THE SOCIAL AND ECONOMIC CAUSES OF KETT'S REBELLION?

The impact of enclosure on Tudor society and why it led to discontent

Enclosure was blamed by many contemporaries for the growth of poverty and vagrancy in Tudor society. The practice of enclosure was at its most common in areas which could be used for either arable or sheep farming in the South East and the Midlands. Under the medieval open-field system of agriculture, land was divided among the inhabitants of the village and used for subsistence farming of crops and animals. The common land was shared by all and was often used to graze animals. The practice of enclosure aimed to create larger profits from the land. Landlords saw the financial opportunities that rearing sheep for the cloth trade could bring. They were also under pressure from rising prices, which meant that they needed to increase their income. Sheep farming needed little manpower, but could bring vast profits and lead to large-scale enterprises, such as that of Sir William Fermour of Norfolk, who owned 17,000 sheep. Enclosure usually took place by erecting walls or hedges which 'enclosed' an area of land for the landlord's use. This practice had

> **KEY TERM**
>
> Protector
> The Duke of Somerset was the Protector for the young king Edward VI, who was just 11 years old when the rebellion of 1549 broke out. As Protector, Somerset acted as a guardian for the king and as a regent; Somerset made decisions and ran the country on Edward's behalf.

1547 – Edward Seymour becomes Lord Protector

1548 – Failure of John Hales' anti-enclosure bills

Enclosure commissions issued by Somerset

1547

1548

been going on since at least the 15th century. Sometimes, enclosure was a practical response to depopulation, where the tenants had left or died and had not been replaced. More seriously, some landlords enclosed village common lands, which affected the poorest members of the community who were most reliant on these to graze their animals. This type of enclosure could have a knock-on effect, because common grazing provided manure for the village crops; without this, it became harder to grow enough food to survive. Some landlords also used the practice of **engrossing**. Other practices by landlords, such as **rack-renting**, also attracted criticism.

Enclosure certainly did cause some social and economic hardship. The most vulnerable were copyhold tenants, whose leases were most open to challenge, and the landless, who were reliant on the common lands for survival. It was these groups who were most likely to find themselves forced out of their homes and into poverty. Contemporary thinkers, such as Thomas More and John Hales, blamed enclosure for many of the social problems of the time, and this led to government action against enclosure. As early as 1489, there was an attempt to pass an Act of Parliament to regulate enclosure. In 1517, Thomas Wolsey issued a commission of inquiry into illegal enclosures. Successive Tudor governments also tried to regulate enclosure and sheep farming. The 1533 Sheep and Farms Act tried to restrict the number of sheep kept per farmer to 2,400; engrossing was allowed, but only to a maximum of two farms. From March to November 1549, a tax on sheep was introduced in an attempt to restrict the size of flocks and discourage landlords from turning to sheep farming.

Linked to enclosure were other practices that were likely to cause increased hardship among the poorest in society. Such practices included rack-renting. Another focus of complaint was increasing entry fines. These methods improved landlord profit margins, but placed more economic pressure on tenants, especially the poorer ones, who were unable to pay. Enclosure and entry fines had already attracted popular criticism before the outbreak of the 1549 revolt. Some rebels in the Pilgrimage of Grace complained about these practices, which were a constant source of potential tension between landlords and tenants.

However, enclosure was not always practised by powerful landlords to the cost of their tenants. The impact of enclosure depended on a region's rural economy. East Anglia, where Kett's rebellion took place, was dominated by sheep farming, with some flocks of sheep numbering well over a thousand, but local practices regarding enclosure varied. In the East of Suffolk, North West Suffolk and North Norfolk, attitudes to enclosure were ambiguous (see Figure 5.1). This was because the soils in these regions were light and encouraged a mixture of sheep farming and arable farming. The presence of large flocks of sheep in these areas provided the necessary manure to fertilise crops which might otherwise have struggled to grow in the light soil. In these regions, the situation was made more complex by the existence of a medieval tradition known as **foldcourse**. Tensions in this region tended to surface when the landlords tried to challenge their tenants' rights to enclose. When rebellion broke out in 1549, some of the rebels' demands focused more on sheep farming than enclosure because of these local conditions. However, in Central Suffolk and South East Norfolk, there was a more densely wooded region with heavier soils. This region tended to be dominated

KEY TERMS

Engrossing
The practice of amalgamating two or more farms together. The buildings on these farms might then either be left to decay, while their former occupants were forced to move elsewhere.

Rack-renting
The practice by landlords of rapidly increasing rents so that the tenants who were unable to pay could be evicted. It also helped landlords to increase their profits.

KEY TERM

Foldcourse
This tradition allowed landlords to use their tenants' lands and the common land to graze sheep. This led to tenants enclosing their arable lands to protect them from their landlord's sheep.

1549 – May–June:
Enclosure riots in the
Midlands and South East

1549 – 6–8 July: Kett's rebellion breaks out
1549 – 31 July: Kett's rebels defeat the
Marquess of Northampton's army

1549

1549 – June: Outbreak
of the Western Rising

1549 – 16 August: Western Rising
put down by government forces
1549 – 27 August: Kett's rebels
defeated at Dussindale

KEY TERM

Godly commonwealth
The commonwealth represented the 'common good' in England. Committed Protestants, such as Hales, Latimer, Crowley and Somerset, believed that the wealthy had a Christian duty, given to them by God, to look after the poor, and that the practice of enclosure led directly to increased poverty and hardship, unemployment and vagrancy. They argued that if the wealthy took responsibility for looking after the poor and needy, this would create a more Christian society in which the common good was upheld.

by sheep farming, while the wooded nature of the countryside made it hard to find suitable areas in which to grow crops. Because land where crops could be grown was at a premium, enclosure was seen as a nuisance, especially when landlords ignored local villagers' rights to use common land. In this region, it was the landlords who enclosed and the tenants who complained about it, the reverse of the situation in the sheep-corn localities. The common element in both the sheep-corn and wood-pasture regions was the impact of sheep farming on local communities, which led to increasing social and economic tensions.

The role of the commonwealth-men

Enclosure was criticised by a group sometimes known by historians as the 'commonwealth-men'. This group of thinkers were often politicians, clergymen and intellectuals, with a strong reformer faith. They saw enclosure not just as a public nuisance, but also as the fundamental source of the poverty, unemployment and vagrancy that plagued mid-Tudor society. In the 1540s, reformers such as the government official John Hales, the writer Robert Crowley and Hugh Latimer, Bishop of Worcester, wrote and preached about the need for social reform and, in particular, the need to control enclosure (Source 1). The commonwealth-men believed that social reform should happen for the good of the commonwealth, though they were not advocating social equality. Their aim was to create a **Godly commonwealth**. Their ideas were important for two reasons. First, Protector Somerset was influenced by their thinking to introduce commissions of enquiry into illegal enclosure. Second, although many of the rebels could not read or write, they could still hear about and understand ideas about the need for a more just society and the greed of landlords; these ideas then influenced the rebels' aims and actions in 1549.

EXTEND YOUR KNOWLEDGE

The 'commonwealth-men' and historians
Historians writing in the early 20th century, such as R.H. Tawney and W.K. Jordan, identified a group of 16th-century thinkers who, they believed, had a coherent set of ideas and policies about social and economic problems. It was thought that these men formulated a cohesive group, which influenced the Duke of Somerset and was very influential in government policy in the late 1540s.

The historian Geoffrey Elton has discredited this idea, arguing that no such coherent group existed. Elton thought that the men identified as commonwealth-men were a disparate group who were not well co-ordinated and did not even agree with each other. Elton was particularly dismissive of the commonwealth-men's ideas about the causes of poverty and social distress.

However, recent work on the so-called commonwealth-men by Catherine Davies has shown that although these men were not an organised group of policy-makers, their ideas were important because they reflected the growing concerns of the period about poverty. This group were also closely linked with Protestantism, and their religious beliefs influenced their ideas about how to do deal with the poor. In sermons and their writings, they attacked the corruption and negligence of the clergy and the landed elites. These men were particularly critical of enclosure because it was an example of how the wealthier in society exploited the poor and vulnerable. They also argued that it was the duty of the wealthy to look after the poor through charity, education and good works. Even if they were not an organised group of policy-makers, these thinkers were the voice of a group with a social conscience. The Duke of Somerset was certainly influenced by some of their ideas.

ACTIVITY
KNOWLEDGE CHECK

1 Research the following 'commonwealth-men': Robert Crowley, John Hales and Hugh Latimer.

   You should try to find out about their backgrounds, their careers and their religious and political ideas.

2 When you have finished your research, write a paragraph to answer the question: how significant was the role of the 'commonwealth-men' in influencing ideas about social and economic change?

SOURCE

Robert Crowley, 'An Information and Petition against the Oppressors of the Poor Commons of this Realm', presented to the parliament of 1548.

If there were no God, then would I think it lawful for men to use their own possessions as they list [want]... But forasmuch as we have a God, and he hath declared unto us by the Scripture that he hath made the possessioners [land owners] but stewards of his riches, and that he will hold a straight account with them for the occupying and bestowing of them, I think no Christian ears can abide to hear that...

Now harken [listen] you possessioners and you rich men lift up your ears, you stewards of the Lord, mark what complaints are laid against you in the high court of the living God... Whiles the wicked wax [grow] proud, the poor man is afflicted and troubled. Would to God the wicked might feel the same things that they invent for others... Behold you engrossers of farms and tenements, behold I say, the terrible threatenings of God whose wrath you cannot escape. The voice of the poor (whom you have with money thrust out of house and home) is well accepted in the ears of the Lord, and hath stirred up his wrath against you...

For when you have multiplied your rents to the highest so that you have made all your tenants your slaves to labour and toil and bring to you all that may be ploughed and digged out of your grounds, then shall death suddenly strike you...

You have showed no mercy: how can you look then for mercy? O, noble counsellors, be merciful to yourselves... learn to know the estate [position] that God has called you to, and to live according to your profession; know that you are all ministers in the common wealth...; know that your office is to distribute, and not to scrape together on heaps...

And if any of them [the poor] perish through your default [failure], know then for certainty that the blood of them shall be required at your hands... If the sturdy fall to stealing, robbing and receiving [stolen goods]: then you are the causes thereof, for you dig in, enclose, and withhold from them the earth out of which they should dig and plough their living.

ACTIVITY
KNOWLEDGE CHECK

1 List the ways in which enclosure was believed to create social and economic problems in mid-Tudor society.

2 Read Source 1 and answer the following questions:

   a) What does Crowley argue is the relationship between God and the 'possessioners'?

   b) What problems does Crowley associate with enclosure?

   c) Crowley was writing to the 1548 parliament: how might this have affected the message he was trying to get across?

   d) How might a potential rebel interpret Crowley's arguments?

A Level Exam-Style Question Section A

Study Source 1 before answering this question.

Assess the value of Source 1 for revealing the problems caused by the practice of enclosure and the attitudes of those advising the Tudor government.

Explain your answer, using the source, the information given about its origin and your own knowledge about the historical context. (20 marks)

Tip
How do Crowley's religious beliefs affect his attitudes and arguments?

However, the commonwealth-men were incorrect about the real causes of poverty in the Tudor period. Poverty in the 16th century was caused by population growth. As the population grew, there was more pressure on the job market; wages fell and prices rose, as demand and inflation increased. Enclosure made these problems worse, but it was not their root cause.

In the 1540s, England faced a series of social and economic crises. Between 1525 and 1551, it is estimated that the population grew rapidly, from about 2.3 million to 3.0 million. As the population grew, it became harder to ensure that there was an adequate food supply. Greater demand for food led to rapid price rises, which hit the poorest in society the hardest. This led to more pressure on the land, which was needed to grow more crops. The need to increase the amount of land in tillage (land used for crop production) encouraged Somerset's government to try to restrict the practice of enclosure. The price rises were also what caused landlords to turn to enclosure to increase their profits; but this only made the lives of the rural poor even harder. A larger population also meant that there was increased competition for jobs and more unemployment. The unemployed were reliant either on charity or on the limited poor relief available at this time (see Chapter 2); those who were unable to find work or help often turned to vagrancy and begging, which alarmed the Tudor authorities. It was these conditions that led to the passing of the vicious 1547 Vagrancy Act, which punished vagrants severely. This government response to hardship can only have added to the resentment felt by the poor.

These problems were exacerbated in the 1540s by poor harvests in 1545 and 1549. This made the problem of food shortages and rising prices even worse. At the same time, the European market in wool and cloth was temporarily booming; this encouraged even more landlords to turn to sheep farming and to raise rents because they needed to boost their profits. Not only did sheep farming require less labour than arable farming, which made the problem of unemployment worse, but the enclosure of common ground hit the poorest peasants hardest, because they were most reliant on it to make ends meet. A further problem was the **debasement** of the coinage to meet the costs of war with France and Scotland in the 1540s. Debasement caused prices to rise still further. As the **price index** shown in Source 2 suggests, the price increases of the late 1540s were particularly severe. Those on a low income or with no job at all suffered the most. Somerset and his advisers realised that something needed to be done about these problems. The result was the 1548 and 1549 commissions on enclosures, which proved to be the catalyst for Kett's rebellion.

The impact of the Duke of Somerset's commission on enclosures

The Duke of Somerset was a committed Protestant and was attracted by the idea of creating a Christian commonwealth in England. He even passed a private parliamentary bill which protected the **copyholders** on his own estates from enclosure. Somerset appointed John Hales to oversee government reform of social and economic problems. In 1548–49, Hales tried to introduce a series of bills encouraging social and economic reform. These bills all failed because parliament tended to represent the interests of the landed elites, who profited the most from enclosure and sheep farming. Hales' only success was to introduce a new tax on sheep in 1549.

KEY TERMS

Debasement
A process by which the gold and silver coinage was melted down and mixed with less expensive metals. This mixture was then used to make an increased number of coins. Debasement was a quick and easy way for the government to raise money, but it led to economic problems. Because the gold and silver was mixed with base metals, there was reduced confidence in English currency. This led to merchants putting up their prices, which added to the problem of inflation.

Price index
Economists and historians sometimes use values rather than prices to show changes to standards of living. An index of 100 is the norm; values under 100 show that prices are falling. Values of over 100 show that prices are rising.

KEY TERM

Copyholder
A tenant who was supposed to have a copy of their lease in the rolls of their manor, as well as keeping their own copy. Copyhold leases could vary; some were by inheritance; others were for life or for a number of years; some were 'by the will of the lord of the manor'. Those tenants who inherited the lease were generally the most secure, though they could still be forced out by the fines that they had to pay when they inherited. The least secure were those who had no fixed terms to their lease, but any copyholder was vulnerable to eviction if the records which proved their right to the lease were lost or destroyed.

SOURCE

2 Prices for the years 1500–50. These are based on the work of the economists Henry Phelps-Brown and Sheila Hopkins, who researched historical wage and price fluctuations. Their work is based on an index where 100 is the norm. Changes to prices were based on the cost of basic raw materials such as wheat (for bread) and hops (for ale), which an ordinary family might buy.

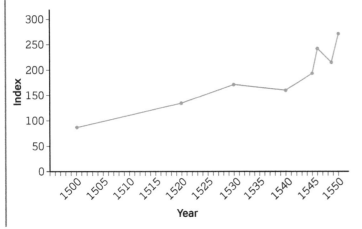

Hales' and Somerset's next action was to issue a series of commissions that were to inquire into illegal enclosures and report the evidence back to the government. However, these commissions did not have the power to order illegal enclosures to be taken down or to punish those found to be in breach of the law. In June 1548, commissioners were appointed, but only one commission actually went ahead. This was in the Midlands and included Hales himself. However, the commissioners found little evidence of illegal enclosure. Hales claimed that this was because of obstruction by local landlords, who refused to co-operate with his commissioners.

The failure of the 1548 commissions did not deter Somerset or Hales. Somerset took the problem of the failed enclosure commissions into his own hands. Where possible, he took direct action against illegal enclosures by ordering the ploughing up of illegal enclosures. The estates of Thomas Howard, Duke of Norfolk, which were currently in the Crown's hands, were among those affected. A park belonging to John Dudley, Earl of Warwick, was also ploughed up. In April 1549, Somerset also issued new enclosure commissions. The commissioners were told that illegal enclosures should be destroyed. However, Somerset's order to the commissioners was illegal. The terms of the commission, which had been set out in 1548 and had not been changed, stipulated that commissioners were to investigate enclosures, not destroy them.

The enclosure commissions had two unintended consequences. The first was that Somerset alienated the landed gentry and nobility who were the targets of his commissions. This was a mistake, as it was this group who were the first line of defence against rebellion. Somerset was also reliant on this group for support in the government of the country. The second unintended consequence was that the commons of England thought that Somerset was on their side. The social and economic conditions of the late 1540s were causing widespread hardship, as well as growing resentment against the landed elites. This resentment was compounded by the idea of the Godly commonwealth, which Somerset himself embraced. Somerset was seen by the commons as the 'Good Duke', who would support them against the greed and corruption of the landlords. His enclosure commissions only encouraged this impression further. Somerset's attempts to inquire into and punish illegal enclosers sent a message to the rebels that any actions that they took to deal with local breaches of the law would be condoned by the Duke. These developments were particularly dangerous because they isolated Somerset from the rest of the landed elites and encouraged a rebellion that soon spiralled out of control.

Figure 5.1 The positions of the rebels' camps during Kett's rebellion.

EXTEND YOUR KNOWLEDGE

John Hales

John Hales' early career was spent in the service of Thomas Cromwell, but he was not affected by Cromwell's fall in 1540. Hales worked in the hanaper, a government office that was responsible for issuing and sealing government writs. A committed Protestant, Hales purchased former monastic land in the Midlands and used some of it to set up a school in Coventry. He was also a scholar and author and became particularly interested in economic issues. Hales' Protestantism meant that he found further favour under Somerset's Protectorate, while his interest in establishing a Godly commonwealth led him to play a key part in Somerset's attempts at social and economic reform in 1548-49.

TO WHAT EXTENT DID KETT'S REBELLION POSE A CHALLENGE TO THE GOVERNMENT?

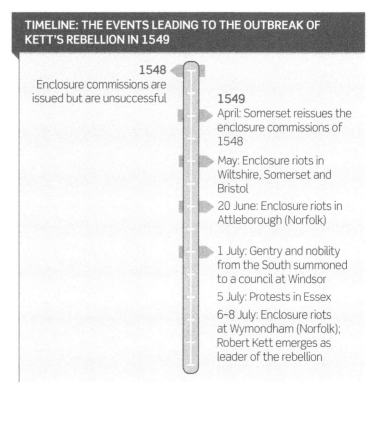

TIMELINE: THE EVENTS LEADING TO THE OUTBREAK OF KETT'S REBELLION IN 1549

1548
Enclosure commissions are issued but are unsuccessful

1549
April: Somerset reissues the enclosure commissions of 1548

May: Enclosure riots in Wiltshire, Somerset and Bristol

20 June: Enclosure riots in Attleborough (Norfolk)

1 July: Gentry and nobility from the South summoned to a council at Windsor

5 July: Protests in Essex

6–8 July: Enclosure riots at Wymondham (Norfolk); Robert Kett emerges as leader of the rebellion

The origins of the rebellion

The origins of the rising in Norfolk, which became known as Kett's rebellion, lay in the social and economic crises of the late 1540s. In 1549, riots against illegal enclosure of common land broke out and spread quickly through Essex into East Anglia. Trouble in East Anglia itself began in Attleborough (Norfolk). On 1 July, many of the local gentry and nobility were summoned by Somerset to a meeting at Windsor Castle. Although this meeting was probably to discuss the serious rebellion in the West Country, it added to the unease of the commons, who perhaps feared they were to be the target of a severe government response. With many of the leading landlords away from the region, the riots gained enormous momentum and support from across East Anglia.

EXTEND YOUR KNOWLEDGE

The Western Rising (1549)

The first serious rebellion to break out in 1549 was in Devon and Cornwall. The Western Rising began in June 1549 and continued until 16 August. The causes of the rising were local resentment over the introduction of a new English Book of Common Prayer, which the rebels in the more religiously conservative South West resented. As in Kett's rebellion, the local gentry were overwhelmed, but unlike Kett's rebellion, some gentry joined the Western Rising. The Duke of Somerset found it difficult to put down the rising because government forces were already overstretched, dealing with enclosure riots across the Midlands and the South East. The situation was made worse by poor communications and a reluctance by Somerset to take the rising seriously. The western rebels were able to march to the county town of Exeter, which they besieged. A government army did not relieve Exeter until 6 August 1549, and the rebels were not finally defeated until a battle at Sampford Courtenay on 16 August, in which it is estimated that about 4,000 rebels were killed.

The timing of two serious rebellions, the Western Rising and Kett's rebellion, at opposite ends of the country, in a period of general social and economic unrest, made it harder for the government to respond to the crisis. It was particularly lucky for Somerset that the western rebels, like Kett's rebels, did not choose to march on London.

Kett's rebellion began at the market town of Wymondham (Norfolk), where the local community had met together for traditional feasting and celebrations. On this occasion, the festivities got out of hand and the crowds started to destroy the enclosures of an unpopular local landowner, Sir John Flowerdew. Flowerdew was a lawyer who had been in dispute with the people of Wymondham over the fate of the local abbey. He had started to demolish part of the abbey, even though the townspeople had purchased it. As a locally unpopular individual who abused his social status for his own gain, Flowerdew was an obvious target for the rioters, especially given the encouragement of Somerset's enclosure commissions. Flowerdew tried to turn the rioters against another Wymondham landowner, Robert Kett. Kett had also followed the practice of enclosing common land and so was another potential target for the rioters. If Flowerdew had been hoping to distract the rebels from his own property by encouraging them to attack Kett, he was mistaken. Kett sided with the rebels. He agreed that he had illegally enclosed the common land and ordered his hedges to be torn down. These actions turned Kett into the leader of an increasingly widespread anti-enclosure movement. Kett then made the decision to march on Norwich, the local county town. By 12 July, Kett and his rebels had set up a camp on Mousehold Heath, a hill that overlooks Norwich.

Kett's rebellion gathers momentum

Norwich was an obvious choice for Kett and his rebels as a focus for their protest. It was the second largest city in England after London. Although Norwich itself was a rich town, about six percent of the population owned 60 percent of the land and goods. This meant that there was a sharp divide between the rich and the poor, which the rebels could exploit to gain sympathy from the townspeople. News of Kett's arrival encouraged some of the inhabitants of Norwich to throw down enclosures on the outskirts of the town. In addition, Norwich was an important administrative centre. Threatening such a vital city was a good way to guarantee the government's attention.

Kett's camp encouraged other camps to be set up, such as Downham Market (Norfolk) and Bury St Edmunds (Suffolk). The local gentry who had not gone to Windsor were overwhelmed by the sheer scale and rapidity of the rising. Unlike the Pilgrims of Grace, however, Kett's rebels did not seek to persuade the gentry to join them. In the rebels' eyes, the landowning elites were the group they were rebelling against, so the idea of inviting them to join the rebellion would have contradicted their stated aims. The size of the rebel camp at Mousehold ensured that Kett had the upper hand in his early dealings with the town officials of Norwich. Realising that they had no real alternative, the mayor and city council tried to co-operate with Kett. They helped Kett to provide for the rebel camp by organising the collection of food and supplies. This uneasy arrangement continued until 21 July, when a government messenger reached Norwich. Encouraged by this, the mayor and council started to fortify the city against the rebels. But the rebels had also been busy acquiring weaponry; they had even hauled in cannon from the coast. Before the messenger could offer a pardon to the rebels, they began to bombard Norwich, but the cannons were too far away to do any damage. On 22 July, the rebels offered the mayor a truce, but the town council refused. This provoked a successful full-scale attack on Norwich by the rebels, which led to the capture of the mayor. The rebels did not choose to remain in the city, however, preferring to withdraw to the safety of their camp at Mousehold.

ACTIVITY
KNOWLEDGE CHECK

1 In your own words, explain why you think Kett's rebellion grew so quickly.

2 Why did the rebellion pose such a threat to Somerset's government?

The government response to the rebellion

The failures of William Parr, Marquess of Northampton

At this stage, Somerset's government was in a very weak position. Norwich had been overrun and the rebels had refused a pardon. In fact, the offer of a pardon had inflamed the rebels, who saw themselves as loyal subjects of the Crown, not rebels at all. Somerset now turned to more forceful methods and sent an army under William Parr, the Marquess of Northampton. Northampton's army contained Italian mercenaries, which provoked the rebels even more, because foreigners were being used by the English government against its own people. The Marquess arrived at Norwich on 30 July. On 31 July, he declared a pardon for anyone who would surrender, but only 20 rebels took up the offer. Instead of surrendering, the rebels launched another attack on Norwich. The Marquess was forced to withdraw from the city and many of the remaining local gentry fled. Norwich was once more in the hands of the rebels and remained so for the next three weeks.

The successes of John Dudley, Earl of Warwick

Following Northampton's humiliating failure to deal with the rebels, Somerset was forced to raise a second army. The new army was placed under the command of the Earl of Warwick. Warwick's army of about 12,000 men reached Norwich on 23 August and negotiations with the rebels began. The government now offered pardons to all except Kett. The offer was angrily turned down, even though Kett himself had been prepared to meet with Warwick personally. On the night of 23 August, the rebels showed their organisation by raiding the carts carrying Warwick's weaponry. The rebels captured guns which they then used against Warwick's army.

Warwick's approach now became more hard-line. On 24 August, he entered Norwich and arrested and hanged some rebels. But the rebels continued their resistance. They used the narrow streets of Norwich to wage a form of guerrilla warfare against Warwick's troops, using tactics such as arson and ambushes. These tactics made it hard for Warwick's men to defend themselves, because they were used to fighting pitched battles on open battlefields. The arrival of 1,000 mercenaries on 26 August to provide back-up for Warwick was the event which proved the turning-point in the rebellion. Warwick succeeded in cutting off the rebels' lines of supply and this caused Kett's leadership to start to waver. Kett made the decision to move the camp from the hill at Mousehold, which had given the rebels good protection against attack. The rebels now took up a new position at Dussindale. On 27 August, Warwick made a final attempt at negotiation. The rebels were asked to give themselves up, but they refused and fired warning shots. This continued defiance was the signal for Warwick to attack. The rebels were not trained fighters and did not have the weapons or skills to defend themselves against a much more experienced royal army. Kett was captured and up to 3,000 of the rebels were killed. Kett himself was executed for treason in December 1549. Once again, it had taken the government considerable amounts of time and military might to put down rebels who were both determined and organised. The 'commotion time' and Somerset's mismanagement also led to his fall from power.

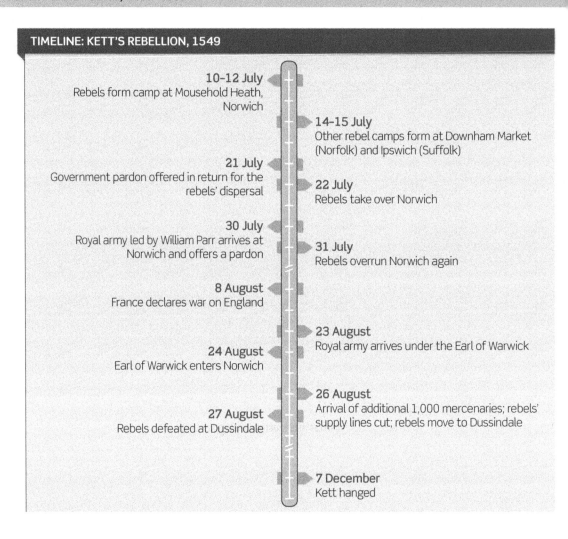

TIMELINE: KETT'S REBELLION, 1549

10–12 July
Rebels form camp at Mousehold Heath, Norwich

14–15 July
Other rebel camps form at Downham Market (Norfolk) and Ipswich (Suffolk)

21 July
Government pardon offered in return for the rebels' dispersal

22 July
Rebels take over Norwich

30 July
Royal army led by William Parr arrives at Norwich and offers a pardon

31 July
Rebels overrun Norwich again

8 August
France declares war on England

23 August
Royal army arrives under the Earl of Warwick

24 August
Earl of Warwick enters Norwich

26 August
Arrival of additional 1,000 mercenaries; rebels' supply lines cut; rebels move to Dussindale

27 August
Rebels defeated at Dussindale

7 December
Kett hanged

ACTIVITY
KNOWLEDGE CHECK

1 Create your own detailed timeline of the events of Kett's rebellion. Using different colours, highlight: successes for the rebels; successes for Somerset's government.

2 Why do you think it took so long for the government to put down Kett's rebellion?

The rebels' actions and their demands

The best sources of information about what the rebels hoped to achieve are their petition and their actions. The trigger for the rebellion was resentment over enclosure, coupled with the encouragement the rebels received from Somerset's enclosure commissions. However, the rebels' demands were also the result of the social and economic difficulties that they were facing, and longer-term resentment over the perceived corruption of the East Anglian gentry. The demands reflected the concerns of rebels who had come from all over Norfolk and Suffolk to join the camp at Mousehold.

The attacks on Flowerdew's enclosed lands at the start of the rebellion reveal the resentment felt in East Anglia. Flowerdew also represented the sort of member of the gentry whom the rebels particularly disliked. As a lawyer, Flowerdew was able to use his legal skills to gain power locally; in doing this, he had upset the established local community at Wymondham. He was also the **escheator** for Norfolk, and as such was responsible for overseeing the Crown's rights over its lands. This post gave Flowerdew, like many other local officials, the opportunity to make extra money through bribes and intimidation. Other unpopular members of the gentry who were often unpaid government officials also had their property attacked. Another lawyer, John Corbet of Sprowston, had his home vandalised. Rabbit warrens and deer parks were also targeted by the rebels. This was because these animals were considered delicacies in Tudor England and were supposed to be eaten only by gentlemen. The rebels particularly resented the abuse of their power and privileges by the local gentry. Occasionally, this resentment boiled over into physical violence. When the rebels captured Lord Sheffield in Norwich on 31 July, he was brutally beaten to death. Although the rebels were keen to maintain a form of social hierarchy, their contempt for the landed elites was clear.

The rebels were also trying to demand better local governance. Apart from a few outbreaks of violence in Norwich, Kett was careful to keep order within the rebel ranks. The rebels saw themselves as creating a new model for the government of their locality. The camp at Mousehold Heath was deliberately set up to be near the county town of Norwich. Kett adopted the system of government writs and commissions to issue orders for supplies of food and drink. The rebels also wanted to show that they could administer law and order effectively. Members of the gentry who were captured were put on trial before Kett under a tree, which the rebels called the Oak of Reformation. These actions were the rebels' attempts to show that they could run local government peacefully and effectively without the local gentry.

SOURCE

3 From Nicholas Sotherton's account of Kett's rebellion, 'The Commotion in Norfolk'. This was written in 1549. Sotherton sought to explain and justify the actions of the Norwich mayor and council in co-operating with the rebels.

They [the rebels] appointed a place of assembly among them in an oaken tree... and the Gentlemen that they took they brought to the tree of Reformation to be seen of the people to demand what they would do with them: where cried hang him and some kill him... and indeed they did press their weapons to kill some of these gentlemen.

ACTIVITY
KNOWLEDGE CHECK

1 Make a list of the rebels' aims. Which of their aims do you think was a) most important to the rebels; b) most threatening to Somerset's government?

2 Read Source 3. How valuable is Sotherton's description of the rebels' actions as evidence of their aims?

The rebels' petition
The rebels' petition is also revealing of what motivated them (see Source 4). Although anger over enclosure had sparked the rebellion, it did not dominate the rebels' complaints. This was because the most important issue for the Norfolk-based rebels was the abuse of the practice of foldcourse used by sheep farmers (see page 109). Although the rebels were encouraged by news of other enclosure riots and Somerset's enclosure commission, their anger was more directly focused on sheep farmers (articles 3, 21 and 23). Resentment over larger landlords' power and lack of respect for the rights of villagers to common land in their pursuit of profit from sheep farming is reflected in the rebels' demands. Linked to these concerns were the rebels' complaints about rises in rents (articles 2, 14, 21). Again, this was an economic complaint which also drew attention to the role of the local gentry, who were blamed for deliberately raising rents to exploit their poorer tenants and increase their own profits.

Other demands focused on the social structure and the role of the gentry in local government. The rebels wanted an end to corrupt government by local gentry. In particular, they cited the roles of escheator and **feodary** (article 12). These officials were accused of lining their own pockets at the expense of central government. The rebels were so angered by this open corruption of the system that they demanded that each officer who had upset them should pay four pence per day for the duration of the rebellion (article 29). They even demanded that local government officials should be chosen by the local people in order to ensure that someone honest was chosen. This was an extremely radical demand for the time, as officials were nominated by the king on the advice of his councillors. Similarly, article 18 of the rebel demands aimed to stop royal officials from inquiring into the lands of less wealthy landowners because this meant extra expense for the landowner. Kett's rebels were also inspired by the first great popular rising of 1381, when, according to oral tradition, the rebels had demanded that all **bondmen** should be made free. Article 16 suggests

KEY TERMS

Feodary
An official employed in the Court of Wards and Liveries, a financial court set up in 1540. The duty of the feodary was to search out potential heirs of landowners who held their land directly from the king.

Like the escheator, the role of feodary was open to bribery and corruption. Kett's rebels complained that these unpaid local officials were taking bribes from landlords to manipulate their findings so that their report would protect the interests of the landlord, but would potentially rob the Crown of income.

Bondman
A peasant (or serf) whose rights were extremely restricted and whose life was controlled by the lord of the manor.

that the rebels had both a sense of tradition and of responsibility to look after the interests of the poorest and most vulnerable in society. The demand may also reflect the practices of the local member of the nobility, Thomas Howard, Duke of Norfolk, who at this time was in prison. Norfolk had continued to use bondmen on some of his estates such as Kenninghall (Norfolk). Kett's rebels had clear views about the current corruption in the system of government, as well as the responsibility of the landowners to treat their tenants and servants well. This explains why some of their demands, such as articles 14 and 28, refer to the reign of Henry VII. The rebels were looking back to a time when they felt that government was more just. However, the rebels were not simply traditionalists who wanted government and society to revert to how they were in the past. Their demands also reflected a new, radical approach to government which was particularly dangerous for Somerset and the local gentry.

Another aspect of the rebels' demands was the state of religion and the clergy (articles 4, 8, 15, 20). Unlike the rebels in the West Country, who wanted a restoration of Catholicism, Kett's rebels were sympathetic to the Duke of Somerset's move towards Protestantism (see Chapter 1). The rebels used the new Book of Common Prayer introduced in 1549 in daily services at their camp. Several of their demands were also focused on the state of the clergy. In particular, the rebels were concerned about the education of the local clergy. They asked that any clergyman who was unable to preach properly should be removed from their position and that the local parishoners or lord should choose a more suitable replacement. These demands suggest that the rebels were particularly concerned that some clergymen did not serve their local communities well, and were either poorly educated at best or greedy and corrupt at worst.

Although many of the rebels' demands sought to change radically the role of the landed elites in government and society, they did not seek the complete overthrow of the government or to change the hierarchical structure of Tudor society. The rebels did not see themselves as traitors. They were also keen to insist that they were loyal to the king and to his government; the wording of their articles is moderate in tone. Nearly every demand started with the phrase 'we pray that…'. In addition, the rebels did not seek to destroy the nobility and gentry. Some of their articles (10, 24) were concerned with the preservation of the rights and privileges which were due to men of rank, such as the right to keep a dovecot or rabbits. However, it is also clear that the rebels resented the local gentry and wanted their role to change. Rabbit warrens were attacked because they represented the status and wealth of the gentry achieved at the expense of the commons. Rabbit warrens were a particular source of grievance because the rabbits could escape and eat local crops. What the rebels wanted was for social hierarchy to remain, but for the landed elites to play a very different role in that hierarchy where they would be prevented from exploiting the commons.

SOURCE

Selected articles from the rebels at Mousehold Heath, 1549, from F.W. Russell, *Kett's Rebellion in Norfolk*, 1859.

2. We certify your grace that whereas the lords of the manors have been charged with certain free rent, the same lords have sought means to charge the freeholders to pay the same rent, contrary to right.

3. We pray your grace that no lord of no manor shall common [enclose] upon the common.

4. We pray that priests from henceforth shall purchase no lands neither free nor bond, and the lands that they have in possession may be let to temporal men, as they were in the first year of the reign of King Henry VII.

8. We pray that priests or vicars that be not able to preach and set forth the word of God to his parishioners may be thereby put from his benefice, and the parishioners there to choose another or else patron or lord of the town.

10. We pray that no man under the degree of a knight or esquire keep a dove house, except it hath been of an old ancient custom.

12. We pray that no feodary within your shores shall be a counselor to any man in his office making, whereby the king may be truly served, so that a man being of good conscience may be yearly chosen to the same office by the commons of the same shire.

14. We pray that copyhold land that is unreasonable rented may go as it did in the first year of King Henry VII. And that at the death of a tenant, or of a sale the same lands to be charged with an easy fine as a capon [chicken] or a reasonable sum of money for a remembrance.

15. We pray that no priest shall hold no other office to any man of honour or worship, but only to be resident upon their benefices [parishes], whereby their parishioners may be instructed within the laws of God.

16. We pray that all bond men may be made free, for God made all free with his precious bloodshedding.

17. We pray that Rivers may be free and common to all men for fishing and passage.

18. We pray that no man shall be put by your Feudatory to find any office, unless he holdeth of your grace in chief, or capite above 10 by year.

20. We pray that every proprietary parson or vicar having a benefice [position in the Church] of 10 or more by year, shall either by themselves, or by some other person teach poor men's children of their parish the book called the catechism and the primer.

21. We pray that it be not lawful to the lords of any manor to purchase lands freely, [freehold lands], and to let them out again by copy or court roll to their great advancement, and to the undoing of your poor subjects.

23. We pray that no lord, knight, esquire, nor gentlemen do graze nor feed any bullocks or sheep if he may spend forty pounds a year by his lands but only for the provision of his house.

24. We pray that no man under the degree of esquire shall keep any conies [rabbits] upon any freehold or copyhold unless he pale [fence] them in so that it shall not be to the commons' annoyance.

28. We pray your grace to give license and authority by your gracious commission under your great seal to such commissioners as your poor commons have chosen, or to as many of them as your majesty and your counsel shall appoint and think meet, for to redress and reform all such good laws, statutes, proclamations and all other your proceedings; which hath been hidden by your Justices of your peace, Sheriff, Feudatories, and other your officers, from your poor commons, since the first year of the reign of your noble grandfather King Henry VII.

29. We pray that those your officers, which have offended your grace and your commons, and [are] so proved by the complaint of your poor commons, do give unto these poor men so assembled 4d. every day so long as they have remained there

SOURCE 5

From Nicholas Sotherton's 'The Commotion in Norfolk', written in 1549 from the viewpoint of the local gentry and after the suppression of the rebellion.

On the 11th of July, Sir Roger Wodehouse, Knt., taking his household servants with him and three carts, two laden with beer and a third with provisions, followed the rebels, with the view of endeavouring to dissuade them from their undertaking, imagining that they being his near neighbours would have had respect to his kindness, and have minded his persuasions; but, on the contrary, they seized him, stripped him of his apparel, took his horses and all he had from him, cruelly tugged and cast him into a ditch of one Morricc's, of Nether-Earlham, by Hellesdon Bridge, and would there have slain him, had it not been for his servant's courage, who could not, however, free him from their hands; but his life was spared, and he was carried off as a prisoner and detained in custody by the insurgents.

ACTIVITY
KNOWLEDGE CHECK

1 On your own copy of the rebel petition, highlight in different colours demands dealing with: sheep farming and enclosure; the role of the gentry; local government; religion; treatment of the poor.

2 Read Source 5 and answer the following questions:

　a) How did the rebels treat Sir Roger Wodehouse?

　b) Why might the rebels have reacted to a member of the gentry in this way?

　c) How far do you trust Sotherton's account of the rebels' actions? Explain your answer.

3 Why did the rebels' demands and actions pose such a challenge to local and national government?

The extent of the threat posed by the rebellion

The weakness of Somerset's government

Kett's rebellion was a very real threat to the government, and especially to the structure of society. The rebellion was large; the Mousehold camp was 16,000 strong, and there were other such camps across East Anglia and beyond. Government resources were already stretched by the outbreak of the Western Rising. Kett's rebellion forced Somerset to divide his forces in order to deal with extensive rebellions at opposite ends of the country. As a result, the government took longer to respond, giving Kett's rebels more time to strengthen their defences and organise themselves. When a royal army did arrive under the Marquess of Northampton, the rebels were able to see off the professional soldiers. The reason for the government's decision to send Northampton was that the local member of the nobility who should have been able to put down the rebellion was the Duke of Norfolk. Norfolk had been arrested for treason in 1546. Since then, he been in prison, and his lands had been forfeited. Norfolk's absence from the region in which he was the most important landowner created a power vacuum. The local gentry lacked leadership from a resident nobleman and the rebellion was able to gather momentum much more quickly.

The organisation of the rebels

The rebels were also well-organised and were able to sustain and supply a large camp of people for six weeks. Worryingly for Somerset's government, the local authorities began to co-operate with the rebels. Kett insisted on using the same form of writs and commissions that were used by the central government. Because the rebels appeared peaceful and well-organised, local administrators who would normally have served the government responded to the rebels' requests. For example, the churchwardens of Carlton Colville (Suffolk) collected money and sent it to the camp at Mousehold. The fact that the rebels' organisation stretched well beyond the camp at Norwich suggests that Mousehold was being seen by local officials as the new centre of administration for the region. This was a real challenge because the rebels were using the Mousehold camp to show how local government should operate, entirely without the help of the local gentry. The success of this rival form of government, run by and for the commons, showed just how resented the traditional gentry had become. The threat to social stability and hierarchy was considerable and was made worse because the rebels believed that their actions were condoned by Somerset. The gentry who were captured faced rough treatment, which suggests that the rebels' traditional respect for the authority of their social superiors was beginning to break down. Furthermore, on 8 August, France declared war on England; this put the government under an even greater strain, as the French started to besiege the English-held town of Boulogne. Kett's rebellion appeared to threaten the complete breakdown of social order, and the government was powerless to do anything about it for most of July and August of 1549.

However, the rebellion was put down and order was restored. Although the social order was severely challenged, it did not break down entirely. Although the rebels were hostile to the local gentry of East Anglia, they did not resent the fact that there was a hierarchy in Tudor society; nor did they want an end to the system of rank and status. The rebels saw themselves as loyal subjects who were merely drawing their rulers' attention to the greed and corruption of local individuals. Moreover, the rebels chose to stay in their camps; they did not march on London as the Cornish rebels did in 1497. This meant that they did not threaten the central seat of government, which would have been particularly dangerous at such of time of social and political tension. Finally, once the government sent reinforcements led by a competent military commander, the Earl of Warwick, the rebels were no match for professional soldiers in a pitched battle. However, even Warwick struggled at first to deal with the extent of the rebellion. The Earl was fortunate that Robert Kett made decisions which made the rebels more vulnerable to attack. The ferocity with which the rebellion was put down suggests that the government had been seriously shaken and was in no mood to treat the rebels mercifully.

A Level Exam-Style Question
Section B

How far do you agree that Kett's rebellion was driven by the rebels' desire for better local government? (20 marks)

Tip

What is meant by 'better local government'? Was this the most important reason for the rebellion?

ACTIVITY
KNOWLEDGE CHECK

1 Draw a grid analysing whether the following factors were evidence of Kett's rebellion threatening, or not threatening, the government: leadership of the rebellion; government weaknesses and mistakes; rebel aims and tactics; and organisation and duration of the rebellion.

2 In your overall judgement, to what extent was Kett's rebellion a threat?

WHAT WERE THE ROLES OF KETT, THE DUKE OF SOMERSET AND THE EARL OF WARWICK?

The role of Robert Kett as a leader of the 1549 rebellion

Robert Kett was a tanner – someone who worked with leather and hides – who had made enough money to buy land in the Wymondham region. Kett was from an emerging social group of artisans and yeomen farmers. Known by contemporaries as 'the middling sort', this group were often literate and were increasingly involved in local government within their own communities. Men like Kett were often held in considerable respect by their local community and could thus gather support and command obedience. Kett himself was prosperous enough to have avoided the social and economic hardships of the late 1540s. This was because he owned land, and so was in a better position to survive price increases than those who were landless or tenants. Although he was not a member of the gentry, Kett's position as a landowner also put him in a group that was the main focus of the rebels' complaints: landlords who enclosed their lands and ignored the rights of villagers to the local common land. But when Sir John Flowerdew tried to turn the rebels' anger on Kett, Kett's response was unexpected. Instead of defying the rebels, he supported them.

Kett's leadership and tactics

Kett's actions were recorded by Nicholas Sotherton (Source 7), a member of the group of families who governed Norwich. Sotherton wrote an account of the rebellion which attempted to explain away the actions of the mayor and council of Norwich in co-operating with the rebels. Although Sotherton's view was always pro-gentry and anti-rebellion, his description of Kett's actions when confronted by the angry mob still gives a clear sense of Kett's role as leader of the rebellion. Kett agreed with the rebels that he had enclosed the common lands illegally and volunteered to destroy his fences himself. But Kett was prepared to go even further than this. Like Robert Aske, the leader of the Pilgrimage of Grace, Kett seems to have been an idealist with a strong sense of social justice. Kett sided with the rebels against the local landowners. He promised to stay with the rebels until they had achieved their aims and he attacked the greed of the gentry. His position within the local community meant that the rebels were prepared to listen to him and accept his leadership. Regardless of whether Kett made the exact speech which Sotherton put in his mouth, he was clearly a charismatic leader. Kett was able to persuade the rebels to follow him and was soon the leader of an army that was about 16,000 strong. He would not have been able to achieve this without considerable skills of persuasion and organisation. Even when government armies arrived, Kett's rebels stayed loyal to him, trusting that his leadership would be enough to protect them.

Kett's leadership was also important because of the way in which he organised and ran the rebellion. Kett insisted on good order within the rebel camp and that the rebels should take the moral high ground by behaving peacefully. His orders were mostly obeyed; the outbreaks of physical violence that did occur were usually the result of provocation by the government, such as the arrival of the Marquess of Northampton with an army. Kett set up a court of justice where captured members of the gentry were put on trial. This court was based at Mousehold, under a tree known as the Oak of Reformation. Kett, with representatives from local communities drawn from across Norfolk, passed judgement on those brought before him. Members of the gentry were imprisoned on the orders of this court. Kett's aim was to show the central government that local government could be run effectively and fairly. This was a clever tactic, as it was designed to cause the gentry as much embarrassment as possible by highlighting their mismanagement of local affairs. Kett's use of writs and commissions probably helped to persuade other local communities and officials to co-operate. If the rebels had demanded food and supplies using violence and threats, they would have lost the moral high ground and the sympathies of those with the power to help them. Kett was also adamant that he was not a rebel. When the government offered a pardon to the rebels, Kett refused because, he argued, he was not a rebel in the first place and so did not need a pardon.

SOURCE
6

Kett giving justice at the Oak of Reformation. This is an 18th-century depiction of Kett and his rebellion, which lived in popular memory long after it ended.

How did Kett's mistakes lead to the defeat of the rebellion?

However, Kett was not a military man, and lacked the tactical awareness to deal with a well-trained army under the leadership of an experienced military campaigner, the Earl of Warwick. The rebels were able to defeat Northampton because he underestimated them and delayed dealing with them while he was entertained by the mayor and council of Norwich. Northampton also chose to remain in Norwich itself, while the rebels had a strong defensive position overlooking the city. These circumstances meant that when Kett ordered an attack on Norwich, the rebels had the upper hand in the fighting that took place in the city streets. Warwick was a different proposition, however. By cutting off the rebels' supply lines, he forced Kett to make a difficult choice. Without supplies, the rebel camp could not survive. At this stage, Kett seems to have panicked. Sotherton claims that Kett started to listen to prophecies that the rebels would be victorious at Dussindale, a village just outside Norwich. It is not clear whether Kett believed these prophecies or was simply uncertain what to do to deal with the threat from Warwick's army. Nevertheless, he gave the order for the rebel camp to be disbanded and for the army to march to Dussindale, where new defences were hastily erected. This decision by Kett

proved to be a tactical disaster. On the hill at Mousehold, the rebels had been well-protected from attack, especially by cavalry. Dussindale was flat and did not have this protection. It was easy for Warwick to use his trained cavalry against the untrained rebels. Sotherton claims that Kett tried to flee and was captured. The Battle of Dussindale put an end to Kett's rebellion. Although the rebellion was almost certainly doomed from the moment that Warwick started to gain the upper hand, Kett's decision to move to Dussindale hastened the end of the rebellion, and perhaps made its final battle bloodier.

ACTIVITY
KNOWLEDGE CHECK

Discuss with a partner:

1 Why was Kett's leadership so important in the 1549 rebellion?

2 To what extent were Kett's mistakes responsible for the failure of the rebellion?

SOURCE
7

From Nicholas Sotherton's 'The Commotion in Norfolk', written in 1549 from the viewpoint of the local gentry and after the suppression of the rebellion. Sotherton is describing how Kett reacted to the attempts to throw down his own enclosures.

Kett easily allowed himself to be won over [by the rebels]... and told them he would not only grant their request, but would stand by them to restrain and put down wholly the power of the nobility and gentry. He hoped... he should shortly be able to bring about such a change that, as they had felt deeply their own misery, so those wretches should have equal occasion to feel deeply the bitter consequences of their pride and haughtiness. He set forth the many shameful things they had for some time past been called on to suffer... 'But be of good courage,' continued he, 'for power so excessive, avarice so great, and cruelty of every kind so unheard of, cannot but be hateful and accursed in the sight both of God and man. Through the covetousness of the gentry the State has suffered grievous injury; while we, by the loss of the commons, have in like manner been wronged; but we will demand... that our wrongs be righted. As regards the field I have enclosed, I will make it common for all men; and not only so, but will make it common with my own hands... if any measure is for your advantage, rest assured I will ever second it to the utmost of my power, not as your companion, but as your general, your standard-bearer, and your chief: in a word, I will not only be present at your councils, but henceforth will preside at them.'

Inflamed by his words, they surrounded him on all sides, and with many shouts testified the joy they felt at having gained so great an acquisition to their cause. They then spread themselves over the field before mentioned, and in accordance with their original design, filled up the ditches and laid it open. When they had done this, they seem to have felt that they had made a good beginning; that now the power of the oppressor would cease, and freedom henceforth be their portion; and, urged on partly by their own daring and present success, and partly by the exhortations of their leader, as Kett now was, whose words acted like fire on their inflammable tempers, they looked upon disturbing the peace as a small matter, and became eager to produce such a change in the government of the country as might be beneficial to themselves.

ACTIVITY
KNOWLEDGE CHECK

1 Why do you think that people such as the artist of Source 6 would continue to commemorate Kett's rebellion 200 years later?

2 Read Source 7 and complete the following exercises:

   a) On your own copy of the source, highlight words or phrases which suggest why Kett emerged as the leader of the rebellion and his leadership style.

   b) What evidence is there in the source that Kett and the rebels had been influenced by the ideas and actions of Somerset and his advisers?

   c) Sotherton was intending to portray the rebels as a real threat to social order. Does this mean that we should distrust his account of Kett's actions?

A Level Exam-Style Question Section A

Study Source 7 before answering this question.

Assess the value of Source 7 for revealing the significance of Robert Kett's role as a leader of the rebellion and the rebels' approaches to local government in 1549.

Explain your answer, using the source, the information given about its origin and your own knowledge about the historical context. (20 marks)

Tip
Consider how the author of this source might affect its value as evidence of Kett's leadership.

SOURCE
8

A portrait of Edward Seymour, Duke of Somerset, by Hans Holbein the Younger, painted before his rise to power in 1547.

The Duke of Somerset's response to the rebellion

Somerset's style of government

Somerset's style of rule was dictatorial. He tended to bypass the Council and relied on a group of his own friends and advisers, such as William Paget, to make policy decisions. Somerset was also careful to control access to the young king. The Protector's power rested on the co-operation of his supporters and his ability to control Edward VI; when these were severely shaken as a result of his handling of the 1549 risings, he fell from power. Somerset's own policies played a key role in creating the atmosphere for rebellion and encouraging Kett's rebels to think that they had the government's support. The Duke liked to portray himself as a friend of the commons, and especially the poor. His anti-enclosure policy had led to the commissions of 1548 (see pages 112–113). He even set up a special court at his own house where the poor could seek justice, though this was another example of Somerset's disregard for the usual systems of Tudor government. The result of Somerset's actions was to send the message to the rebels that he was on their side; at the same time, his actions also alienated other members of the landed elites whose support he needed, such as the Earl of Warwick.

Somerset's negotiations with the rebels

Somerset's response to Kett's rebellion made the situation worse. When the Duke was eventually brought down by his enemies at Court, he was accused of endangering the social and political order of England by negotiating with the rebels and offering them concessions. The work of historian Ethan Shagan has shown that these accusations had basis in fact. A series of letters between Somerset and the various rebel camps survive which suggest that Somerset's actions in the summer of 1549 gave further encouragement to the rebels. Although the letters emphasised the importance of the existing social order and obedience to those of a higher rank, Somerset made promises to the rebels which showed that he was sympathetic to their complaints. For example, when Kett's rebels sent their list of demands to the government, Somerset replied saying of the demands, 'indeed we will not dissemble [deceive] with you, we see for them for the most part founded upon great and just causes.' Somerset's actions further encouraged the rebels because the new enclosure commissions reissued in 1549 continued their work throughout the summer. The fact that commissioners appointed by the Protector were busy inquiring into and taking action against one of the main causes of resentment sent a message that the government was supporting them against the landlords. Finally, Somerset inflamed the situation still further by promising the rebels that the parliament that was due to meet on 4 November would be moved forward a month to 4 October. Somerset's intention in moving the parliamentary session forward was that the rebel complaints could be discussed more quickly. In fact, the rebellion was put down before this could happen, but in the short term, Somerset's offer only encouraged the rebels even more.

How did Somerset make Kett's rebellion worse?

Somerset made the situation even worse in the summer of 1549 because he was giving mixed messages to Kett's rebels. On the one hand, he appeared to be encouraging them in their rebellion, but on the other hand, he was also trying to bring the rebellion to an end. Somerset first offered a pardon. Because Kett and his followers did not see themselves as rebels, but as men who were acting in line with Somerset's own policies, this offer was rejected. Somerset then had to resort to force. He was unfortunate in that the Marquess of Northampton bungled the first attempt at dealing with the rebellion, and that this gave the rebels even more time to organise themselves. These events led the rebels to believe that Somerset had betrayed them and only hardened their determination to resist. The eventual violent end to the rebellion was a result of Somerset's mishandling of the overall situation. He had first seemed to encourage the rebels and then he tried to disperse them by force. His intentions were honourable and were based on his strong Protestant faith, but the results were disastrous, both for the rebels and for his own political position. Somerset's bungling led to his downfall in October 1549. The Council resented Somerset's power and blamed him for the serious social and political crises that had threatened England. They had him arrested and removed from his position as Protector. He was eventually replaced in this position by the man who had put down Kett's rebellion, the Earl of Warwick.

SOURCE

9 From a letter written by William Paget to the Duke of Somerset on 7 July 1549. Paget was one of Somerset's closest advisers, but in this letter he warns Somerset of the dangers of his social and religious policies.

I told your Grace the truth, and was not believed; well, now your Grace sees it. What says your Grace? Marry, the King's subjects out of discipline, out of obedience, caring neither for Protector nor King, and much less for many other mean [lesser] officer. And what is the cause? Your own levity, your softness, your opinion to be good to the poor. I know, I say, your good meaning and honest nature... society in a realm does consist and is maintained by means of religion and law... Look well whether you have either law or religion at home, and I fear you shall find neither... Now, Sir, for the law: where is it used in England at liberty? Almost nowhere. The foot taketh upon him the part of the head, and commons is become a king... I know in this matter of the commons every man of the Council has misliked your proceedings, and wished it otherwise.

ACTIVITY
KNOWLEDGE CHECK

Read Source 9 and answer the following questions.

1 What does the source reveal about Paget's attitude to Somerset's style of government?

2 Why was Paget so concerned about the effects of Somerset's policies?

3 From what you know of Somerset's beliefs and actions, was Paget correct in his criticisms of Somerset's rule?

The Earl of Warwick's role in suppressing the rebellion

EXTEND YOUR KNOWLEDGE

John Dudley, Earl of Warwick
John Dudley was an experienced military commander. He had been admiral of the king's navy and had served in Henry VIII's wars with Scotland and France in 1544. Dudley was capable of great ruthlessness both on the battlefield and in politics. He had been promoted to the title of Earl of Warwick in 1547 as reward for supporting Somerset's bid to become Protector. In 1549, however, Warwick turned on Somerset and was instrumental in removing him from power. Warwick then went on to replace Somerset as Edward's Protector for the rest of the reign. He made himself Duke of Northumberland in 1551.

Warwick's actions were quite cautious in the early stages of the rebellion. A ruthless politician, he had probably realised that the rebellions would pose a real challenge to Somerset's leadership and might even lead to his fall. Warwick's actions were dictated by the fact that he had been a political ally of Somerset, but with the possibility of Somerset falling from power, he was concerned to secure his own position at Court. He did not want to be brought down if Somerset fell. In addition, Warwick had been one of the targets of Hales' enclosure commission in 1548; the Earl had no reason to support Somerset, although, like all members of the landed elites, he was concerned about the threat to his property posed by the rebellions. As a result of these circumstances, Warwick's attitude to the rebellion was ambivalent. He did not want the rebels to succeed, but he had no desire to prop up Somerset's position as Protector.

Warwick's initial failures
Despite his mixed loyalties, Warwick was a good choice to lead the army. Initially, he was appointed to lead the royal army against the rebellion in the South West, but news of Kett's rebellion led to a change of plan and Warwick was sent to East Anglia instead. Warwick was a particularly good

choice to deal with Kett's rebels. The manor of Wymondham, where the trouble in Norfolk had first broken out, belonged to the Earl. Robert Kett was even one of Warwick's tenants. Warwick's eventual role in dealing with the rebellions of 1549 was very similar to the repressive role played by the Duke of Norfolk in 1537. Following the failure of the Marquess of Northampton in July 1549, Warwick was sent at the head of the new royal army. Warwick's army contained a contingent of German mercenaries who had been persuaded to fight with the offer of a month's pay for one day's work. When the rebels saw the royal army coming, there was considerable panic. However, Warwick was prepared to negotiate; he offered a pardon to all but Kett. The rebels were reluctant to accept this, but they were prepared to welcome Warwick's messengers into their camp in an attempt to find a peaceful settlement. Unfortunately for both sides, there was an incident between the rebels and Warwick's troops which resulted in a young rebel boy being shot and killed – this hardened attitudes on both sides. Although Kett was still prepared to trust Warwick and negotiate with him, he was dissuaded from doing so by other rebels, who feared Warwick's intentions towards them.

Why was Warwick able eventually to defeat the rebels?

Following the failure of this initial meeting, Warwick took action. He ordered that the gates of Norwich should be opened. When the rebels inside refused, he ordered his army to open fire on the main gate. The strength of Warwick's army was such that they were able to break through the city defences. The Earl and his men were able to overrun the city, capturing and executing some rebels on the spot. However, Warwick's success was not decisive and he had put himself and his men in a dangerous position. Like Northampton, Warwick was not a native of Norwich and did not know the layout of the streets. This allowed the rebels, who had local knowledge, to launch a counter-attack during which some of Warwick's ammunition was captured. However, despite fierce attacks by the rebels, which left much of the city on fire, Warwick and his troops were able to resist. The Earl even ordered that his men should take an oath which bound them to remain in the city until they had defeated the rebels or died in the attempt.

Warwick's leadership was helped by the arrival of additional Swiss mercenaries and by the gradual reduction of the rebels' supply lines, which made them increasingly desperate and which made Kett make the rash decision to leave Mousehold Heath for Dussindale on 26 August. Warwick then took advantage of the fact that the rebels now had to make new defences at Dussindale. He decided to attack the following day (27 August). Following a final offer of pardon to the rebels, which was refused, Norfolk's men charged. This caused the front line of the rebels, including Kett, to scatter and try to flee. The remaining rebels picked up the weapons that the front line had thrown away and tried to carry on fighting. Warwick was so impressed by their courage that he offered another pardon, which he had to confirm in person before the rebels would stop. Up to 3,000 rebels were killed at Dussindale by Warwick's army; it is estimated that Warwick lost about 40 men. Warwick had managed to turn a potentially difficult and dangerous situation to his advantage and he had succeeded in suppressing the rebellion where Northampton had failed.

ACTIVITY
KNOWLEDGE CHECK

Why do you think Northumberland was able to put down Kett's rebellion when the Marquess of Northampton had failed to do so?

The extent of repression

Like the Pilgrimage of Grace, Kett's rebellion was put down with considerable force, though government retribution was immediate in 1549, where it had been delayed in 1536. Warwick was prepared to hang 49 rebels captured in Norwich on sight. Up to 3,000 rebels were also killed at Dussindale. The following day, Warwick ordered nine rebels to be hung, drawn and quartered at the Oak of Reformation in a symbolic act of revenge. As a deterrent, the heads of these men were displayed on the city walls of Norwich, while their bodies were sent to local communities which had been involved in the rebellion. The severest punishment was reserved for the rebel leader, Robert Kett. He was taken to Newgate jail in London; on the way, he was paraded through the streets of the capital city. Kett was found guilty of treason and was sentenced to be hung, drawn and quartered in London. However, the government then changed its mind. He was sent back to Norfolk instead, where his death could be witnessed by the local communities who had supported him, as a deterrent to further rebellion. Kett was hanged in chains from the walls of Norwich Castle, and his body left to rot. The government suppression of the revolt was severe; there was no more trouble in East Anglia.

However, the government did not seek to end the rebellion solely by repression. There were repeated attempts to get the rebels to disperse peacefully by offering them pardons. These government attempts at a peaceful solution were possibly partly inspired by the Duke of Norfolk's successes in 1536 in persuading a very large group of rebels to go home without a fight. Somerset and the rebels both seemed to be aware of these tactics, and the betrayal of the promise of pardon by Henry in 1537. In his correspondence to the rebels, Somerset had to reassure the rebels that the pardon was genuine and would not be retracted at a later date. Similarly, once the initial blood letting was over, Warwick himself restrained the local gentry from taking further revenge. On 29 August, a church service was held in Norwich in which Warwick himself spoke, giving thanks to God for an end to the rebellion. Furthermore, although Kett's rebellion was put down forcibly, other rebel camps which had been set up in East Anglia were dissolved by the armies of Northampton and Warwick without the need for violence. The government also used propaganda to persuade the rebels that to rise up in revolt was against the laws of God and England. In particular, prominent clergymen such as Thomas Cranmer, Archbishop of Canterbury, preached against rebellion and the ideas encouraged by those who believed in a Godly commonwealth (Source 10). It was the scale, organisation and leadership of the rebels at Mousehold Heath that led to the severity of the eventual government response against it. Even then, violence tended to be a last resort; Somerset's government did not have the men or resources to approach the rebellion in any other way.

SOURCE 10

Thomas Cranmer's sermon against rebellion, given at St Paul's, London, 21 July 1549.

It is reported that there be many among these unlawful assemblies that pretend knowledge of the gospel, and will needs be called gospellers; as though the gospel were the cause of disobedience, sedition, and carnal liberality, and the destruction of policies, kingdoms, and commonweals, where it is received. But if they will be true gospellers, let them be obedient, meek, patient in adversity and long suffering, and in no wise rebel against the laws and magistrates.

ACTIVITY
KNOWLEDGE CHECK

Read Source 10. What was Cranmer's view of rebellion? Why might he hold these views? How effective do you think his sermon was likely to be? Explain your answer.

A Level Exam-Style Question Section B

How far were the growing social and economic problems of the 1540s responsible for the outbreak of Kett's rebellion in 1549?

How far do you agree with this statement? (20 marks)

Tip

Think about the extent to which social and economic problems were the root cause of the rebellion. What role did Somerset's policies play in encouraging social unrest?

 EXTRACT 1

From the *Encyclopedia Britannica's* article on the Peasant's Revolt of 1381.

The Peasants' Revolt of 1381 is one of the most dramatic events of English history. What began as a local revolt in Essex quickly spread across much of the South East of England, while some of the peasants took their grievances direct to the young King, Richard II, in London.

SOURCE 11

From *The Vision of Piers Plowman*, by William Langland, a 14th-century English poet. The poem includes accounts of the growing disparities within society.

The needy are our neighbours, if we note rightly;

As prisoners in cells, or poor folk in hovels,

Charged with children and overcharged by landlords.

What they may spare in spinning they spend on rental,

On milk, or on meal to make porridge

To still the sobbing of the children at meal time.

Also they themselves suffer much hunger.

 SOURCE 12

John Ball's sermon at Blackheath. Ball was a priest and one of the leaders of the rebellion. This is a speech John Ball is believed to have delivered to the rebels in 1381.

When Adam delved and Eve span, Who was then the gentleman? From the beginning all men by nature were created alike, and our bondage or servitude came in by the unjust oppression of naughty men. For if God would have had any bondmen from the beginning, he would have appointed who should be bond, and who free. And therefore I exhort you to consider that now the time is come, appointed to us by God, in which ye may... cast off the yoke of bondage, and recover liberty.

 SOURCE 13

From the *Anonimalle Chronicle*, a 14th-century English chronicle, cited in C. Oman, *The Great Revolt of 1381*. Wat Tyler was another leader of the 1381 rebellion. He may have earned his living as a roof tiler.

Wat Tyler of Maidstone came to the King with great confidence, mounted on a little horse, that the commons might see him... And when he had dismounted he half bent his knee, and then took the King by the hand, and shook his arm forcibly and roughly, saying to him, 'Brother, be of good comfort and joyful, for you shall have, in the fortnight that is to come, praise from the commons even more than you have yet had, and we shall be good companions.' And the King said to Walter, 'Why will you not go back to your own country?' But the other answered, with a great oath, that neither he nor his fellows would depart until they had got their charter such as they wished to have it. And he demanded that there should be no more villeins [serfs] in England, and no serfdom..., but that all men should be free and of one condition.

THINKING HISTORICALLY   Cause and consequence (6c)

Connections

Extract 1 and Sources 11–13 demonstrate some typical aspects of medieval ideas about rebellion, from the first popular revolt in 1381.

1 Read Extract 1. How might this be seen as similar to the actions of Kett's rebels?

Read Source 11.

2 What did Kett's rebels believe about the state of English society and the economy?

3 How is this similar to Langland's claims about 14th-century England?

Look at Sources 12 and 13.

4 What did Kett's rebels copy from the rebellion of 1381?

5 Make a list of other similarities between the rebellion of 1381 and Tudor popular revolts. How did their understanding of Wat Tyler's rebellion affect the attitudes and actions of Tudor rebels?

6 Why is it important for historians to see these links across time and be able to explain how causal factors can influence situations much later in time?

EXTRACT

2 From John Guy, *Tudor England* (1988).

The 1549 revolts were the closest thing Tudor England saw to a class war. No single cause was responsible: agrarian, fiscal, religious, and social grievances fused... The East Anglian revolt was of the 'camping' variety... Their leaders were just outside the magisterial orbit: Kett was a yeoman freeholder... Although their articles emphasised their antagonism to the governing class, they wanted 'alternative government', not mob rule. They sought to exclude the gentry... from their world...

EXTRACT

3 From M. L. Bush, *The Government Policy of Protector Somerset* (1975).

The bulk of the stirs tended to embarrass the government by seeking to implement rather than resist its policy... If anything the aim was to aid the government against the aristocracy...

EXTRACT

4 From D. MacCulloch and A. Fletcher, *Tudor Rebellions*, 5th edition (2008).

Social tension was undoubtedly very strong in Norwich at the time of the rebellion. The city's marked inequality of wealth made it vulnerable to class antagonism when times seemed bad. About 6 per cent of the population owned approximately 60 percent of the lands and goods. By the 1540s the worsted industry was in decline and some craftsmen were emigrating... The instability of Norwich society at a time of economic readjustment helps to explain the ease with which Kett took control of the city.

THINKING HISTORICALLY Change (8a, b & c) (II)

Judgements about change

If two professionals were asked to track a patient's health over time, one might approach this task by measuring heart rate, weight and cholesterol, while the other professional might assess the patient's mental well-being, relationships and ability to achieve their goals. Both are valid approaches, but result in different reports. What is true in this medical case is true in historical cases. Measuring change in something requires: (a) a concept of what that something is (e.g. What is 'health'? What is an 'economy'?); (b) judgements about how this thing should be measured; and (c) judgements about what relevant 'markers of change' are (how we distinguish a change from a temporary and insignificant fluctuation).

Historians have differed in their emphases on the impact that social and economic change had on the structure of Tudor society, and the extent to which these changes caused a breakdown in the traditional hierarchy. This has led them to interpret the threat posed by Kett's rebellion in different ways.

Look at Extracts 2–4 about Kett's rebellion above and answer the following questions:

1 Do all three accounts agree that Kett's rebellion represented a breakdown in Tudor social hierarchy?

2 Do all three accounts agree in the chronology of change? (Do they see it happening in the same time periods and at the same pace?)

3 Do all three accounts agree in characterising change as (a) rapid, (b) dramatic and (c) impacting society as a whole?

4 Do the historians all think of the social and economic change in the same way (for example, do they all focus on the national situation or on local variations)?

5 Generalising from these examples, to what extent do historians' judgements about change depend on what historians decide to look at and how they decide to measure change?

ACTIVITY
SUMMARY

Below is a set of causes and events related to Kett's rebellion. Make your own copy of these cards and complete the activities below.

Sir John Flowerdew and Robert Kett were local rivals.	The practice of enclosure had been criticised by commonwealth-men such as John Hales.	The Duke of Somerset passed a private Act of parliament protecting his own copy-holders.
The Duke of Somerset was sympathetic to the ideas of the commonwealth-men.	There had been bad harvests in 1545 and 1549.	Debasement of the coinage had led to inflation.
John Hales introduced several parliamentary bills which aimed to deal with enclosure.	Sir John Flowerdew was a member of the local gentry who had upset the people of Wymondham with his enclosures.	In July 1549, Somerset ordered the enclosure commissions to investigate and prosecute cases of illegal enclosure.
Prices of staple goods rose rapidly in the 1540s.	Sheep farming was a very profitable source of income in the 1540s.	Landlords reacted to inflation by increasing rents and enclosing land.
There were enclosure riots in 1548 and the spring of 1549 across the Midlands and South East.	Somerset wrote to the rebels offering them concessions.	The Marquis of Northampton was unable to suppress the rebellion.
The rebels set up their own system of local government with which local authorities co-operated.	The rebels resented the power and greed of the gentry landlords.	The rebels thought that the government was on their side.
The imprisonment of the Duke of Norfolk created a power vacuum in East Anglia.	The local gentry were unable to deal with the rebellion; many fled and some were captured.	About 3,000 rebels were killed at the Battle of Dussindale.

1 Arrange these cards to show (not all cards will be relevant):

   a) the causes of Kett's rebellion: long-term, short-term and the trigger

   b) why the rebellion was such a threat to the Tudor government.

2 Now use the cards to help you create a plan for the following question: 'How far do you agree that Kett's rebellion represented a serious threat to the stability of the Tudor government in 1549?'

WIDER READING

Heard, N. and Turvey, R. 'Change and Protest,1536–88: Mid-Tudor Crises?' *Access to History* (2009)

Ross, J. 'Was Lord Protector Somerset ("The Champion for the Commonwealth") Responsible for Kett's Rebellion?' *History Today* (2011)

Shagan, E.H. *Popular Politics and the English Reformation*, Cambridge (2003)

3.6

Queen takes queen? The Revolt of the Northern Earls, 1569–70

KEY QUESTIONS

- To what extent was the arrival of Mary, Queen of Scots the main reason for the Northern Rising?
- How serious was the threat posed by the Revolt of the Northern Earls to Elizabeth I?
- Why did the rising fail and what were the results of this failure?

INTRODUCTION

In 1569, a revolt broke out against Elizabeth's rule in the North of England. The rebellion was potentially very serious for Elizabeth because it was led by two members of the traditional northern nobility, the Earls of Northumberland and Westmorland. The Northern Rising had both political and religious dimensions, which made it particularly serious for Elizabeth. The arrival of Mary, Queen of Scots, a rival Catholic claimant to the throne, united those in the North who were alienated from Elizabeth's government. Eventually, the rising was put down with considerable force, but its events were to have longer-term consequences for both Protestants and Catholics for the rest of Elizabeth's reign.

TO WHAT EXTENT WAS THE ARRIVAL OF MARY, QUEEN OF SCOTS THE MAIN REASON FOR THE NORTHERN RISING?

Why did Mary, Queen of Scots pose a problem for Elizabeth?

Mary, Queen of Scots posed a double threat to Elizabeth. Mary had a legitimate claim to be Queen of England. She was also Catholic and was a potential figurehead for those Catholics in England and abroad who wanted to see the end of Protestant rule in England.

Mary was born in 1542 and was the only surviving child of James V of Scotland, who died in the same year. Mary's claim to the English throne came from her grandmother, Margaret Tudor. Margaret was the daughter of Henry VII, and she had been married to James IV of Scotland (see Chapter 3). Mary's Tudor blood meant that she and Elizabeth were cousins; Mary's children would have a claim to both the English and Scottish thrones. Mary's claim to be Queen of England was strengthened because there was no doubt about her legitimacy. Mary had been born in wedlock, while Elizabeth was the daughter of Henry VIII and his

| 1559 – Elizabeth introduces her religious settlement | 1566 – Birth of James VI of Scotland | 1568 – Mary, Queen of Scots flees to England | 1570 – Publication of papal bull *Regnans in Excelsis* that excommunicates Elizabeth I |

1560   **1565**   **1570**

| 1561 – Mary, Queen of Scots returns to Scotland | 1567 – Arrival of Spanish troops to suppress Dutch Revolt | 1569 – November–December: Revolt of the Northern Earls |

second wife, Anne Boleyn. Some, especially good Catholics, considered Elizabeth to be illegitimate because they believed Henry's marriage to Anne Boleyn was not valid. This was also a view that was held by Elizabeth's potential foreign enemies. France and Spain were both Catholic countries who might be persuaded to support a challenge to remove the Protestant Elizabeth from the throne. One of the biggest concerns for Elizabeth was the possibility of a Catholic crusade, led by a coalition of powerful foreign rulers and backed by the pope, the aim of which would be to replace Elizabeth with Mary. Although the political situation in Europe was favourable to Elizabeth's position for much of the early 1560s, this began to change later in the decade.

The international context of the threat posed by Mary

Mary, Queen of Scots began to pose a real threat to Elizabeth's position as queen from the mid-1560s, and this threat developed rapidly in 1568–69. Mary had spent her youth in France. This was because there had been repeated attempts by the English to capture her and she was removed to France (her mother's country) for safety. Mary was brought up at the French court and eventually married the heir to the French throne. Mary's continuing connection with France actually enhanced Elizabeth's security. This was because France's great rival, Spain, would not support a French candidate to be queen of England. If Mary, supported by France, became queen of England as well, it would give the French too much power. In addition, if Mary were to become queen of England, the French would be able to control the English Channel, which would prevent the Spanish King Philip II reaching the lands he controlled in the Netherlands. As long as Mary was associated with France, Philip would continue to support Elizabeth as queen, even though she was Protestant and he was Catholic. For Philip, this was a better option than allowing French power to increase.

SOURCE

1

A 16th-century portrait of Mary, Queen of Scots.

1572 – Massacre of St Bartholemew's Eve; execution of the Dukes of Norfolk and Northumberland

1584 – Assassination of William of Orange

1587 – Execution of Mary, Queen of Scots

1575   1580   1585   1590

1580 – Philip II annexes Portugal

1585 – England goes to war with Spain

1588 – Spanish Armada

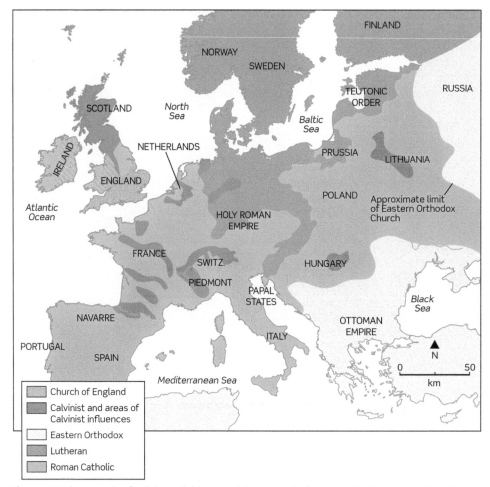

Figure 6.1 The growth of religious divisions and the spread of more radical Protestantism (known as Calvinism) in Europe.

Guise family

The House of Guise was the most powerful family in France and was a key supporter of the Catholic faith. Mary's mother was a member of the Guise family. This meant that Mary, Queen of Scots was related to French Catholic nobility. Mary's cousin, Henry, Duke of Guise (1550–88), founded the French Catholic League to try to prevent the spread of Protestantism in France. Mary's connection with the Guise, made her even more of a threat to the Protestant Elizabeth.

After Mary's French husband died in 1560, she returned to Scotland and began to rule as queen in her own right. Even though she was no longer in France, Mary's links with that country were still strong because she was related to the most powerful nobles in France, the **Guise family**. This meant that Philip II would continue to back Elizabeth to counterbalance the Franco-Scottish alliance. By 1565–66, however, Mary's rule in Scotland had gone disastrously wrong and she was faced with a Protestant noble revolt in Scotland. By 1567, Mary was imprisoned in one of her own castles, Loch Leven. She was then forced to abdicate in favour of her young son, James. In 1568, Mary managed to escape from Scotland. She arrived in England in May 1568.

EXTEND YOUR KNOWLEDGE

Mary, Queen of Scots and the Scottish nobility

Mary, Queen of Scots found herself in a difficult position on her return to Scotland. She had been brought up a Catholic, but when she returned to Scotland, she found that many of the Scottish nobility were Protestant. At first, Mary was prepared to tolerate Protestantism in Scotland. She worked with her illegitimate half-brother, the Earl of Moray, who was Protestant, and the majority of her councillors were also Protestant.

However, relations with the Scottish nobility started to unravel when Mary chose to marry her first cousin, Henry, Lord Darnley. Darnley also had a claim to the English throne, so any children of this marriage would have a right to rule both England and Scotland. Mary's marriage to Darnley caused the Protestant nobility, led by the Earl of Moray, to revolt. The marriage also went badly. Despite the birth of a son and heir, James, in 1566, Darnley and Mary quarrelled continually. In 1567, Darnley's body was found in the ruins of his house, which had been blown up. He had been strangled. Mary herself came under suspicion, as did another member of the Scottish nobility, the Earl of Bothwell. Mary did not help her situation by eloping with Bothwell. However, she still had some Catholic supporters in Scotland who helped her to escape in 1568.

1 In your own words, explain why you think Mary posed a threat to Elizabeth.

2 Imagine that you are one of Elizabeth's councillors: how would you advise Elizabeth to deal with the threat from Mary? Explain why you would give this advice.

Court politics and faction

The deterioration of relations with Spain

The Northern Rising in 1569 had its roots in the development of tensions at Court between rival groups of Elizabeth's nobility. Elizabeth I herself was reliant on the advice of her most trusted councillor, William Cecil. Cecil and Elizabeth had worked together since her accession to the throne in 1558 to create a moderate religious settlement which aimed to keep both Protestants and Catholics happy. However, some members of the nobility at Court resented Cecil's influence with the queen. This was because Elizabeth, advised by Cecil, seemed to be leading the country into a war with Catholic Spain. By 1568, Anglo-Spanish relations were starting to deteriorate. A Protestant-led rebellion had broken out against Spanish rule in the Netherlands, but this had been put down with considerable brutality by the Spanish in 1567–68. This put Philip II of Spain in a stronger position, and the presence of Spanish forces in the Netherlands, just across the Channel from England, created fears in England of a possible invasion. The situation was made worse in December 1568, when four Spanish ships carrying bullion (gold and silver) to pay the Spanish troops in the Netherlands took refuge from pirates in England. Cecil ordered that the bullion should be seized. This cut off the Spanish army's pay and the Spanish government reacted angrily. By the end of 1568, it looked like England was about to be dragged into a war with Spain, a much larger and more powerful country. Cecil's policy was blamed for this, and a Court plot emerged to try to remove him from power.

Philip II and the Netherlands

The Netherlands was under the control of the kings of Spain. Before Philip II came to the Spanish throne in 1556, the Netherlands had been allowed considerable autonomy by Spain, but this began to change as Philip tried to impose more direct Spanish rule. In the 1560s, tension began to mount between the Dutch and their Spanish rulers. The tensions were not helped by the fact that Protestantism had spread to the Netherlands. In 1566, riots broke out against Spanish rule, led by Protestants. In 1567, Philip II sent an army of 10,000 men to suppress the revolt. Initially, he was successful, and by 1568, the rising had been suppressed. However, more trouble broke out in 1572 and was to continue for the rest of the 16th century.

The Dutch revolt caused problems for Elizabeth. England needed Protestant allies; it would not be in Elizabeth's best interests to allow the Dutch to be defeated. Furthermore, the Netherlands was an important export market for English wool and cloth. Finally, the presence of a large Spanish Catholic army just across the English Channel was a cause for concern for Protestant England.

The Court plot against William Cecil

The Court nobles who became involved in the plan to remove Cecil did not intend to remove Elizabeth from power. They saw themselves as loyal subjects of the queen who were concerned by the influence that Cecil had over her. The men involved in the attempt to get rid of Cecil included Thomas Howard, Duke of Norfolk, and two members of the northern nobility who had their own personal grudges against Elizabeth and Cecil, the Earls of Northumberland and Westmorland. Northumberland and Westmorland were both Catholic, while the Duke of Norfolk was nominally Protestant, but was suspected of having secret Catholic sympathies. These men were motivated initially by the desire to end the threat of war with Spain and to remove William Cecil.

The aim of the plot which emerged in 1568–69 was that the Duke of Norfolk, who was the most senior noble in the realm, would marry Mary, whom many members of the nobility considered to be Elizabeth's heir. Elizabeth's consistent refusal to marry or to name her successor worried her advisers, who feared the political instability that would occur if she were to die suddenly without an heir.

One solution to the problems of the succession and what to do with Mary was for her to marry the Duke of Norfolk. Supporters of this idea at Court thought that this alliance would secure the English succession and control Mary through marriage to someone who was at least nominally Protestant. Norfolk was considered the most suitable person to marry Mary because he was the most powerful member of the English nobility. It was also thought better for Mary to marry an Englishman and stay in England, where her actions could be more easily controlled. Once Norfolk was married to Mary, the plan was that he would use his enhanced political position to ensure that Mary was recognised as Elizabeth's heir. This would protect Mary's own claim to the throne and settle the question of the royal succession. Philip would also be able to use his power to topple Cecil from his position as Elizabeth's chief minister and to end the potential slide into war with Spain.

EXTEND YOUR KNOWLEDGE

Why did Elizabeth refuse to marry or name an heir?

In the 1560s, despite pressure from her Council and parliament, Elizabeth had consistently refused to agree to marry or to name a successor. Elizabeth felt that to name a successor would undermine her own position and create a potential rival for the throne. Elizabeth was also reluctant to marry because a husband would potentially undermine her power as queen, particularly since women were considered to be inferior to men. Elizabeth might have preferred to marry her favourite, Robert Dudley, but marrying an Englishman would cause jealousy among other English nobles. In addition, by remaining unmarried, Elizabeth could use her marriage as a bargaining chip in negotiations with foreign powers.

This plan was popular not just among resentful Catholic courtiers. Even Elizabeth's favourite, the Earl of Leicester, was prepared to support the plan, even though he was a committed Protestant and probably did not want to get rid of Cecil. Leicester thought that Mary could be restored to the Scottish throne with Norfolk at her side and that Mary would convert to Protestantism in order to keep her Scottish crown and ensure the friendship of England. Leicester was probably mistaken in his assumptions, however. Mary had done nothing to suggest that she would be prepared to convert, and Norfolk himself only followed the Protestant faith because it was politically safer for him to do so.

Unfortunately for the plotters, by September 1569 Elizabeth had heard about the plan. She was furious and forbade any further discussion of the marriage. The marriage of her most powerful nobleman to a rival claimant to the throne would have been politically dangerous for Elizabeth. Norfolk's power and wealth, coupled with Mary's claim to be queen, could have led to a challenge to Elizabeth's right to be queen. Mary's Catholicism and the suspicion that Norfolk was sympathetic to the Catholic faith were also dangerous. A marriage between them might have encouraged discontented English Catholics to try to overthrow Elizabeth. Most of the men who had been involved in the plot, including Dudley and Norfolk, eventually submitted to the queen and admitted their part in the plot. However, Norfolk's actions had aroused suspicions among the queen's advisers that there was more to the plan than a marriage to Mary.

The role of the Duke of Norfolk

Thomas Howard, the fourth Duke of Norfolk, was the grandson of the Duke of Norfolk who had negotiated with the rebels in the Pilgrimage of Grace in 1536. He was brought up in the Protestant faith, but his sympathies seem to have lain with Catholicism. In the early 1560s, Norfolk served Elizabeth loyally. In 1560, he even led the English army against French Catholic intervention in Scotland.

SOURCE 2 Portrait of Thomas Howard, fourth Duke of Norfolk, painted in 1562 by an unknown English artist.

The Duke of Norfolk's role in the events of 1568–69 was ambiguous. In 1568, he was the leading member and the chief beneficiary of the plot to marry Mary and remove Cecil. Norfolk was the most powerful member of the nobility; a rising led by him would be particularly dangerous. Norfolk's actions and links with disgruntled members of the nobility, such as Northumberland and Westmorland, was enough to put him under suspicion at Court. On 26 September 1569, he decided to leave the Court at London. Fortunately for Elizabeth, Norfolk decided not to go to the North to raise rebellion with Westmorland and Northumberland. Instead, he went to his estates at Kenninghall (Norfolk) while he decided what to do. On 1 October, he had made up his mind that his best option was to remain loyal to Elizabeth. Norfolk wrote to Westmorland telling him not to rebel. Norfolk then returned to Court at the queen's summons and was imprisoned in the Tower.

Norfolk's actions in 1568–69 were an indirect cause of the rebellion of 1569. His leadership in the Court plot stirred up the resentment of men such as Northumberland and Westmorland. In 1569, Norfolk does not seem to have been plotting to take the throne, but he may well have been thinking about it during the time he spent at Kenninghall. Norfolk may also have been motivated by a more general concern about the declining role of the traditional nobility. In the eyes of men like Norfolk, Northumberland and Westmorland, upstarts like William Cecil, who did not have a title or a great landed inheritance, were taking over Tudor government. However, in 1569, Norfolk's decision to remain loyal to Elizabeth undermined the potential threat of the Northern Rising and left Westmorland and Northumberland feeling increasingly isolated.

The economic and religious insecurities of the northern earls

The religious concerns of the northern earls

Both the Earl of Northumberland and the Earl of Westmorland were openly Catholic, as were many others who lived in the North of England. Despite the break with Rome under Henry VIII, and further moves towards Protestantism under Edward VI and Elizabeth (see Chapter 1), many living in the North preserved traditional Catholic practices and beliefs. In the 1560s, about 75 percent of the leading families of Yorkshire were Catholic, and there was a similarly high percentage in counties such as Durham and Lancashire. The survival of Catholic traditions was made possible partly by Elizabeth's own policies in the early 1560s. Elizabeth created a settlement that would allow most moderate Catholics to conform. The 1559 Settlement and the Thirty-Nine Articles (1563) kept the doctrine of the Church of England as moderate as possible. In particular, the liturgy of the Communion was made deliberately ambiguous so that both moderate Protestants and Catholics would be more likely to accept it. This policy led to the development of a group known as **church papists**. In addition, until the threat of a Catholic rebellion became serious from 1568, recusancy continued to flourish. This allowed the Catholic faith to persist in the North.

KEY TERM

Church papist
One of a moderate majority of Catholics who conformed outwardly to the Church of England by going to Church services.

However, as relations with Spain deteriorated from 1566, Catholics started to come under suspicion. The government feared that Catholics would have divided loyalties – to the queen and to the pope – and so could not be trusted. The increasing threat of a Catholic-led rising was exacerbated by the remoteness of the North, which made it harder for the central government to react quickly to potential threats. The government response to this threat was to introduce a more hard-line approach to religious conformity.

As government fears of a Catholic rising increased, the authorities started to enforce the religious settlement more strictly. Elizabeth's government appointed a series of men with strong Protestant convictions to positions in the northern Church and government. The aim of these appointments was to spread Protestant ideas in the region while clamping down on Catholic activity. The most important Church appointment was James Pilkington as Bishop of Durham. Pilkington had radical Protestant views and preached against both Catholicism and the power of the traditional nobility. Pilkington and his followers among the clergy began a campaign to eradicate traditional practices in the diocese of Durham. In particular, they attempted to remove church furniture and religious imagery which they thought represented a Catholic approach to worship and belief. These policies made Pilkington and his followers unpopular locally.

Government intervention in the North

Another cause of the growing resentment among Catholic nobles and gentry in the North was the appointment of Protestant outsiders to key posts in the North. This led to both religious and political tensions, as the incomers attempted to enforce Elizabeth's rule. The change was also felt more acutely because Mary I had appointed members of the traditional northern nobility to important strategic and political posts in the region between 1553 and 1558. Nobles who had benefited from these policies now found themselves deprived of their positions or overlooked, in favour of Protestant outsiders. For example, Elizabeth's cousin, the Protestant Lord Hunsdon, became Warden of the East March in 1568, a position that had traditionally been held by the Earls of Northumberland. Hunsdon had no lands or connection with the region; his appointment was a deliberate attempt to extend royal control in a region where Elizabeth feared a challenge to her authority. Another unpopular figure was Sir John Forster. Although he was from the North, he was a rival to the Earl of Northumberland's local power and was completely loyal to Elizabeth, to whom he owed his promotion. Forster was appointed Warden of the Middle March, a position that had also previously belonged to Northumberland. Finally, the Council of the North was also run by an outsider, Thomas Radcliffe, Earl of Sussex, who was appointed as president of the Council in July 1568. Radcliffe was another cousin of the queen, who had served her loyally in Ireland. All of these appointments had the effect of extending royal control more extensively into the North. Although this was a trend that had been apparent since the reign of Henry VIII (see Chapter 2), the growing religious and political tensions in the North of England during the 1560s magnified the significance of these appointments and the resentment felt by the northern Catholic nobles and gentry, who felt increasingly under pressure.

The economic concerns of the northern earls

The lack of opportunities in government also had economic consequences for the Earls of Northumberland and

Westmorland. The appointment of their rivals to key positions which had once been theirs meant that they lost the incomes these posts had brought. Both earls were suffering financially in the 1560s and government policy was making their situation worse. In 1562, Northumberland wrote to the Earl of Pembroke, asking him to ask the queen for a grant of £1,000, an enormous sum by the standards of the time. The Earl of Westmorland was forced to borrow £80 from Sir George Bowes in 1568. In the same year, Northumberland tried to claim compensation for the rights to a copper mine that had been discovered on his estates; the Crown refused to pay him anything. These financial worries added to the earls' grievances, though they were not enough on their own to provoke them to rebel. Their rebellion in 1569 was caused by a combination of increasing government intrusion into the North, both religiously and politically, and Elizabeth's own actions, which convinced the earls that they had nothing to lose by rebelling.

ACTIVITY
KNOWLEDGE CHECK

1 Draw a spider diagram with the title, 'Why did the northern earls resent Elizabeth's government?' Use the headings in the section above to create your diagram.

2 Which was the most important reason in explaining the growing resentment of the northern earls: religious grievances, government intervention or economic issues? In your own words, explain the reasons for your choice.

Mary, Queen of Scots' arrival

The arrival of Mary in England in May 1568 was particularly awkward for Elizabeth. Mary was expecting refuge and help in regaining the Scottish throne. She was treated well, but her potential claim to the English throne made her a serious threat. Mary could not be allowed to live freely in England. Her presence in the country made her a potential figurehead around whom discontented Catholics might rally. With the deteriorating relationship with Spain at this time, there was also the threat of foreign intervention, though Philip II was still reluctant to help someone with links to France. Mary was placed in comfortable imprisonment; in 1569 she was moved to Tutbury Castle (Staffordshire). This was because the political and religious situation at this time was so tense that she could not be allowed to stay anywhere near London or the Scottish border.

Elizabeth was now in a very difficult position. Mary was an anointed queen who had been deposed by her own disobedient subjects. Elizabeth had very strong views about the importance of the royal prerogative and the need for all subjects to obey their monarch. If Elizabeth were to execute another anointed monarch, it would set a dangerous precedent for her own English subjects. However, it was not particularly practical to help Mary regain her Scottish throne. Having a minor (James VI) on the Scottish throne would weaken the potential threat of invasion from over the border because the Scots would lack the necessary leadership of a strong adult monarch. Furthermore, the Earl of Moray, the regent who now controlled Scotland and its baby king, was

Protestant. England's security in the North would be enhanced if it had a neighbour with the same religious outlook. Even though Elizabeth viewed the actions of the Scottish nobility with considerable distaste, political necessity meant that she was not prepared to overturn the political situation in Scotland.

The result of Elizabeth's dilemma was that Mary remained in captivity in England. While this helped the Anglo-Scottish relationship, Mary's presence in England rapidly became a focus for those members of the nobility who were discontented with Elizabeth's rule and who sought a return to Catholicism. Elizabeth's position was weakened still further by the fact that she herself was not married and had no children of her own. Mary's arrival in England was thus a threat to Elizabeth's position, especially as Mary already had a son and heir, James VI, whose existence meant that there was a ready-made dynasty waiting to succeed Elizabeth. Mary's physical presence in England put additional pressure on Elizabeth to make the succession to the throne clear. This was why nobles with a range of religious sympathies, from the Catholic-leaning Duke of Norfolk to the very Protestant Earl of Leicester, were prepared to support Mary's marriage to the Duke of Norfolk and an acknowledgement of Mary's right to be Elizabeth's heir. The plot to arrange a marriage between Mary and Norfolk also coincided with growing resentment at Court against William Cecil, and the fears of the northern Catholic nobility about their futures. The result was, first, the failed attempt to remove Cecil, and then, the rebellion by the two earls who were the most alienated from Elizabeth's government, Westmorland and Northumberland.

SOURCE

3 William Cecil, 'A Short Memorial of the State of the Realm', written in early 1569, probably for Elizabeth I. In this document, Cecil sets out the problems facing England.

The perils are many, great and imminent. Great in respect of the persons and matters.

Persons
The Queen's Majesty herself...

The Pope, the king of France, and Spain... and their associates.

The Queen of Scots...

Matters
The eviction of the crown of England from the Queen's Majesty, to set it upon the head of the Queen of Scots...

Changing the estate of England to Popery: which cannot be accomplished while the Queen's Majesty lives, nor so assuredly and plausibly any way, as by putting the Crown of England upon the Queen of Scots' head.

The exalting of the Queen of Scots shall please the Pope, the two monarchs, and all the Papists in Christendom, England and Scotland...

The weakness of the Queen's Majesty estate grows from lack of:

1. Marriage 2. Children 3. Assistance from other foreign powers...

The... near approaching of these perils appears [because of]...

The persecutions made by the Kings of Spain and France of their subjects for religion... The inward troubles in Scotland these eight years as by the unlucky marriage of the Queen of Scots with the Lord Darnley. [And] By the fame of the murdering of her husband...

SOURCE

4

Notes sent by Sir Thomas Gargrave, the Protestant vice president of the Council of the North, to Sir William Cecil, 2 November 1569.

Upon the first rumour of a marriage between the Duke of Norfolk and the Scottish Queen, the

Papists much rejoiced, and imagined that religion would be altered, and took encouragement to speak against the Protestants, whereby much fear rose among the people.

Then news came that the Duke had left the Court, and gone into Norfolk, and that there upon the Earls of Northumberland and Westmorland had caused their servants to take up their horses and be in readiness; where upon the people imagined that the earls would assist the Duke; but whether they caused their men to be in readiness, or had any such meaning, is unknown. I have heard since that the Earl of Northumberland has scarcely sufficient horses for his own family. There was another rumour that the confederates intended to deliver the Scottish Queen from the Earl of Shrewsbury.

When the Duke returned to Court, it was rumoured that the plotters, moved that religion should be the cause of their stir, upon which point it was said they disagreed and so departed; but neither the place where the assembly was held, nor the persons that attended are known, save that Robert Bowes and Francis Norton were the persons that disagreed; yet I have heard by one of their friends that there never was any such matter.

The persons named as great doers in these matters be all evil of religion.

ACTIVITY
KNOWLEDGE CHECK

1 Read Sources 3 and 4 and answer the following questions:

   a) What problems does William Cecil identify for Elizabeth and England at the start of 1569?

   b) How far does Source 3 support Source 4 about the problems facing Elizabeth I?

2 Imagine that you are one of Elizabeth's councillors in May 1568 on the arrival of Mary, Queen of Scots in England. What would be the strengths and weaknesses of each of the following options?

   a) Returning Mary to Scotland

   b) Sending Mary to France

   c) Allowing Mary to remain in England

   d) Allowing Mary to marry the Duke of Norfolk

3 If you were to choose just one of these options, which would it be, and why?

> **A Level Exam-Style Question Section B**
>
> How far do you agree that the arrival of Mary, Queen of Scots in England in 1568 was the primary cause of the Northern Rising in 1569? (20 marks)
>
> **Tip**
> *What is meant by 'primary' cause?*

HOW SERIOUS WAS THE THREAT POSED BY THE REVOLT OF THE NORTHERN EARLS TO ELIZABETH I?

The beginnings of the Northern Rising in 1569

TIMELINE: THE GROWTH OF TENSION, 1568–69

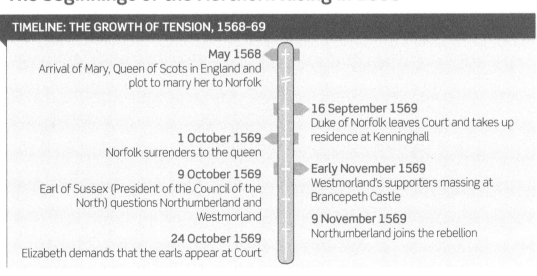

May 1568
Arrival of Mary, Queen of Scots in England and plot to marry her to Norfolk

16 September 1569
Duke of Norfolk leaves Court and takes up residence at Kenninghall

1 October 1569
Norfolk surrenders to the queen

9 October 1569
Earl of Sussex (President of the Council of the North) questions Northumberland and Westmorland

Early November 1569
Westmorland's supporters massing at Brancepeth Castle

9 November 1569
Northumberland joins the rebellion

24 October 1569
Elizabeth demands that the earls appear at Court

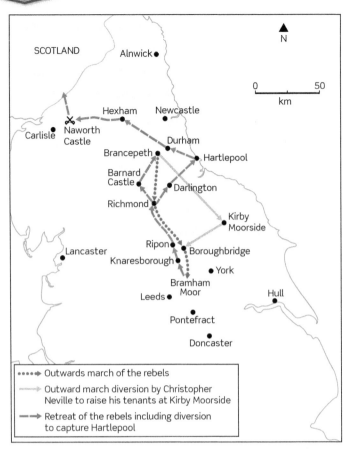

Figure 6.2 The Northern Rising in 1569–70.

Legend:
- •••••➤ Outwards march of the rebels
- ——➤ Outward march diversion by Christopher Neville to raise his tenants at Kirby Moorside
- ━━━➤ Retreat of the rebels including diversion to capture Hartlepool

Early tensions in 1569

After Norfolk's initial withdrawal from Court (see pages 134–135), Westmorland and Northumberland were confident that he was planning to rebel; this led them to plan a rising of their own. By the time that news of Norfolk's surrender reached them, their plans for a rebellion that was to begin on 6 October were already well-advanced and had to be hastily abandoned. Without Norfolk's support, the earls wavered. But rumours of a rising aroused the suspicions of the president of the Council of the North, the Earl of Sussex. Sussex himself was in a difficult position because he was a friend of the Duke of Norfolk, who was now in disgrace. Sussex was worried that his own loyalties to Elizabeth might be called into question. To show that he was completely loyal to Elizabeth, Sussex decided to call Westmorland and Northumberland for questioning before the Council of the North. Westmorland and Northumberland claimed that they were innocent of any plotting; Sussex decided to accept their claims and allowed them to go free, but he was still cautious about the rumours that continued to circulate.

However, Elizabeth remained suspicious of Westmorland and Northumberland, who were out of reach in the North, and decided to take further action against them. On 24 October, she ordered Westmorland and Northumberland to come to Court in London. This was against the advice of the Earl of Sussex, who thought correctly that such an order would provoke the earls to open revolt. On 9 November, the earls, who feared what would happen to them if they went to London, finally rebelled. Elizabeth's actions had forced them into rebellion because they thought that

they had no other alternative. However, the earls were not alone in their resentment of Elizabeth's religious policies and her rule of the North. In the first week of November, supporters of the Earl of Westmorland were beginning to mass at his castle at Brancepeth in County Durham. The Northern Rising was not just a rebellion by disgruntled members of the northern nobility; it also attracted support from the commons, who also resented Elizabeth's religious policies. The Earl of Northumberland, who was always the more reluctant of the two rebel nobles, was actually persuaded to join the rebellion by his followers, who convinced him that he was about to be captured by the Earl of Sussex. Meanwhile, gentry who were loyal to the queen started to gather at Barnard Castle, which was also in County Durham. These gentry were under the leadership of Sir George Bowes, the steward of Barnard Castle, who remained loyal to Elizabeth throughout the rising, despite coming under severe pressure from the rebels.

SOURCE 5

From the examination of the Earl of Northumberland, after his capture in 1572. This is a record of Northumberland's own account of the rising. It takes the form of a series of questions put to him by the president of the Council of the North, Lord Hunsdon, and Northumberland's replies. In this section, Northumberland explains how the rebellion began.

Then old Norton and Markenfield came to me and said we were already in peril, through our often meetings, and must either enter the matter without the Earl [of Westmorland], or depart the realm; and it would be a great discredit to leave off a godly enterprise that was looked for at our hands by the whole kingdom, many of whom would assist us. I bade them take time to consider; they were away 14 days, and then returned with other gentlemen of the bishopric, and some belonging to the Earl, who were forward in the matter. I objected that my Lord President suspected us, and would not let us escape; but I offered to write to the gentlemen of the country to know their mind... I wished to consult the Earl of Derby, Queen of Scots and Spanish ambassador. The first did not answer; the other two thought it better not to stir.

ACTIVITY
KNOWLEDGE CHECK

1 Read Source 5. What does it reveal about the reasons for the Northern Rising?

2 What does the source reveal about the level of threat posed by the rebellion?

3 Northumberland was giving evidence about his role in the rising to the English authorities following his capture. How might this affect his account of events?

The rebellion, which began on 9 November, was based on the county of Durham, and particularly on the Earl of Westmorland's fortress at Brancepeth. The rebels marched to Durham Cathedral, where they celebrated Catholic Mass and destroyed all signs of Protestantism. They then returned to Brancepeth, where they were better able to defend themselves. On 15 November, they marched again, but this time they went South.

The main events of the Northern Rising

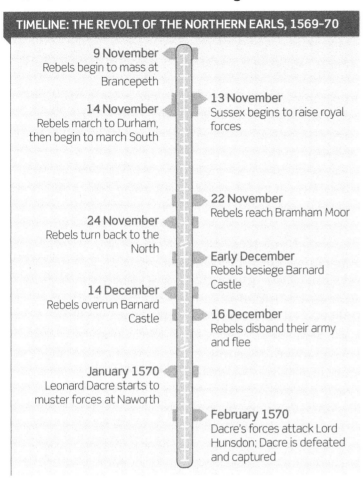

TIMELINE: THE REVOLT OF THE NORTHERN EARLS, 1569–70

9 November
Rebels begin to mass at Brancepeth

13 November
Sussex begins to raise royal forces

14 November
Rebels march to Durham, then begin to march South

22 November
Rebels reach Bramham Moor

24 November
Rebels turn back to the North

Early December
Rebels besiege Barnard Castle

14 December
Rebels overrun Barnard Castle

16 December
Rebels disband their army and flee

January 1570
Leonard Dacre starts to muster forces at Naworth

February 1570
Dacre's forces attack Lord Hunsdon; Dacre is defeated and captured

SOURCE 6

The proclamation of the northern earls, issued at Darlington on 16 November 1569 by the earls of Northumberland and Westmorland.

Thomas, Earl of Northumberland and Charles, Earl of Westmorland, the Queen's most true and lawful subjects, and to all her highness' people, send greeting: Whereas divers new set up nobles about the Queen's Majesty, have and do daily, not only go about to overthrow and put down the ancient nobility of this realm, but also have misused the Queen Majesty's own person, and also have by the space of twelve years now past, set up, and maintained a new found religion and heresy, contrary to God's word. For the amending and redressing whereof, divers foreign powers do purpose shortly to invade these realms, which will be to our utter destruction, if we do not ourselves speedily forfend [prevent] the same. Wherefore we are now constrained at this time to go about to amend and redress it ourselves, which if we should not do and foreigners enter upon us we should all be made slaves and bondsmen to them. These are therefore to will and require you, and every of you, being above the age of sixteen years and not sixty, as your duty towards God does bind you, for the setting forth of his true and catholic religion; and as you tender the common wealth of your country, to come and resort unto us with all speed, with all such armour and furniture as you, or any of you have. This fail you not herein, as you will answer the contrary at your perils. God save the Queen.

ACTIVITY
KNOWLEDGE CHECK

Read Source 6.

1 What did the Earls of Westmorland and Northumberland claim were their aims in rebelling?

2 Why might the earls' proclamation have been a danger to Elizabeth I in 1569?

The rebels' aim was to raise the county of Yorkshire in rebellion. As they moved South, the earls issued proclamations (Source 6). In these proclamations, the earls claimed that they were Elizabeth's loyal subjects, who were defending her from advisers such as William Cecil, who had persuaded her to enforce Protestantism and attack Catholicism. By claiming that they were loyal to Elizabeth, the earls were presenting themselves not as rebels, but as concerned subjects who wished to free her from bad advice. Like the Pilgrims of Grace, the earls made reference to the idea of the commonwealth, reinforcing the idea that they were acting for the good of the country.

By 22 November, the rebels had marched to Bramham Moor. This was a particularly important strategic junction. At Bramham, the road which joined York to the towns of Tadcaster and Ilkley further West was met by the great Roman road which linked London to the North. Gaining control of this junction meant that the rebels were able to threaten York itself, an important centre of northern government, as well as blocking any government troops marching North from London or South from Newcastle. Even more worryingly for the government, the rebels could have marched South to rescue Mary, Queen of Scots from Tutbury Castle, just 40 miles away. By late November, the rebels had attracted around 3,800 foot soldiers and 1,600 horsemen. The horsemen were also a particular threat to the government since this meant that the rebels were well-equipped.

Meanwhile, officials who remained loyal to the queen found it difficult to act because of the scale of the rebellion they now faced. The Earl of Sussex, who as president of the Council of the North was in charge of maintaining order, was trapped in York with only 400 horsemen. Sussex had tried to raise a larger army of 1,500 footmen, but he had not been able to attract the support he needed from the local gentry. The rebels controlled so much of the North that Sussex stopped sending letters to London because he feared that they would fall into the wrong hands. However, Lord Hunsdon did manage to send a message to William Cecil in London, warning him of the rebels' advance south, and advising Cecil to move Mary from Tutbury, which Cecil did.

But on 24 November, the luck of the government supporters began to change. On this date, the rebels made the decision to retreat to Brancepeth. The rebels' decision seems to have been due to a combination of reasons.

- They had heard rumours of a large royal army that was being organised further South under the Earl of Warwick.

- They may also have heard that Mary, Queen of Scots had been moved from Tutbury to Coventry and was out of their reach.

- The rebels realised that if they marched further South they would not receive as much support; the Earls of Westmorland and Northumberland were well-known in Yorkshire and Durham, where they commanded respect and loyalty, but they would not have been able to rely on this elsewhere.

- The rebels had hoped to raise Cheshire and Lancashire in rebellion, but this had not happened because the most important member of the nobility in these regions, the Earl of Derby, chose to remain loyal to Elizabeth.

The result of these circumstances was enough to convince the rebels to turn back to County Durham, where the rebellion began and their support was strongest. However, this did not signal the end of the rebellion. The rebel army was still large; a rebel army of 3,200 footmen and 1,500 horsemen was able to besiege Barnard Castle in early December. Meanwhile, another group of rebels marched East and captured the port of Hartlepool. They had received a message promising them support from Spain, and they hoped that Spanish troops would land at the port, but this support never came.

The failure of the Northern Rising and Leonard Dacre's revolt, 1570

It was not until 16 December, when the large royal army finally reached the river Tees, that the rebel earls disbanded their army and fled. The earls got as far as Hexham before they were challenged by Sir John Forster. On 19 December, the remaining supporters of the rebels and Forster's army fought a brief skirmish, the only real conflict of the rebellion, but the earls escaped further North. Northumberland fled over the border into Scotland, where he hoped to find more supporters. Instead, he was handed over to the pro-English regent of Scotland, the Earl of Moray. Eventually, Northumberland was returned to England in 1572 and he was beheaded in York. Westmorland managed to escape to the continent and remained in exile for the rest of his life.

Although the rebellion of 1569 was put down, there were still further threats to Elizabeth's government. Another potential rebel, Lord Dacre, had travelled to London during the rebellion and professed his loyalty to Elizabeth. Dacre had come under suspicion because he was in correspondence with Mary, Queen of Scots. Dacre managed to convince the authorities in London that he was loyal and he was allowed to return to his estates around Naworth Castle (Cumbria), where he began to fortify its defences. He also gathered an armed force of about 3,000 men. By early 1570, Dacre's actions had made the government suspicious and an order was issued for his arrest on 15 February. Lord Hunsdon was sent to take Dacre into custody, but was attacked by Dacre and his troops. In the battle that followed, about 500 rebels were killed or captured. Hunsdon and his troops were victorious, but Dacre managed to escape across the border to Scotland. Eventually, Dacre made his way to the continent, where, like the Earl of Westmorland, he remained in exile. Westmorland's and Dacre's lands were confiscated and given to Elizabeth's loyal supporters. With the execution of Northumberland in 1572, the destruction of the power of the traditional northern nobility was complete.

ACTIVITY
KNOWLEDGE CHECK

Write a brief explanation of why you think it took so long for Elizabeth's government to put down the Northern Rising.

The capture of Durham and the siege of Barnard Castle
The capture of Durham

Although the rising ultimately failed, the rebels did have some notable successes, especially in County Durham, where the rebellion began. In November 1569, they were able to march into the city of Durham. At this time, Durham was an important administrative centre in the North, but it was not heavily fortified, which is why the rebels were able to capture the city so easily. Durham was also the focus of the rebellion because of the religious and political tensions that existed there. The actions of the Bishop of Durham had upset many of the local Catholic gentry (see page 135). Of the recorded participants in the Northern Rising, 794 came from the county of Durham. The cathedral at Durham had been used by the bishop to symbolise the move to Protestantism. One act that had caused particular resentment among Catholics was the destruction of the banner representing the local saint, St Cuthbert, which had been kept at the cathedral. When the rebels entered the city, it is significant that they went to the cathedral to hold a Catholic mass and to destroy the Protestant symbols they found there. For the rebels, what the cathedral looked like and how its services were conducted symbolised what they saw as an attack on their traditional beliefs and practices. The importance of Durham was such that when the Council of the North was reorganised in 1572, the city and its region were brought under the Council's direct control.

The siege of Barnard Castle

The siege and capture of Barnard Castle in December 1569 was perhaps even more alarming to Elizabeth's government. Barnard Castle was a fortress in the South West of County Durham which guarded the river Tees. It had been Crown property since the late 15th century and was an important stronghold, which had been entrusted to George Bowes as its steward. Barnard Castle was one of the keys to controlling the surrounding region. Whoever held the castle would be able to use it as a refuge and as a place from which attacks could be launched. At the start of the rising in County Durham, Barnard Castle rapidly became a rallying point for those loyal to Elizabeth. As the rebellion progressed and the rebels seized control of the county of Durham, the castle became a refuge for government supporters.

In early December, the castle came under siege from nearly 5,000 rebels. By 14 December, Bowes reported that the supplies were so low within the fortress that its defenders were reaching the point of starvation. Such was the desperation of his men that 226 leapt over the walls to join the rebels. Another 150 of the defenders then turned on Bowes and opened the gates of the castle. Bowes was forced to surrender to the rebels, but he was then allowed to leave with 400 of his men. The temporary capture of Barnard Castle was significant because it showed just how weak and isolated Elizabeth's supporters had become. Bowes was unable even to control his own supposedly loyal men within the castle. However, the capture of Barnard Castle did not represent anything more than a temporary success for the rebels, as they were forced to flee two days later. In addition, the rebels do not seem to have wanted to cause physical harm to Bowes or his men. Like the capture of Durham, the rebels were more concerned about attacking the places that symbolised the aspects of Elizabeth's government which they resented the most, such as her religious policy and her neglect of the traditional noble families in favour of men such as Bowes. The rebels do not seem to have wanted to cause physical harm to the men who represented Elizabeth; in this respect, the rebellion was almost entirely peaceful, like the Pilgrimage of Grace before it. Most of the violence that did occur happened in the government repression following the failure of the revolt.

ACTIVITY
KNOWLEDGE CHECK

What does the capture of Durham and Barnard Castle suggest about the extent of the threat posed by the Northern Rising to Elizabeth's government?

The role of the northern earls in the revolt

The two northern earls who became involved in the revolt of 1569, Northumberland and Westmorland, both had good reason to feel aggrieved at Elizabeth's management of the North. However, their initial attitudes to the plot to marry Norfolk to Mary were rather different. Westmorland, who was Norfolk's brother-in-law, was one of the main supporters of the planned marriage. Westmorland's close family relationship with Norfolk meant that Westmorland expected increased patronage and favour from Norfolk and Mary if the marriage went ahead. This was particularly inviting for Westmorland, who hoped to have his power and influence in the North restored. However, Northumberland was never in favour of the marriage. Although he was in contact with both Mary and the Spanish ambassador, he opposed Mary's marriage to Norfolk. This was because Norfolk was nominally Protestant; Northumberland was determined to restore the Catholic faith and he did not think that the marriage of Mary to someone who was not fully committed to Catholicism was the way to achieve this. Northumberland even suggested that a better marriage for Mary would be to Philip II of Spain, but this idea was not well-received because Philip had no real desire to get involved in English affairs. In November 1569, Northumberland was slow to commit to open rebellion. When rebel troops began to mass, it was at Westmorland's stronghold at Brancepeth. Northumberland did not join the rebellion until 9 November, when the momentum of events persuaded him to support the rising.

Even if Northumberland was reluctant to get involved in the marriage plot and open rebellion, the issue that persuaded him was his commitment to his Catholic faith. Northumberland and Westmorland both wanted to see the restoration of Catholicism in England. They thought that the best way of achieving this was to ensure that Mary, Queen of Scots was next in line in the royal succession, though neither seems to have wanted to go as far as deposing Elizabeth. However, the earls' plans were not well-thought through. Their initial attempt at a rising in early October had been abandoned following the news of Norfolk's arrest. The pattern of the rebel movements also suggests that the earls were uncertain about how to proceed. The rebels went first to Durham, before moving South to Bramham Moor, and then back North again. These movements suggest that the earls did not have a clear strategy, particularly once they realised that they had no chance of releasing Mary, Queen of Scots.

However, the role of the earls was important because of the potential danger they posed to Elizabeth's government, even if they claimed that they were her loyal subjects. Both Northumberland and Westmorland had been in contact with people who were potential enemies of Elizabeth, especially Mary herself and the Spanish ambassador. Their letters reveal their determination to restore Catholicism, in direct contradiction to Elizabeth's own moderate Protestant settlement. The earls' involvement was also dangerous because of the leadership they provided among the local communities, where they were well-known and where traditional loyalties remained strong. The earls were not alone in resenting Elizabeth's religious settlement or the actions of Protestant intruders from the South. When the earls rose, they were able to rely on the support of many other Catholic gentry, many of whom had long-standing connections with the earls and their families. The earls were also able to use their landed estates to recruit their own tenants. The strength of their support meant that they were able to control the counties of Durham and Yorkshire for nearly a month, while Elizabeth's local officials struggled to contain the rising and found themselves surrounded.

SOURCE

7 From the examination of the Earl of Northumberland, 1572. Here the captured earl explains the divisions among the rebels in their discussions about whether to rebel.

Then our company was discouraged. I left my house on a false alarm, and went to Lord Westmorland's on my way back to Alnwick. I found with him all the Nortons, Markenfeld, his two uncles, the two Tempests... and Sir John Neville, all ready to enter forthwith. We consulted; my Lord, his uncles, old Norton, and Markenfeld were earnest to proceed. Francis Norton, John Swinburne, myself and others thought it impossible, so we broke up and departed, every man to provide for himself. Lady Westmorland, hearing this, cried out, weeping bitterly, that we and our country were shamed for ever, and that we must seek holes to creep into. Some departed, and I wished to go... but when I found I could not get away, I agreed to rise with them.

ACTIVITY
KNOWLEDGE CHECK

1 What does Northumberland's account in Source 7 reveal about the problems faced by the rebels?

2 How does Northumberland explain his own eventual involvement in the rebellion? Do you trust his account?

The extent of the threat posed by the Northern Rising to Elizabeth

In some ways, the Northern Rising posed a direct threat not only to the stability of the North, but to Elizabeth's position on the throne. There was a threat that the northern rebels might get support from the Catholic Philip II of Spain or the pope. Moreover, the presence of Mary, Queen of Scots led to increasing pressure on Elizabeth to settle the royal succession. Mary herself was in contact with English members of the Catholic nobility and her remaining supporters in Scotland.

The Northern Rising could have led to an attempt not just to restore Catholicism, but to depose Elizabeth altogether.

The rising was also dangerous to Elizabeth because it showed the extent to which her religious settlement had failed to take root in the more religiously conservative North of England. The settlement had been in place for ten years, yet in the North, Catholicism remained the dominant belief among many members of the nobility and gentry, who were prepared to rise up in support of their faith. The rising also exposed the weaknesses in the monarchy's ability to control the more remote regions of England effectively. Even though the Council of the North had been reorganised in 1537, its members were not able to prevent the rebellion from breaking out. The Northern Rising exposed the weaknesses in Elizabeth's policies towards the North, and the dangerous resentment she had created with the imposition of Protestant outsiders. It took over a month for a large royal army to reach the county of Durham. Even the mustering and movement of this army showed the weaknesses in Tudor government. The army was so large and expensive to move that it took a long time to reach Durham. Although Sussex and Hunsdon repeatedly asked William Cecil for a small, mobile force of 800 men, including 500 cavalry, they were ignored.

However, Elizabeth did survive the rebellion and it was to be the last of the reign in mainland England. The rebellion did not spread further west into Cheshire or Lancashire, even though these were areas with strong Catholic sympathies. This was mostly because the dominant noble in these areas, the Earl of Derby, remained loyal. In addition, once the Duke of Norfolk had decided to throw himself on Elizabeth's mercy, the rebels were deprived of support from his estates further south. The rebels were also not prepared to use their strength in numbers to force a battle when they had the advantage in November. When the royal army eventually arrived in December, the news of its approach was enough to make the rebel army disperse.

SOURCE

Sir Ralph Sadler writing to Sir William Cecil from York, 6 December 1569, explaining why the Earl of Sussex would not be able to trust his forces to fight the rebels.

I perceive her Majesty is to believe that the force of her subjects of this country should not increase, and be able to match with the rebels; but it is easy to find the cause. There are not ten gentlemen in all this country that favour her proceedings in the cause of religion. The common people are ignorant, superstitious, and altogether blinded with the old popish doctrine, and therefore so favour the cause which the rebels make the colour of their rebellion, that, though their persons be here with us, their hearts are with them. And no doubt all this country had wholly rebelled if, at the beginning, my Lord Lieutenant had not wisely and stoutly handled the matter. If we should go to the field with this northern force only, they would fight faintly, for if the father be on this side, the son is on the other; and one brother with us and the other with rebels.

ACTIVITY
KNOWLEDGE CHECK

How far does Source 8 suggest that the Northern Rising was a threat to Elizabeth? Explain your answer.

WHY DID THE RISING FAIL AND WHAT WERE THE RESULTS OF THIS FAILURE?

Reasons for failure

Failures in the leadership of the Northern Rising

The leadership of the Northern Rising lacked the co-ordination and clear objectives of earlier risings. Compared to the Pilgrimage of Grace or Kett's rebellion, where one charismatic leader emerged with a clear set of aims and methods, the leadership of the Earls of Northumberland and Westmorland was less focused. Although Westmorland was committed to the Norfolk–Mary marriage, he still had to be convinced to rebel by his uncle, Christopher Neville. Northumberland needed even more persuading to join the rebellion and did not agree with the Norfolk–Mary marriage to begin with, although he was prepared to plot to achieve Mary's freedom from imprisonment. This suggests that there were disagreements among the rebel leaders about their aims and methods, and this may well have weakened their leadership of the rebellion.

The government response to the Northern Rising

Although local government officials struggled to cope initially, ultimately, the Tudor government had the strength to reinstate order. Elizabeth's policy of giving local office to loyal Protestant outsiders and local men such as John Forster, who were reliant on royal favour for their position, helped to bring about the rebellion, but it also helped to end it. Men such as Forster, George Bowes and Lord Hunsdon remained entirely loyal to Elizabeth. These men were in constant contact with the government in London and were responsible for relaying the situation on the ground to the men organising the response to the rising. Their information led to the organisation of a counter-attack and the removal of Mary, Queen of Scots from the rebels' reach. Finally, the news of the arrival of the enormous army from the South was enough to deter the rebels from advancing further South. The government response may have been slow initially, but when it did materialise in early December, the threat posed by the size of the royal army was enough to scare the rebels, who did not wish to fight.

The lack of widespread support for the Northern Rising in England

The Northern Rising also failed because it did not attract wider support from within England or from abroad. Although the rising itself was still a threat because of the numbers involved and the time it took to put down, it failed to attract support from other members of the nobility. Nobles with Catholic sympathies decided that rebellion was too risky. For example, Henry Clifford, the Earl of Cumberland, had been in trouble in the early 1560s for protecting Catholic priests. However, in 1569, Clifford was not prepared to take the risk of open rebellion. Instead, he helped to defend Carlisle from a rebel attack. Similarly, the Earl of Derby, who controlled much of Lancashire and Cheshire and had Catholic sympathies, preferred to stay loyal. Even in the heartlands of Neville and Percy support in Yorkshire and Durham, there were still members of the local gentry who preferred to remain neutral or even support Elizabeth. For example, John Sayer was a member of the Durham gentry who was usually a supporter of the Earl of Northumberland. However, Sayer chose not to follow the earl into rebellion, but to help George Bowes in the defence of Barnard Castle instead. The example of Sayer suggests that the rebellion did not automatically attract the support of all of those who had grievances against Elizabeth's government. This was because, for some, the fear of what would happen to them if they supported a failed rebellion overrode any resentment that they felt.

Another problem the rebel leaders faced was attracting the wider support of ordinary men and women. Although the rebel earls were able to attract about 5,000 supporters for the rebellion from their own estates, the rebellion never gained the level of popular support seen in the Pilgrimage of Grace, which attracted an estimated 30,000 people. The reasons for this seem to have been a combination of the earls' lack of influence beyond the regions where they were the dominant landlords and popular apathy on the part of the commons. Without the support of other members of the nobility, the earls were not able to raise support outside Yorkshire and Durham. In addition, popular attitudes to religion had started to change. Although the Catholic masses held at Durham Cathedral attracted a large congregation, this did not translate into mass support for the rebel army. The Catholic ceremonies at Durham Cathedral appealed to the commons' sense of tradition, but a full-scale rebellion did not. Popular dislike and suspicion of foreigners meant that a return to a Church controlled by the pope in Rome was not widely supported. The result was that when the earls tried to rally popular support for a return to Catholicism and the papacy, they were met with indifference.

The lack of international support for the Northern Rising

The rebellion also failed because there was no support from foreign Catholic powers. The rebels believed that Philip II of Spain was going to send troops to help them, but this was a false belief. Although relations between England and Spain had deteriorated by 1568, Philip remained reluctant to help Mary because she had too many connections with France. Despite Elizabeth's Protestantism and Mary's Catholicism, Philip preferred an England that was Protestant and free of French control than one that was Catholic and dominated by France. The rebels also hoped that Scottish Catholic supporters of Mary might invade from the North, but this was prevented by the pro-English regent of Scotland, the Earl of Moray. Finally, the rebellion lacked legitimacy in the eyes of some Catholics because Elizabeth had not yet been excommunicated by the pope. If Elizabeth had been excommunicated, all loyal English Catholics would have been released from their obligation to obey her and would have been encouraged to try to remove her from power. The pope did eventually excommunicate Elizabeth in February 1570, but this was too late for the rebels of 1569.

ACTIVITY
KNOWLEDGE CHECK

1 Create a spider diagram entitled, 'Why did the Northern Rising fail in 1569?' Use the headings provided in the section above to add detail to your diagram.

2 In your opinion, what was the most important reason for the failure of the 1569 rising? Explain your answer.

SOURCE

9 Letter from Guerau de Spes, the Spanish Ambassador in England, to the Duke of Alba, who was in charge of Philip II's army in the Netherlands. The letter was sent from London on 1 December 1569.

The people in the North are strong and have 12,000 infantry and 3,000 horse together. They intended to go towards Tutbury to release the queen of Scotland, but as they hear she has been conveyed to Coventry they have stopped with the intention of giving battle to the queen's forces, for which purpose the northern people will gather 30,000 men… The queen has appointed as her general the Earl of Warwick, brother of Leicester, and they say they intend to raise 15,000 men and 5,000 horse, although few horses can be got… Great efforts are being made on behalf of the queen to borrow money from all the merchants, particularly foreigners… The French ambassador has been here to say that if I could help these people [the Catholics] in their just cause he would be a faithful comrade to me on his King's behalf without jealousy or suspicion. I excused myself by saying that I had no orders from his Majesty on the subject. [The Ambassador] thinks that, if these people in the North were to march straight here there would be nothing to withstand them, seeing the confusion of the Court, while their other friends would have greater chance than at present of moving. I will do nothing without orders from your Excellency. Not a word is said now about sending anyone to Spain. It was nothing but a fiction from the first, and the Council only wishes to see the Marquis [the French Ambassador] gone in order that no one shall stand in the way of the queen's purpose. She is now so completely in accord with them for the defence of their sect that she seems to have lost sight of the danger of ruin, both for her and them. I expect, as soon as the Marquis has gone, they will give me but little chance of taking part in any affairs. Lord Montague and the Earl of Southampton have sent to ask me for advice as to whether they should take up arms or go over to your Excellency. I told them I could not advise them until I had due instructions to do so. I said my letters had been seized because there were rumours about them lately, and I therefore did not know what they ought to do.

ACTIVITY
KNOWLEDGE CHECK

1 Read Source 9. On your own copy of the source, highlight in two colours:

   a) Evidence that suggests that the Northern Rising was a threat to Elizabeth I

   b) Evidence that suggests that the Northern Rising was not a threat to Elizabeth I.

2 How far do you trust de Spes' version of events in the North? Explain your answer, using your knowledge of the Northern Rising.

A Level Exam-Style Question Section B

'Both the Pilgrimage of Grace in 1536 and the Northern Rising in 1569 show the weakness of the Tudor monarchy in the North of England.' How far do you agree with this statement? (20 marks)

Tip
You will need a structure that allows you to compare the two rebellions.

A Level Exam-Style Question Section A

Study Source 9 before answering this question.

Assess the value of Source 9 for revealing the extent of the threat of the Northern Rising to Elizabeth's position on the throne and the approaches of her government to dealing with this threat.

Explain your answer, using the source, the information given about its origin and your own knowledge about the historical context. (20 marks)

Tip
Note the date and author of the source. How would de Spes' position as Spanish ambassador affect his view of events?

Government repression following the revolt

During the rebellion of 1569 itself, there was very little bloodshed, mainly because there was no pitched battle between the rebel army and the government forces. The 1570 clash between Dacre and Hunsdon resulted in the deaths of about 500 rebels. But despite the relatively non-violent approach of the rebels, Elizabeth I was determined to exact revenge. Her determination suggests that she was severely shaken by the revolt and wanted to prevent further attempts at opposition by making an example of those who had supported the Northern Rising. Although both Northumberland and Westmorland escaped, eight other ringleaders were executed in the aftermath of the revolt. Northumberland suffered the same fate when he was handed over to the English authorities in 1572.

However, Elizabeth wanted to send out an even stronger message. She ordered that 700 ordinary rebels should be executed as well. Compared to the punishments meted out after the Pilgrimage of Grace, which had been an even more threatening rising, Elizabeth's demands were more severe. However, there is evidence that Elizabeth's orders were not fully carried out. In particular, Sir George Bowes appears to have tried to soften the impact of Elizabeth's orders. His papers show that Bowes only punished a small proportion of those accused. For example, in Richmondshire, just 57 executions were carried out from a list of 215 victims. Bowes claimed that he was unable to carry out the executions because many of the intended victims had escaped. Although Bowes was loyal to the queen, he also had to live in the region where he was being asked to carry out severe punishments. The result was that he seems not to have tried very hard to search for those who had disappeared. The Earl of Sussex also helped to decrease the severity of the punishments. Sussex was under pressure from the queen to prove his loyalty. This led to Sussex trying to keep Elizabeth happy by telling her that Bowes had completed the executions in a particular region long before Bowes had actually finished his work. As a result of the actions of Bowes and Sussex, it is estimated that 450 of the 700 executions were actually carried out. This was still more than in the aftermath of the Pilgrimage of Grace, but the impact was not as severe as Elizabeth had originally intended.

The government response to the rebellion also took a political form. In 1572, the Council of the North was reorganised once again. The Puritan Henry Hastings, Earl of Huntingdon, was appointed as president of the Council, which was given extended powers over the North of England (see Chapter 2). Huntingdon remained in charge of the Council until his death in 1595. Huntingdon's continued presence in the North helped to stabilise the region. He was helped by the confiscation of the lands of the rebels. For example, the exiled Earl of Westmorland had all his estates confiscated. These policies helped to decrease the power and influence of the traditional northern nobility and to strengthen the power of the Crown in the North. Finally, the Northern Rising helped to establish Protestant rule in Scotland. In 1570, the Scottish regent, the Earl of Moray, was assassinated by a supporter of Mary, Queen of Scots. This was a potential blow for English security in the North. However, the recent rebellion in the North gave the English government the excuse to launch a series of raids across the Scottish border. The English claimed that they were pursuing the rebels who had escaped there in 1569, but in fact they were using the invasion to undermine Mary's supporters in Scotland. The result was that Mary's supporters in Scotland were not able to take advantage of Moray's assassination, and the Protestant leadership of Scotland was able to re-establish itself successfully.

EXTEND YOUR KNOWLEDGE

The role of the Earl of Moray in Scotland (1567–70)

James Stuart, Lord Moray, was the illegitimate brother of Mary, Queen of Scots. Since 1567, he had been acting as regent in Scotland for his nephew (and Mary's son), James VI. In 1568–69, Moray was carrying out campaigns in Scotland against supporters of Mary, who continued to fight for her right to be queen. On 23 January 1570, Moray was shot and killed by James Hamilton, one of Mary's supporters.

The implications of the revolt for Catholicism and Protestantism in England

KEY TERMS

Politique
A person who preferred to support a moderate form of religion and some religious toleration in order to promote national unity.

Papal bull
An order issued by the pope which all Catholics were expected to obey.

After the Northern Rising, government attitudes towards both Catholicism and Protestantism became more hard-line. However, Elizabeth, who was a **politique**, tended to prefer caution and resisted attempts by her councillors and parliament to introduce legislation which she thought went too far in compelling her subjects to attend Church of England services. Elizabeth wanted to defend the religious settlement of 1559–63. She distrusted radicalism on both ends of the religious spectrum – both hard-line Catholicism and the godly zeal seen in Puritanism. However, the 1569 rising made it harder for Elizabeth to maintain a moderate approach, especially once the **papal bull** *Regnans in Excelsis* arrived in 1570, which excommunicated her. Elizabeth also came under pressure because of the deteriorating situation on the continent. Protestant rebellions in France and the Netherlands put Elizabeth in a difficult position. She was reluctant to go to war in support of the Dutch or French Protestants, but if she did nothing, there was a real danger that the more powerful Catholic rulers of Spain and France would triumph. If Protestantism was extinguished on the continent, then England would be isolated and in danger of a Catholic invasion. These fears led to increasing anti-Catholic paranoia. The arrival of Catholic missionary priests in England only added to this paranoia, which in turn fed an increasing pressure for action to be taken against Catholics and for more support to be given to those who wished to spread a more radical Protestant faith.

SOURCE

10 From the papal bull, *Regnans in Excelsis*, which excommunicated Elizabeth in 1570. From William Camden's *History of Elizabeth I*, 1688.

This very Woman, having seized on the Kingdom, and monstrously usurped the place of Supreme Head of the Church in all England, and the chief Authority and Jurisdiction thereof, hath again reduced the said Kingdom into a miserable and ruinous Condition, which was so lately reclaimed to the Catholic Faith and a thriving Condition... declared the aforesaid Elizabeth, as being an Heretic and Favourer of Heretics... to have incurred the Sentence of Excommunication and to be cut off from the Unity of the Body of Christ. And moreover We do declare her to be deprived of her pretended Title to the Kingdom aforesaid... and We do command and charge all and every the Noblemen, Subjects, People, and others aforesaid, that they presume not to obey her, or her Orders, Mandates and Laws.

ACTIVITY
KNOWLEDGE CHECK

Read Source 10. Why would the papal bull of excommunication have posed a threat to Elizabeth?

Which Catholics posed a threat to Elizabeth?

Part of the problem for Elizabeth's government after 1569 was identifying which Catholics posed a real threat to Elizabeth. The majority of English Catholics chose loyalty to their queen and country rather than to a foreign power. However, there were some Catholics whose loyalties were split because they were also obedient to the pope in Rome. It was these Catholics whom the English government was most worried about, especially once the bull of excommunication was issued. The bull not only released Elizabeth's Catholic subjects from any oaths of obedience they had taken to her, but also threatened the excommunication of any Catholic who continued to obey her. The northern earls had wanted a return to Rome and full Catholicism, but had not gone so far as to try to depose Elizabeth. With Elizabeth's excommunication, English Catholics were actively encouraged by the papacy to consider this option. The result was that, as tensions mounted in the 1570s and 1580s, a minority of committed Catholics plotted to assassinate Elizabeth and replace her with Mary, Queen of Scots, who remained in prison in England. Although this group was a minority, their activities led to wider suspicion of recusants. After 1569, recusants began to be treated more harshly. The appointment of the Puritan Earl of Huntingdon as president of the Council of the North in 1572 signalled the beginning of this harsher approach. Huntingdon was not prepared to tolerate any open Catholic activity. He enforced the existing government legislation against recusants much more vigorously than had been done previously. He also made sure that Protestant preachers were appointed to northern churches in order to spread Protestant ideas and discourage Catholic beliefs and practices. Huntingdon was even prepared to protect the more radical Puritan preachers who arrived in York and Durham. Although Elizabeth disliked and distrusted Puritanism, Huntingdon argued that the presence of these preachers was the best way to ensure the decline of recusancy.

At the same time, the Catholic threat seemed to be increasing as a result of the arrival of English Catholic priests in England from 1574. These priests had been trained in a Catholic seminary, specially set up in Douai (in the Netherlands) in 1568 by the English Catholic William Allen, who had fled England. Allen's example was followed in Rome, Valladolid and Seville, with the intention that Catholicism could be reintroduced to England through their trainees' work. During the reign, these seminaries sent about 800 priests to England, who were supported in secret by Catholic recusants. English trained **Jesuit** priests also began to arrive in England, including Cuthbert Mayne and Edmund Campion. These highly trained men, and those who sheltered them, were seen by Elizabeth's government as a threat to political stability and were harshly dealt with when caught.

The government response to the Catholic threat

In 1571, Elizabeth was forced to summon her first parliament for five years in response to the growing religious and political crises in England and abroad. Subsequent parliaments were called in 1572, 1581, 1584 and 1586, in response to the increasing threat that Catholicism was felt to pose. Each of these parliaments followed news of the discovery of Catholic plots to assassinate Elizabeth and replace her with Mary, Queen of Scots, whom Elizabeth refused to execute until 1587.

KEY TERM

Jesuit
The Jesuit order of priests was founded in the 1530s as a Catholic response to the growing popularity of Protestantism. A Jesuit takes a vow of obedience to the papacy and their aim is to spread the Catholic faith, even in difficult or dangerous conditions.

Parliament attempted to increase punishments for recusants in order to deter plots against Elizabeth. Some of these attempts were unsuccessful because Elizabeth herself opposed them, but even she was forced to accept an increasingly hard-line approach as threats from some English Catholics and foreign Catholic powers increased. For example, in 1571, parliament made it a treasonable offence to obtain or publish the papal bull of excommunication. In the same year, the Treason Act was extended to include those who tried to claim that Elizabeth had no right to be queen. In 1572, parliament met in the aftermath of the massacre of St Bartholemew's Eve in France. This event heightened fear and suspicion of English Catholics, and especially the role played by Mary in encouraging further plots against Elizabeth.

SOURCE

11   Sir Walter Mildmay, a Protestant member of Elizabeth's Council, speaking to parliament in November 1584.

I beseech you to consider what a change there would be if, in the place of the present rulers, those priests, rebels, fugitives, and Papists, known to be cruel and dissolute and vain, were set at the helm of the Church and commonwealth. And if any doubt what a miserable change this would be, let him but remember the late days of Queen Mary [I], when... the Pope's authority was wholly restored, and for the continuance thereof a strange nation, proud and insolent, brought into this land to be lords over us.

The 1572 parliament attempted to pass an Act that would have banned Mary from the English succession, but Elizabeth would not agree to this. But further threats followed with the arrival of the seminary and Jesuit priests. In 1577, Cuthbert Mayne was the first to be captured and executed. In 1581, Elizabeth agreed to stricter laws against recusants, including a huge increase in the fine for non-attendance of Church of England services to £20 a month or imprisonment. Anyone who was caught attending Mass could also be imprisoned. In 1584, fears of Catholic plots increased still further following the assassination of the Dutch Protestant rebel leader, William of Orange. Mary's continued survival and role in plots against Elizabeth added to these tensions. In 1584, a document known as the Bond of Association was circulated by Elizabeth's Council. Those who signed the Bond pledged to put to death anyone who tried to gain the throne by harming Elizabeth. The parliament of 1584–85 once again sought to tighten controls on Catholic priests and their recusant supporters. This led to the Bond being made law in the Act for the Queen's Safety. An Act against Catholic priests also ordered them to leave the country within 40 days or be executed for treason. Anyone found guilty of helping them would also face the death penalty. In 1585, England was finally drawn into a war with Spain, after years of increasing tension. This meant that there was a strong possibility of a foreign Catholic invasion force combining with Catholic recusants and Mary, Queen of Scots to remove Elizabeth. In 1586, these fears became justified when Sir Francis Walsingham, Elizabeth's spy master, discovered another plot to assassinate Elizabeth involving Mary and English and French Catholics. Parliament was called to condemn Mary, and the Council forced the reluctant Elizabeth into signing Mary's death warrant, though she was furious when she found that her orders had been carried out.

EXTEND YOUR KNOWLEDGE

The massacre of St Bartholomew's Eve and the assassination of William of Orange
English paranoia about the threat posed by Catholicism was heightened by events on the continent. In both France and the Netherlands, Catholic and Protestant forces were at war, and news of Catholic massacres of Protestants led to fear of a Catholic crusade against England and similar violence against English Protestants. In the massacre of St Bartholomew's Eve in 1572, violence against Protestants began in Paris, but spread rapidly throughout France. An estimated 10,000 Protestants were killed. In 1584, the assassination of the Dutch Protestant leader of the rebellion against Catholic Spanish rule, William of Orange, led to fears of a similar event in England. William of Orange was shot by a Catholic who had gained access to William's circle by posing as an ally. The assassination showed just how vulnerable a ruler could be.

SOURCE

12 A letter from one of the Protestant spymaster Sir Francis Walsingham's agents, written to him in February 1585, describing the threat from the Catholics.

I have revealed the miserable and perfidious design of the enemies of the state, who desire nothing but its total ruin, and to raise and stir up the people of England against their princess by a civil war. This they do by means of evil rumours and defamatory books, popish and contrary to religion, which are transported into England from France at the instance of those who are in flight from their country, and also of the Spanish ambassador and of others who favour them: such as Mass-books, other defamatory books written by Jesuits... and other books serving their purpose.

ACTIVITY
KNOWLEDGE CHECK

Read Sources 11 and 12.

1 What do they suggest about the seriousness of the threat posed by Catholics to Elizabeth and her government?

2 How might the authors and purpose of these sources affect their view of the Catholic threat?

TIMELINE: CHANGING ELIZABETHAN ATTITUDES TO CATHOLICS FOLLOWING THE 1569 RISING, 1570–87

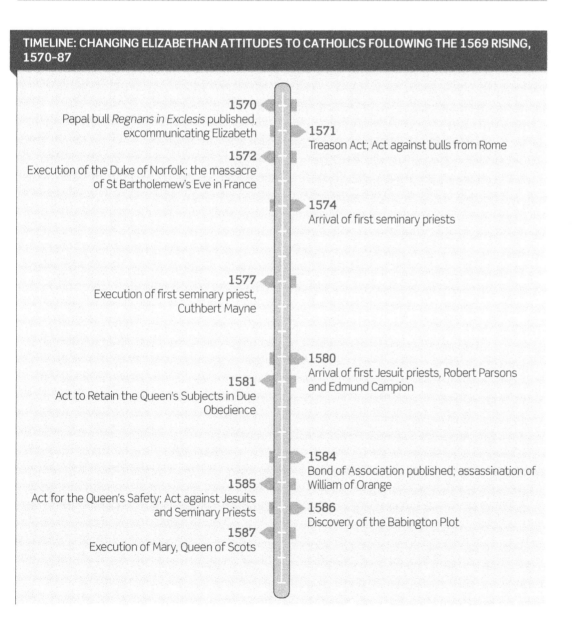

1570
Papal bull *Regnans in Exclesis* published, excommunicating Elizabeth

1571
Treason Act; Act against bulls from Rome

1572
Execution of the Duke of Norfolk; the massacre of St Bartholemew's Eve in France

1574
Arrival of first seminary priests

1577
Execution of first seminary priest, Cuthbert Mayne

1580
Arrival of first Jesuit priests, Robert Parsons and Edmund Campion

1581
Act to Retain the Queen's Subjects in Due Obedience

1584
Bond of Association published; assassination of William of Orange

1585
Act for the Queen's Safety; Act against Jesuits and Seminary Priests

1586
Discovery of the Babington Plot

1587
Execution of Mary, Queen of Scots

The decline of Catholicism in England

By the end of the reign, practising Catholics were a minority. It has been estimated that by 1603, only 50,000 Catholics, including Church papists, remained in a population of about five million. The decline in Catholicism after 1569 was hastened by the lack of access to priests who were prepared to perform masses in secret. Although Jesuit and seminary priests did their best to sustain the Catholic faith, they were not able to reach the majority of the Catholic population in England. By the 1580s, the English clergy who had been appointed in the reign of the Catholic Queen Mary were also starting to die out. These clergymen had helped to keep older traditions and practices alive. However, the longer that Elizabeth survived, the more likely it was that her religious settlement would continue and reach wider acceptance. By the late 1580s, a whole generation of English people had grown up with the Church of England. This undermined the older Catholic tradition, though without the stricter laws and suspicion of recusants that was brought about by the Northern Rising, Catholicism might have remained a stronger force in England for much longer. Ironically, by the late 1580s, it was Puritanism that was considered to be more of a threat to the political stability of England.

Protestantism in England after the Northern Rising

The increasing fear of Catholicism after 1569 also led to a growing desire among Protestants to reinforce their own beliefs and practices. Some Puritans saw the opportunity to push for a more radical religious settlement as a means of making English Protestantism secure and counter-balancing the threat from Catholic recusants.

As a reaction to the Northern Rising, the personnel on Elizabeth's Council began to change. New councillors in the 1570s included Sir Walter Mildmay, Ambrose Dudley, Earl of Warwick and Sir Francis Walsingham. All of these men had Protestant sympathies and aimed to strengthen the Protestant faith in England. Some of these men, including Robert Dudley, Earl of Leicester, favoured sending an army to help the Dutch Protestant rebels against Catholic Spain. Creating a Protestant-controlled Netherlands would have increased the number of potential English allies. It would also have had the advantage of driving out potentially hostile Spanish troops from the Netherlands, denying them a base from which to launch a Catholic invasion. Elizabeth consistently overruled these plans, preferring a more cautious approach. She was not persuaded to help the Dutch openly until 1585, which led to the outbreak of war with Spain. In 1588, English Protestant fears of a Catholic invasion reached new heights, with the arrival of the Spanish Armada off the English coast. The Armada was defeated, but the threat of Spanish intervention, which had not materialised in 1569, remained a constant problem for the rest of the reign.

Within England, Elizabeth's Protestant councillors tried to ensure the growth of Protestantism as a way to ensure loyalty to Elizabeth. Elizabeth herself wanted to ensure the growth of moderate **Anglicanism**, but some of her councillors, such as the Earl of Leicester, supported and protected more radical Puritan preachers such as Thomas Cartwright. The spread of Protestantism was also helped by the growth of printing, which allowed cheap religious tracts and ballads to be produced. These tracts were strongly antipapal and xenophobic, but they emphasised the idea that support for the Church of England was the duty of all loyal Englishmen.

Elizabeth's Protestant councillors were also behind much of the anti-Catholic legislation that was passed from 1571. They used parliament to try to put pressure on the reluctant Elizabeth to put Mary on trial, though she resisted until 1586. Puritan MPs in parliament also saw the threat from Catholicism as an opportunity to argue for a more radical religious settlement. In 1571, for example, a Puritan MP, William Strickland, tried to introduce a bill that would have created a more radical Book of Common Prayer. He was defeated because Elizabeth refused to consider any changes to her moderate religious settlement, but this did not deter other Puritans from trying to alter the structure and liturgy of the Church of England. Ironically, by the late 1580s, Puritanism was seen as more of a threat than Catholicism. A tiny minority of Puritans, known as separatists, tried to break away from the Church of England altogether by setting up their own independent churches. These groups were forcibly suppressed, but their persistence led to the Act against Seditious Sectaries, passed in 1593. The development of radical Protestantism in the wake of the increased threat posed by Catholicism from 1569 was also a threat to Elizabeth. Some Puritans seemed to want to challenge her right to be governor of the Church of England, and even to break away from the Church altogether. Although most Puritans did not go this far, any challenge to Elizabeth's authority after 1569 was suppressed. The 1569 rising showed that any radical religious beliefs were a potential threat to Elizabeth's position as queen; after this date, any attempt at further challenges, either legal or illegal, were suppressed.

EXTRACT 1

From N. Fellows, *Disorder and Rebellion in Tudor England* (2001).

The two Earls had many reasons for leading the rising... fear appears to be an important factor: they had already suffered a loss of status under the Elizabethan regime...

EXTRACT 2

From C. Haigh, *Elizabeth I* (2013).

Elizabeth I had blundered: she forced the Earls to choose between flight and rebellion, when rebellion was still (just) a realistic option. They chose rebellion, because of the Catholic enthusiasm of their followers... so the Earls rebelled, more in sorrow, than in anger: men who had been planning a rebellion for weeks, even months, were forced into an unplanned rising.

EXTRACT 3

From A. Fletcher and D. MacCulloch, *Tudor Rebellions*, 5th edn (2008).

So secular as well as religious tensions in northern society deserve consideration in the context of this rebellion. It may be that political resentment at the extension of Tudor authority in the North was more important in attracting support to it than hatred of Protestantism. Bowes was hated not for his religious feelings but for his strident loyalty... When Elizabeth summoned the earls to Court she precipitated a crisis in northern society, but the cause of Catholicism proved inadequate to sustain the rising that followed.

ACTIVITY
SUMMARY

1 Design a poster showing the causes and main events of the Northern Rising. You may use illustrations on your poster, but you should ensure that there is plenty of factual detail (e.g. dates, examples).

2 Explain in your own words the consequences of the Northern Rising for each of the following:

   a) Elizabeth I and her Council

   b) moderate Catholics in England

   c) recusants

   d) moderate Protestants in England

   e) Puritans.

WIDER READING

Doran, S. *Elizabeth I and Religion*, Lancaster Pamphlets (1993)

Guy, J. *My Heart is My Own: the Life of Mary, Queen of Scots*, Harper Collins (2004)

Kesselring, K. *The Northern Rebellion of 1569: Faith, Politics and Protest in Elizabethan England*, Palgrave Macmillan (2007)

THINKING HISTORICALLY   Evidence (6b)

The strength of argument

Read Extract 1.

1 What is weak about this claim?

2 What could be added to it to make it stronger?

Read Extract 2.

3 Is this an argument? If yes, what makes it one?

4 How might this argument be strengthened?

Read Extract 3.

5 How have they expanded their explanation to make the claim stronger?

6 Can you explain why this is the strongest claim of the three extracts?

7 What elements make an historian's claims strong?

3.7 | Troublesome Ireland: Tyrone's rebellion, 1594–1603

KEY QUESTIONS
- Why did the Nine Years' War (Tyrone's rebellion) break out?
- How extensive was support for rebellion in the years 1594–1603?
- Why did the war last so long?

INTRODUCTION

In 1595, rebellion against English rule in Ireland broke out. The reasons for the revolt were a mixture of longer-term and shorter-term problems. The English monarchy had long attempted to extend its control in Ireland; the need to do this was increased as a result of the break with Rome in the 1530s, which created additional religious tensions. Meanwhile, the **Anglo-Irish lords**, who traditionally ruled most of Ireland, felt increasingly alienated and threatened by English policy. The result was a rebellion that the English authorities struggled to contain, which was made worse by the wider context of England's ongoing war with Spain and the threat of Spanish intervention in Ireland.

WHY DID THE NINE YEARS' WAR (TYRONE'S REBELLION) BREAK OUT?

The reasons for the Nine Years' War

Long-term problems in Anglo-Irish relations

Ireland and its relationship with England was a problem for all of the Tudor monarchs. The Tudor monarchs did not rule Ireland, although they claimed to have the right to do so. In the Tudor period, England controlled Dublin and its **Pale** through a Lord Deputy. The situation beyond the Pale was complex. Most of Ireland was controlled by Anglo-Irish members of the nobility, such as the O'Neills, who, as Irish chieftains, maintained their own private armies and acted as quasi-kings in the regions under their control.

Another problem was that the government and traditions of the Irishry were very different from those of England and could seem threatening to English observers, especially those living in Dublin and the Pale. The Irish practised a custom known as **tanistry**, which was used to organise the inheritance of lands and titles. In addition, the Irish nobles did not adopt English titles such as 'earl'; for example,

KEY TERMS

Anglo-Irish lord
A descendant of earlier English settlers who had intermarried with the indigenous Irish. Over hundreds of years, these Anglo-Irish nobles had developed their own identity. Most spoke the native language of Ireland, Gaelic, and were proud of their independent status.

The Pale
The area that surrounded Dublin. Traditionally, English rule did not extend 'beyond the Pale'. Lands beyond the Pale were known as 'the Irishry'.

1530s – England breaks with Rome

1541 – Irish chieftains acknowledge Henry VIII as king of Ireland

1556 – The Earl of Sussex begins policy of plantation in Ireland

| 1530 | 1535 | 1540 | 1545 | 1550 | 1555 | 1560 | 1565 |

Hugh O'Neill, who became the head of the O'Neill clan, was known as 'the O'Neill'. Although this practice ensured that the clan was always led by a strong, adult male, it also led to feuds, as rivals for the chieftainship struggled for power. This system, coupled with the apparent lawlessness and primitive nature of the Irish way of life when compared to that of the English, led some of the English living in Ireland to argue that the best way to control Ireland was to anglicise its laws and customs.

KEY TERM

Tanistry
The Irish system that governed the inheritance of titles and land. Under this system, all those who bore the family name, known as a clan, were ruled by a leader chosen from among the adult males of that clan. This meant that inheritance of land and titles did not necessarily move from father to eldest son, as it did in England; the tanist (heir) could be a nephew, a cousin or a more distant relative from the same family.

SOURCE
1 Chief of the Mac Sweynes seated at dinner and being entertained by a bard and a harper, plate 3 from *The Image of Ireland* by John Derricke, an English artist, 1581 (woodcut).

ACTIVITY
KNOWLEDGE CHECK

1 What does Source 1 reveal about the customs and lifestyle of the Anglo-Irish lords?

2 This picture was made by an English artist; how might this affect the way the Anglo-Irish are depicted?

Timeline

- **1570** – Elizabeth I excommunicated
- **1579–83** – Rebellion in Munster and plantation of Munster begins
- **1588** – Defeat of the Spanish Armada
- **1596** – English expedition to Cadiz and second Spanish Armada
- **1600** – Mountjoy sent to Ireland
- **1603** – Death of Elizabeth I; Tyrone surrenders

1570   1575   1580   1585   1590   1595   1600   1605

- **1569–71** – Introduction of English-style councils in Connaught and Munster
- **1574–76** – Failure of English plantations in Ulster
- **1585** – England goes to war with Spain
- **1594** – Outbreak of rebellion in Ulster
- **1599** – Earl of Essex sent to Ireland
- **1601** – Spanish force lands at Kinsale; Tyrone defeated

Policy of conciliation
A peaceful method in which a compromise was reached between the English and Anglo-Irish.

Tenants-in-chief
Under the medieval system of land ownership in England, technically all land was owned by the king. His nobility were his tenants; their rent was usually paid through military service in the king's armies. The monarch could also exercise rights over the lands of tenants-in-chief, including the right to administer their estates if the tenant died while the heir was a minor. Lands that were forfeited by a tenant-in-chief who was executed also reverted to the Crown.

Long-term causes of the rebellion

The problem of Ireland became potentially more serious from the 1530s, when Henry VIII broke with Rome (see Chapter 1) because Ireland remained Roman Catholic. This created an additional problem for the Tudor monarchs because Irish Catholic sympathies might lead them to support a Catholic crusade against England. The Tudor monarchs were now faced with a choice: they could either follow a **policy of conciliation**, or they could try to intervene more directly in Ireland. In the 1540s, Henry VIII chose the first course of action.

- In 1541, the Irish chieftains agreed to recognise Henry's right to be king of Ireland; the English government also encouraged the Anglo-Irish nobility to surrender their lands to the Crown. These lands were then re-granted to the Anglo-Irish; the Irish nobility were to be **tenants-in-chief** of the English Crown and they were given English titles.

- However, the Anglo-Irish nobility continued to remain semi-independent. In response, Mary appointed an English Lord Deputy, the Earl of Sussex. Sussex started a new trend in the English response to the problem of Ireland. He fortified the Pale and then encouraged English settlers to move into territory just outside the Pale. The idea was to 'civilise' the Irish by introducing English customs and practices; this system was known as plantation.

Elizabeth's rule of Ireland, 1559–94

As a Protestant queen, Elizabeth faced the potential threat of an Irish-Catholic rising against her rule. This threat started to become a reality from 1569, with the Revolt of the Northern Earls in England (see Chapter 6). The response of the English government was to pursue a more hard-line policy in which the traditions and laws in Ireland were to be replaced with English ones. For example, the English government tried to establish councils to govern the regions of Connaught and Munster, in 1569 and 1571 respectively. These councils were modelled on the Councils of the North and Wales and were led by a president. In a further attempt to anglicise Irish government, the traditional Irish regions were subdivided into English-style counties, which were run under traditional English methods, using officials such as sheriffs.

The policy of more direct intervention by the English government led to unsuccessful rebellions in Munster in 1569 and 1579–83. The second rebellion was brutally suppressed, the rebels were hunted down and executed and their lands were used to encourage plantation by English settlers. These plans were based on similar plans for the colonisation of the New World by Sir Walter Raleigh. By 1592, there were 775 English settlers in Munster. These settlers were outnumbered by the indigenous Irish in the region, but their presence was still a cause of resentment.

Sir Walter Raleigh, Ireland and the colonisation of the New World
In 1584, the explorer and adventurer Sir Walter Raleigh was instructed by Elizabeth I to explore and set up an English colony in North America. Raleigh never went to North America himself. Instead, he and a group of friends funded two expeditions to found a colony at Roanoke in North Carolina, in 1584 and 1587. These early attempts at colonisation (although they were unsuccessful) encouraged similar plans for Ireland. Raleigh himself took advantage of the confiscation of the Desmond lands to acquire extensive Irish estates (about 160,000 hectares) for himself. He then tried to encourage English settlers to become his tenants, although he was not very successful. Raleigh took up residence at Killua Castle and spent some time there until he sold his estates in 1602.

Composition
Traditionally, landowners in Ireland had had to pay various charges to both the English and their Irish overlords. Landlords had to pay money to the English known as a 'cess', to cover the cost of garrisons (troops who were stationed permanently in a town or fortress). The same landlords also had to give money to their Irish chieftain to cover the cost of his private army and household. The English plan was to commute (transfer) these payments into one single payment to the English authorities; this system was known as composition.

The arrival of new English settlers to take over estates that had once belonged to Anglo-Irish nobles caused additional tensions in the Irishry. The new settlers saw the indigenous Irish as backward and superstitious; this assumption was fuelled by many of the settlers' commitment to a radical Protestant faith. The new settlers thought it was their God-given duty to convert the Irish, whom they saw as being little better than pagans. Meanwhile, the Irish Catholics began to link protection of their religious beliefs with protection of 'Irish' values and traditions.

Even in regions of Ireland where there was no open revolt, English policy was leading to increasing tension with the Anglo-Irish nobility. From 1585, the English government used a technique known as **composition** to try to increase their hold over Ireland. In 1585, for example, Connaught landowners were persuaded by English commissioners to agree to the commutation of their traditional payments. The Irish landlords agreed that they would pay a yearly rent to the Council of Connaught of 10 shillings for every 50 hectares of inhabited land that they owned. Superficially, this seemed like a better deal for Irish landowners, as it appeared to reduce the often arbitrary financial demands that were made on them. In return, the Anglo-Irish chieftains were supposed to accept English-style law and government in their territories, which increased English control there.

SOURCE

2

From Edmund Spenser's treaty, *On the View of the Present State of Ireland* (1596), cited in *The Dublin Review*, vol. 17 by W. Spooner. Spenser was an English poet who acquired lands in the Munster plantation. He spent time in Ireland in the 1580s and 1590s, campaigning against Irish unrest. He favoured complete anglicisation.

Wherein it is great wonder to see the odds which are between the zeal of the Popish priests and the ministers of the Gospel. For they spare not to come out of Spain, from Rome and from Rheims, by long toil and dangerous travelling hither, where they know peril of death awaits them and no reward or riches are to be found, only to draw the people unto the Church of Rome: whereas some of our idle ministers, having a way for credit and estimation thereby opened up to them, and having the livings of the country offered to them without pains and without peril, will neither for the same, nor any love of God, nor zeal of religion, nor for all the good they may do by winning souls to God, be drawn forth from their warm nests to look out into God's harvest, which is even ready for the sickle and all the fields yellow long ago.

SOURCE

3

A description of Ireland written by Captain Francisco de Cuellar in 1589, cited in H. Allingham, *Captain Cuellar's Adventures*, 1897. De Cuellar had been in the Spanish Armada in 1588. His ship escaped the English but was wrecked off the Irish coast. The Spanish who survived the shipwreck were beaten and robbed by the Irish.

The custom of these savages is to live as the brute beasts among the mountains... carry on a perpetual war with the English, who here keep garrison for the queen... The chief inclination of these people is to be robbers, and to plunder each other; so that no day passes without a call to arms among them... These people call themselves Christians. Mass is said among them, and regulated according to the orders of the Church of Rome. The great majority of their churches, monasteries, and hermitages, have been demolished by the hands of the English... In short, in this kingdom there is neither justice nor right, and everyone does what he pleases.

ACTIVITY
KNOWLEDGE CHECK

1 Make your own timeline showing the main events in Anglo-Irish relations from 1509 onwards.

2 On your timeline, use different to colours to show the religious, political and international causes of the deteriorating relations with Ireland.

3 Read Sources 2 and 3. What does Edmund Spenser think are the main problems facing the English in Ireland? How far does Francisco de Cuellar agree with Spenser?

4 In what ways do the backgrounds and experiences of the authors of Sources 2 and 3 affect their view of the situation in Ireland?

English incursions into Ulster from the 1570s

Many of the issues affecting other parts of Ireland also affected Ulster. In the late 16th century, Ulster remained the most Gaelic part of Ireland, where English control was extremely limited. Ulster was controlled by the O'Neill clan, although their power was traditionally disputed by a rival clan, the O'Donnells. In the past, it had suited the English government to allow the O'Neills and O'Donnells to govern Ulster between them. However, from the 1570s, the English began to encroach into Ulster territory. Two English courtiers, the Earl of Essex and Sir Thomas Smith, were granted a contract to establish a settlement in Eastern Ulster. This plantation failed, but not before the situation had spiralled into violence. The plantations were resisted by both the O'Neills and the O'Donnells, uniting them against a common enemy. The English responded with violence. In 1574, 200 members of the O'Neill clan were massacred at a feast to which they had been invited by the English; in 1575, 500 members of the O'Donnell clan were killed in a surprise raid. Elizabeth called off the plantation in 1576, but the damage had already been done to Anglo-Irish relations.

The resentment of the Earl of Tyrone and other Ulster lords

Although the English attempted a more conciliatory approach to Ulster in the 1580s, with Hugh O'Neill accepting the English title of Earl of Tyrone in 1585, this was only a temporary peace. Tensions grew with new attempts by the English to settle Ulster. From 1585, the chieftains of Ulster had started to agree to commutation and to the re-granting of their estates to the English Crown, so that they became tenants of the English monarchy and subject to English law. From 1590, the English government in Dublin took advantage of the new settlement of the Anglo-Irish estates. The initial Ulster plantation was made possible by the execution in 1590 of the chief of the MacMahon clan, Hugh Roe MacMahon, and the forfeiture of his lands to the Crown. The MacMahon lands in Ulster were then given to English settlers such as Sir Henry Bagenal. Meanwhile, the Anglo-Irish lords realised that the commutation and re-grant agreements they had made concealed a trap. Anyone who failed to keep their side of the agreement with the English could now be charged with treason under English law.

EXTEND YOUR KNOWLEDGE

The MacMahon clan, the Earl of Tyrone and English rule in Ireland

The MacMahons were traditionally tenants of Hugh O'Neill in Ulster. Under Irish custom, the MacMahon lands should have reverted to O'Neill. However, the MacMahons had been persuaded to surrender their lordship of Oriel to the English Crown, which had then been re-granted to them, and changed into an English-style county, called County Monaghan. But Hugh Roe MacMahon was only prepared to accept commutation, surrender and re-grant; he was not prepared to accept English-style rule, something that the English government insisted was essential. The result of this dispute was that MacMahon was tried and executed for resisting English rule, and his estates were forfeited to the English Crown, not O'Neill.

Tyrone began to feel increasingly under threat from English rule. Before 1590, he had been prepared to work with the English government in Dublin when it suited him. Tyrone was in a feud with the overall head of the O'Neill clan, Turlough Luineach O'Neill, over Tyrone's right to be the next chieftain. This explains why Tyrone had been prepared to accept an English title; English support was important to him as he attempted to assert his right to be O'Neill's heir. However, from 1590, English attitudes to Tyrone began to change, as the government sought to assert its power more directly in Ulster. Tyrone became a potential obstacle to complete English dominance in Ulster. Tyrone tried to neutralise the threat from the English by making a marriage alliance with the sister of one of the new English incomers, Sir Henry Bagenal. Although Sir Henry refused to allow the marriage to go ahead, Tyrone and Mabel eloped. This created personal enmity between Tyrone and Sir Henry.

Other Ulster chieftains were also coming under threat in the 1590s. Hugh Roe O'Donnell had been kidnapped and imprisoned in Dublin Castle by the English. O'Donnell was held prisoner to make his father obey English rule. After four years of imprisonment, O'Donnell managed to escape in 1591 and began

to plot against them. Another Ulster lord, Hugh Maguire, was also increasingly resentful about English intrusions into Fermanagh, a region he had previously controlled. Both Maguire and O'Donnell had links to the Earl of Tyrone because they were married to Tyrone's daughters. Maguire and O'Donnell's plotting against the English in the early 1590s made it increasingly hard for Tyrone to remain neutral, even if he had wanted to.

English mismanagement of the Anglo-Irish chieftains

In May 1593, Hugh Maguire launched an attack on English officials in Sligo. Tyrone, as the leading lord in the region, was ordered by the Lord Deputy to arrest Maguire, but Tyrone refused. Maguire then attacked the English garrison based at Monaghan (Ulster). Forced to co-operate with Sir Henry Bagenal, who was in charge of English forces in the region, Tyrone helped to capture Maguire in October 1593. Tyrone then retired to his estates at Dungannon, complaining that Bagenal had failed to acknowledge the help he had given. Tyrone felt himself to be increasingly under threat from English rule. He wanted the English to give him overall charge of Ulster, in return for which he would accept English-style government, such as sheriffs and English law courts.

Tyrone was not alone in feeling that he was being overlooked in favour of Englishmen with connections to Elizabeth's Court. For example, the Earl of Ormond was one of the most influential of the Anglo-Irish nobility, but he was never appointed to the position of Lord Deputy, even though he was Elizabeth's cousin. Appointments to office in Ireland were increasingly dominated by minor English officials who had access to Court patronage and who used their position for personal gain. This situation increased the resentment of the Anglo-Irish.

Tyrone's decision to rebel

However, it was Tyrone's resentment and his links to O'Donnell and Maguire that caused Elizabeth and her Council to become increasingly concerned about the situation in Ulster.

- In 1593, O'Donnell had been in touch with the Catholic Philip II of Spain to ask for support, but this was not forthcoming because Philip was too busy dealing with trouble in the Netherlands.

- In June 1594, O'Donnell and Maguire besieged the English-held Enniskillen Castle; in August, Maguire, helped by Tyrone's brother, ambushed an English relief force heading for Enniskillen, killing 56 English soldiers.

- In August 1594, Tyrone presented himself to the new and inexperienced Lord Deputy in Dublin, Sir William Russell, and promised to restore peace in Ulster and to co-operate with the English government. In return, Tyrone wanted complete control over Ulster.

- Russell was prepared to believe Tyrone's promises and did not arrest him; crucially, Tyrone was also allowed to keep his private army, which was normally used for keeping local order. However, Elizabeth's government was not prepared to give Tyrone the control he wanted because they distrusted his intentions. The result was that Tyrone's grievances continued to grow, and in May 1595 he rebelled.

Men such as Hugh O'Neill, Earl of Tyrone, had spent time in England, had English connections and spoke English fluently. However, as the demands he published in 1599 show (Source 4), he also had loyalties to his Irish roots and resented increasing English intervention. In addition, religious tensions also played their part in persuading the Catholic Tyrone and his followers to rebel. The influx of Protestant settlers created an additional threat for those loyal to Catholicism which led them to look for support from England's enemy, Spain. Ultimately, Tyrone's loyalties to his Irish roots and Catholic faith were stronger than his newer links to an English government that seemed to be increasingly untrustworthy. The result was that he chose to rebel and challenge English control of Ireland.

ACTIVITY
KNOWLEDGE CHECK

1 Copy and complete the table to show how the English handling of the situation in Ulster led to rebellion.

Problem	What happened?	How did this make revolt in Ulster more likely?
English plantations in Ulster		
Tyrone's grievances		
Grievances of other Ulster lords		
Mistakes of the English government		
Religion		

2 In your opinion, what was the most important reason for the outbreak of Tyrone's revolt? Explain your answer.

EXTEND YOUR KNOWLEDGE

Hugh O'Neill, Earl of Tyrone and his connections with England
Tyrone had been fostered by an English settler family and had made visits to Court in 1567–68, 1587 and 1590. During these visits, he built up links with influential men, such as the Earl of Leicester and Elizabeth's spymaster, Sir Francis Walsingham. Even the queen had been impressed by Tyrone. By the early 1590s, however, the situation at Court had changed. Walsingham and Leicester had both died and they were replaced by men with whom Tyrone had no connections.

A Level Exam-Style Question Section B

How significant were the grievances of Hugh O'Neill, Earl of Tyrone, in bringing about rebellion in Ireland from 1594? (20 marks)

Tip
You will need to compare the significance of Tyrone's grievances with the wider causes of the revolt.

SOURCE
4

A selection from Tyrone's demands made in 1599. A copy of these demands reached Sir Robert Cecil, the queen's Secretary, who wrote the word 'Ewtopia' [Utopia] on them.

That the Catholic, Apostolic and Roman religion be openly preached and taught throughout all Ireland, as well in cities as borough towns, by Bishops, seminary priests, Jesuits, and all other religious men.

That the Church of Ireland be wholly governed by the Pope...

That all Irish priests and religious men, now prisoners in England or Ireland, be presently set at liberty, will all temporal [lay] Irishmen, that are troubled for their conscience, and to go where they will without further trouble...

That there be erected an university upon the Crown rents of Ireland, wherein all sciences shall be taught according to the manner of the Catholic Roman Church.

That the Governor of Ireland be at least an Earl, and of the Privy Council of England...

That the Lord Chancellor, Lord Treasurer, Lord Admiral, the Council of State, the Justices of the laws... and all other officers appertaining to the Council and law of Ireland, be Irishmen.

That all principal governments of Ireland, as Connaught, Munster, etc., be governed by Irish noblemen...

That no Irishmen's heirs shall lose their lands for the faults of their ancestors...

That no children nor any other friends be taken as pledges for the good abearing of their parents, and, if there be any such pledges now in the hands of the English, they must presently be released...

That the Queen nor her successors may in no sort press an Irishman to serve them against his will.

That O'Neill, O'Donnell, the Earl of Desmond, with all their partakers, may peaceably enjoy all lands and privileges that did appertain to their predecessors 200 years past...

That all Irishmen, of what quality they be, may freely travel in foreign countries, for their better experience, without making any of the Queen's officers acquainted withal...

That all Irishmen that will may learn, and use all occupations and arts whatsoever...

ACTIVITY
KNOWLEDGE CHECK

1 Read Source 4. Using different colours, highlight the different types of complaints made by Tyrone. Which are religious? Political? Cultural?

2 Tyrone produced these demands in 1599, when he was at the height of his power and his successes against the English. How might this have affected his demands?

3 What do you think Robert Cecil meant by writing 'Utopia' on Tyrone's demands? What does this suggest about the attitudes of the English government towards Tyrone's revolt?

KEY TERMS

Musketman
Member of the army carrying a musket (a firearm).

Pikeman
Member of the army carrying a pike (a long pole with a metal tip).

Support for Tyrone within Ireland

Tyrone's revolt was a serious challenge to England. Tyrone's rebel army was large and well-organised. He used English and Spanish captains to train his men, and imported weapons and ammunition. In 1595, Tyrone led an army of 1,000 cavalry, 4,000 **musketmen** and 1,000 **pikemen**. He also had the support of other Ulster chieftains, including his two sons-in-law, Hugh Roe O'Donnell and Hugh Maguire. Traditional feuds were forgotten as the Irish united against a common enemy, the English. Moreover, rather than using traditional weapons such as spears and axes, Tyrone's troops were equipped with modern weapons such as muskets and pikes. His force was supplemented by deserters from the English army. These were Irishmen who had been recruited by the English because they were experienced fighters, but these men found that their loyalties were ultimately with the Irish rebels, not the English. Even Tyrone's cavalry was better-trained than the English horsemen.

Tyrone's successes encouraged other Irish chieftains outside Ulster to join his rebellion. The rebellion spread first to Connaught in 1595; in 1598, Leinster and Munster joined the rebellion. Key supporters included James FitzThomas and Florence MacCarthy. By 1596, the rebels claimed to have 6,000 foot soldiers and 1,200 cavalry, compared with the English forces of 5,732 footmen and 617 cavalry. The rebel armies consistently outnumbered the English forces until Elizabeth was finally persuaded to send the largest army of her reign to Ireland in 1599, under the leadership of Robert Devereux, the second Earl of Essex.

Spanish support for Tyrone's rebellion

The role of Philip II of Spain

Philip II of Spain saw it as his duty to help fellow Catholics against Protestant forces. The Spanish monarchs also saw an opportunity to destabilise the English war effort. England and Spain had been at war since 1585; the **Spanish Armada** had failed in 1588, but this did not deter the Spanish. English forces had been sent to help the Dutch Protestants who were rebelling against Spanish Catholic rule in the Netherlands and there had also been an English attack on the Spanish port of Cadiz.

KEY TERM

Spanish Armada
An armada was a fleet of warships. The most famous example of an armada was the fleet sent against England by Philip II in 1588, which was intended to provoke Catholic rebellion in England, but was defeated. There were further Spanish armadas in the 1590s.

Irish-Spanish contact had begun as early as 1593. In September 1595, there were further negotiations with the Spanish for money and men. In 1596, Philip agreed to send a second Armada, this time to Ireland. The Spanish fleet intended for Ireland was large – 100 ships; there was also an additional fleet that was sent to attack England itself. Luckily for Elizabeth, the Spanish fleet was dispersed by strong winds; 32 ships were lost and the rest had to return to Spain.

Spanish support for Tyrone under Philip III

On Philip II's death in 1598, his successor, Philip III, was prepared to continue the Spanish policy of intervention in Ireland. However, Philip III was uncertain about the best policy to adopt. Sending troops and ships was expensive and dangerous. However, sending a Spanish army to Ireland might encourage Elizabeth to withdraw her troops from the Spanish Netherlands as she tried to deal with the increasing problems in Ireland. Moreover, Philip III hoped that sending an army to Ireland would allow him to establish a base there from which he could invade England itself. However, before 1601, he never had enough available troops to send to Ireland.

In January 1601, Philip finally had enough troops to send to Ireland. However, the Spanish encountered problems on their voyage; some of the ships in the fleet became separated during a storm. These included the ships carrying some of the weapons and ammunition. When the Spanish army eventually reached Kinsale, there were only 3,400 men left out of the 6,000 Tyrone had requested. If Tyrone had been able to meet up with the Spanish army, their combined forces would have outnumbered the English army again, but the actions of the English Lord Deputy Mountjoy prevented this from happening. Ultimately, although Spanish support for Tyrone's rebellion was significant in that they were prepared to provide money and men, their support was more of a threat than a reality. The Spanish kings were too busy fighting the Dutch rebels and the English to be able to give more than temporary and limited support to the Irish rebels. Bad luck played a part in the ending of the 1596 Armada, and the invasion force that finally arrived in 1601 was too late to make a significant contribution to a rebellion that was already weakening.

ACTIVITY
KNOWLEDGE CHECK

1 Why do you think Tyrone was able to command such support in Ireland?

2 Why was the English response to Tyrone's revolt weakened?

3 How significant was the role of Spanish support?

4 What was the significance of key events and individuals?

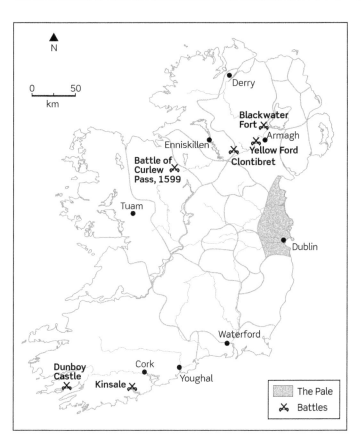

Figure 7.1 The main events and sites of battles in Ireland, 1594–1603.

HOW EXTENSIVE WAS SUPPORT FOR REBELLION IN THE YEARS 1594–1603?

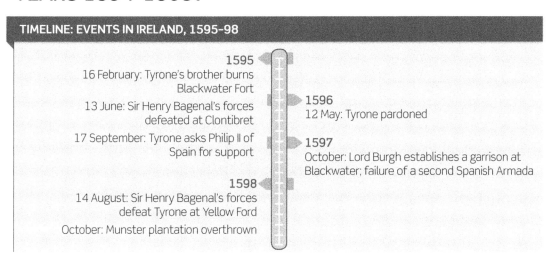

TIMELINE: EVENTS IN IRELAND, 1595–98

1595
16 February: Tyrone's brother burns Blackwater Fort

13 June: Sir Henry Bagenal's forces defeated at Clontibret

17 September: Tyrone asks Philip II of Spain for support

1596
12 May: Tyrone pardoned

1597
October: Lord Burgh establishes a garrison at Blackwater; failure of a second Spanish Armada

1598
14 August: Sir Henry Bagenal's forces defeat Tyrone at Yellow Ford

October: Munster plantation overthrown

The Battle of Clontibret, 1595

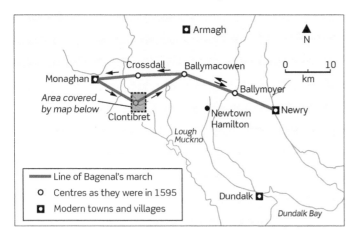

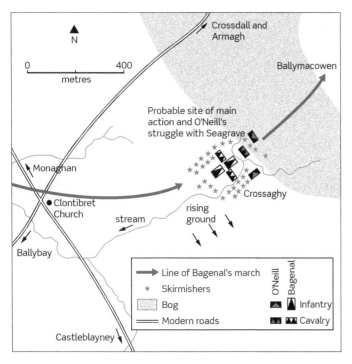

Figure 7.2 Bagenal's march and Irish movements at Clontibret.

The early stages of the Nine Years' War were focused on the English garrison forts on the borders of Ulster. The English fort at Blackwater was attacked by the rebels and the English commander surrendered. Meanwhile, Lord Deputy Russell found that his forces were outnumbered; he had just 1,100 men to use for the defence of English possessions. The government in London responded by withdrawing English troops from Brittany, where they had been fighting Spanish forces; 2,000 men were promised, but only 1,616 arrived, and many of these were in poor condition.

Meanwhile, the rebels were continuing to challenge the English with some success. In May 1595, the Irish captured Enniskillen Castle and began to besiege Monaghan Castle. Sir Henry Bagenal, who was **marshal** of the English army, attempted to help the besieged garrison. He marched with 1,750 men from the English stronghold of Newry, with the aim of delivering men and supplies to Monaghan Castle. Tyrone now used his well-trained

troops to launch a series of assaults on the English troops; this became known as the Battle of Clontibret. As Bagenal and his troops approached Monaghan, they were ambushed by Tyrone's men. Bagenal's army was forced to fight, using up much of the gunpowder that they were bringing to supply the garrison at Monaghan. The English troops eventually reached the safety of the castle, but they were faced with a problem. Their supplies were now very low, so they had little to leave in the fort or to defend themselves with on the return journey to Newry.

> **KEY TERM**
>
> **Marshal**
> The man responsible for the organisation and equipment of the English army.

On 27 May 1595, Bagenal and his men set out to return to Newry. Once again, they were ambushed by Tyrone's forces, which were about 4,000 strong. Tyrone's tactics were particularly effective; his well-trained musketmen were hidden on both sides of the road and were able to fire on Bagenal's column of men from these positions. The English column was forced to slow down as it came under attack, which made it even more vulnerable. Eventually, the English had to stop just outside Newry. By this time, they had very little ammunition left and had suffered at least 31 deaths, with 109 wounded. However, Tyrone did not press his advantage further, because his troops had run out of gunpowder as well. Bagenal and his men were eventually rescued by sea, but the battle had shown the English that they faced a well-organised Irish force who outnumbered them, and who were able to take advantage of their knowledge of the terrain to ambush vulnerable English troops.

SOURCE

From the Irish chronicles known as the *Annals of the Four Masters*, describing the ambush at Clontibret. These accounts were compiled by Irish Franciscan monks in the 1630s from earlier existing accounts.

For some time [in 1595]... the English did not dare to bring any army into Ulster, except one hosting which was made by Sir John Norris and his brother, Sir Thomas Norris, the President of the two provinces of Munster, with the forces of Munster and Meath, to proceed into Ulster. They marched to Newry, and passed from thence towards Armagh. When they had proceeded near halfway, they were met by the Irish, who proceeded to annoy, shoot, pierce and spear them, so that they did not suffer them either to sleep or rest quietly for the space of twenty-four hours. They were not permitted to advance forward one foot further; and their chiefs were glad to escape with their lives to Newry, leaving behind them many men. Horses, arms and valuable things... Sir John Norris and his brother Sir Thomas, were wounded on this occasion. It was no ordinary gap of danger for them to go into the province after this.

> **ACTIVITY**
> **KNOWLEDGE CHECK**
>
> 1 What does Source 5 suggest about the relative strengths and weaknesses of the Irish and English armies?
>
> 2 How valuable is this source for revealing the reasons why the English were unable to suppress the rebellion?

The Anglo-Irish truce and renewed fighting, 1596–98

The English responded to the humiliation of Clontibret by retaking Blackwater. However, by the end of 1595, the situation had reached a stalemate. The rebels found that their tactic of capturing and garrisoning small fortresses was making them vulnerable. This was because it was too expensive and dangerous to keep supplying these garrisons. In addition, Elizabeth I was also keen to negotiate, which was cheaper than expensive warfare. By March 1596, an apparent settlement had been reached. Tyrone agreed to submit, to pay damages, to stop demanding freedom of worship for Catholics and to accept English sovereignty. The English agreed to remove their garrisons; Tyrone would keep control in Ulster and was to arrest any rebels who caused trouble.

However, by May 1596, negotiations had broken down. This was because in the autumn of 1595 and early 1596, the rebels and Philip II of Spain had begun negotiations of their own. In September 1595, Tyrone and O'Donnell offered the crown of Ireland to Archduke Albert, the Spanish Catholic governor of the Netherlands, and a nephew of Philip II. In return, the rebels wanted a Spanish army, plus money and weapons. In the summer of 1596, Philip offered further encouragement by sending representatives to discuss a Spanish invasion. These discussions led to the unsuccessful armada sent in October 1596. Nevertheless, encouraged by Spanish support, the rebels were prepared to fight on. The spread of the rebellion was helped by the use of propaganda distributed by the rebels that encouraged all good Catholics to join the fight (Source 6).

SOURCE

6

An example of a circular written by the Earl of Tyrone that was distributed to Irish lords. This copy, written on 15 November 1599, fell into English hands, and is entitled 'Copy of a traitorous writing delivered throughout Ireland by the arch-traitor Hugh... Earl of Tyrone'.

Using... more than ordinary favour towards all my countrymen both for that generally you are by your profession Catholics and that naturally I am inclined to affect you, I have for these and other considerations abstained my forces from tempting to do you hindrance [harm]. And the matter that I did expect that in process of time, you would enter in consideration of the lamentable estate of our poor Country most tyrannically oppressed and of your own gentle consciences in maintaining, relieving and helping the Enemies of God and our country... But now seeing that you are so obstinate... of necessity I must use severity against you whom otherwise I most entirely loved, in reclaiming you by compulsion when my long tolerance and happy victories by God's particular favour doubtless obtained could work no alteration in your consciences...

Hereby, I thought good and convenient to forewarn you requesting every of you to come and join with me against the enemies of God and our poor country: if the same you do not, I will use means not only to spoil you of all your goods but according to the utmost of my power shall work what I can to dispossess you of your lands: because you are means whereby wars are maintained against the exaltation of the Catholic faith: contrariwise whosoever you shall be that shall join with me upon my conscience... I will employ myself to the utmost of my power in their defence and for the extirpation [destruction] of heresy, the planting of the Catholic Religion, the delivery of our country of infinite murders, wicked and detestable policies by which this kingdom was hitherto governed... And seeing these are motives most laudable... I thought myself in conscience bound seeing God has given me some power to use all means for the reduction [return] of this our poor afflicted country into the Catholic faith, which can never be brought to any good pass without... your... helping hands... giving you to understand... that chiefly and principally I fight for the Catholic faith to be planted throughout all our poor country... I have protested and do hereby protest if I had gotten to be king in Ireland without the Catholic Religion which before I have mentioned I would not the same accept.

ACTIVITY
KNOWLEDGE CHECK

1 Read Source 6. What arguments does Tyrone use to persuade the Anglo-Irish nobility to join his rebellion?

2 Which of his arguments do you think were likely to be the most effective and which the least effective?

A Level Exam-Style Question Section A

Study Source 6 before answering this question.

Assess the value of Source 6 for revealing the causes of rebellion in Ireland and the part played by Hugh O'Neill, Earl of Tyrone, in leading this rebellion.

Explain your answer, using the source, the information given about its origin and your own knowledge about the historical context. (20 marks)

Tip
What does the source reveal about Tyrone's leadership style and use of propaganda to spread his ideas?

As the rebellion continued to spread in the years 1596–98, Tyrone adopted more aggressive tactics. Once the government proclaimed him a traitor in 1595, Tyrone had little to lose. He now claimed that he had the right to grant lordships and positions in other regions of Ireland, beyond the lands he controlled in Ulster. Tyrone was attempting to unite all the Anglo-Irish chieftains throughout Ireland in defence of Catholicism. To reward his supporters and emphasise his control over the rebellion, Tyrone was prepared to claim the right to give titles to his followers, overriding both existing English appointments and Irish tanists. For example, James FitzThomas, who had become alienated from the English regime, was created Earl of Desmond by Tyrone.

EXTEND YOUR KNOWLEDGE

James FitzThomas, Earl of Desmond

Jame FitzThomas claimed the right to be the heir of his uncle, the previous Earl of Desmond, whose estates had been confiscated following his involvement in rebellion against the English in 1579-83. In an attempt to get himself reinstated, FitzThomas had turned to Elizabeth's government for help, but had found none. Tyrone was able to exploit FitzThomas' resentment by giving him the title he wanted; in return, FitzThomas joined the rebellion.

By 1597, the English hold on Ireland seemed to be slipping away. The English government decided to replace the Lord Deputy, Sir William Russell, and the commander of the English army, Sir Henry Norris, with one man, Thomas, Lord Burgh. Burgh was an experienced soldier and administrator. He decided that the best tactic was to try to undermine Tyrone's power base by attacking his estates in Ulster. The result was another disaster at Yellow Ford.

The Battle of Yellow Ford and the collapse of the Munster plantation, 1598

Mistakes by the English government and military commanders

Burgh's initial plan in 1597 was to march into Ulster itself, where he would aim for Tyrone's estates at Dungannon. However, Burgh found himself outnumbered by Tyrone's forces. By October 1597, the English offensive had been halted. Burgh now decided to build a new series of fortifications along the Blackwater river in Ulster. The new fort at Blackwater was intended to give additional protection to the English garrison at Armagh in southern Ulster. It was also meant to provide a base for further attacks against Tyrone's stronghold, which was just a few kilometres away.

Burgh's decision presented the English government with more problems. In October 1597, Burgh died suddenly which meant that the English lacked both a Lord Deputy and an overall leader of the army. To make matters worse, the previous commander of the English army, Sir Henry Norris, had also died. Burgh had also made a crucial mistake in reverting to the use of small garrison forts. Moreover, the fortress at Blackwater had a garrison of just 150 men and was defended only by earthworks. On top of this, the English government was distracted by news of another Spanish Armada in October 1597; one of the most experienced military commanders left in Ireland, Sir Thomas Norris, was sent to Munster to deal with the potential threat, which came to nothing when the Spanish fleet was dispersed by a storm. Meanwhile, the English army was put under the command of the Anglo-Irish Earl of Ormond.

EXTEND YOUR KNOWLEDGE

The Earl of Ormond

Thomas Butler, Earl of Ormond, was a member of the Anglo-Irish nobility and a cousin of Elizabeth I. He was also an important landowner in County Tipperary, Munster, and a committed Protestant. Despite being passed over for the office of Lord Deputy, Ormond remained loyal to the English government and helped to put down the rebellion.

Elizabeth I was now left with the problem of what to do about Blackwater Fort. The Council wanted to abandon the fortress, but Elizabeth was keen to try to divide the rebels by offering further negotiations. In December 1597, Tyrone agreed to a truce, but he was using this breathing space to prepare his forces for another attack. When the truce came to an end in June 1598, Tyrone began to besiege Blackwater Fort. Ormond tried to respond, but his army was full of Irish soldiers who could not be trusted to stay loyal. Faced with a full-strength rebel army of about 5,000 men, Ormond had to accept help from Sir Henry Bagenal, the English military leader who had been humiliated at Clontibret. Bagenal offered to bring an extra 4,200 men and began to march to Blackwater.

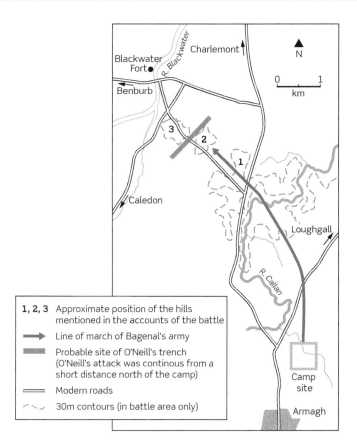

Figure 7.3 Bagenal's march and the ambush at Yellow Ford, August 1598.

The English defeat at Yellow Ford and the collapse of the Munster plantation

On 11 August 1598, Bagenal and his troops were attacked at Yellow Ford by Tyrone. In a repeat of what had happened at Clontibret, the English found themselves under fire on both sides from the Irish musketmen lying in wait to ambush them. As the English army struggled to keep moving forward, its progress was slowed by its attempts to cross the ford. Heavy English **artillery** also became stuck in the boggy ground near the river. When Bagenal rushed to the scene of the fighting, he himself was killed, along with about 830 of his men; 400 more were wounded and 300 Irishmen in the English army deserted to join the rebels. The surviving Englishmen also lost most of the supplies and equipment that they were taking to Blackwater. Of the 4,200 men that Bagenal had started out with, only 2,000 made it back to Armagh. The English authorities feared that Dublin itself could come under attack, though Tyrone was too cautious to take this opportunity. However, the results of the English defeat at Yellow Ford were still extremely serious for the English position in Ireland. Discontented Irishmen in Munster were finally encouraged by Tyrone's successes to rebel. The Munster plantations were

KEY TERM

Artillery
Heavy weaponry such as cannons and siege engines, used to break down fortifications.

overthrown very rapidly. The English authorities had been so busy worrying about the situation in Ulster that they had ignored the fears of the English settlers in Munster that trouble was brewing. The 3,000 Munster settlers were faced with a sudden uprising by their tenants. Most of the settlers either fled, or were captured and killed by the rebels. In just a few days, the Munster colony, which had taken 14 years to establish, had been destroyed.

The shock of the defeat at Yellow Ford forced Elizabeth into action. She sent 1,900 troops to protect Dublin and backed these up with 6,300 more men, who were sent between October 1598 and January 1599. These troops helped Ormond to stop the Munster rebellion from spreading any further. However, the queen still prevaricated about choosing a new Lord Deputy to replace Burgh. Finally, in March 1599, she appointed Robert Devereux, second Earl of Essex, as Lord Lieutenant of Ireland. The use of the title Lord Lieutenant was meant to echo the Lieutenancy system that had existed in England since 1585 (see Chapter 2), but Essex proved to be ill-suited to the role he had been given.

SOURCE

7 An Irish account of the Battle of Yellow Ford from the *Annals of the Four Masters*.

When O'Neill had received intelligence that this great [English] army was approaching him, he sent his messengers to O'Donnell, requesting him to come to his assistance against this overwhelming force of foreigners who were coming to his country. O'Donnell proceeded immediately, with all his warriors... to assist his ally... The Irish of all the province of Ulster also joined the same army, so that they were all prepared to meet the English before they arrived at Armagh. They then dug deep trenches against the English in the common road...

As for the English, after remaining a night at Armagh, they rose next morning early... They then formed into order and array as well as they were able, and proceeded... in close and solid bodies... till they came to the hill which overlooks the ford... After arriving there they perceived O'Neill and O'Donnell... having drawn up one terrible mass before them, placed and arranged on the particular passages where they thought the others would march on them...

As for the Marshal and his English [forces], when they saw the Irish awaiting them, they did not show any symptom whatever of fear, but advanced vigorously forwards, until they sallied across the first broad [and] deep trench that lay in their way; and some were killed crossing it. The Irish army then poured upon them vehemently and boldly... The [English] van was obliged to await the onset, bide the brunt of the conflict, and withstand the firing, so that their close lines were thinned, their gentlemen gapped, and their heroes subdued...

ACTIVITY
KNOWLEDGE CHECK

What does Source 7 reveal about the reasons why the Irish were able to defeat the English at Yellow Ford?

The Battle of Curlew Pass, 1599

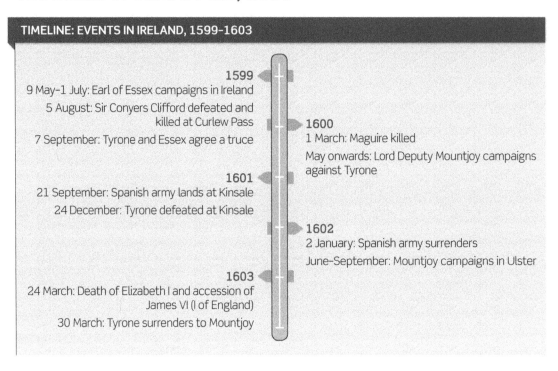

TIMELINE: EVENTS IN IRELAND, 1599–1603

1599
9 May–1 July: Earl of Essex campaigns in Ireland
5 August: Sir Conyers Clifford defeated and killed at Curlew Pass
7 September: Tyrone and Essex agree a truce

1600
1 March: Maguire killed
May onwards: Lord Deputy Mountjoy campaigns against Tyrone

1601
21 September: Spanish army lands at Kinsale
24 December: Tyrone defeated at Kinsale

1602
2 January: Spanish army surrenders
June–September: Mountjoy campaigns in Ulster

1603
24 March: Death of Elizabeth I and accession of James VI (I of England)
30 March: Tyrone surrenders to Mountjoy

On his arrival in May 1599, Essex was faced with a dire military situation in the North of Ireland. An Irish attack on Sir Donough O'Connor at Collooney Castle (Connaught) presented Essex with a particularly difficult challenge. O'Connor was one of the few Irish chieftains who had continued to support the English government during Tyrone's rebellion. O'Connor came under siege from one of the leading rebels, Hugh Roe O'Donnell. Essex could not afford to allow one of the few English supporters among the Irish to be captured, so he ordered Sir Conyers Clifford, the president of Connaught and an experienced military campaigner, to rescue O'Connor.

Clifford obeyed orders, and began to march to O'Connor's rescue at the head of an army of about 1,490 footmen and 205 cavalry. Unfortunately for Clifford, he and his men had to cross the Curlew Mountains to get to Collooney. On 15 August 1599, as the English army approached the pass that led through the mountains, they were ambushed by an Irish force. As at Yellow Ford, the English were trapped in unfamiliar geography. There were mountains to either side, and they could not escape from the road they were following because it was surrounded by woods and bogs. As the English army came under attack, the troops began to panic and flee. Clifford himself was killed, along with about one-third of his army. The surviving army was forced to turn back to safety. The result of this was that the besieged O'Connor was forced to surrender to the rebels and a valuable English ally was lost.

The impact of the English loss at Curlew Pass
As a result of the loss at Curlew Pass, Essex decided that it was no longer possible to attack Tyrone. The English army was suffering from sickness and many of their Irish soldiers were deserting. When Elizabeth heard of this decision, she was furious, and ordered Essex to march North to Ulster. Essex obeyed; when he reached Louth, he encountered Tyrone, whose army was much larger. Instead of fighting, Essex made the decision to negotiate with Tyrone in private. Essex and Tyrone agreed on a truce, during which the rebels were to be allowed to continue to occupy all the lands and fortresses they possessed or had captured.

ACTIVITY
KNOWLEDGE CHECK

1 Make a list of reasons why the English were not able to defeat the Irish rebels in the years 1595–1600.

2 Which do you think is the most important reason for the English lack of success, and why?

The role of Sir Henry Bagenal

Sir Henry Bagenal was a member of the English gentry whose family also had estates in Ireland at Newry (Ulster). From the 1570s, the Bagenals were keen to expand their estates and interests in Ulster; this brought them into conflict with the Earl of Tyrone. For example, both Tyrone and the Bagenals claimed that they had the right to be overlords of the O'Hanlon clan and their estates in southern Ulster. To Tyrone and his supporters, the Bagenals represented the type of grasping and unscrupulous English incomers who used their connections with the Court in London to acquire more land and power in Ireland. Certainly, Bagenal was a troublemaker; he even managed to upset the English authorities in Ireland by getting into disputes with other settlers. In 1586, Bagenal was summoned to Court to explain his disagreements with the Dublin authorities. As part of a justification for his actions, Bagenal produced a series of documents to convince William Cecil, the queen's Secretary, that English policy in Ireland needed to change. One of these, 'The Description and Present State of Ulster' (Source 8) shows the English settlers' concerns about the growing power of Tyrone and the weakness of the English Crown in Ulster. Bagenal's recommendations to the government included a division of O'Neill's lands and for Ulster to have its own council and president. Although he did not achieve many of his demands, the power struggle between the ambitious Bagenal and Tyrone helps to explain why Tyrone was increasingly alienated from the English authorities in the early 1590s. An English captain who knew Tyrone well wrote to Elizabeth I that it was Bagenal's actions that provoked Tyrone to rebel. However, the Nine Years' War cannot be blamed on the personal feud of two men. The tensions between Tyrone and Bagenal were a reflection of problems that were afflicting Ireland because of the increasingly interventionist style of English rule. But Ulster was one of the last provinces to remain outside English control and Tyrone was the most powerful chieftain in Ulster; under these circumstances, alienating Tyrone was a particularly dangerous thing to do.

Apart from his political role, Sir Henry also had a military role to play in the English extension of power beyond the Pale. Bagenal's role as marshal from 1591 meant that he was responsible for the organisation of the royal armies. Bagenal does not seem to have been a good military tactician and was unable to learn from his mistakes. He led his men into two humiliating defeats, at Clontibret in 1595 and at Yellow Ford in 1598 (see pages 160–163); in both cases, his troops were ambushed by the Irish, who knew the territory better. At Yellow Ford, Bagenal lost control of his troops entirely, as parts of his army panicked, turned and fled; he himself was killed in the confusion.

SOURCE

8 Marshal Henry Bagenal's description of the problems facing Ireland, written in 1586 to justify his actions to the English government, from 'The Description of the Present State of Ulster'.

It may easily be perceived by this slender and brief description of Ulster, what hath been and are the reasons why this Province hath been from time to time more changeable to Her Majesty than any other, as namely, the want of good towns and fortified places... And next the sufferance of the O'Neills to usurp the government of the several Captains and freeholders, and by little and little to exceed the bounds of their own and so increase upon the possessions of others; whereby they were made stronger than otherwise they could have been, and abled thereby to wage and maintain the greater number of Scots... Fourthly... the want of due exercises of religion and justice... is the occasion of much impiety and barbarousness ...

Remedies.

Considering Her Majesty's excessive charge... as well for the defence of this her realm as in other parts beyond the seas, for the necessary strengthening of her whole dominions: it is not convenient to desire Her Majesty greater expense, but only that such revenues as this Province may be made to yield to Her Majesty may be employed upon fortifications in places most needful... And to the second: like as in former time of good government it was a thing most regarded in all treaties to weaken the force of the O'Neills by withdrawing from them their Uryaghes [rights]... Therefore the way is, to apportionate [divide] both to Turlough Luineach and the Earle of Tyrone... lands on the North side of Blackwater to them and their heirs males... As for the fourth: it might doubtless be remedied if these countries were as well brought to the nature as to the names of Shires; that is, that the Shires being perfectly bonded, Sheriffs of English education may be appointed in every county, and in certain convenient places some preachers and free schools. And for the whole Province a Council were established, of the wisest, gravest, and best disposed, dwelling within the same... That also Assizes, Quarter Sessions, and such other like... should... be in every county observed; which all require not so great charge and travail [work] in the beginning, as they yield both profit and honour in the end.

ACTIVITY
KNOWLEDGE CHECK

Read Source 8 and answer the following questions.

1 What does Bagenal think are the main problems facing Ireland and what solutions does he propose?

2 What does the source suggest about the relationship between the English and the Irish in the 1580s?

3 From what you know about Bagenal and his career, how far would you trust his judgement about the situation in Ireland?

The role of Florence MacCarthy

Florence MacCarthy was born Finian MacDonagh MacCarthy, but he later anglicised his first name to Florence. The MacCarthy family were dominant in West Cork and Kerry in Munster, where they could command a powerful fighting force. The English authorities calculated that the MacCarthy clan could muster about 5,000 fighting men. In the 1580s, the MacCarthys had a friendly relationship with the English; they had even helped the English to put down the Munster rebellions. Under the tanist system, MacCarthy also expected to become the next leader of his branch of the MacCarthy clan, known as the **MacCarthy Reagh**.

MacCarthy's grievances against the English

As English influence expanded into Munster in the 1580s, MacCarthy started to come under suspicion. He was a Catholic who had learnt Spanish and was suspected of being in contact with Spaniards who were present on the South coast of Ireland. In 1589, he was arrested for the first time. The main reason for his arrest was that the English president of Munster felt that MacCarthy posed a potential threat to English interests in the region. MacCarthy had made a marriage alliance that would allow him to claim the title of **MacCarthy Mor**; this would have given him even more power in the Munster region because he would have been chieftain of all the different branches of the MacCarthy family. MacCarthy spent two years in the Tower of London and did not return to Ireland until 1593. By this time, his relations with the English had soured. He also faced a rival for his claim to be the MacCarthy Mor, Donal MacCarthy. The English were prepared to support Donal MacCarthy in his claim because it was a way to stop Florence from becoming more powerful.

By 1598, Tyrone was trying to extend the rebellion by recruiting potential supporters who had grievances against the English. MacCarthy was an obvious target for Tyrone. Tyrone recognised Florence as the MacCarthy Mor, but Florence was not easily convinced to join the rebellion, perhaps because, in the past, Tyrone had backed his rival, Donal MacCarthy. Florence played O'Neill off against the English by trying to negotiate with both sides. Florence even promised the English authorities that the MacCarthys would support them if he was given the title of MacCarthy Mor.

MacCarthy's role in the rebellion

MacCarthy's military role in the Nine Years' War was relatively limited. He was prepared to allow some of Tyrone's mercenaries onto his lands. Kinsale, where the Spanish troops eventually landed in 1601, was in MacCarthy territory. At the same time, MacCarthy continued to write to Elizabeth I, claiming that he was loyal to her. In the period 1598–1601, during the fighting in Munster, he did not commit troops to help either Tyrone or the English. The one exception to this was when his men ambushed English troops who were destroying his estates at Carbery. The English president of Munster, Sir George Carew, granted MacCarthy a pardon, but his suspicions of MacCarthy's motives and loyalties continued to grow. By August 1601, the Munster rebellion was nearly suppressed and Carew felt safe to move against MacCarthy. MacCarthy was arrested and sent back to imprisonment in England. MacCarthy's papers were found to contain correspondence with Tyrone and other rebels. His arrest and removal from Ireland just before the decisive campaign that ended the rebellion was an important blow for the English. Although MacCarthy was reluctant to commit to open military opposition, he was still an important threat to the English in Munster. He was another member of the Anglo-Irish nobility who felt resentful of their treatment by the English and were prepared to work with the Spanish in order to undermine English rule of Ireland in the name of Catholicism.

1 Explain in your own words why Florence MacCarthy was prepared to support Tyrone's rebellion.

2 How far do you think MacCarthy's support for Tyrone increased the challenge to the English government? Explain your answer.

The role of the Earl of Essex

Robert Devereux, the second Earl of Essex, was one of Elizabeth's Court favourites, and the stepson of the Earl of Leicester, another of Elizabeth's favourites. In 1599, after persuasion from the earl, she appointed him Lord Lieutenant of Ireland, at the head of a large force.

EXTEND YOUR KNOWLEDGE

The rise of the Earl of Essex (1590s)
Young, athletic and handsome, Devereux had risen to prominence because of his ability to flatter the ageing queen. Essex was also ambitious; he saw himself as a military leader and argued for England to take a more positive approach to its war with Spain. In 1596, Elizabeth allowed Essex to lead a raid on the Spanish port of Cadiz; while this was not as successful as Essex claimed, he still received a hero's welcome on his return to England. However, Essex's military talents did not match his ambitions. He was also a divisive influence at Court. Essex was trying to build up his faction. The cautious Elizabeth was reluctant to trust Essex with too much responsibility. In 1597, Essex had disobeyed her orders during a naval mission; instead of defeating the Spanish navy, which is what he had been asked to do, Essex chose to pursue the valuable Spanish treasure ships instead, without success.

Essex's lack of skill as a military commander was soon exposed when he reached Ireland in May 1599.

- Poor organisation meant that he did not have the equipment necessary to follow his planned attack on Ulster. The plan was to trap Tyrone though simultaneous advances from the South and the North, but the earl did not have the necessary ships or gun carriages. This was the fault of the English Privy Council, not the earl.

- Essex's strategic decisions were poor. While waiting for the equipment he needed, he sent half of his large army to bolster English garrisons across Ireland. Essex may have arrived with the largest army Elizabeth had ever sent, but he wasted this valuable resource by splitting it up.

- Essex then decided to campaign in Munster. This was also unwise, because it wore out his troops and created unnecessary expense without achieving any serious military gains. At the same time, English troops were continuing to suffer losses, such as at Curlew Pass. Again, these losses were not entirely Essex's fault, but they reflected badly on him as Lord Lieutenant.

Elizabeth held Essex directly responsible for these disasters and his lack of progress in engaging Tyrone in battle, and she wrote to him in July 1599 expressing her anger. Now Essex found himself caught between the furious queen who wanted to see Essex giving value for money by dealing with Tyrone, and the Council in Dublin who advised that marching North to face Tyrone was foolhardy. In August 1599, Essex decided to obey Elizabeth; by now, his military mismanagement meant that he only had a force of 4,000 men left out of the 17,200 he had arrived with. The result was that when he met Tyrone and his army, Essex and his men were outnumbered. Essex now made another mistake by choosing to meet with Tyrone in private without any witnesses. This played into the hands of Essex's enemy at Court, Sir Robert Cecil, who was able to claim that what Essex had discussed with Tyrone had been treasonous. On 24 September 1599, Essex hurriedly left Ireland, disobeying Elizabeth's orders that he was not to abandon his post without her permission. Essex's disobedience and incompetence led to a trial before the Privy Council. He was replaced in Ireland by Lord Mountjoy.

The role of Lord Mountjoy

Charles Blount, Lord Mountjoy, managed to succeed in suppressing Tyrone's revolt where others had failed. Mountjoy was another English courtier, with considerable experience fighting in the Netherlands and France. When Mountjoy arrived in Ireland in February 1600, he faced many difficulties. After the truce with Tyrone expired in January 1600, Tyrone marched South into Munster with 2,000 men and then set up at camp near the port of Kinsale.

However, Mountjoy was a decisive and imaginative military leader. He had 13,200 men in his army and he used his resources well. Mountjoy's job was made slightly easier because he was helped by the new president of Munster, Sir George Carew, who was an experienced military commander. But even before Carew's arrival, the English commanders had some luck; Tyrone's son-in-law and fellow rebel, Hugh Maguire, was killed in a skirmish. This weakened rebel control in Ulster, where Maguire was a chieftain, and Tyrone decided to withdraw from Kinsale rather than face the English forces who were preparing to surround him. Carew, with 3,000 reinforcements, then began the process of suppressing the rebellion in Munster.

With Carew regaining English control in Munster, Mountjoy could concentrate on Ulster. His first tactic was to distract Tyrone by marching towards the Blackwater river. While Tyrone was focused on Mountjoy's forces, an English force of 4,000 men sailed to Lough Foyle on the northern coast of Ulster and landed successfully, helping to surround Tyrone. In September 1600, Mountjoy took on Tyrone himself, but Tyrone was still too strong for the English forces. When the armies met at Moyry pass, Tyrone was able to resist the English attack. During his campaign, about 75 of Mountjoy's men were killed and 300 wounded. He had not yet managed to defeat Tyrone, but he had succeeded in surrounding the earl in Ulster, something no other military commander had managed to do. With the help of Carew, Mountjoy had also managed to bring the rebellion in Munster to an end. These successes meant that the Irish were now reliant on support and reinforcements from Spain.

WHY DID THE WAR LAST SO LONG?

The Battle of Kinsale, 1601, and the arrival of Spanish support

The Spanish troops who arrived in 1601 were highly trained and brought siege guns with them. But when Philip III first agreed to send the troops in January 1601, the rebellion was still alive in Munster. By May 1601, Carew had succeeded in suppressing most of the unrest in Munster. When the Spanish troops finally arrived at Kinsale, they were too late to help the rebels and were cut off from Tyrone, who was still surrounded in Ulster, at the other end of the country.

However, the arrival of the Spanish troops was still very dangerous for Mountjoy and the English government. Mountjoy feared that the presence of the Spanish would encourage former rebels in Munster to rise again. He also needed to stop Tyrone from joining up with the Spanish. Mountjoy decided that the best course of action was to defeat the Spanish at Kinsale as soon as possible. He marched South from Ulster, gathering forces as he went. By the end of October 1601, Mountjoy had reached Kinsale and was besieging it with 7,000 men. The removal of Mountjoy's army from Ulster freed Tyrone to march South as well. Tyrone knew that if he wanted to regain his military advantage, he needed to win a decisive victory over the English; to do this, he needed the additional Spanish troops at Kinsale. This was why Tyrone was prepared to take the risk of marching in mid-winter, when poor weather was likely to make military campaigning very difficult. Tyrone and his ally Hugh Roe O'Donnell eventually arrived at Kinsale on 21 December 1601, with an army of 6,500. Mountjoy's army, which was still besieging Kinsale, was now trapped between the Spanish and Irish armies. The English were in a desperate position; they lacked proper defences, they were cold and exhausted and supplies were running low; disease and desertion had also reduced their numbers to 6,600.

Thinking that he would be able to defeat the English, Tyrone prepared for battle. He and the Spanish planned a joint attack by land and sea. Tyrone had always preferred to avoid open battle, but he was prepared to take the risk because he was also hoping that Irishmen in the English army would desert and join him instead. But on 24 December, as Tyrone's army were making the final preparations for their attack, Mountjoy launched a surprise attack on the Irish. As the English cavalry charged, the Irish horsemen panicked, turned round and ran into the main body of their own army, causing it to scatter. The battle was over very quickly. The Spanish in Kinsale did not join in because they had been waiting for the Irish to appear at a pre-arranged meeting point, but the Irish never got there. The battle at Kinsale was the last major military engagement of the rebellion, although it took another 15 months for the rebellion to finally come to an end. Tyrone retreated back to Ulster, O'Donnell fled to Spain, and in January 1602 the Spanish troops who were still in Kinsale surrendered to the English.

SOURCE

9

From an account of Mountjoy's leadership at Kinsale by Fynes Moryson, in *An History of Ireland*. Moryson was Mountjoy's private secretary and his official historian of the Nine Years' War. Moryson's account tends to show the English in the best light possible and is very disparaging of the Irish.

The 24th of December: some half hour before the day, the Lord Deputy in his house sitting at Council with the Lord President... as thinking the intended enterprise of the enemy by some accident to be broken, suddenly one of the Lord President's horsemen called him... and told him that Tyrone's army was come up very near to our camp... and his Lordship being always in readiness... (seldom going to bed by night)... when he heard that they were advanced within three quarters of a mile of our camp, caused all our men to draw into arms... and himself... advanced... to take view of the enemy...

ACTIVITY
KNOWLEDGE CHECK

1 Read Source 9. What does this suggest about Mountjoy's leadership and military skills?

2 Why do you think Mountjoy was successful in dealing with Tyrone's rebellion when Essex was not?

3 Apart from his leadership, what other factors contributed to Mountjoy's success?

4 'Mountjoy's successes in Ireland were the result of luck rather than judgement.' Write a paragraph explaining whether you agree with this view.

The siege of Dunboy

One of the bloodiest episodes of the Nine Years' War was the siege of Dunboy Castle in June 1602. Dunboy Castle was on the coast of the Beara peninsula on the south west coast of Ireland. The castle was held by the Irish rebel Donnell O'Sullivan Bere in the name of the Spanish king, and it was thought that its defences were impossible to breach.

In April 1602, Carew decided to organise a siege of Dunboy. He planned to transport his troops by water, using Bere Island as a base, which lay just off the coast on which the castle was situated; this was to avoid a land crossing through mountainous territory. The Constable of Dunboy, Richard MacGeohegan, came to speak with Carew. Carew offered MacGeohegan the chance to surrender, but the Constable refused, saying that he had only come to warn Carew about the dangers he and his men faced in attacking an impregnable fortress. However, MacGeohegan made a vital mistake. He mentioned to Carew that if his soldiers tried to land on the beach in front of the castle, they would be trapped. Carew reconnoitred the area around the castle and managed to find another beach that was undefended. The English started to build their own defences on this beach, including gun placements for their cannon. Carew's determination to attack was increased by the arrival in the region of a Spanish ship carrying gold and weapons. He wanted to take the castle before the Spanish could get there and reinforce it.

What was the significance of the siege of Dunboy?

On 16 June, the English had finished building their defences and used their cannon to open fire on the castle. The cannon fire began to break down the walls of the castle and MacGeohegan was badly wounded. The English now launched an assault on the castle itself, trapping the remaining defenders in its vaults. Carew showed his ruthlessness by ordering the cannon to keep firing, in an attempt to bury the defenders in the rubble. Cornered and desperate, the rest of the defenders surrendered, although MacGeohegan tried to blow up the castle with the defenders' remaining gunpowder.

After the siege, Dunboy was destroyed, to make sure that it could not be used to resist the English in the future. Although they had surrendered, 58 of the defenders were executed in the local market place. Of the 143 men in the Dunboy garrison, not a single one survived. The siege of Dunboy ended the last of the Irish resistance in Munster. Mountjoy pursued Tyrone into Ulster with 3,000 men. Tyrone did not try to fight back, but used his local knowledge to take refuge in the woods. The rest of his followers gradually submitted to the English. In February 1603, Elizabeth allowed Mountjoy to open negotiations with Tyrone.

Ironically, when Tyrone finally submitted to Mountjoy on 30 March 1603, he received very generous terms. He was pardoned and was recognised as the Chief Lord of Ulster under the English Crown, almost the very title that he had been trying to get from Elizabeth in the first place. The reason for Mountjoy's generosity was linked to events at the English Court. Elizabeth had died six days before, and Mountjoy was keen to return to England in order to ingratiate himself with the new King James VI. Mountjoy may therefore have offered the concessions that he did in order to reach a settlement as quickly as possible. This was to cause problems for James in the future, but for now, the trouble in Ireland was at an end.

SOURCE 10 Contemporary map showing Dunboy, from the *Pacta Hibernia* by Sir Thomas Stafford, c1633.

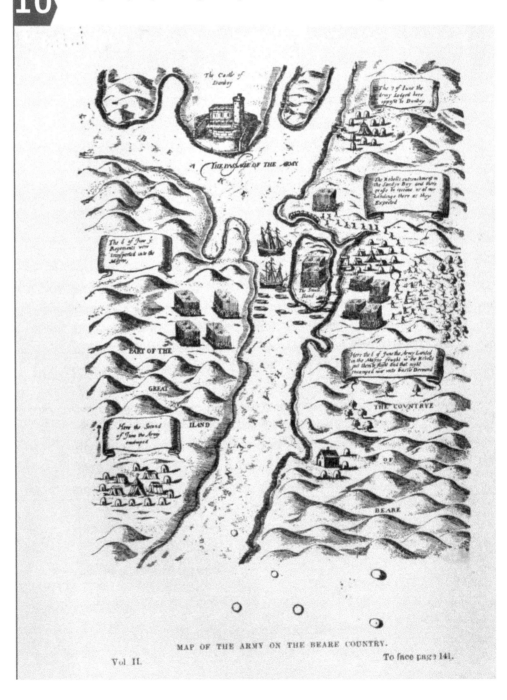

ACTIVITY
KNOWLEDGE CHECK

Copy and complete the table. Why did the Irish rebellion eventually collapse?

Cause	What did they do?	How did this lead to the end of the rebellion?	How important were their actions? (Give a mark out of 10)
Actions of Mountjoy and Carew			
Actions of the Earl of Tyrone			
Role of the Spanish			

Costs to the English government

England was a small country of just over four million people, and it did not have the resources to sustain a successful war against the Spanish and the Irish for a long period of time. Elizabeth's government had an income of about £300,000 per annum, which was not nearly enough to deal with the heavy financial demands of war. For example, maintaining English forces in the Netherlands alone cost £100,000 per year. The Irish revolt put additional strain on the finances, as the costs of garrisoning there rose to £5,000 per month. On top of this, the English government had to fund the armies and their weapons; by 1597, Elizabeth had spent £300,000 on campaigns in Ulster. All of these costs had to be borne by the English parliament and taxpayers.

By 1596, the war in Ireland had become the largest single expense for the English government. The government had to keep sending troops to Ireland, but before 1600, it never managed to send enough at one time to make a significant difference. Between 1594 and 1602, 30,592 soldiers from 36 English counties were sent to Ireland in groups of between 1,000 and 6,350. Although some of these soldiers were experienced, the majority were untrained and undisciplined new recruits. The English government was so desperate to find more troops to send to Ireland that it even started to send members of the **trained bands**. Ireland was seen as a frightening and dangerous place, and there was great reluctance to serve there. In 1600, there was very nearly a mutiny of Kentish cavalry who were waiting at Chester to be shipped to Ireland. Such was the fear of Irish service that the local gentry and yeomen made sure that they avoided the musters for service in Ireland; this reduced the quality of the soldiers in the army still further, as Source 11 suggests.

KEY TERM

Trained band
A group of well-trained soldiers who were used for defence in each county and were usually exempt from service abroad.

SOURCE
11
Summary of a letter dated 21 October 1596, written by local government representatives in Chester to William Cecil, Elizabeth's Secretary, explaining their concerns about the mustering and state of the army to be sent to Ireland. From the Calendar of State Papers of Elizabeth I, Vol. 6.

Having... mustered the ten horses and their riders, sent out of the diocese of Gloucester, and finding divers defects of... pistols etc... one Hall, who conducted the said horsemen hither to Chester, undertook before us that all should be supplied forthwith... Since which time, those horsemen have made much stir, clamour, and complaint, some of them resorting to me bare-legged and barefoot, and showing how they wanted shoes and stockings; others affirming that they lacked shirts, doublets, hose etc (which wants were not mentioned, nor could be discovered at the Musters, for that their armour and horsemen's coats covered their bodies, and on their legs they had boots); whereupon I sent for the said Hall their conductor, requiring him to supply their defects of apparel. Who answered, that he had already paid them all the allowance which was delivered to him for their uses, concluding that he could not yield them any supply of apparel. Moreover, one of the soldiers being seen and searched by a chirurgien [doctor], is found to be dangerously diseased of the foul sickness (called Morbus Gallicus[syphilis]), so as, for fear of infecting the rest, I have thought it most requisite to discharge him. He is also most poor and needy, wanting money and divers necessaries... I have not seen so many difficulties and defects in the setting forth of so small a number of horsemen. Pleaseth it your Lordship to appoint some good and speedy order herein.

ACTIVITY
KNOWLEDGE CHECK

1 What does Source 11 suggest about the problems facing the English government in dealing with the rebellion in Ireland?

2 How valuable is this source as evidence of the reasons for the English failure to deal with Tyrone's rising?

English financial weaknesses

Most of the cost of providing for the armies fell on the English counties. In Kent, for example, the county was responsible for sending 56 cavalry and 600 footmen to Ireland between 1595 and 1602. This cost the county taxpayers £3,324. On top of this, the central government was levying increasing amounts of taxation to try to meet the demands of war. The 1590s was a period during which there were poor harvests, famine and epidemics of disease, which led to social and economic hardship. On top of demands placed on them to find and fund soldiers to send to Ireland, landowners had to bear the increasing costs of poor relief, as well as high levels of taxation. The result was increasing levels of complaint and attempts to evade the payments; in 1596, the men of Middlesex refused to contribute to local payments for their musters of men and equipment.

These financial pressures meant that although English resources were more extensive than Tyrone's, the English armies sent to fight in Ireland were not large enough, and were poorly equipped and trained. In contrast to the English financial problems, Tyrone had developed an efficient financial system that allowed him to fund a well-trained and well-equipped army. He had reorganised the Ulster economy to increase his income. As a result, he had an income of £80,000 per annum. Even when he had all of his army assembled in 1598, which cost him about £500 a day, Tyrone was able to afford this expense.

However, the length of the war was not just the result of England's financial crisis. The English army was fighting in unfamiliar territory, which meant that it was always at a disadvantage. Tyrone and his followers used their knowledge to wage a form of guerrilla warfare on the English troops, preferring ambush and occasional sieges to pitched battles where they were likely to be at a disadvantage. The English war effort was further hampered by the logistical problems of transporting men, horses and equipment to Ireland. Communications were slow and it took time to get reinforcements to the right locations, which gave the Irish more time to prepare and to plan, meaning that it was not until 1601 that the English began to gain the upper hand.

A Level Exam-Style Question Section B

How accurate is it to say that it was English weaknesses that account for the long duration of Tyrone's rebellion in Ireland? (20 marks)

Tip

You need to define what is meant by 'English weaknesses' – this could include financial pressures and military leadership and strategy.

ACTIVITY
KNOWLEDGE CHECK

Make a spider diagram to show the reasons why Tyrone's rebellion lasted so long. Your headings could include: English military weaknesses; English financial weaknesses; Irish strengths; role of the Spanish.

SOURCE

An account of Mountjoy's tactics in Ulster, written c1606 by Fynes Moryson, who was secretary to Mountjoy. Moryson was an eyewitness to Mountjoy's campaign against the Irish rebels in 1600–03. He provides an English Protestant view of the ending of the rebellion.

... where other deputies used to assail the rebels only in summer time, this lord prosecuted them most in winter... This broke their hearts; for the air being sharp, and they naked, and they being driven from their homes into the woods [which were] bare of leaves, they had no shelter for themselves. Besides that, their cattle were also wasted by travelling to and fro. Add to that they were... troubled in the seed time [and] could not sow their ground. And in the harvest time both the deputy's forces and the [English] garrisons cut down their corn before it was ripe, and then in winter time they [the English troops] carried away or burnt all the stores of food in the secret places where the rebels had conveyed them.

EXTRACT

Wallace MacCaffrey, *Elizabeth I* (1993), whose account of Tyrone's rebellion draws heavily upon the account of Fynes Moryson, Mountjoy's secretary.

With Tyrone's capitulation, Elizabeth finished the task set by her father 80 years earlier, the completion of the English conquest of Ireland… it was achieved in agony and pain through the misery and deaths of countless of the Queen's subjects… it evoked on both sides a venomous outpouring of hatred which would permanently poison relations between the two islands.

EXTRACT

Steven G. Ellis, *Tudor Ireland* (1985), whose account of Tyrone's rebellion also draws upon Moryson's account.

Undoubtedly, the planning, preparation and execution of Mountjoy's campaign was an extraordinary feat of government. Yet… the cost of victory was unexpectedly high. Large parts of Ireland had been devastated, crops burned, cattle slaughtered, or buildings razed. Ulster was almost a wilderness, Munster, West of Cork almost uninhabited, trade disrupted…, towns ruined or declining, and the population decimated by famine.

THINKING HISTORICALLY Evidence (6c)

Comparing and evaluating historians' arguments

What can we say, credibly, about Fynes Moryson's account of the impact of Tyrone's rebellion (Source 12) and the English response to it on the basis of source materials such as these? We need first to consider the context from which the sources emerge (this is a history written by a seasoned traveller several years after he had witnessed the events) and the wider context (Tyrone's rebellion had caused a serious threat to the stability of Elizabeth's government). A credible account needs also to avoid going beyond what the evidence allows us to claim.

Extracts 1 and 2 are two historians' accounts of the impact of Tyrone's rebellion, both of which draw heavily on Moryson's account.

1 Compare the two accounts and identify factual statements or claims that they both agree on. Make a list of these points.

2 Look carefully at how the historians use language. Do they both use equally cautious language in making their claims or is one more confident and assertive than the other? Is one (or both) of the historians over-claiming?

3 Look back at Source 12. Do both historians in Extracts 1 and 2 appear to have made equally effective use of Moryson's evidence?

4 Are both of the historical accounts equally credible or are there reasons to prefer one account to another?

ACTIVITY
SUMMARY

1 Design your own diagram or flow chart to show: the causes of Tyrone's revolt; the key events; the reasons for its eventual failure.

2 Write one side of A4 to answer the following question: 'How far do you agree that the Nine Years' War posed a serious challenge to the English government in the years 1594–1603?'

 WIDER READING

Brigden, S. *New Worlds, Lost Worlds: The Rule of the Tudors, 1485–1603*, Penguin (2001)

Ellis, S.G. *Ireland in the Age of the Tudors, 1447–1603*, Longman (1998)

Morgan, H. *Tyrone's Rebellion: The Outbreak of the Nine Years' War in Ireland*, Boydell (1999)

Preparing for your A Level Paper 3 exam

Advance planning

Draw up a timetable for your revision and try to keep to it. Spend longer on topics that you have found difficult, and revise them several times. Aim to be confident about all aspects of your Paper 3 work, because this will ensure that you have a choice of questions in Sections B and C.

Paper 3 Overview

Paper 3	Time: 2 hours 15 minutes	
Section A	Answer 1 compulsory question for the option studied, assessing source analysis and evaluation skills	20 marks
Section B	Answer 1 question from a choice of 2 on an aspect in depth for the option studied	20 marks
Section C	Answer 1 question from a choice of 2 on an aspect in breadth for the option studied	20 marks
	Total marks =	60 marks

Section A questions

There is no choice of question in Section A. You will be referred to a source of about 350 words long, printed in a Sources Booklet. The source will be a primary source or one that is contemporary to the period you have studied, and will relate to one of the key topics in the Aspect of Depth. You will be expected to analyse and evaluate the source in its historical context. The question will ask you to assess the value of the source for revealing something specific about the period, and will expect you to explain your answer, using the source, the information given about its origin and your own knowledge about the historical context.

Section B questions

You will have a choice of one from two questions in Section B. They will aim to assess your understanding of one or more of the key topics in the Aspect of Depth you have studied. Questions may relate to a single, momentous year, but will normally cover longer periods. You will be required to write an essay evaluating an aspect of the period. You may be asked about change and continuity, similarity and difference, consequences, significance or causation, or you may be given a quotation and asked to explain how far you agree with it. All questions will require you to reach a substantiated judgement.

Section C questions

You will have a choice of one from two questions in Section C. Questions will relate to the themes of the Aspects of Breadth you have studied, and will aim to assess your understanding of change over time. They will cover a period of not less than 100 years and will relate either to the factors that brought about change, or the extent of change over the period, or patterns of change as demonstrated by turning points.

Use of time

- Do not write solidly for 45 minutes on each question. For Section B and C answers, you should spend a few minutes working out what the question is asking you to do and drawing up a plan of your answer. This is especially important for Section C answers, which cover an extended period of time.

- For Section A, it is essential that you have a clear understanding of the content of the source and its historical context. Pay particular attention to the provenance: was the author in a position to know what he or she was writing about? Read it carefully and underline important points. You might decide to spend up to 10 minutes reading the source and drawing up your plan, and 35 minutes writing your answer.

Preparing for your A Level exams

> ## Paper 3: A Level sample answer with comments

Section A

These questions require you to analyse and evaluate source material with respect to its historical context.

For these questions remember to:

- look at the evidence given in the source and consider how the source could be used in differing ways to provide historical understanding
- use your knowledge of the historical context to discuss any limitations the source may have
- use your historical understanding to evaluate the source, considering how much weight you would give to its argument
- come to a judgement on the overall value of the source in respect to the question.

Study Source 4 in Chapter 3 (page 70) before you answer this question.

Assess the value of the source for revealing how secure Henry was on the throne in the early years of his rule and his approaches to government. Explain your answer using the source, the information given about it and your own knowledge of the historical context. (20 marks)

Average student answer

When Henry VII came to the throne in 1485, he faced many challenges and threats because he was a usurper and there were other people with a better claim to the throne. Polydore Vergil was in England during Henry's reign and was commissioned by Henry to write a history. This means that Vergil would most likely be biased in favour of Henry and would show him in a good light so he might not always be reliable. Vergil describes the problems that Henry faced at the start of his reign, mentioning Edward Earl of Warwick who had a claim to the throne. Vergil shows that Henry dealt with the threat from Warwick very well by putting him in the Tower of London. Warwick remained in prison for the rest of his life until he was executed in 1499; this shows that Henry dealt very effectively with the threats he faced.

Vergil also describes how Henry dealt with another potential threat to his position when he talks about 'Elizabeth, elder daughter of Edward IV'. Elizabeth had a claim to the throne and represented the Yorkists, the rivals to Henry for the throne. Elizabeth's brothers had disappeared during the reign of Richard III, which made him very unpopular. There were also rumours that Richard intended to marry Elizabeth, his own niece, which made him even more unpopular. Elizabeth's mother arranged with Henry's mother that Henry would marry Elizabeth. When Henry won against Richard at Bosworth and Richard was killed, Henry agreed to go through with the marriage which helped him to become more secure on the throne at the start of his reign and to deal with the threat from Yorkists who might have wanted the throne for themselves.

Henry was also helped by Richard's unpopularity. As Vergil says, 'in the places through which he passed was greeted with the greatest joy by all'. This suggests that people were pleased that Henry was now king; Richard had been accused of murdering his own nephews and was not well-liked, even by his own nobility. Henry had some support from important nobles such as his uncle, Jasper Tudor, and his friend, the Earl of Oxford. He also had considerable support from Yorkists who were unhappy with Richard's rule. Henry was careful to reward these people to ensure that they stayed loyal to him; 'he would give complete pardon and forgiveness to all those who swore obedience to his name' as Vergil says. This made him more secure on the throne. He was even prepared to forgive Yorkists such as the Earl of Lincoln. However, Vergil

Although the context of the source is mentioned and Vergil's motives considered, these are not well explained. A better approach would be to explain that although Vergil needed to please his patron, he did research his topic carefully and was not always favourable in his view of Henry.

The point is valid, but tends to narrative and needs more developed explanation.

There is some use of accurate detail here to explore Vergil's claims, but it needs to be more clearly focused on how secure Henry was on the throne at the start of the reign.

cannot be trusted entirely because he was paid by Henry to write about his reign, so he is likely to exaggerate Henry's popularity.

Henry also managed to make himself secure by his approach to government. Vergil says that 'he summoned a Parliament, as was the custom, in which he might receive the crown by popular consent'. This was important for Henry because parliament was one of the places where he could communicate with his subjects. By summoning parliament he was showing that he intended to rule fairly and to take into account the views of his subjects. Parliament was the only place where laws could be made and taxation raised. By summoning parliament very promptly after Bosworth, Henry was trying to get his subjects on his side and show that he was not a tyrant like Richard III. Henry also used parliament to make his claim to the Crown stronger. This was important because his claim was so weak and he had become king after beating Richard at Bosworth. Henry used parliament to declare himself king. He also used parliament to make his reign start the day before Bosworth so that everyone who fought against him was a traitor. This made his claim to be king stronger.

Henry was also 'shrewd and prudent, so that no one dared to get the better of him through deceit or guile... He cherished justice above all thing'. Vergil is showing that Henry was very keen to ensure that the laws of England were obeyed and that the nobility could not use their position to challenge his position as king. Henry made the Lords and Commons in parliament swear an oath not to retain illegally. He also passed an Act of Resumption which increased the wealth of the Crown and was careful not to give away too many lands to his supporters which made him stronger. This is why Vergil calls him 'distinguished, wise and prudent'. However, Vergil is not entirely accurate when he says that 'no one dared to get the better of him'. Henry faced challenges from John, Earl of Lincoln, in 1486 who began to plot against him. Henry had trusted Lincoln and had even allowed him to be on his Council. Henry also faced a challenge from other Yorkists such as the Staffords and Sir Francis Lovell who tried to rebel against him. This is another example of Vergil exaggerating in order to please Henry as he does not mention the problems Henry faced.

In conclusion, the source is quite valuable for showing how secure Henry was on the throne and how he ruled England. Vergil shows that Henry managed parliament very cleverly and got the people on his side. He also acted fast to deal with the threat from the Earl of Warwick and the Yorkists by arresting Warwick and marrying Elizabeth of York. However, Vergil was writing to please Henry so he tends to exaggerate how successful Henry was in dealing with the threats he faced.

> This section is more clearly focused on the question of Henry's approach to government. The evidence on how he used parliament is accurate, but needs more detailed explanation of what this suggests about how secure he was.

> Own knowledge is used to show that Henry attempted to strengthen his position on the throne, but that he also made mistakes. The comment about Vergil's motives in portraying Henry in a positive light is assertion. It could be improved by an explanation of how Henry made mistakes and faced challenges, but was able to overcome them.

There is an attempt at a judgement with some consideration of the nature of the source, but this is not well-developed.

Verdict

This is an average answer because:

- it shows a basic understanding of the source material and identifies some key points, although there is a tendency to drift from the question set
- it shows some knowledge of context, but this could be developed
- it has some evaluation of the source material, but this tends towards assertion and would benefit from specific development about Vergil and the value of his account as evidence
- there is some overall judgement, but it needs more development to make it substantial.

Use the feedback on this essay to rewrite it, making as many improvements as you can.

Paper 3: A Level sample answer with comments

Section A

These questions require you to analyse and evaluate source material with respect to its historical context.

For these questions remember to:

- look at the evidence given in the source and consider how the source could be used in differing ways to provide historical understanding
- use your knowledge of the historical context to discuss any limitations the source may have
- use your historical understanding to evaluate the source, considering how much weight you would give to its argument
- come to a judgement on the overall value of the source in respect to the question.

Study Source 4 in Chapter 3 (page 70) before you answer this question.

Assess the value of the source for revealing how secure Henry was on the throne in the early years of his rule and his approaches to government. Explain your answer using the source, the information given about it and your own knowledge of the historical context. *(20 marks)*

Strong student answer

Polydore Vergil's account of Henry's rule is very valuable for revealing his style of rule and approach to government. It is also helpful for understanding how secure Henry was on the throne in the early years of his rule, though the nature of the source (pro-Tudor propaganda) means that it does not fully take into account the full extent of the problems Henry faced or the level of the threats to his security. Polydore Vergil was commissioned by Henry to write a history of his reign. Because Vergil spent time in England, he was well-placed to observe how Henry ruled England. Although he was not a witness to the events at the start of Henry's reign, Vergil did research his topic carefully. This means that while he had to present a favourable account at times, his account of Henry's early years is likely to be relatively accurate and a valuable source of information about Henry's security and his approach to government.

Vergil is clear that Henry was not very secure on the throne at the start of his reign. Vergil refers to Henry 'quelling the insurrections'; this implies that there were attempts to rebel against Henry and that he was not entirely secure. Vergil goes on to give the example of one such threat, Edward, Earl of Warwick. Vergil claims that Henry 'was fearful lest, if the boy should escape and given any alteration in circumstances, he might stir up civil discord'. This is a good example of the challenges Henry faced to his security. Henry had won the throne from Richard III by defeating and killing Richard at Bosworth in 1485. However, Henry's own claim to the throne was very weak; he was descended from Edward III via an illegitimate branch of the family who had no right to claim the throne. Vergil talks about 'Edward, the fifteen-year-old earl of Warwick, sole survivor of George, duke of Clarence'. Clarence was the brother of Richard III and Warwick was his nephew. Warwick had a strong claim to the throne. This is why Vergil claims that Warwick might 'stir up civil discord'. Although some Yorkists such as John Morton, Bishop of Ely, and Sir Giles Daubeney had been prepared to support Henry because they had become alienated by Richard's rule, there was no guarantee that they would continue to support Henry once Richard was dead and there was a chance of putting a Yorkist monarch back on the throne. This suggests that Henry was not at all secure to begin with and that it was vital for him to deal with the potential threat posed by the Yorkists.

Vergil is also a valuable source for showing that Henry did have some advantages in 1485 which helped him to become more secure. Vergil claims that Henry was greeted 'like a triumphing general… Far and wide the people hastened to assemble by the roadside, saluting him as king'. Vergil is somewhat embellishing the response to Henry in order to show how popular Henry was and how unpopular Richard was. However, it is true that Richard's rule had been unpopular and that many

The introduction is clearly focused on the question of what the source reveals about both the threats to Henry's security and his style of government. It also deals with the nature of the source.

Additional factual detail is used to give detailed context to the source and to examine the validity of Vergil's claims.

members of the nobility and gentry were no longer prepared to support him. Richard was generally believed to have murdered his own nephews in order to get the throne; this caused widespread anger and helps to explain why some Yorkists were prepared to turn against Richard. However, the attitude of the nobility at Bosworth again shows that Henry was not secure. He was fortunate that Sir William Stanley and his men rescued him on the battlefield; although Stanley had helped Henry in 1485, there was nothing to stop him and other members of the nobility from plotting to remove Henry in the future. Vergil's over emphasis on the popularity of Henry's victory is Tudor propaganda. Vergil was trying to show that Henry had a right to rule because he had defeated a tyrant and his victory was genuinely popular. Because of this, Vergil's claims should not be taken at face value, although he also acknowledges the threats posed to Henry by rival Yorkist claimants.

Vergil's account of Henry's approach to government in the early years is very valuable because it shows how Henry attempted to deal with potential enemies while making his position as king more secure. Vergil emphasises the early use that Henry made of parliament: 'he summoned a Parliament, as was the custom, in which he might receive the crown by popular consent. His chief care was to regulate well affairs of state…' Henry called parliament after he had already been crowned as king. When Vergil talks about Henry receiving the crown 'by popular consent' he is suggesting that Henry used parliament to enhance his position as king. Henry's management of parliament was particularly clever; he asked them to declare that he was king but he was careful not to suggest that parliament was giving him the right to be king. This was a clever move because he was showing that parliament was going to be important to him in his rule but he was not going to let it control him. This use of parliament showed that Henry was good at manipulating the system to make his position stronger. Henry was also careful in the early months of his rule to try to keep Yorkist support. As Vergil claims, 'in order that the people of England should not be further torn by rival factions, he publicly proclaimed that (as he had already promised) he would take for his wife Elizabeth daughter of King Edward'. By keeping his promise to marry Elizabeth, Henry was able to neutralise one Yorkist claimant and make his own position stronger by marrying an heir to the throne. Vergil also shows how Henry attempted to win over his potential enemies by giving them 'pardon and forgiveness to all those who swore obedience to his name'. An example of this policy was Henry's forgiveness of the Earl of Lincoln; when Lincoln swore an oath of loyalty to Henry he was even allowed to join the Council. This suggests that Henry was a bit naive in his treatment of potential rivals for the throne as Lincoln rebelled against Henry in 1487. However, Vergil's claim that 'in government he was shrewd and prudent… He cherished justice above all things' is partly accurate. Henry wanted to ensure that the nobility could not use their private armies to overthrow them, so he made the Lords and Commons in parliament promise not to retain men illegally. Henry's approach was also cautious in his use of rewards to his supporters; he did not give away large amounts of lands or money which would have made the nobility more powerful. Instead, he preferred to reward his supporters with cheap options such as giving them the Order of the Garter. This supports Vergil's claim about Henry's prudent approach to government in the early years.

Overall, Vergil's account is very useful for revealing Henry's approaches to government. Although Vergil somewhat exaggerates Henry's right to be king and the popularity of his rule, his account does give an accurate impression of the cautious way in which Henry tried to establish himself on the throne and in particular Henry's use of parliament and his marriage to Elizabeth of York. Vergil tends to downplay the extent of the challenges posed to Henry, but he does admit that there were threats to Henry's security from rival claimants and the Yorkist faction which Henry had to manage carefully.

> This section provides more context and explains and illustrates the attitude taken by Polydore Vergil.

> The judgement is clearly focused on the question and evaluates the weight of the source as evidence.

Verdict

This is a strong answer because:

- it identifies and illustrates the key points in the source

- it deploys some effective own knowledge to develop these points and provide context
- it reaches a clear and substantiated conclusion.

Paper 3: A Level sample answer with comments

Section B

These questions require you to show your understanding of a period in depth. They will ask you about a quite specific period of time and require you to make a substantiated judgement about a specific aspect you have studied.

For these questions remember to:

- organise your essay and communicate it in a manner that is clear and comprehensible
- use historical knowledge to analyse and evaluate the key aspect of the question
- make a balanced argument that weighs up differing opinions
- make a substantiated overall judgement on the question.

To what extent was Kett's rebellion simply a reaction to the Duke of Somerset's enclosure commissions in 1548–49? (20 marks)

Average student answer

Kett's rebellion was very serious for the Duke of Somerset and his government. Riots broke out across the south and east of England in 1549 and reached Norfolk in early July. At Wymondham, rioters threw down the hedges of men who had enclosed the common land. Robert Kett became the leader of these riots. He marched with the rebels to Mousehold Heath outside Norwich where the rebellion became even more serious because it attracted up to 16,000 men. It took the government until the end of August to put the rebellion down by force at Dussindale. There were several causes of the rebellion including Somerset's enclosure commissions but there were also other important reasons for the rising.

The Duke of Somerset was known as the 'Good Duke'. He was very interested in helping the poor in society and he thought that enclosures were the root of the problems affecting Tudor society. Enclosure was where greedy landlords put hedges or ditches around their lands so that they could use them for sheep farming. Often, landlords were enclosing common land that was used by the poor. Enclosure was blamed by men like Somerset and his advisers for causing poverty and vagrancy and he was determined to do something about it. In 1548, Somerset appointed John Hales to inquire into enclosure. Hales was a reformer and was influenced by the ideas of the 'commonwealth-men'. In 1548, Hales tried to introduce several bills into parliament to deal with sheep farming and enclosure. He was not very successful, but in 1548, he led a commission inquiring into enclosure in the Midlands. This was not very successful either, but Somerset was determined. In 1549, he issued more commissions into enclosure and encouraged them to act against members of the nobility who had enclosed illegally. This encouraged men such as Kett to rebel because enclosure had caused a lot of problems in East Anglia and there was a lot of resentment there.

There were also other reasons for the outbreak of Kett's rebellion in 1549. England was going through a severe economic depression in the late 1540s. The population of England had grown rapidly and there was not enough food to feed everyone. This led to price rises which affected the poorest in society who could not afford to buy enough food to live on. Parliament was worried about the increasing numbers of vagrants and beggars and had passed an Act in 1547 which punished them severely.

The introduction is mostly narrative and focuses only briefly on the question of the role of the enclosure commissions in starting the revolt. It could be improved by a clearer focus on the different causes of the rebellion and an initial judgement about whether it was 'simply' the enclosure commissions that caused the rising.

This paragraph is mostly accurate, but lacks detailed development. It tends to narrative and would be improved by an explanation of how and why Somerset's commissions led to riots in Norfolk.

This section is accurate, but could be improved with some precise statistics about population growth and price rises. The punishments introduced in the 1547 Act could also be explained to show the pressures that were being placed on the poor and the reasons for their resentment of the ruling elites.

The poor in society had nowhere to turn for help. The economic situation was made worse because of the government's policy of debasement which forced prices up even higher. There were also several bad harvests in the 1540s which meant that the crops failed and prices rose even higher. These problems meant that the people were angry with the government. They were also angry with the rich landowners who were enclosing land for sheep farming, especially the common land which the poor relied on to survive. This was a particularly common practice in East Anglia which is why there was more anger there which grew until rebellion broke out in 1549. Therefore, the social and economic conditions were a more important reason for Kett's rebellion than the enclosure commissions.

This section deals with a second reason for the outbreak of revolt, the social and economic crisis of the period. While the material is mostly accurate, it could do with some more detailed examples. The section ends with an assertion which attempts to focus on the question. This could be improved by an explanation of why social and economic problems were a more important reason for the rebellion than Somerset's commissions.

Finally, another reason for the outbreak of Kett's rebellion was local anger at corrupt government officials who were also members of the gentry. This was linked to Kett's charismatic leadership because he was the one who turned the riots at Wymondham into a more organised protest. The rebels were angry that members of the local gentry took advantage of their position and local offices to make themselves richer at a time when the poor were getting poorer. An example of a local official was Sir John Flowerdew who had used his position as a lawyer and escheator to demolish parts of the abbey at Wymondham which the townspeople claimed was theirs. Flowerdew had also enclosed come of the common land locally so it was not surprising that the rioters first attacked his fences. Flowerdew tried to distract the rioters by turning their anger against Robert Kett who had also enclosed land. But Kett took the side of the rioters and agreed to throw down his fences. He then organised the rebels to march to Norwich, which was a very large town; Kett was a very good leader and he attracted up to 16,000 men to join his rebellion. Kett and the rebels showed their anger at corrupt and greedy landlords in several ways. In their demands, they complained about local officials abusing their powers, the problems of enclosure and sheep farming. One demand even complained that some landlords still did not allow their tenants any freedom and that they were like medieval serfs. An example of this was the Howard family who were very unpopular in the region because of their harsh treatment of their tenants. They also captured and imprisoned local members of the gentry and town officials in Norwich. Kett also set up a people's court under a tree, called the Oak of Reformation, where landlords could be tried and disputes settled. The rebels were also very well organised under Kett. They were able to get food and supplies from Norwich and elsewhere to show that they could run local government better than the gentry. This was very dangerous for Somerset and his government because Kett and his followers were rejecting the local gentry and nobility. This was also an important reason for Kett's rebellion.

This paragraph tends to drift into detailed narrative in places, although it does attempt to introduce a third reason for rebellion. It is also in danger of answering a different question about the extent of the threat posed by the rebellion. It could be improved by a clearer focus on why the rebels were so angry about local government and how Somerset's commission seemed to be encouraging the rebels to air their grievances.

In conclusion, there were several reasons for Kett's rebellion in 1549. These included Somerset's commissions, the social and economic situation and local anger about gentry and noble landlords. All of these reasons were very important in causing the rebellion.

This is a very brief conclusion, which does not reach a judgement on the question. It could be improved by an explanation of which was the most important reason and whether Somerset's commissions were 'simply' to blame.

Verdict:

This is an average answer because:

- there is some analysis of the question, but the answer tends to description in places
- the material used is accurate and has some range, but lacks depth of detail
- there is some attempt to answer the question, but this is not well-explained
- the final judgement lacks substantiation.

Use the feedback on this essay to rewrite it, making as many improvements as you can.

Paper 3: A Level sample answer with comments

Section B

These questions require you to show your understanding of a period in depth. They will ask you about a quite specific period of time and require you to make a substantiated judgement about a specific aspect you have studied.

For these questions remember to:

- organise your essay and communicate it in a manner that is clear and comprehensible
- use historical knowledge to analyse and evaluate the key aspect of the question
- make a balanced argument that weighs up differing opinions
- make a substantiated overall judgement on the question.

To what extent was Kett's rebellion simply a reaction to the Duke of Somerset's enclosure commissions in 1548–49? (20 marks)

Strong student answer

Kett's rebellion in 1549 was certainly triggered by the Duke of Somerset's enclosure commissions, but to say that it was 'simply' a reaction to these commissions is an understatement. Kett's rebellion was caused by a complicated mixture of factors which included Somerset and his advisers' attitudes to poverty and social reform, the social and economic hardship of the later 1540s and popular anger in the Norfolk region about the abuses of members of the local gentry and nobility of their positions in local government. Somerset's commissions helped to bring about the outbreak of riots in Norfolk, but the development of these riots into a full-scale rebellion can be better explained by longer-term social and economic problems.

> The introduction is focused on the question and deals with the word 'simply'. The overall argument is clear and the candidate uses criteria such as 'trigger' and 'longer-term' to explain the outbreak of rebellion.

Somerset's enclosure commissions in 1548–49 were an attempt to deal with what many Tudor thinkers thought was the main cause of poverty and vagrancy. Enclosure was often used in sheep farming which was the main industry in England and was very profitable, particularly in the 1540s. As landlords, who were often members of the nobility and gentry, enclosed their lands, they sometimes took areas of common land; others forced their tenants out by raising rents. The common land was important for the poorest villagers because they could use the land to graze their animals; the loss of this land made it hard for these poorer members of society to survive. Somerset's response was to issue commissions of inquiry in 1548, although only one of these was active. Somerset then reissued the commissions, but gave them additional powers to act against illegal enclosers, which he was not supposed to do. This led to the destruction of illegal enclosures belonging to members of the nobility; for example, a park belonging to John Dudley was ploughed up. Somerset's enclosure commissions led to riots across the Midlands and south east. This was because the practice of enclosure was widely resented and Somerset's commissions seemed to be encouraging those with grievances to believe that the government was on their side. The riots that began in Wymondham in Norfolk started with attacks on the enclosures made by an unpopular member of the local gentry, Sir John Flowerdew. Enclosure was a cause of resentment in East Anglia because of the importance of sheep farming in the region. Local landlords such as Sir William Fermour owned 17,000 sheep and it was men such as him who used enclosure to increase their profits at the expense of poorer tenants and smaller farmers.

> These paragraphs show a sustained analysis of the question supported by accurate and well-selected detail.

However, although the enclosure commissions encouraged the initial riots at Wymondham, it was not 'simply' the commissions that caused such large and dangerous rebellion to break out. In parts of Norfolk, the regions known as 'foldcourse', it was the smaller landlords who were carrying out enclosure, not the gentry or nobility. It was not just enclosure that was the issue in Norfolk; it was sheep farming more generally. The rebel demands show that in some cases they were in favour of enclosure, but what they really resented was the power of the landed gentry and nobility and the wider problems caused by sheep farming in the region. Somerset's social policies from 1547 had attacked not just enclosure but sheep farming as well; for example, in March 1549 John Hales, supported by Somerset, had introduced a tax on sheep in an attempt to discourage the keeping of huge flocks. It was not 'simply' the enclosure commissions that caused the rebellion in 1549; it was also Somerset's more general social and economic policies which made the rebels think that the government would support their actions.

Kett's rebellion also had longer-term causes which Somerset's enclosure commissions were also attempting to solve. In the later 1540s, there was an economic downturn. The population grew very rapidly from 2.3 to 3.0 million in a short period of time. Population growth made it harder to provide enough food and prices started to rise quickly. By 1549, prices were more than double what they had been in 1500. These changes affected the poorest in society the most. These people were reliant on the common land in their village to survive; however, the practice of enclosure led to less access to this common land. By the late 1540s, there was severe social and economic hardship and a massive divide between the richest and poorest in society. This helps to explain why Kett's rebellion broke out, especially as Somerset seemed to be portraying himself as a champion of the poor.

A second factor is examined and considered as a longer-term reason for the rebellion.

To argue that Kett's rebellion was 'simply' a reaction to Somerset's enclosure commissions also ignores the growing dissatisfaction with the role of the gentry and nobility in the government of Norfolk and Suffolk. The rebels' complaints and actions show that they were angry about what they saw as the greed and corruption of the landed elites. For example, the first person to be targeted at Wymondham was Sir John Flowerdew. Flowerdew had enclosed lands illegally but he had also been in dispute with the local community about the ownership of the abbey. Flowerdew had used his power as a local official (escheator) and his legal knowledge to buy part of the abbey. Somerset and his advisers encouraged these complaints by seeming to target powerful members of society in their enclosure commissions and by their rhetoric in sermons preached and published by men such as Robert Crowley which criticised wealthy landowners for not looking after the poor. The rebels' actions also showed their long-standing resentment about greedy and corrupt members of the gentry; for example, another unpopular local official, John Corbet of Sprowston had his property vandalised. The rebel actions and demands show the real reason for the outbreak of rebellion in 1549. Resentment over the actions of the landed elites had developed over several years. To the rebels, the gentry seemed to be corrupt and greedy; illegal enclosure was one of the symptoms of this corruption. When Somerset launched his commissions of inquiry, he triggered the outbreak of riots against enclosure, but these were fuelled by a wider sense of resentment against the ruling elites.

Clear focus on the question and knowledge is well-deployed to assess the relative importance of the causes.

In conclusion, Kett's rebellion was not 'simply' the result of Somerset's enclosure commissions. The commissions sparked the initial riots, but the rebellion that emerged in East Anglia grew so quickly because of the social and economic depression and long-term resentment against the members of landed society who governed East Anglia. The enclosure commissions encouraged the rebels to think that Somerset would support their actions, but it was his more general attitude to the creation of a Godly commonwealth that encouraged Kett and his followers to continue in their rebellion and to demand such radical change in local government.

An overall judgement is reached using valid criteria.

Verdict

This is a strong answer because:

- the argument is sustained throughout
- criteria for making a judgement on the question are well selected and used
- the answer is well-organised and well-supported by precise and well-selected detail.

Paper 3: A Level sample answer with comments

Section C

These questions require you to show your understanding of a subject over a considerable period of time. They will ask you to assess a long-term historical topic and its development over a period of at least 100 years, and they require you to make a substantiated judgement in relation to the question.

For these questions remember to:

- organise your essay and communicate it in a manner that is clear and comprehensible
- use historical knowledge to analyse and evaluate the key aspect of the question covering the entire period
- make a balanced argument that weighs up differing opinions
- make a substantiated overall judgement on the question.

How far do you agree that the 1513 subsidy marked the most significant improvement in the government of the localities in the years 1485–1603? (20 marks)

Average student answer

The 1513 subsidy was very important in improving the government of the localities in the years 1485–1603, but there were also other reasons for these improvements.

Thomas Wolsey introduced the subsidy in 1513 to try to increase the amount of money the government received by making the way it was assessed and collected more fair. The subsidy was set up to assess people on their ability to pay. This was based on their wealth or income. Each person had to take an oath to show that they were telling the truth about how much they were worth and local commissioners went round and checked the assessments. The nobility also had to pay a tax based on their rank. This system was fairer because people only paid what they could afford, so more people paid the tax. This increased the amount of money the government received and so made the system more efficient. Later governments built on Wolsey's idea. For example, Thomas Cromwell introduced the idea that people should pay tax in times of peace as well as war. But by Elizabeth's reign the system was not working very well. Many people were avoiding taxation altogether or were lying about how much they were assessed. Elizabeth was partly to blame for this because she allowed the system to become stale. For example, assessments became fixed and no one checked the assessments that were given to the authorities. This meant that the subsidy became less successful over time.

Another way in which the government of the localities was improved in the years 1485–1603 was by better use of the Justices of the Peace. Justices of the Peace had been used in government for hundreds of years but under the Tudors they became increasingly important in local government. Henry VIII began to increase the power of the JPs and this was continued under Edward and Elizabeth. For example, under Edward VI, JPs were made responsible for overseeing religious changes in local churches such as enforcing the Book of Common Prayer. They also became responsible for enforcing local order, for example regulating alehouses. By Elizabeth's reign, there were more JPs than there had ever been, doing a wider range of jobs. Elizabeth's government made the JPs responsible for overseeing the new poor laws. This made them very important in improving the government of the localities.

The introduction attempts focus on the question, but it could be improved by mentioning what other improvements were made other than the 1513 subsidy and an initial judgement focusing on which was the 'most significant'.

This section is accurate, but lacks detailed support. It could be improved by an explanation of how the subsidy improved on the older system seen under Henry VII and how this improved the government of the localities.

This section contains assertions about the JPs under Henry VIII, which could be better explained and substantiated. There is no reference to the role of the JPs under Henry VII, which would strengthen the point.

This section looks at another reason for the improvement of local government. It is accurate, but lacks detailed support. It could be improved by an explanation of how the increasing role of the JPs helped to improve local government, especially through their involvement in social and religious control of the localities.

The government of the localities was also improved through the increasing amount of laws passed to deal with poverty and beggars. The Tudor government feared the increasing number of poor who wandered around the country because they could spread disease and disorder. The population of England was growing rapidly in the Tudor period; prices were also going up and wages were going down, meaning more people were at risk of falling into poverty. At first, the government tried to control the poor by punishing those who they thought were able-bodied but lazy. For example, in 1531, a Poor Law was passed which ordered vagrants to be whipped. In 1547, the Vagrancy Act was passed. Vagrants could be punished by being branded or being forced to work as slaves. However, this law was too harsh, so the government was forced to look for other options. This led to the passing of the Statute of Artificers in 1563 which was a new way of trying to deal with the problem of poverty. Under this Statute, all unmarried people under the age of 30 had to work and to accept any job offered to them. The Statute also focused on getting more people to work on the land and protected recruitment into skilled occupations. In 1598, there was another Act dealing with the problem of poverty. The Act introduced the post of overseer of the poor for each parish, who looked after the local payments for poor relief. Another law in the same year, the Vagabonds Act, dealt with punishments for dangerous vagabonds. These acts all helped to improve local government.

> The detail used in this section is accurate, but tends towards a description of what the government did. It could be improved by an explanation of how this helped improve local government, with a comparison of the significance of this legislation compared to the 1513 subsidy. There is also no reference to legislation passed under Henry VII.

Another way in which local government was improved in the Tudor period was by improving control over regions where there was not much law and order, such as the North and Wales. In 1537, a new Council of the North was introduced which had increased powers and was led by an outsider. This helped to improve government in the North. Elizabeth I continued this process after the Revolt of the Northern Earls in 1569.

In Wales, there were two laws which brought the region under the control of England. English laws and systems of government were to be used. New counties were created with MPs who were to be elected for the English parliament. There was also a new form of Council in Wales which was used to make government in this region work more effectively. All of these changes made local government work better and were more important than the 1513 subsidy.

> This section would benefit from more detailed development; for example, an explanation of what the new powers of the Council of the North were, how this helped to improve government of the localities, and how Elizabeth I built on this system after 1569. There also needs to be some reference to the government of the North before 1537 and especially under Henry VII.

In conclusion, the 1513 subsidy was not very significant in the improvement of local government in the period 1485–1603. This is because other changes had more of an effect. The most significant improvements in local government were the changes to poor relief.

> This conclusion is very brief and offers an unsubstantiated judgement on the question. It could be improved by an explanation of why the changes to poor relief had more of an effect; for example, did improved management of poverty and vagrancy lead to less local unrest? How lasting were the changes brought about by the subsidy?

> This section ends with an assertion which attempts to answer the question. This could be improved by an explanation of why the use of conciliar government in the North and in Wales was a more important improvement in the government of the localities than the 1513 subsidy.

Verdict

This is an average answer because:

- the topic in general is partly addressed, but the answer lacks enough detailed explanation and analysis
- there is some deployment of own knowledge, but it does not cover the full date range of the question; in particular, there is no reference to the reign of Henry VII

- there is a judgement, but it is not substantiated.

Use the feedback on this essay to rewrite it, making as many improvements as you can.

Paper 3: A Level sample answer with comments

Section C

These questions require you to show your understanding of a subject over a considerable period of time. They will ask you to assess a long-term historical topic and its development over a period of at least 100 years, and they require you to make a substantiated judgement in relation to the question.

For these questions remember to:

- organise your essay and communicate it in a manner that is clear and comprehensible
- use historical knowledge to analyse and evaluate the key aspect of the question covering the entire period
- make a balanced argument that weighs up differing opinions
- make a substantiated overall judgement on the question.

How far do you agree that the 1513 subsidy marked the most significant improvement in the government of the localities in the years 1485–1603? (20 marks)

Strong student answer

The 1513 subsidy was an important landmark in Tudor local government because it improved the efficiency with which taxation was collected. However, it was not the most significant improvement in the government of the localities across the whole period 1485 to 1603 because it did not lead to such lasting change as other innovations. Tudor local government also improved in other ways during the period, especially the management of law and order across England and particularly in the remoter regions of the country which had always been troublesome. These improvements were more lasting than the subsidy and had a greater impact on the government of the localities because they improved how effectively the localities were controlled by the Crown.

The subsidy introduced by Wolsey in 1513 was an important innovation in how the Tudor government was able to raise money from the localities. Before 1513, the government had been reliant on an old-fashioned system called fifteenths and tenths. However, as Henry VII found, the way that tax was assessed had been set in 1334 and took no account of changes in property values or price rises. The result was that the Tudor government was using a system that took no account of inflation. It was also not a very fair system because responsibility for paying the amount set for a community was passed on to those who did not have the influence to avoid paying tax. The result was that the poorer members of society paid more than the richer ones. Under Henry VII, this system had led to tax rebellions in 1489 and 1497. Wolsey's subsidy changed this system by introducing a new method of assessment and payment. This was significant because the new system was fairer; everyone was now assessed on how much property or income they had. A new tax was also introduced for the nobility which was based on their rank. Subsidy commissioners were appointed for each region to check that taxpayers assessed their wealth honestly; for the first time, each individual paid according to their wealth. This was particularly important for poorer regions of the country such as the North and South West, where high levels of taxation had provoked protest under Henry VII. Initially, the new subsidy was very effective in creating more income for the Crown. Between 1513 and 1523, Wolsey raised £322,099 through the new subsidy. In comparison, fifteenths and tenths raised between 1512 and 1517 raised just £117,936. However, in the later Tudor period, the subsidy had less of an impact on local government and became a reason for more local tension. Under Elizabeth I, the levels raised by the subsidy fell. This was because Elizabeth permitted the rates at which tax was paid to become fixed. Another problem was that the system became increasingly corrupt because there was less checking of each person's assessment of their wealth. This allowed the wealthy and powerful in Tudor society to evade taxation, just like they had done under Henry VII. For example, William Cecil had an income of around £4,000 per year, but he claimed that it was only £133 6s 8d. This meant he paid less tax. This corruption in the system meant that the Tudor government continued to rely on the unfair system of fifteenths and tenths as well as the subsidy. The result was that although the 1513 subsidy brought a temporary improvement to local government, it was not sustained and the old problems of enforcing a system that was fair for everyone returned. Therefore, the 1513 subsidy was not as significant in improving local government as it first appeared.

The introduction is clearly focused on the question and introduces criteria by which a judgement can be reached, which change had the more lasting impact.

This section deals with the 1513 subsidy; it ranges with some confidence across the period and analyses the extent to which the subsidy brought about a lasting or significant improvement to local government.

The most significant improvement to local government was the better management of law and order through increased use of the JPs and through more effective handling of the problems of poverty and vagrancy. JPs had been used in Tudor government since the Middle Ages, but from Henry VII's reign, their role in local government began to grow. Henry VII made the JPs responsible for dealing with over-powerful nobles. By the 1540s, population growth and price rises had created increasing numbers of vagrants and beggars. The government responded by increasing the powers of JPs to deal with local order; for example, in 1552, JPs were given the power to license alehouses which were considered to be a particular cause of social unrest. Under the Statute of Artificers in 1563, JPs were given additional powers to ensure that everyone who was able to work was made to do so. Under Edward and then Elizabeth, JPs were also given powers to enforce the religious changes which the government had enacted through parliament. This role was particularly important in regions which remained loyal to Roman Catholicism such as the North and the South West. Because the JPs were drawn from the local gentry and nobility, they had the status in local society to ensure that the central government's policies were enforced effectively. Their success can be seen in the declining level of rebellion in England during the Tudor period; after 1569, there were no more popular rebellions in England. Even in the 1590s, when there was a social and economic crisis, there was no widespread unrest. This suggests that the increasing role of the JPs in local society meant that the government had better control of local order. This helped to reduce the amount of social tension and created better order in local government. These changes were more lasting than the 1513 subsidy and so were more effective in the longer term.

Local government was also improved by the increase of control in Wales and the North. These were regions that were traditionally militarised and often quite lawless, especially because they were dominated by powerful members of the nobility. The most important developments to improving the government in these regions were in the 1530s and 1540s. In this period, the Council of the North was reorganised and placed under the control of a president who came from outside the region; the aim was to undermine the power of the regional nobility and to improve royal control following the very serious Pilgrimage of Grace. In Wales, the Laws in Wales Acts (1535 and 1542) brought the government and laws of Wales into line with English ones. Wales was divided into English-style counties, and English-style officials, such as JPs, were introduced. The re-organisation of Wales was so effective that there was no further unrest in the region for the rest of the period. However, the re-organisation of the Council of the North was less effective before 1569, suggesting that there had been fewer improvements in the government of the North, and effective local government of this region remained a problem for all Tudor monarchs, despite attempts to deal with issues such as unfair taxation, poverty and disorder. Even in the North, however, local government improved after 1569 because the power of the traditional noble families such as the Percies and Nevilles, who had caused trouble for Henry VII and Henry VIII, had been completely destroyed. They had been replaced by southerners and some northerners loyal to the Crown who were appointed to the Council, and their power was extended across the North. Significantly, many of the Council's members were also JPs, showing the importance of the enhanced role of the JP across England and Wales. These developments had very little to do with the changes made by the 1513 subsidy but had a lot to do with the use of JPs and the Council system to enforce the policies of the central government on even remote localities.

In conclusion, the introduction of the 1513 subsidy resulted in some improvements to local government, especially in introducing a method of tax assessment that was fairer and improved government income. However, the changes brought about by the subsidy were not lasting and so cannot be described as the most significant improvement. In comparison to the subsidy, the growing role of the JPs was the most important improvement in local government. This is because the JPs were members of the local gentry and nobility who had enough status to keep order; by giving more power to them, local government improved across all of England and Wales, even in regions where local order and stability had traditionally been a problem.

These sections range across the whole period and evaluate the significance of other reasons for improved local government. There is clear analysis and a good level of detailed development.

The final judgement answers the question set and reaches a substantiated conclusion.

Verdict

This is a strong answer because:

- it is focused on the question and establishes criteria through which the most significant improvement can be judged
- it has a suitable range of points that cover the whole date range
- there is evaluation of and comparison between the key features of the period.

Index

Acknowledgements

The authors and publisher would like to thank the following individuals and organisations for permission to reproduce photographs and text in this book.

Photographs

(Key: b–bottom; c–centre; l–left; r–right; t–top)

Alamy Images: National Geographic Image Collection 6, Pictorial Press Ltd 8, SOTK2011 122; **Bridgeman Art Library Ltd:** Edinburgh University Library, Scotland/With kind permission of the University of Edinburgh 153, His Grace The Duke of Norfolk, Arundel Castle 91, 104, 134, Mary Queen of Scots House, Jedburgh, Scotland/Neil Holmes 131, National Portrait Gallery, London UK/Stefano Baldini 67, Private Collection 9, 15b, 61, Private Collection/Ken Welsh 15t, 23, The Trustees of the Weston Park Foundation, UK 123; **Columbia University Archives:** 170; **The Art Archive:** British Library 68; **TopFoto:** British Library Board 62, 87, Fotomas 53

Cover image: Getty Images: Culture Club

All other images © Pearson Education

Figures

Figure 3.1 adapted from www.royal.gov.uk, Contains public sector information licensed under the Open Government Licence (OGL) v3.0. www.nationalarchives.gov.uk/doc/open-government-licence.

Maps

Map 6.2 from *Tudor Rebellions*, rev. 5th ed. by A. Fletcher and D. MacCulloch, Longman, 2008, p.xxiv, Copyright © 2008. Reproduced by permission of Taylor & Francis Books UK; Maps 7.2, 7.3 adapted from *Irish Battles: A Military History of Ireland* by G. A. Hayes McCoy, Appletree Press Ltd, 1990. Reproduced with permission.

Text

Extracts pp.16, 17, 18, 42 from *The Tudor Constitution: Documents and Commentary,* 2nd edn by G. Elton, Cambridge University Press, 1982 Copyright © Cambridge University Press, reproduced with kind permission from Cambridge University Press and the Royal Historical Society; Extract p.20 from *Parliament Under The Tudors* by J. Loach, Clarendon Press, 1991, p.x, By permission of Oxford University Press; Extracts p.27, 'Extract 2' p.128, quote p.108 from *Tudor England* by J. R. Guy, Oxford University Press 1988, pp.135, 208–09, 208, By permission of Oxford University Press; Extract p.33 from *William Roper's Life of Sir Thomas More, Knight,* modernised by Mary Gottschalk, © Center for Thomas More Studies, www.thomasmorestudies.org/docs/Thomas%20More%20 Petition%20for%20Free%20Speech%20Modern.pdf; Extract p.45 from *Elizabethan Parliaments 1559–1601* by M.A.R. Graves, Longman, 1987, p.90, Copyright © 1987, reproduced by permission of Taylor & Francis Books UK; Extract 'Source 3' p.48 from *Tudor and Constitutional Documents A.D. 1485–1603* by J.R. Tanner, Cambridge University Press, 2013, p.50, Copyright © Cambridge University Press; Extracts 'Source 4' p.48, p.52 from *Tudor Government* by T.A. Morris, Routledge, 1999, p.69, pp.142–43, Copyright © 1999 Routledge, reproduced by permission of Taylor & Francis Books UK; Extract p.69 from *Henry VII* by R. Lockyer, Longman, 1983, p.95, Copyright © 1983, reproduced by permission of Taylor & Francis Books UK; Extract p.70 from *Sources and Debates in English History,*

1485–1714 edited by Newton Key and Robert Bucholz, Wiley Blackwell, 2009, pp.32–33, republished with permission of John Wiley & Sons; permission conveyed through Copyright Clearance Center, Inc., Extracts pp.72, 83 from *The Wars of the Roses and Henry VII* by Colin Pendrill, Heinemann, 2004, p.203, p.204, reproduced with permission from the author; Extract p.74 from 'Milan: 1497' in *Calendar of State Papers and Manuscripts in the Archives and Collections of Milan 1385–1618* edited by Allen B. Hinds, 1912, pp.310–341, www.british-history.ac.uk/cal-state-papers/milan/1385-1618/pp310-341 [accessed 12 January 2016], reproduced with permission from British History Online; Extract 'Source 3' p.90 from 'Henry VIII: August 1535, 21–25' in *Letters and Papers, Foreign and Domestic, Henry VIII, Volume 9, August–December 1535*, edited by James Gairdner, 1886, pp.40–57. British History Online., www.british-history.ac.uk/letters-papers-hen8/vol9/pp40-57 [accessed 7 November 2015], reproduced with permission from British History Online; Extract 'Source 4' p. 90 from *The Pilgrimage of Grace and the Politics of 1530s* by R.W. Hoyle, Oxford University Press, 2001, pp. 457–58, By permission of Oxford University Press; Extracts pp.94, 103, 124, 'Extract 4' pp.128, 138, 139, 142, 143, 'Extract 3' p.151 from *Tudor Rebellions*, rev. 5th ed. by A. Fletcher and D. MacCulloch , Longman, 2008, pp.142, 36, 78, 82–83, 163–64,163, 164–65, 163–64, 115, Copyright © 2008, reproduced by permission of Taylor & Francis Books UK; Extract pp.95–96 from 'Henry VIII: October 1536, 11–15' in *Letters and Papers, Foreign and Domestic, Henry VIII*, Volume 11, *July–December 1536*, edited by James Gairdner, 1888, pp.257–284. British History Online., www.british-history.ac.uk/letters-papers-hen8/vol11/pp257-284 [accessed 12 November 2015], reproduced with permission from British History Online; Extract p.111 from *The English Renaissance: An Anthology of Sources and Documents* by Kate Aughterson, Routledge, 2002, p.155, Copyright © 2002 Routledge, reproduced by permission of Taylor & Francis Books UK; Extract p.117 from *Authority and Disorder in Tudor Times* by P. Thomas, Cambridge University Press, 1999, p.42, Copyright © Cambridge University Press; Extract 'Source 10' p.127 from *Miscellaneous Writings and Letters of Thomas Cranmer* by Thomas Cranmer, Regent College Publishing, 2001, p.195, reproduced with permission; Extract 'Extract 1' p.127 from The History of the Peasants' Revolt by Jeff Hobbs, www.britannia.com/history/articles/peasantsrevolt. html, reproduced with permission; Poetry 'Source 11' p.127 from *The Vision of Piers Plowman* translated by H.W. Wells, Sheed and Ward, 1935, reproduced with permission from Rowman & Littlefield Publishing Group; Extract 'Source 13' p.127 from *The Great Revolt of 1381* by C. Oman, Clarendon Press, 1906, pp.200–201, By permission of Oxford University Press; Extract 3 on p.128 from 'Social Policy 2: The Government and the Peasant Risings' by M.L. Bush in *The Government Policy of Protector Somerset,* print, Montreal: McGill-Queen's University Press, 1975, p.95, reproduced with permission; Extract p.137 from 'Addenda, Queen Elizabeth – Volume 15: November 1569' in *Calendar of State Papers Domestic: Elizabeth, Addenda, 1566–79,* edited by Mary Anne Everett Green, 1871, pp.93–130. British History Online. www.british-history.ac.uk/cal-state-papers/domestic/edw-eliz/addenda/1566-79/pp93-130 [accessed 17 January 2016], reproduced with permission from British History Online; Extract p.145 from 'Simancas: December 1569' in *Calendar of State Papers, Spain (Simancas)*, Volume 2, 1568–1579, edited by Martin A.S. Hume, 1894, pp.213–224. British History Online. hwww.british-history.ac.uk/cal-state-papers/simancas/vol2/pp213-224 [accessed 15 November 2015], reproduced with permission from British History Online; Extract p.149 from *Giordano Bruno and the Embassy Affair* by John Bossy, Yale Nota Bene, 2002, pp.228–9, Copyright © 1991 by John Bossy, reproduced with permission; Extract 1 on p.151 from *Disorder and Rebellion in Tudor England* by N. Fellows, Hodder and Stoughton, 2001, p.89, reproduced by permission of Hodder Education; Extract 2 on p.151 from *Elizabeth I* by C. Haigh, Routledge 2013, p.69, Copyright © 2013 Routledge, reproduced by permission of Taylor & Francis Books UK; Extract p.160 from www.ucc.ie/celt/online/T100005F/text007.html, reproduced with permission; Extract p.161 from 'Faith and Fatherland or Queen and Country? An Unpublished Exchange Between O Neill and The State at The Height of the Nine Years War' by Hiram Morgan in *Dúiche Néill*, No. 9, 1994, pp.8–65, reproduced with permission; Extract p.163 from www.ucc.ie/celt/online/T100005F/text010. html, reproduced with permission; Extract 1 on p.173 from *Elizabeth I* by W. MacCaffrey, Princeton University Press, 1992, p.432, Copyright © 1992 Princeton University Press; Extract 2 on p.173 from *Tudor Ireland* by Steven G. Ellis, Longman, 1985, p.315, reproduced with permission from author.